The Revc  ıg of the ıgıoıaııı

A Study of the Bircham Riots 1835 and their aftermath

David Adams

Larks Press

Published by the Larks Press
Ordnance Farmhouse, Guist Bottom, Dereham,
Norfolk NR20 5PF
01328 829207
Larks.Press@xlnmail.com
Website: www.booksatlarkspress.co.uk

Printed by Short Run Press, Exeter
November 2013

British Library Cataloguing-in-Publication Data
A catalogue record for this book is available
from the British Library

Picture credits

Pictures on p.53 and 94 are reproduced by courtesy of Gressenhall Farm and
Workhouse Museum of Norfolk Life.
Grateful thanks to Susan Fernandez for the pictures of the Kitton family on
pp.18-19, 114 and 172.
Pictures on pp. 23, 27, 33, 36, 77, 104, 215, 272 are reproduced from Joseph Hill's
Survey of Houghton in 1800 by kind permission of Lord Cholmondeley.
The picture of Sir Edward Parry on p.99 is taken from 'Parry of the Arctic'
by Ann Parry.
Photographs on pp. 15, 39, 113, 134, 148, 150, 179, 237, 238, 333 were taken by
the author in 2011.
Maps by Rob Adams.

Preface

A quarter of century or more has now elapsed since I first made the journey across the Cheshire Plain, over the Pennines and across the Lincolnshire flatlands into Norfolk. It was my first visit to the county from which my maternal grandparents had migrated at the end of the nineteenth century. My grandfather and three generations before him had lived in the planned village of New Houghton, close to the Palladian masterpiece built for Robert Walpole. My first visit to Houghton included the Hall; and besides the tour of the splendours of the house, I was able to view some of the old documents from the Muniments Room. The then agent, Percy Baldwin, had kindly laid out rent books and other dusty volumes containing references to my ancestors. Thus began my love affair with this most wonderful of places, and over the years I have been privileged to have been able to explore some of the treasures carefully stored away in the nineteenth century, and now slumbering on shelves away from the familiar routes taken by visitors to the Marquess of Cholmondeley's Norfolk home.

It was David Yaxley, the Houghton Archivist, who suggested on one of my visits that I might care to look at some of the bundles of bills that had been written in the 1830s, and more or less forgotten since that time. Over the years I copied out many of these bills, and lever-arch files began to bulge on my bookshelves. The heading of one of the bundles caught my eye, just one word: 'Riots'. A glance at the contents indicated that there had been serious damage to some farmhouses in the neighbouring parish of Great Bircham. An injured policeman had also been conveyed in a chaise to Walsingham.

I could not leave the matter there, but had to find out as much as I could about the event which history has recorded as the 'Bircham Riots'. Books were ordered from my local library, and then visits were made to the British Newspaper Library and to the Public Record Office, as it was then called, in Kew. A new file was created…and then forgotten. I suppose it was advancing years that made me reopen those lever-arch files and consider whether anything might be converted into a published work. It soon became apparent that this was a story worth telling. I have been surprised that so little of the riots is known among many present-day Norfolk residents, and for that reason alone it has perhaps been worth taking a rather large slice out of my life to write this book. I should declare I am no professional historian; but I can

3

hardly expect this study to be judged any less critically on that score. Any imperfections contained herein must be my responsibility alone.

A visit to Bircham was made in 2010 and some of the farms were photographed. A plan was conceived. Little did I realize how long it would take to bring it to fruition. The journey has been full of activity: further visits to Kew – and this time with a camera as well as a pencil and notebook – and other record repositories and libraries. Many books have been read and many (too many) words have been scribbled down. And then there is the Internet. I must be grateful to the Church of the Latter Day Saints for putting Norfolk parish registers on their Family Search website; but I am not entirely sure whether their inclusion of Norfolk Poor Law Records should receive the same degree of gratitude. From the beginning I had decided to include Chapter 2 for those readers not familiar with the Poor Laws, but the Docking Union Guardians' Minutes proved to be a rich vein of new information, which considerably increased the size of the text. To the revolt of the 'ignorant', a title which arose from one of the newspaper reports, I now added their taming. These minutes gave me much about life in the workhouse and amongst the poor of the Docking Union, and they were too fascinating to cast aside.

I have no idea whether any of my ancestors gathered in Great Bircham on that June night. They were certainly within walking distance of the scene. It is possible that John Pilgrim, the verse on whose gravestone helped to shape my conclusion, was closely related to my great, great grandmother, Avis Pilgrim. They would have both been classed by many contemporary observers as belonging to that vast body of the 'ignorant', despite their strong Primitive Methodist faith and the undoubted literacy of the rioter. A rather large gathering of agricultural labourers found a frightening voice in the summer of 1835 and it is that which has given rise to this study. Nevertheless, the contemporary sources for an account of those few days in June 1835 probably number no more than a handful of people, and their accounts cannot escape being biased. None are biased towards the agricultural labourers who so dramatically sought the attention of their social superiors.

Many people have helped me in the quest. First I must thank Lord Cholmondeley for allowing me to consult the records kept at Houghton. On all my visits there I was assured of a friendly welcome from Susan Cleaver, who succeeded Percy Baldwin. I cannot thank David Yaxley enough for all the help he has given me, not just with my research, but also in connection with my visits over the years.

I thank the staff of the Norfolk Record Office, the Norfolk Heritage Centre in the Millennium Library, Norwich; the staff and volunteers at Gressenhall Farm and Workhouse Museum; and volunteers at the Library of the Norfolk Family History Society. All in their different ways gave me valuable assistance. I also thank staff at the National Archives, the British Newspaper Library and the Library of the University of Chester.

I must also mention two writers. I am extremely grateful to John Archer, whose unpublished PhD thesis I read during my early research into the riots, for allowing me to visit him. He encouraged me to press on with my plan and persuaded me that perhaps even a retired modern linguist could write a history book. John also read my enormous first draft and offered much useful advice. Secondly, I was most pleased to track down Barbara Allen of South Creake. Barbara, unknown to me, had already been a long way down the road I have been treading, and I am very grateful to her for copying for me her dissertation on the effects of the Poor Law Amendment Act in the Docking Union.

No descendants of Bircham Rioters responded to my appeal in the journal of the Norfolk Family History Society, but that is compensated for by contributions from descendants of some of the farmers. Very close to publication I made contact with Gerry Kitton, a direct descendant of the tenant of Church Farm in 1835; and through the kindness of his niece, Susan Fernandez, I received photographs and fascinating information about the Kitton family. I am grateful to Peter Davies of Newport, a descendant of James Howlett, for telling me about the connection with shoemakers Howlett and White; Linda Johnson sent me the very interesting link between Daniel Denny's wife and William Cobbett; Sarah Robinson supplied information on the Hebgin family and further details on the riots; Judy Mitchell of Thunder Bay, Ontario, was able to tell me something of the Doughtys after their emigration and Steve Tomlin clarified how much hay could be cut with a scythe in a day.

It was particularly interesting for me and my wife to spend some time in the former Church Farm, Bircham in the summer of 2011. Mr and Mrs Viney looked after us well in their guesthouse. The dining room must surely have been the room which, in June 1835, was piled high with broken furniture and books ready to be ignited. Sitting by the pond in Bircham Tofts listening to a hen peewit calling to her young seemed in that summer far removed from June 1835, but a visit to the village today can still say much about life in the Birchams in the nineteenth century. I thank the Sandringham Estate and the owner of

Pond Farm for allowing me to publish photographs of properties in Bircham.

I am especially grateful to the Walsingham Estate Company for allowing me to photograph the old Bridewell and the Courthouse. The rioters, if they were able to return to Walsingham in 2013, would find little that has changed. For any student of the Bircham Riots a visit to Walsingham is highly recommended. I am grateful, too, to Gressenhall Farm and Workhouse Museum for allowing me to print a photograph of the punishment cell and for supplying photographs of Docking Workhouse and of farm labourers. The maps in Chapter 5 have been created using GenMap.

I must thank Rob Adams for the production of the maps of the area and the village, and for his encouragement and advice. Above all, two people must be thanked for reading the text and offering much help: John Jewsbury and my wife, Iona. The latter deserves very special thanks, because it was through her chance look in the Great Bircham Church Visitors' Book that I was able to make contact with Gerry Kitton and Susan Fernandez.

I have, incidentally, left the original punctuation and spellings in quotations from manuscript sources.

I have often been asked if there is any similarity between the riots in London, Manchester and elsewhere in 2011 and the Bircham Riots. Both were very ugly affairs, and the appalling events of 2011 brought to the attention of us all the dreadful effects of the destructive orgy. There was also destruction in Bircham, but thankfully no fatalities. It is far too early to judge the 2011 riots objectively, but huge differences in wealth exist now as they did in 1835. In addition, nobody today can fail to be aware of current political thinking on welfare benefits; and exactly the same questions were being asked in 1835 as they are in 2013. What has changed for the better is that the eradication of 'ignorance' has proceeded apace since the nineteenth century. There has been a distinct levelling in the standard of living enjoyed by many descendants of the farmers on the one hand and of the labourers on the other. Universal education has had much to do with that. Nevertheless deprivation still exists and so does the tendency to riot.

Finally, I must especially thank my publisher, Susan Yaxley. I fear I have given her much to do, including the elimination of some appalling errors; but she has pursued her task with extreme diligence, thoughtfulness and determination.

David Adams, Chester, September 2013

CONTENTS

Preface p.3
A Note on Money and Weights and Measures – p.8
Abreviations – p.9

INTRODUCTION
Mr Lewis Writes a Letter p.11

PART I – BACKGROUND
Chapter 1. The Birchams in 1835 p.13
Chapter 2. Poor Laws Old and New p.77

PART II – REVOLT
Chapter 3. The Rising of the 'Ignorant' p. 96
Chapter 4. Trials and Punishment p. 133
Chapter 5. A Riot from Nowhere? p.154

PART III – TAMING
Chapter 6. The Imposition of Deference p.195
Chapter 7. The Docking Union Gets to Work p.217
Chapter 8. The 'Ignorant' are to Know their Place p.234
Chapter 9. Women p.253
Chapter 10. Good Intentions p.273
Chapter 11. Tamed at Last? p.297

CONCLUSION
Mr Groom Pays a Visit p.305

Appendices
A. The complete list of rioters who appeared in court p.310
B. Relief in the Docking Union p.324
C. Thomas Hebgin and Mary Anne Spanton p.327
D. The dietary used in Docking Workhouse p.329
E. The sale of Hebgin's stock, utensils and furniture p.331
F. Details of Bircham farms p.332

A Note on Money and Weights and Measures

Nineteenth century money values have not been given their modern equivalents anywhere in the text; and no conversions such as those of distance or area into metric values have been made.

Money
It is difficult to make a comparison between 1835 and today as regards monetary values. A rough equivalent can be found in the 2005 National Archives Currency Converter.

1835	2005
£1	£44. 10
£100	£4, 410
£1000	£44, 410

Before 1971 the pound was divided into 20 shillings. A shilling was divided into 12 pennies. Sometimes prices were given in guineas. One guinea was 21 shillings.

Measurements – Linear and Area

Imperial	Metric
1 inch (1 in)	2.54 cm
12 inches = 1 foot (1 ft)	30.48 cm
3 feet = 1 yard	91.44 cm

Area The standard measurement was the acre, about 40% of the hectare.

Imperial	Metric
perch (or rod or pole)	25.29 m^2
40 perches = 1 rood	1011.71 m^2
4 roods = 1 acre	

Weight

Imperial	Metric
16 ounces (16 oz) = 1 pound (1 lb)	0.45 kg
14lb = 1 stone (1 st)	6.35 kg
2 st = 1 quarter (1 qtr)	12.7 kg
4 qtr = 1 hundredweight (1 cwt)	50.80 kg
20 cwt = 1 ton	1016 kg

Volume
For grain the word most often encountered in Norfolk was coomb.
However, as density varied so did the weight of a coomb. For barley a coomb was 16 st and for wheat 18 st.

Imperial	Metric
1 peck	9.09 l
4 pecks = 1 bushel	36.37 l
4 bushels = 1 coomb	145.48 l

Abbreviations

BNP	*Bury and Norwich Post*
BPP	British Parliamentary Papers
CRO	Cheshire Record Office
DUGM	Docking Union Guardians' Minutes
EA	*East Anglian*
HH	Houghton Hall
NC	*Norfolk Chronicle*
NM	*Norwich Mercury*
NRO	Norfolk Record Office
PLC	Poor Law Commission/Commissioners
TNA	The National Archives

The Bircham area on Bryant's Map of Norfolk in 1826

Introduction - Mr Lewis Writes a Letter

It was on 3 July 1835 that Lewis Jarvis, a King's Lynn solicitor, sat down and wrote a letter to Richard Groom in London. Mail coaches by this time would not have taken long to reach the capital, and it is likely that Richard Groom read the letter on the following day. He was used to letters from Norfolk, most of them to do with farms, tenancies and matters relating to the business of a large estate. He acted as the agent for the Second Marquess of Cholmondeley, who had an important and substantial estate centred on Houghton in the north-west of the county. His principal seat, however, was in Cheshire. The splendid Palladian mansion of Houghton Hall had been built for Sir Robert Walpole, usually regarded as Britain's first prime minister. The contents of Jarvis's letter were somewhat different from run of the mill business, and must have given him much cause for reflection, even if conveyed in an unemotional style. His employer, the Noble Lord George Horatio Cholmondeley, himself a direct descendant of Robert Walpole through his daughter Mary, would need to be informed as soon as possible.

Houghton Hall in 1800 from Joseph Hill's Survey *(Plate I)*

What, then, did Lewis Jarvis wish to tell Lord Cholmondeley's agent in London? As Cholmondeley's rent collector he often sent letters to London, and this one started with very routine business: he enclosed an Abstract of Copyholds in the Manor of Ingoldisthorpe in Snettisham. He asked to be informed if Groom wished a Manorial Court to be held. The second and third paragraphs had nothing to do with copyholds or manorial courts although the writer was clearly wishing to draw the attention of the agent to the state of some of the Cholmondeley properties. They read:-

I'm very sorry to say that serious Riots have taken Place in Great Bircham by the Poor of that and adjoining Parishes by the Overseers commencing upon the New Poor Law Bill - They have destroyed all the Windows of three Farm Houses belonging to the Marquis of Cholmondeley, destroyed parts of the Tenants Furniture and burnt the Books and Papers, and the Families obliged to escape from their Houses.

This has been communicated to me by a Gentleman who has been at Bircham, but I have not seen or heard from Mr. Reeve [the Houghton land agent] *– I understand it occur'd on Monday or Tuesday Morning and that the Military are now there.*

The letter conveyed the essence of what have come to be known as the Bircham Riots. There is much more to tell, however. A visitor to Great Bircham today might glance at the village sign and be reminded that we are in Royal Country, parts of the village now belonging to the Sandringham Estate; the ox on the sign recalls the great importance of arable farming in this part of Norfolk over many centuries. Yet nothing speaks of anything remotely resembling a riot. The same visitor might sit outside the nearby King's Head in the midsummer sunshine enjoying a quiet drink; yet such a visitor would probably have no idea that, just before Lewis Jarvis wrote his letter, scenes of violence, which might easily have resulted in death, had been played out on that very spot a couple of years before Queen Victoria came to the throne. The barn conversions close-by seem remote from the nineteenth century poor of Great Bircham and the adjoining parishes, and our visitor would very likely not be aware that a vast crowd of agricultural labourers came to those very farms intent on causing mayhem one summer's night in 1835.

Note

This letter sent to Richard Groom is in the archives at Houghton Hall, among a group of papers known as Cellar Documents. Its reference is 910L.

Chapter 1. The Birchams in 1835

But the landlord's influence for good or evil extends to his tenants and labourers, and in its general results regulates, in no unimportant degree, the productiveness and welfare of the country. Yet of all classes in the community he is the only one who receives no special training....He comes to it frequently without knowledge of its duties, and, with a consciousness of his own inability to perform them, he resigns all into the hands of his agent.

English Agriculture, James Caird (1852)

His business is to grow the heaviest crops of the most remunerative kind his soil can be made to carry, and, within certain limits of climate which experience has now defined, the better he farms, the more capable his land becomes of growing the higher qualities of grain, of supporting the most valuable breeds of stock, and of being readily adapted to the growth of any kind of agricultural produce. ...In this country the agricultural improver cannot stand still. If he tries to do so, he will soon fall into the list of obsolete men, being passed by eager competitors, willing to seize the current of events and turn them to their advantage.

English Agriculture, James Caird (1852)

But the agricultural labourer in the southern counties, while he derives from his labour the means of a very scanty existence, is almost everywhere felt as a burden instead of a benefit to his employer.

English Agriculture, James Caird (1852)

I The Three Birchams

The three Birchams, Great, Tofts and Newton, were originally separate manors which came into the Houghton Estate at various times. Thus, in 1835, Lord Cholmondeley was the lord of all the manors, and owned all the land and properties in the three villages. This made the villages typical closed parishes, that is to say ones closed to new development. There were many such parishes in North-west Norfolk. Much of the land was given over to arable farming and the soil was generally light, mainly on a bed of gravel or sand, but sometimes on marl. The latter was often used to fertilize the land in the same way as lime does.

The populations of the three parishes, taken from the 1831 census, were:

Great Bircham – 451: Bircham Tofts – 130: Bircham Newton – 95.

At the beginning of 1835, for administrative purposes, the parishes were in the Hundred of Smithdon. The Docking Union then took over the administration of the Poor Law.

The population of the three parishes grew steadily, but not dramatically, through the first half of the nineteenth century, and then declined. The figures here are for Great Bircham, but the other two smaller parishes show the same pattern.

1801	1811	1821	1831	1841	1851	1861	1871	1881	1891	1901
325	330	398	451	511	503	489	484	450	392	383

Any present-day Bircham resident, returning to the village in 1835, would recognize much. Perhaps one major difference would be the large number of young people - a complete contrast to the demographic profile of the village today. At the time of the 1851 census over half of the people were aged twenty and under. In the 1830s the expectation of life for those born between 1775 and 1840 hovered between thirty-five and forty, and therefore any visitor travelling back through time to Bircham in 1835 would not expect to see many older people. Deaths in Great Bircham have been plotted for the years 1813-1851. The numbers include nonagenarians, and we might be surprised by the fact that no fewer than fifty-nine people had survived to at least the biblical three score years and ten. This was not untypical; as Alan Armstrong has observed: 'the outstandingly high proportions of those aged sixty-five and over – in town and country alike, but particularly the latter – were a remarkable feature of Norrfolk's age profile'.[1]

II The Bircham Farmers

In Great Bircham there were five farmers: John Kitton, Daniel Denny, Thomas Hebgin, John Nurse and Anthony Beck.

Bircham Tofts had two farmers: James Warnes Howlett and Philip Jarrett.

Bircham Newton also had two farmers: John Barker and William Blyth.

The farmers of the latter place seem to have had no involvement with the Bircham Riots, but the other farmers, apart from Beck and Jarrett, played their part; one of them more conspicuously than the rest.

1. Town Farm

In Great Bircham it is still possible to see two former farmhouses near the King's Head, on opposite sides of the road. On the road coming from Hillington and Flitcham on the left-hand side, close to the village sign, there is a large barn conversion, and then, parallel to the road, there is a substantial house. This is Town Farm, and in 1835 it was occupied by Thomas Hebgin. In 1834 the annual rent was £260. By the time of the Tithe Award (1838) there were over 600 acres in total. In 1834 the rental is for Hebgin and Nurse; the latter must have occupied a smaller house on the same farm. In 1838 there is no mention of John Nurse in Great Bircham, and in 1836 he was paying rent for a farm in Bircham Tofts. Nurse, however, was definitely involved in the events of 1835. He was Thomas Hebgin's brother-in-law.

Town Farm, Great Bircham
(Photo 2011)

The Thomas Hebgin at Town Farm in 1835 was the second of that name. His father married Sarah Sewell in 1782 in Shouldham Thorpe (north of Downham Market) and Thomas junior was born there in 1789. Thomas and Sarah had a large family, and the first to be baptized at Great Bircham was Ann, who later married John Nurse. Her baptism was in January 1798, so it must have been around that time that the Hebgins moved to Town Farm. Thomas Hebgin senior died in 1809. In his will he provided for his widow, allowing her £30 a year, and he put everything in trust for his children still under twenty-one. His effects were sworn under £1,500. It is probable that Thomas Hebgin junior, as the eldest son, became the farmer soon after the death of his father; however, from 1812 to 1826 it is Sarah Hebgin paying the land tax. The land tax of 1832 is in the name of 'Thos Hebgin and Nurse'. Sarah Hebgin was buried in Great Bircham in 1839, but by then she was a resident of Flitcham Hall, the residence of her daughter, Elizabeth. At the time of the riots Hebgin had been married for three years and had one infant son, William, who had been baptized in January 1835. Hebgin married Susanna Wright, of the parish of Fincham, in Saham Toney, in 1832. He died in 1850, and Susanna in 1865.

Preserved amongst the muniments at Houghton Hall is a wonderful survey of all the properties on the Houghton Estate. It was done in 1832 by Habbakkuk Englestown, who was then living at the New Inn (later King's Head), Houghton. The Survey gives a good description of Hebgin's farmhouse:-

46 feet by 21 feet the Walls built wth Bks the Roof cover'd with pantiles consist of Entrance and stair case, kitchen & parlour on the ground floor and three chambers with Atticks over the same.

The farm buildings were extensive and the barns huge.
(See Appendix F.)

2. Church Farm

On the other side of the road is the former Church Farm; in 1835 the tenant was John Kitton. The farm consisted of 825 acres in 1838, and the rent in 1834 was £400. John Kitton was born in Sprowston in

1780, the son of John and Lucy Kitton, but he must have spent nearly all his life in the north-west of Norfolk. John Kitton senior, of Beeston (near Norwich), married Lucy Blyth at Eaton, a parish south of Norwich, in 1772. The Blyths were an important and influential family. A Samuel Blyth (1707-1783) had been born in the parish of Horsford and had married, in 1729, Elizabeth Kitton (1710-1784), of Horsham. This Samuel Blyth came to farm in Bircham Tofts. A descendant of Samuel was Henry Blyth of Sussex Farm, Burnham Westgate; and Henry's first son, Henry Etheridge Blyth, was to become a man of some distinction in Norfolk farming and the wider community.

Seven children in total were baptized at the church of St Mary, Sprowston, the last one, Samuel Blyth Kitton, in 1781. The Kittons, with their young family, came to Pond Farm in Bircham Tofts some time after the birth of Samuel. Just one child was baptized in Bircham Tofts: Lydia in 1783. She lived only five days, however, and was buried on 12 January 1783, the same day as her father. Thus, Lucy Kitton was a young widow when she began to run the farm on her own.

A survey of the Houghton Estate done by Joseph Hill in 1800 names Lucy Kitton as the tenant of the Bircham Tofts farm. John Kitton junior was certainly the tenant of the same farm by 1815, when a rental of Houghton Estate properties was drawn up; his mother did not die until 1821, but was by then living in Fakenham. He married Rebecca Maria Blyth, the youngest sister of Henry Blyth of Sussex Farm, at Sedgeford in 1805; she was his second cousin. John and Rebecca had eleven children in all, of whom ten survived into adulthood. It is difficult to be completely sure when the Kittons moved to Church Farm, but it was probably around 1825 or 1826. In 1835, Kitton, as well as being the principal farmer in the parish, was also a churchwarden and overseer.

Of the other children of John Kitton junior and Rebecca we can note that they included six daughters. One of these, Ellen, born in 1818, was blind, according to the 1851 census. And even though it is not recorded in the earlier censuses, two other daughters, Mary (born 1812) and Rebecca (1813), were also blind, or at least poorly sighted.

The Kitton Family

The Kitton family

Opposite - John Kitton (1780-1848) and Rebecca Maria Kitton (1778-1856). They married in 1806 and were living at Church Farm in 1835. Six of their children (left to right): Juliana Tillyard (1806-1879); Elizabeth, Lucy, Howlett (1808-1872); Rebecca Kitton (1813-1892); Revd John Kitton (1814-1882) later Ketton; Ellen Kitton (1818-1885); Henry Kitton, Archdeacon of British Kafraria, South Africa.

Margaret Tillyard (1822-1891) and Edward Wright Kitton (1823-1878), the youngest children at the time of the riots

The Kitton Household with servants in front of Church Farm c. 1872. Possibly taken after the marriage of Edward Wright Kitton to Ellen Jane Cutter.

There were probably at least four children in the household in 1835, the youngest being Edward (aged nearly twelve).

Three of the Kitton daughters married (but only one became a farmer's wife); the others lived out their long lives as spinsters, all of them eventually moving away from Bircham. For women of their status, unable to find a husband, life offered little in the way of fulfilment, apart from supporting parents and unmarried brothers, being a maiden aunt or doing good works in the community. Life was even more complicated for these blind spinsters. Their married sisters would not necessarily have found life a great deal more fulfilling, except in their restricted roles as wives and mothers. The sons, of course, had a much greater chance of pursuing careers. The only son to maintain his position as farmer to the end of his life was Edward, and he ran Church Farm until his death in 1878, which came only six years after his marriage. By 1851, the other farmer son, Charles, had become a commercial agent in Heigham, and he died in London five years later. Two more sons, John and Henry, became clergymen, the former living out his life in Lancashire; in 1871 he was the headmaster of Hutton Grammar School. By the time of his death in 1882, he had changed his name to Ketton, in imitation of his distant cousin, the owner of Felbrigg.

Kitton died in 1848, and the announcement of his death in *The Norfolk Chronicle* declared he had been 'a much-respected inhabitant' of Great Bircham for many years. His will reveals the extent of his personal wealth: it was sworn to be under £4,000. Rebecca died in 1856, and her effects were sworn under £800.

3. Heath House Farm

Daniel Denny's farm was called Heath House Farm, a property which any visitor coming along the road from Flitcham would encounter first, on the right-hand side of the road. It is situated some distance from the centre of the village. In 1800, when Joseph Hill surveyed the Houghton Estate, the farm had 647 acres of arable and 244 acres of pasture; by 1838 the total acreage had grown to nearly 950 acres. It was the largest farm in Great Bircham. In 1834 the rent was £450, which had dropped to £400 two years later. In March 1836, Denny gave notice to quit unless the rent was reduced.[2]

In 1835 Denny was a comparatively young man of thirty-eight. He came from the corner of South-east Norfolk, on the Suffolk border; he was probably born in Gillingham about 1797. He appears to have had a good start in life, as his uncle, also called Daniel, left him 'messuages, farmlands and premises situate in the parish of Raveningham' in his will of 1803. Young Daniel had married Bridget Eleanor (Ellen) Clarke in Bergh Apton in 1826. The Marriage Register states he was from the nearby parish of Stockton. Exactly where he was before 1832 is not known. He had two daughters, aged ten and eleven according to the 1841 census, but their baptisms are not to be found in the Great Bircham Parish Register. A son, Samuel Denny, was baptized in Great Bircham parish church in 1836. By 1841, they were all living in Stanford, near Thetford, but on 20 October of that year Daniel Denny was lying in Stanford churchyard. He had not died before making a will, and here we can see how rich he was: £1,000 to be invested in Government securities for each of his four young children, and £2,000 for his widow.

One fascinating aspect of Ellen Clarke's background was that her father, Samuel Clarke, a farmer of Street Farm, Bergh Apton, had had some connection with William Cobbett's *Rural Rides*.[3] Cobbett stayed for some time in Bergh Apton in 1821 and Samuel Clarke accompanied him on various journeys in Norfolk. The nearest Cobbett came to Bircham was Holt. He came away with a good impression of farming in Norfolk, calling it 'a county of most excellent cultivators'. One must wonder to what extent, if any, Cobbett's political opinions, and especially his defence of agricultural labourers in the riots of the early 1830s and his implacable opposition to reform of the Poor Law, had come down to Ellen Denny. It seems extremely unlikely that Daniel Denny, farmer of Heath House Farm, was a secret Cobbetite. The radical and anti-Government journalist was in many ways attempting the impossible: the progress of the Industrial Revolution, which brought so much change to all sections of society, was never going to be halted. Even though the farmers and labourers in this part of England were far removed from industrial centres of manufacture, they could not avoid being caught up in the upheaval, and its attendant political reforms. Mrs Denny of Heath House Farm might well have been influenced by William Cobbett and absorbed some of his resistance to change in rural England, but it would soon become apparent that her husband was no friend of the labouring poor.

4. Moor Farm

Anthony Beck was the tenant of Moor Farm and his farmhouse was situated by the Docking road. He had a brother Edward, who appeared in the rental for 1836, but in 1841 he farmed in Harpley. Anthony Beck was born in East Bradenham, near Swaffham, in 1787. He married Kitty (or Catherine) Cruso in 1813 in King's Lynn; the first child to be baptized in Great Bircham was Fanny in 1823, which must have been roughly when he became the tenant of Moor Farm; but several children had already been born at Great Massingham. By the time of the riots, Beck was a widower, and in 1841, he was still living in Great Bircham with daughters Mary, Fanny and Margaret. Enumerated at the Church Close Academy in Burnham Westgate in 1841 was 14-year-old Frederick Beck, Anthony and Kitty's son. Another pupil was John Nurse, the son of farmer Nurse. Anthony Beck died in 1850.

5. Pond Farm

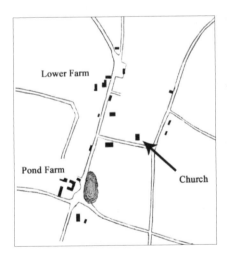

In Bircham Tofts, the 1835 tenant of Pond Farm was James Warnes Howlett. He was the son-in-law of John Kitton, tenant of Church Farm, Great Bircham having married Elizabeth Lucy Kitton in January 1827. The pond, which gives the farm its name, is still there, in front of the farm. It is situated on the road leading out of the village towards the Construction Industry Training Centre. It is also nearly opposite the road leading to the now ivy-clad ruins of Bircham Tofts Church. Hill's Survey of 1800 gives 191 acres arable and 273 acres pasture; the 1851 census has 510 acres. The house today is still an impressive one, although inevitably there will have been changes over the years.

James Warnes Howlett was born in King's Lynn in 1800, the son of James and Sarah Howlett. His father was a wine and spirit merchant, and the address in Pigot's Directory of 1830 was 11 Norfolk Street. The death of James Howlett senior, on 26 May 1841, was reported in *The Bury and Norfolk Post,* and his age was given as eighty-two. We must assume the son became the tenant of Pond Farm before the time of his marriage in 1827, and after John Kitton, moved to Church Farm. He certainly was in Bircham Tofts in August 1826, because one of his horses was stabbed then; he was also paying land tax there in 1826. He died in 1872 at Great Ringstead, but was buried in Bircham Tofts; his wife followed him four months later. At the time of his death he was living at the Lodge, Ringstead, but he had lived in Sedgeford Hall prior to that. In 1871, James Warnes Howlett and his wife were enumerated along with their unmarried daughter, Sarah, and Rebecca Kitton, Elizabeth's sister. He was then farming in a much more modest way (a mere 120 acres).

Pond Farm in 1800 when Lucy Kitton was tenant.
(From Hill's Survey Plate XXIX)

In 1841 the farmer at Pond Farm was Charles Kitton, his wife's brother; Howlett was in King's Lynn with his wife, and he was still a farmer. He was living in Norfolk Street with his sister, Elizabeth Quincey, and her children; his brother-in-law and other sister, Ann Godfrey, were also living at the same address. With Charles Kitton, in Bircham Tofts, were the two young Howlett daughters, Sarah and Fanny. This was certainly only a temporary arrangement and the three siblings, together with their spouses, must have gathered in the Norfolk Street house after their father's death. There appear to have been at least six children born to James Warnes and Elizabeth: the first was another James Warnes, baptized in 1828. There were apparently, and most unusually, two Johns: besides John Kitton Howlett (born in 1830) there had also been John Godfrey (or Godfery) Howlett (1829).[4] The rest were daughters, and two of them died as young children. There were probably five small children in the Howlett household in 1835.

The name Howlett was later carried far from Bircham Tofts to Norwich, and then beyond. In 1846 James Warnes Howlett invested the then very large sum of £10,000 in the Norwich leather-currying business of Robert Tillyard, which soon became Tillyard and Howlett. One wonders where he got the money; possibly Kittons and Blyths had an input. The second forename, Godfrey, of the first John is intriguing. The only reason for this name seems to come from the marriage of Ann Warnes Howlett to John Godfrey in St Margaret's Church, King's Lynn in 1827, but it is possible that there had been connections between Godfreys and Howletts in previous generations. Nothing has been found, however. Perhaps John Godfrey had been particularly generous to his brother-in-law. Godfrey appears as 'yeoman' and as 'gentleman' in later censuses, and it would appear that he was a man of some wealth. Nevertheless, there remains an element of mystery surrounding the name of this son.

James Howlett senior's effects, according to his will, were sworn under £2,000; and James Warnes, as the only son, was the main beneficiary. Thus, by 1846, Howlett was very probably a rich man, his wealth having come from various sources, and certainly not merely from farming. It would not appear that there had been any history of farming with these Lynn Howletts; but James Howlett senior did mention 'Corn and Hay live and dead stock' in his will. It is also apparent, from various advertisements in the press, that he acted as some kind of agent in the letting of properties in Norfolk. Evidently he had been more than a wine and spirit merchant, and his business interests had diversified.

James Warnes Howlett undoubtedly displayed great foresight and perceived that the future of making boots and shoes would no longer lie in the cottage workshops of Norfolk villages. Howlett encouraged his son, John Godfrey Howlett, to take an interest in the business: some time later, in the 1850s, he met George White, who joined the company of Tillyard and Howlett in 1856. The two men then set up their manufacturing base – Howlett and White – on St George's Plain, Norwich. This grew into a major centre of shoe-making, later becoming part of the Norvic Shoe Company.

Here, then, was a wonderful Victorian success story which shows that enterprising men of business did much better to take their chance with manufacturing rather than with agriculture. James Warnes Howlett remained a sleeping partner in the company, not involving himself with anything more than financial matters, but he was clearly anxious for his son to play a full part in a growing business. The move from country to city, albeit via Alabama, was a big one for a self-styled 'clod-hopping farmer's son' and somebody of a retiring nature.

John G. Howlett later became a Baptist – another break with the past. More remarkable was his partner: George (later Sir George) White had had no formal education in his childhood, but once he was working closely with Howlett he saw what had to be done to create an efficient factory system for making shoes. He was a Liberal in his politics and served for a time as Lord Mayor of Norwich and MP for North West Norfolk. He looked after his workers well and when he died, in 1912, it is said that the city came to a standstill, so great was the crowd of people who came to pay their last respects to this man of the people. Both Howlett and White had strong streaks of philanthropy, underpinned by their deep Christian faith. Early on in their partnership, they saw the need to end the deplorable working and living conditions of the Norwich shoe-makers.

Both these men had a strong sense of the ultimate decency and dignity of the ordinary common man – the working man. Their desire to end this system was at least as much for a moral as for a business reason.[5]

6. Lower Farm

John Daniel Nurse was the other farmer in Bircham Tofts, but not at the time of the riots, because he was still in Great Bircham farming with Thomas Hebgin. Nurse moved to Lower Farm, which was just beyond Pond Farm, in 1836, and paid a rent of £315. This had been reduced from the 1834 rent of £440, an amount judged too high by the Houghton agent, Stephen Reeve, especially as he felt the land not healthy enough for sheep.

Nurse was born in East Rudham, where he was privately baptized, but he was publicly baptized on 5 October 1800 in Great Bircham. He was still farming Lower Farm in 1871, together with his son, who was also called John Daniel. Nurse senior died in 1878; he was buried at Bircham Tofts.

The tenant at Lower Farm before Nurse was Philip Jarrett, who later moved to a farm in Bircham Newton. Before doing so he advertised a sale of his stock, implements and utensils, and it is from the press advertisement that we can appreciate the extent of the farms in the three parishes. On sale were no fewer than 600 sheep: Norfolk and Southdown or Leicester and Southdown. The horses included twenty 'prime working carthorses and mares'. There were forty-four store pigs and eight cows. The latter were the famous Norfolk red polls, described as 'blood red' and 'handsome'.[6]

7. Differences in status between Hebgin and Kitton

The Hebgins do not seem to have been quite as elevated socially as some of the other farmers. At least the evidence of the 1871 census points to something of a decline. The younger Thomas Hebgin died in 1850, and his widow and son, William, continued to run Town Farm. They were still doing so in 1861. After Susanna's death, in 1865, William became a butcher, although he still lived with his wife and family in the farmhouse. By 1881, he was a farm steward in Easton, Norfolk. Looking a little wider than Town Farm, it can be noted that a brother of Thomas Hebgin junior, Robert, was a cattle dealer in Docking in 1851; and another brother, John, although a farmer at Hillington, farmed fewer acres than were available in Great Bircham.

As shown below, their financial troubles were evident by 1817 and undeniable by 1826.

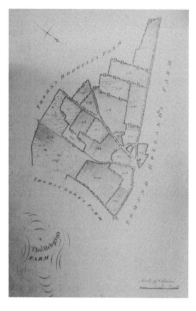

Hebgin's Farm in 1800, from Hill's Survey *(Map IVa.)*

However, Thomas Hebgin junior did endeavour to keep up his role as the scion of an important farming family, even if he needed to diversify into something other than farming: in 1837 he announced that he would be taking advantage of the closure of the New Inn, Houghton and letting out post horses and chaises. Later, those wishing to attend auctions in the area would be able to avail themselves of this service; but in 1852 Mrs Hebgin had to inform the public that the omnibus to Lynn would cease. By 1848, he was playing some part in the formation of a Church Missionary Society in Great Bircham; and he had been serving as a guardian of the Docking Poor Law Union for several years before that. In comparison with most of those in trade, his position in Great Bircham society remained a high one; even if he became the proprietor of an omnibus business.[7]

The Kittons, on the other hand, had more wealth and better connections behind them. Both had much to do with the Blyths who came from further east in the county to North-west Norfolk in the eighteenth century. In 1872, Edward Kitton, the son of John and Rebecca, married into another important farming family, the Cutters; and it was the latter who then came to dominate Great Bircham farming.

It is also probably true that John Kitton felt himself to be superior to the Hebgins in other ways. Not only had he greater wealth and important connections, but he probably had more intellectual rigour. Two of his sons became clergymen: Henry became an archdeacon in South Africa; John Kitton junior, who had a Master of Arts degree from the University of Cambridge, was a curate in Preston.[8] Rebecca Kitton also had Blyth nephews who were clergymen. It is very likely that Church Farm was a highly literate and educated household. Furthermore, as we shall see later, he had every reason to feel he inhabited a higher moral sphere than Hebgin. Nevertheless, we know from a sale advertised in *The Norfolk Chronicle* in 1826 that the young Thomas Hebgin had grown up in a household with 'many volumes of books'. (See Appendix E.) And, as mentioned below, he and his siblings had all been educated at some cost.

Denny, too, was obviously a wealthy man; and so was Howlett. Nevertheless, despite these inevitable differences, the farmers were all considerably richer than those working at the various trades, and especially those struggling to survive by working on the land. The only class of Bircham inhabitants who could equal them were the clergymen. The 1843 sale of the furniture of the Rev. Edward Pidsley, who occupied Great Bircham Rectory, lists a superior range of modern furniture, with chintz and mahogany.[9]

III A Superior Class but a Precarious Existence

The farmers formed a close-knit group, and were further connected by marriage. Even if there were differences between them, they were all wealthy tenants of large farms and it is clear they lived in some style. Three of them were under forty; only Kitton was in his fifties. Given that their noble landlord lived elsewhere, and that there were no other gentry or professional men in the Birchams (apart from the clergymen), they were undoubtedly at the top of their social pyramid. The farmers were the only men in Great Bircham who were registered electors in 1835, apart from Bloom Humphrey, miller, and the Rector. They must have felt they were the natural leaders of the community. Some were churchwardens and overseers of the poor, and also served as special constables; all were employers of the village labourers. Kitton and Hebgin had lived in Bircham since childhood and must have felt supremely confident in their knowledge of the workings of a large arable farm, including the handling of large groups of labourers. Their power and influence were immense.

We can gauge the extent of the wealth of the successful farmers from farm sales advertised in the newspapers. There are several good examples from Great Bircham ranging from 1807 to 1826. Four-poster beds were standard, and so were goose featherbeds. Carpets were Scotch, Venetian or Kidderminster and there was much mahogany furniture. In 1822, the goods of the late Mrs Rodwell, who had lived at Church Farm, included 'a handsome mahogany dining table with circular ends 10 feet by 4'. There was also a 'looking glass in a gilt frame with a very superior cut plate 24 by 40 inches'. The walls had been adorned by '4 hunting prints in gilt frames' and tea had been served on 'very handsome japanned tea-trays'.

The farmhouses were not places devoid of culture. Edmund Holland had 'an excellent well-toned piano forte' and William Beck had 'a secretary and bookcase, with satin and cedar drawers'. His books comprised such items as sixteen volumes of *Hume and Smollett's History of England,* four volumes of *Thornton's Biology,* two volumes of *Sheridan's Dictionary,* as well as volumes of Dryden, Homer, Milton, Pope and others. There were also card-tables and bagatelle boards.

We know that the farms had a good many working horses, but those for personal use had impeccable pedigrees. Holland had a 'filly rising 3 years old, by Mr Read's Fireaway', and the livestock of Thomas Hebgin senior included 'a bay mare five-year-old by Shales' and 'a fast trotter by Golden Ball'. [10]

However, theirs was a precarious existence. The price they could obtain for their produce might fall and, at the same time, their costs rise dramatically. They perceived labour as particularly expensive: according to Richard Noverre Bacon, who in the 1840s produced a report on Norfolk agriculture, the cost of labour per acre on west Norfolk farms in 1800 was 11s.; it rose to 23s. 2d. in 1835 and 26s. 7d. in 1840. For farms on light soil in Norfolk the same writer gives great variations in the price of wheat. During the Napoleonic Wars it was very high: as much as £60 per coomb in 1812; it had fallen to £32 9s. in 1820 and £20 in 1835. He gives the average weekly wages for labourers on the same farms between 1804 and 1843, and there is also a difference, an equally dramatic one, from as high as 15s. (1812) to as low as 8s. (1804 and 1822). [11]

Farmers had a vital role to play in feeding the nation, but they had to be ever vigilant. They could very easily face ruin if they mismanaged their farms. The landlord had entrusted the keeping of his real estate

29

to the farmer, and he wanted it to be farmed well. It was left to the tenant to put his capital into the farm, to stock it properly and to use his resources wisely. The Bircham farmers, along with others with large arable farms, might not have performed any manual tasks, but there is no evidence to point to any inefficiency amongst them, except perhaps with the Hebgins, as we shall examine below. However, we must question the ability of all of them to manage their workforces. Nineteenth century farmers increased their wealth during the early years of the century, and they gradually pulled away materially and socially from those toiling in the fields; yet frequently they were lacking in the way they treated their workers, who were perceived to be more of a burden than a benefit.

In the archives at Houghton Hall there is a letter,[12] probably to Lord Cholmondeley's agent. It is written by Elizabeth, sister of Thomas Hebgin junior, the tenant of Town Farm at the time of the riots. The letter was written in 1817, before the period covered by this book, but it nevertheless reveals much about the difficulties faced by farmers. Thomas Hebgin senior was dead by this time, but his widow was still in the farmhouse. Elizabeth Hebgin complained that the farm did not wholly support the family, given the cost of educating nine children. Her litany of complaints extended over several headings: the current valuation of the farm was much too high; tithes and poor rates (5s. in the pound) were excessive; tradesmen's bills had soared; and the farm could not be worked any more profitably than when they first took it. She wanted the recipient of the letter to appeal directly to the Marquess. Her mother would 'give her last shilling to stay there', she wrote, even though any livelihood to be made would have needed the 'strictest economy'. She further complained that they had suffered great losses of horses and sheep over the previous seven years; indeed the previous year, just before the sales, they had lost half their lambs, and had been forced to sell the rest at much reduced prices. Whether her appeal to the leniency of the landlord had any direct effect we do not know, but there were still Hebgins at Town Farm in 1861.

However, the Hebgins declined in the 1820s. By October 1826, the family, according to the advertisement of the sale of goods in *The Norfolk Chronicle*, had decided not to carry on the farm any longer. (See Appendix E.) The land tax payments between 1801 and 1826 remained the same, first for Thomas Hebgin senior and then, after 1809, for his widow Sarah. It must have been after he married Ann Hebgin that John Nurse came to run Town Farm, with his brother-in-law as a partner, but after the younger Thomas Hebgin's marriage to Susanna Wright his fortunes must have picked up again. It is, nonetheless, far from clear exactly what was happening at Town Farm from 1826 to 1832.

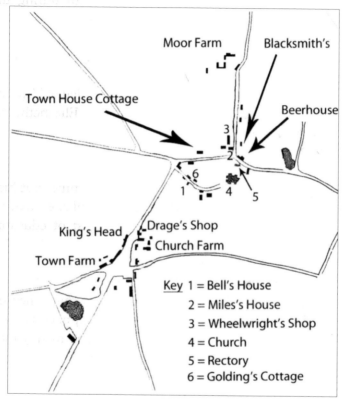

Moor Farm
Blacksmith's
Town House Cottage
Beerhouse
3
2
6
1
4
5
King's Head
Drage's Shop
Church Farm
Town Farm
Key 1 = Bell's House
2 = Miles's House
3 = Wheelwright's Shop
4 = Church
5 = Rectory
6 = Golding's Cottage

The layout of Great Bircham in 1835

IV The Tradespeople

1. General

Virtually all the tradespeople were in Great Bircham, and they mostly lived and worked in the part of the village near the church. They were:

31

John Drage, grocer and draper
John Groom, blacksmith
Bloom Humphrey, corn miller
James Lack, machine maker
William Lack, saddler
Robert Miles, shoemaker
Robert Ransome, shoemaker
Edmund Rice, shoemaker
John Shilling, blacksmith
Martha Spooner, grocer
Robert Spooner, wheelwright and beer-house
Susan Tovell, joiner

They did not form an entirely homogeneous group. Some of the properties they occupied were rather grand, and John Drage and Bloom Humphrey were registered electors, but they were mostly at a distinctly lower social level than the farmers. Their trades were exactly what one would expect in a village of the size of Great Bircham in an agricultural area, and they fulfilled a vital role in the rural economy. Blacksmiths always had plenty of work in an age when farmers had several horses and there was much ironwork to repair. Farm carts and farm properties needed constant attention, so Widow Tovell would always have been in demand. The riots certainly gave her extra work. Rare would have been the families who made their own shoes, and fewer and fewer people repaired them; the shoemakers, therefore, were always kept busy.

2. John Drage

John Drage's shop was near Church Farm. The Tithe Award mentions a cottage, shop and garden. In 1836 the rent was £20 p.a. John Drage, born around 1793 in London, had a shop in East Rudham, where he lived. His name appeared very frequently in the Houghton Accounts Books; his family had been supplying goods of all sorts to the Hall since the eighteenth century. His position in Bircham society was higher than others in trade, and closer to that of the farmers, as is clear from his having been a witness at a marriage of one of the Nurse family.

Drage's shop
(Plate XI in Hill's Survey of 1800)

3. Bloom Humphrey

The Humphrey family occupied the mill for many years. There is no indication of how much rent was paid in 1835, if any; and the 1832 survey does not include the mill. At the time of the riots it was a post mill, which had been there since at least 1761; the present mill dates from 1846.

4. William Lack

Given the number of large farms in the three parishes there would have been much work for anybody dealing with horses. One such was William Lack, appearing as a saddler in *White's Directory*. In the 1841 census he was described as a collar maker, which makes sense. The many heavy horses in the village would have needed collars as well as harnesses, and that would have been his trade. The 1832 survey gave him as the tenant of a house and collar-maker's shop. The brick and flint house was 60 ft by 15 ft. On the ground floor were kitchen, parlour, shop, staircase and pantry; there were three chambers above. There was another building attached, described as in 'bad repair'. In 1836 William Lack paid £8 8s. for a house, shop and garden.

The Directory might suggest three independent shoemakers, but it appears that at least two worked together and all three were connected in some way. Edmund Rice, shoemaker, should be Edmund Royce. He paid £2 6s. in rent for his brick and flint cottage and shoemaker's shop.

6. Robert Miles

However, there was a definite connection between Edmund Royce and Robert Miles, another shoemaker. In the 1832 Survey Robert Miles was living in a treble tenement with Dewing Chapman and Robert Rumbold, but the shoemaker's shop was attached to a double tenement, and here were living William Miles and Thomas Marsters. This might be a mistake, but it does seem likely, from the evidence of the 1841 and 1851 censuses, that William (who was Robert's brother) was living in the tenement next to the shoemaker's shop. Robert might well have wanted his brother, with his growing family, to live in the larger tenement; but he was obviously able to continue his trade in the old shop.

In 1836 Robert's rent was £2 6s.; his name was bracketed with that of Edward Carrington in the 1836 and 1837 rentals. In an account book for1836, Edward Carrington was shown as paying 6s. for land, and in brackets there was written 'Miles & Co'. Carrington was Robert Miles's brother-in-law.

That Robert Miles was also in some kind of partnership with Edmund Royce is evident from some bills kept at Houghton Hall. Royce had secured the lucrative business of supplying boys' shoes to Houghton. In February 1834 Robert Miles acknowledged the settlement of a bill for £8 14s. 4d for 20 pairs of shoes, varying in price from 7s. to 10s. a pair.[13]

It seems very likely that the cottage (divided into two tenements by 1832) and shop were the premises shown more or less opposite the old Great Bircham Rectory, on the road leading to Bircham Tofts, in Hill's 1800 survey. It was the only shoemaker's shop shown by Hill, and as the Miles family had been in Great Bircham for over one hundred years before the survey was made, it seems very probable that this was the location of Robert Miles's shoemaker's shop in 1835. In the 1851 census William Miles's address was Docking Road, and he was enumerated between the Great Bircham curate (who appeared next to Edward Carrington) and John Groom, blacksmith (on Tofts Road).

The family of Miles had been in Great Bircham for well over one hundred years. An earlier Robert Miles had died in 1817 aged 96 and had been Parish Clerk for 48 years. There had been an even earlier Miles, also a parish clerk. The most likely candidate for the shoemaker in the directory, however, was Robert Miles born in 1784, the son of Robert Miles and Elizabeth (formerly Bowman), and brother of William, the agricultural labourer. He married Jane Maria Fox, from Bagthorpe, at Great Bircham in 1808. She made her mark, but Miles signed his name. In the 1841 census, by which time Jane Maria was dead, Robert Miles was given as a shoemaker and he was living next to William Miles, who surely must have been his brother.

The fact that Robert Miles made a will and inserted the notice of his first wife's death in *The Norfolk Chronicle* of 16 January points to a status not rivalling that of the farmers, but not greatly below it. (See Appendix A.)

7. Robert Ransome

Robert Ransome was the third shoemaker. In 1832 he lived in a double cottage, the other tenant being John Golding. He too was related to shoemaker Robert Miles: he was his first cousin. His mother was Dinah Miles, who had married Thomas Ransome in 1780.

8. Susan Tovell

Hill's Survey also mentioned a carpenter's shop, and as it was the only one depicted there and described in the 1832 Survey, we can be much more confident in pinpointing its precise location. There was just one carpenter in Great Bircham in 1851, as in 1835. He was Nelson Garlett, a Suffolk man, who was the son-in-law of the head of the carpentry business at the time of the riots, John Tovell. The latter was not born in the parish, but his wife's family, the Robinsons, were Bircham people. Habbakkuk Englestown records Tovell as living in a small brick and flint house. There was just one room and a pantry on the ground floor, and two chambers above, quite sufficient for John, his wife Susan (or Susanna) and their daughter Martha, who later married Nelson Garlett. In the 1836 rental Widow Tovell was recorded as paying £2 for a cottage and garden. At Michaelmas that year she was in arrears by the same amount. Her husband had died in November the previous year, but it was always Susan Tovell's name that appeared on the bills generated by the riots, of which there are several in the Houghton Hall Archives. She was unable to write, and her husband was equally incapable of doing more than make his mark when the two married in 1810. However, in 1831, John signed his name as a witness at a Great Bircham marriage, and so did his daughter. It is not clear when Nelson Garlett arrived in Great Bircham. His and Martha's first child was baptized in June 1836.

The Carpenter's Cottage and garden
(Plate XIX in Hill's Survey of 1800)

By 1841, Susan Tovell had apparently switched her business, as she was given as a baker when the census was taken. It was Nelson Garlett who was carrying on the carpentry business. She died in 1850, and her daughter Martha died before her, in 1846.

9. John Shilling

John Shilling was one of the two blacksmiths mentioned in the 1836 directory. Just like Susan Tovell, he appeared very many times in the Houghton accounts. Shilling's property was quite extensive: a house, land and a separate smithy. All three were on the road to Docking, not far from Great Bircham parish church. In 1836 he paid £10 in rent. The house was of brick and flint, with a pantile roof. Another brick and flint building, 30 ft by 19 ft, was attached. The detached blacksmith's and shoeing shop was also in brick and flint, and measured 45 ft by 17 ft.

Neither John Shilling nor his wife Hannah had been born in Great Bircham. They came from the Shipdham area, and from at least 1800 they lived in Houghton. The first child to be baptized in Great Bircham was George, in 1809. George died in 1826, but John and Hannah's other two sons became blacksmiths: Horatio (born 1805) was working with his father in 1841 and the youngest child, John Shilling junior, was next door. Neither was in the village in 1851, but they were both still blacksmiths: Horatio in Brancaster and John in Gaywood. John Shilling senior died in 1849 (aged 79), and his wife died in 1836 (aged 61).

One other fact of interest about John Shilling was that, later in the 1830s, he ran a carrier's business. Every Tuesday a cart came from the Black Swan in St Peter's parish, Norwich, to Great Bircham. There was also a carrier's business between the Labour-in-Vain in the same parish, run by somebody called Marsham, a name we shall meet again later. In White's 1836 Directory there was just one carrier between Norwich and Bircham: John Sharp, also every Tuesday from the Black Swan, and leaving at 4 p.m. There may not have been many news-paper readers in the Birchams in 1835, but news from Norwich would have come to the parishes every week, so the people living in the Birchams were far from being cut off from the wider world. (See also Appendix A.)

10. John Groom

The other blacksmith was John Groom, and he too had come from Houghton. He paid £2 10s. in rent for a cottage in 1836, and was still carrying on a blacksmith's business in 1851, from premises on the Tofts road. He appears in the Great Bircham baptismal register as both blacksmith and preacher. He was a Primitive Methodist. His wife, Mary, was given as schoolmistress in the 1851 census. She was born Mary Spooner in 1799 in the nearby village of Stanhoe; and she married John Groom in Great Bircham in 1817. They were both able to sign the register.

11. Robert and Martha Spooner

The Spooners and John Groom were thus connected by marriage. There might have been a business connection too: Mary Spooner's father, Robert, was the wheelwright in the 1836 directory, and he most likely relied on John Groom to supply his tyres. This Robert Spooner was probably born in Stanhoe. He married Catherine Brinn (or possibly Bunn) in Docking in 1798. Two of Mary Spooner's brothers were William (born in 1802) and Robert (1805). Both were born in Great Bircham, so it must have been around the turn of the century when Robert and Catherine arrived in the parish. In 1851, in Groom's household, was his unmarried brother-in-law, William Spooner, wheelwright. The association between the two families thus continued.

In 1832 Robert Spooner senior lived in a brick and flint house 34 ft by 16 ft. There was a small lean-to and the detached wheelwright's and blacksmith's shop was large: 63 ft by 18 ft. The back and end walls were of brick and flint, and the front of stud and board. Robert Spooner junior was occupying a house and grocer's shop, 43 ft 6 ins by 20 ft.

Robert junior married Martha Jervis, of Great Bircham, in 1827. The marriage was by licence, which was normal for the farmers but not for those in trade. He died at the age of 30 in 1834, and so it was his widow Martha Spooner whose name appeared in the directory. She also died young, in April 1836. The grocer's shop mentioned above must have been managed by Robert and Martha Spooner, and then Martha on her own until she died. In 1836, after Martha's death, Robert Spooner senior was paying £8 8s. for a public house and wheelwright's shop.

V Beer-house and Inn

Of some interest to us is the mention of a beer-house in the directory. This is perhaps a more accurate description than the 'public house' of the 1836 rental. Beer-houses sprang up everywhere after the passing of the Beer Act of 1830. This act was designed to counter the excessive drinking of gin. Beer, in contrast, was not held to be harmful, and was even given to children, and for medicinal purposes. There are examples of beer being prescribed – quite a large number of pints over a short period – to the Houghton villagers by a local doctor in the 1830s.[14] Under the terms of the Beer Act all that was required for anybody to open a beer-house was to be a ratepayer, and to hand over two guineas. It must be assumed that the Spooner beer-house had been opened since the passing of the act.

Site of Spooner's Beer-house *(Photo 2011)*

We shall see in Chapter 5 that many of a higher social standing than the labourers, or those in trade, regarded beer-houses as a great evil. Their specific role in generating crime is further discussed below (XIV Crime). James Obelkevich, writing about agrarian society in Lincolnshire in the nineteenth century, gives a counter view of the beer-house:

Yet to labourers it had a positive appeal. It was a thoroughly working-class institution, a cottage opened by a labourer for his fellow labourers, and it offered them one of their few opportunities to escape the surveillance of the dominant classes. In a society under moralizing inhibitions it preserved something of the public frankness of the older society, providing an enclave in which sexual and aggressive impulses could be freely expressed.[15]

Occupying a higher place in the social order of the Birchams was the King's Head. As an inn, it may have offered accommodation. It would certainly have served food. The farmers would probably not have drunk at Spooner's beer-house, but might well have patronised the King's Head. They had the chance to drink wine and spirits there too, something not allowed in a beer-house. However, it was possible that some of the Bircham rioters had been drinking at the King's Head before mounting their attacks on the farmhouses. (See Chapter 5, IV.) In 1835 the King's Head occupied the same site as the inn of the same name today; however, it was totally rebuilt in 1860. Only the much altered stables to the south are part of the original inn premises.

In 1835 the inn was run by George England. In 1836 and 1837, he paid £42 in rent for a public house and lands. It is difficult, from the description in 1832, to work out just what was being offered in the way of accommodation. The other King's Head, in Houghton (formerly New Inn), was possibly the nearest inn where visitors might stay. In 1832 the tenant of the King's Head, Bircham, was William England, the father of George.

William England and his wife Martha came from the neighbouring village of Bagthorpe to run the King's Head. They were certainly not in Great Bircham in 1811, but William England was paying land tax in 1820. By the time of the 1845 White's Directory they had gone. With William and Matha came unmarried children: George, Frances, Nicholas, Martha and Elizabeth. The latter married James Lack, the machine maker. William died in 1832, and Martha, in 1834. Nicholas married Matilda Mitcheley in 1826; a witness was Thomas Hebgin. Elizabeth married James Lack, the machine maker, in 1831, and the announcement of the marriage appeared in the local press, something that was normal with the families of the farmers. Here are two incidents showing that the Englands, like John Drage, were of a higher social status than many in the village. The last England in Great Bircham seems to have been Frances, a farmer in the 1841 census. In the same year she was selling up prior to moving away.[16]

VI Basket-maker

There was a basket-maker, William Taylor, in Bircham Tofts in White's Directory. Baskets would have been very much in demand on the local farms, so this is yet another example of an important village trade. William Taylor was still running a basket-maker's business in 1851, and he was employing three of his four sons. He came to Bircham Tofts from Stanford, the now deserted village some seven or eight miles north of Thetford. He married Mary Toll from Bircham Tofts. It was his second marriage. From the 1851 Religious Census it is clear he was a Wesleyan Methodist.

VII Church and Chapel

Each parish had its own Anglican church, although Bircham Tofts and Bircham Newton shared the same rectory. The Rector of Great Bircham was William Pratt, but he lived in Harpley; the curate, Edward Priest, lived in Bircham Parsonage. There were certainly Primitive Methodists in all three places as well. In April 1832, John Smith, a Primitive Methodist Minister from King's Lynn, registered a house in Bircham Newton as a place of worship. He did the same in Great Bircham and Bircham Tofts in February 1833. In addition, in January 1833, Luke Duffield registered a dwelling house at Great Bircham

The 1851 Religious Census showed a variety of Methodist congregations in the three parishes: Primitive Methodists were in all three places, and there were Wesleyan Reformers and Wesleyan Methodists in Bircham Tofts. The largest nonconformist attendances were always for the Primitives, however, and their premises were larger than the other Methodist meeting-houses. Of all the places of worship in the three parishes it was only the Parish Church of Great Bircham that recorded an attendance larger than a Primitive Methodist meeting-house. This was in keeping with many villages in North-west Norfolk, where Primitive Methodism was strong.

In the Birchams the Ranters, as the Primitives were often called, were particularly numerous. Between 1838 and 1844 class-lists in the parishes of the Lynn Circuit were drawn up and in 1839 there were seventy-eight members (men and women) in two classes across the three parishes. For centuries the Anglican bishops had been arranging periodic inspections, in order to determine the spiritual and temporal state of their dioceses. The records which these inspections generated, the Visitation Records, make interesting reading. As early as 1813, there were in Great Bircham, according to the answers to the questions supplied by the Rector, 'a very few Dissenters of low rank, who call themselves Methodists'. In 1820 the same Rector, Christopher Spurgeon, recorded at the Visitation:

There are some few dissenters of the poorer order of people but it is with pleasure, I assure your Lordship, they attend church regularly every Sunday, and are well disposed in their whole conduct.

By the time of the 1838 Visitation the strength of the Ranters was evident. They were described as increasing in all three places. Moreover, in Great Bircham four schools were mentioned. One, supported by the Rector, was strictly connected with the Church; but the others, two day-schools and one night-school, all supported by the Marquess of Cholmondeley, had heads who were 'decidedly Ranters: one indeed the principal Ranter preacher'.

For Eric Hobsbawm, the Primitives were one of his Labour Sects, and above all a sect that found its greatest support amongst the working-class populations of the villages.[17] The Church of England attracted people from all classes, but congregations were very much under the control of those of the higher social classes. To some extent this applied also to the Wesleyans. Primitive Methodism, in contrast, was genuinely open to the poor, the illiterate and oppressed. There were also women who took leading roles. In a Bircham class-list of 1841 there were Susanna Golding, the wife of an agricultural labourer, and Ann Claxton, the wife of James Claxton, carpenter of Bircham Newton. If an Anglican service was predominantly cerebral and controlled, Primitive Methodist worship was the opposite. It was an emotional and passionate experience. Often conversion involved much writhing on the floor and loud confession of sins. Yet here were preachers known to all the members of the group, people who spoke the same local dialect, and had the same experiences at work or in their homes. They were grouped into classes – an important aspect of their organization – and the class-leaders took on the responsibility of caring for their members, and not solely in spiritual terms. There was thus a natural solidarity even if no unifying political ideology.

We must not overplay the political role of the Methodists, of whatever persuasion. The fervour of the Primitives must have had an appeal to both men and women, and they did thrive in this period of discontent. They would never have condoned the burning of ricks or any sort of violence directed at persons and property. Drunkenness and idleness were condemned as well as anything which put the things of this earth ahead of the storing of treasures in heaven; in this they differed in no way from the teachings of other branches of Methodism or of the Established Church. Yet, the men and women in Primitive Methodist class-meetings found a sense of worth that was rarely communicated to them by their social superiors, and not a few of them, on thinking deeply about the scriptures, would have felt that God's purpose was not to shackle them to their inferior state.

VIII Education

No school was mentioned in the 1836 Directory. A new elementary school was built by the Marquess of Cholmondeley for the children of the three parishes in 1842, a couple of years before the Houghton school was built. However, as the Visitation Records made clear, there was certainly provision for some kind of education before then, for both boys and girls. The Houghton Accounts contain several references to payments to teachers in the three parishes around the time of the Bircham Riots. The provision of schools was a typical feature of all the Cholmondeley parishes, in Norfolk as well as in Cheshire.

Despite some educational provision it is undoubtedly true that illiteracy was common among the villagers in 1835, especially those from labouring families. If we compute the levels of illiteracy from the number of couples who made their mark in the marriage registers, then the situation is quite bleak. There were one hundred and four marriages in Great Bircham between 1802 and 1832; fifty-six grooms and sixty-four brides failed to sign their names. This was far from untypical. Things had not greatly improved several years later. For the years 1839-45, according the Registrar General's Report of 1845, the mean percentage of Norfolk men who signed the register with a mark was forty-four, slightly lower than for Essex and Suffolk, but considerably higher than the mean for the whole of England, which was around thirty-three. For Norfolk women the mean was fifty per cent, which was virtually the same as that for England.

There were also quite a few witnesses who signed with a cross in the Bircham registers, which suggests weddings attended by guests only two of whom could write their names, the clergyman and the Parish Clerk. The farmers signed their names, and so usually did the tradesmen; it was overwhelmingly the labourers who had to make their mark. Much has been made of the use of marriage registers as a way of determining levels of illiteracy, but it is a crude instrument. Considering the general lack of writing implements in the homes of labourers and the rarity of the need to write, it is hardly surprising that so few could do so. However, that did not imply an inability to read. Gradually standards of literacy began to improve, and by 1851 some eighty children were attending the Cholmondeley Free School. [18]

IX Agricultural Labourers

Naturally the above does not give the complete picture. The overwhelming majority of tenants in the 1836 rental or the 1832 survey were not farmers or people in trade. They were nearly all agricultural labourers; there was little other work for the villagers to do. The shoemakers, blacksmiths and the like were essentially family businesses. According to the 1831 census, out of one hundred and ten labourers aged twenty and above there were sixty-two employed in agriculture in Great Bircham. There were twenty-six employed in retail trade or in handicrafts, but that did include masters. There were just five occupiers in the parish (the farmers) and they were the only ones employing agricultural labourers. There were no male servants of any age, and just eight female servants. The figures for Bircham Tofts and Bircham Newton, although based on much smaller overall populations, were very similar. All this is entirely compatible with a community where virtually all the land was given over to arable and sheep farming. Under the heading 'Capitalists, Bankers, Professional and other Educated Men' there was just one in the three parishes, the

Rector of Bircham Newton and Bircham Tofts. Little had changed by the time of the 1851 census.

1. Employment

The term 'agricultural labourer', however, does not entirely cover the working men and women of the three parishes. While the men, and boys as soon as they became old enough, mainly worked on the land, they might have taken on other casual work to feed themselves and their families. Women's employment is notoriously under-recorded in the censuses. It would be quite wrong to assume that girls either helped their mothers in the home or worked as servants – and did nothing else. Of course, the farmers, and the some of the tradespeople too, needed servants and that was the obvious job for a girl as soon as she became thirteen or fourteen. Young children needed plenty of attention and mothers and elder girls undertook that duty. However, women and children, both boys and girls, also did farm work, and not just at the harvest.

We can dismiss the bucolic images of eighteenth and early nineteenth century painters. This was no Arcadian idyll. Most labourers in the 1830s would have looked distinctly unattractive figures, even intimidating. They were scruffy, dirty and lacking in the finer aspects of more genteel society. These men and women, then, were at the bottom of the Bircham social heap. This is precisely the image that has come down to us. Many of those from a much higher order of society consistently disparaged and despised the working men and women who toiled for long hours on their land, who were frequently ill from the back-breaking work, who often had to bear insults, and even blows, from farmers in order to feed the nation. These people did not have a voice, even though a few were perfectly able to read and write, and all were capable of articulating their feelings; but in the summer of 1835 many of the working people of the Birchams, and of the neighbouring parishes, forced those in authority in the Smithdon and Brothercross Hundreds, and some in London, to open their ears.

A misconception often held is that the farm labourers were always in work. There were large farms in Bircham, as we have seen, and on the

Houghton Estate home farm, plantations and, at times, the roads of Houghton there was much to do. The 1851 census gives the acreage of the farms and the number of men who worked on them. It all looks very impressive, but when a farmer was recorded as employing so many men and boys it did not mean they worked all the time. When the work had been done the farmer could not give a man anything else to do. Besides, the number of labourers was increasing. Given that there was a surplus of labour in the Birchams, as elsewhere in agricultural districts at this time, life was particularly hard for the labourers. In the *The Bury Post* of 5 March 1834 it was reported that in the Hundred of Smithdon there were 'two hundred and fifty labourers out of employ, and totally dependent on parish relief'. The parishes were not named but Great Bircham must have been one of them. The farmers had thus no reason to pay generous wages, even when they needed the work doing on their farms.

It is also often forgotten that farm labourers could frequently turn their hands to a great variety of tasks. Those who worked with horses were skilled, and a good teamsman, the person in charge of a team of horses, was very much prized. Most of the Bircham men, when employed, would have worked on the village farms. Yet some of them also found regular employment at the home farm in Houghton; or possibly in the tree plantation there. These were perhaps the lucky ones, as their employment was likely to be more secure; but even the Houghton labourers did not work all the time. Below are some examples, taken from 1834, that appear in a ledger kept by the land agent, Stephen Reeve. They show the variety of jobs done. All the men are known to be residents of Great Bircham or Bircham Tofts.

Month	Names	Work done	Payment
January	Wanford	3 days on farm	6s. 6d.
	Sandford	6 days ditto	12s. 6d.
	Williamson, Chapman, Pilgrim	Filling and spreading 275 loads of marl	£3 8s. 9d.
February	Two Boys Royce	10 days each after turnips	8s. 9d.
	John Chapman	11 days ploughing	£1 2s.
	Dewing Chapman	14 loads of oats at 9d.	10s. 6d.

	Dewing Chapman	10 days threshing	£1 2s. 3d.
	Chapman	Loading straw	6s.
April	Chapman	6 days chopping flagg on common	1s.
	Chapman	Dressing 57 combs of barley at 14d.	£3 6s. 6d.
May	Wandford	12 days ploughing	£1 2s.
	Chapman	3 days after potatoes and hay	5s. 8d.
June	Boy Royce	2 weeks	5s.
	Rippingale & partners	32 days hoeing turnips	3s. 6d.
	Williamson	4 days cutting peas	9s.
	Rippingale & partners	Filling and spreading 120 loads of clay at 3d. a load	£1 10s.
July	Pilgrim	6 days after peas	11s. 9d.
	William Chapman	2 weeks keeping crows	15s.
	William Williamson	12 days cutting peas at 2s. 6d.	£1 10s.
August	Chapman	3 days after corn	7s. 6d.
		9 days threshing rye and oats	£1 2s. 6d.
	Gave Chapman and son for frolic		3s. 6d.
September	John Chapman	9 days at plough	15s.
		2 days at drill	3s. 4d.
	Chapman	12 days threshing with flail rye, oats and barley	£1 2s.
December	Chapman	12 days with team	£1 2s.
	Williamson and Pilgrim	Throwing down fence on common	£1 6s.
	Pilgrim	5 days fencing 11 acres	8s. 6d.

Just a few of the Bircham labourers feature in these accounts; presumably they had proved themselves good workers. The work at Houghton, at least in the period when Reeve wrote up his farm accounts, was always organized by the piece. When there was no work they had to remain idle. Some were undoubtedly lazy or incompetent, but it would be extremely unjust to label them all as poor or indolent workers.

Unfortunately we do not have farm accounts for any of the Birchams. The above are somewhat untypical in that they feature men more or less in regular employment, and were compiled before the riots. Even so they have some value. One Bircham man, Wanford (or Wanfer), was virtually in constant employment at Houghton from May 1833 to May 1834; and his average weekly earnings were more or less 11s.

2. Wages

Earnings are difficult to give with any degree of precision. There are historians who quote average weekly wages for whole counties, thus hiding huge local variations in rates of pay. What really matters is the actual amount of money making up the weekly, or daily, income of an individual family; of paramount importance was to put food into clamouring mouths. The figures are not readily available. By the 1830s, engaging labourers by the week was less common than hiring them by the day, or even the hour. We cannot be sure that the other Bircham labourers, or the Houghton labourers not working at the home farm, were earning what the men above were being paid according to Reeve's ledger. They are, however, the closest idea we can get of farm labourers' earnings on one of the Cholmondeley farms just before the Bircham Riots. George Bate, of the Village Farm in Houghton, gave, in 1832, the figure of 12s. for the average weekly wage in Houghton. Bate also indicated that seven or eight men were able to earn as much as 15s.-18s. threshing corn in winter; and in summer twenty-four men worked for six weeks hoeing turnips and making hay at 20s. The same men's harvest earnings amounted to 30s. per week.[19] It is far from clear that the Bircham men earned these amounts, although harvest pay was always higher than for the rest of the year. Wage rates varied even on the same farm, according to age experience and competence. Seasonal variations were also inevitable.

What is beyond doubt, however, is that generally Norfolk wages for agricultural labourers were low, although there were counties where they were lower still (see below); they were also, on average, 1s. a week higher in the west than in the east of Norfolk, according to Anne Digby.[20] It was a perpetual struggle to maintain a family on these

48

earnings, and it only needed a bout of illness or injury, or a prolonged period of bad weather, to cause severe distress.

The all-important harvest wages made a considerable difference. James Kay, who conducted a survey in 1838 of the earnings of agricultural labourers in Norfolk and Suffolk, calculated the average annual harvest earnings of men was £5 8s. This closely matches what Reeve noted in the summer of 1834: eight men had £5 12s. 6d each; and there was also 5s. each for a 'frolic'. As for wives, Kay found that those without children earned the most: their average annual earnings amounted to £3 8s. 9d. The earnings of women with young children were a third lower than those without. In the case of children, their number and ages certainly influenced their own earnings. In cases where all children were under ten the average annual earnings were £2 4s., but with families with four children above ten the average annual earnings were £20 3s. 8½d. The earnings of women and children can easily be overlooked, but they were often vital to a family's survival. Gleaning was also a source of income, and when Kay put everything together (and excluded the single men) he calculated that the average income of all the other families was £36 4s. or 13s. 9d. a week. For the man alone the average weekly wage was 7s. 3d.[21]

There are two other sources of labourers' earnings that are of relevance to us. Bacon, in his 1844 Report, examined a number of Norfolk farms of various acreages and on a variety of soils. For all the farms the average weekly wage was 9s. 7d. One very large farm on light soil paid 9s. per week; another, of 1,000 acres, paid 11s. Caird (1852) gave the wages of agricultural labourers for the whole country for the years 1850-51. For Norfolk he gave 8s. 6d. as the average weekly wage. However, as Keith Snell has pointed out, these were significantly lower than those of 1833 and 1837. There were counties with lower wages than Norfolk, but labourers in the north of England were much better paid.[22]

Women and children, then, must not be forgotten. Bircham farm accounts might not have survived, but we can at least see what boys could earn: about 2s. 6d per week in the case of the boys Royce. After 1834 there were more records concerning the relief of the poor, and from these we can have some idea of what was being paid in Great

Average Weekly Wages of Agricultural Labourers (from Snell)			
	1833	1837	1850
Wiltshire	9s. 5d.	8s.	7s. 3d.
Dorset	8s. 8d.	7s. 6d.	7s. 6d.
Essex	10s. 9d.	10s. 4d.	8s.
Norfolk	11s.2d.	10s. 4d.	8s. 6d.
Suffolk	10s.2d.	10s. 4d.	7s.

Bircham. In June 1839 three of Thomas Bell's children earned 3s. 6d. per week; and by October 1843 this had risen to 4s. In July of the same year, two of John Hunt's children earned 6s.; and, in April 1843, a child of Rebecca Harrison's was earning 2s. 6d. Two years earlier Hannah Marsham, aged 22, was looking after her siblings. She earned 3s. 10d and the two children 1s. 6d.[23] It all depended on the age, strength and ability of the child, and the availability of work. Reeve also gave details of women's work, but as he did not go as far as giving names we cannot tell whether any Bircham women featured. Gathering stones off the fields was a hated job, but at Houghton in the 1830s it was always done by women. Or there were jobs like weeding, cutting peas, burning quicks or mending sacks. There is one intriguing item in Reeve's ledger: the payment to 'Mrs Golding' of the large sum of £8 17s. 6d. 'for fowls' in May 1834. It is important not to forget the varied possibilities for supplementary income open to women as well as men.

One thing is certain: wages in the mills of Lancashire and North Cheshire were much higher. In October 1836, the guardians of the Docking Union, formed in the previous summer, drew the readers' attention to the notice that they had given to the poor of the district: that families of good character and having a sufficient number of children above the age of twelve, if they agreed to be engaged for three or four years, could earn much higher wages than anything farmers might pay:

Wages per week as follows: for a father 12s. 6d. for a son 18 years of age 6s., 14 do., 3s. 6d. to 5s. 6d. for a girl 18 years of age 6s. 6d. 16 do. 6s. 14 do. 5s. 12 do. 4s.[24]

3. Boys

Life for all labouring families was difficult. For boys in particular their introduction to working life was frequently a harsh and cruel one. They were thrust into the unforgiving working conditions of the farm at a very early age – as young as six sometimes - and soon learnt to swear like adults. Augustus Jessop, the Rector of Scarning, writing in 1882, recounted his talks with the old people of the village. One man recalled a period much earlier in the century when, still in his teens, he had been so severely whipped by a farmer for being late that his clothes were cut to pieces.[25] Such treatment, in varying degrees of viciousness, was frequently meted out by employers or fathers. This was an age when nobody thought such physical chastisement was abnormal. It was a brutal age, peopled by brutes. If they had been asked why they were cruel, farmers would have undoubtedly responded that if young boys, and young men, were not to run wild, severe discipline was required. Without it nothing much would have been done on the farm.

Things improved but slowly. George Edwards, in his auto-biography, tells how he started work scaring crows in 1856, at the age of six. The work soon exhausted him, and one day he fell asleep. The farmer saw him and gave him a severe thrashing, as well as deducting 2d. from his weekly wage of 1s. (for a seven-day week). Four years later, working as a horseman, he was struck on the knuckles by the farm steward for not ploughing straight. Edwards threatened later revenge, but for that he was given such a severe beating that he was left in a badly bruised state. He retaliated and kicked the man in the face. When he told his mother she too attacked the steward, but her maternal devotion earned her a 5s. fine.[26] Labourers were indeed often badly treated, and it was of little use having recourse to the law. As the old man who spoke to Jessop said, 'What was the use of my going to the magistrates? There wasn't a labouring man for miles round would have dared to appear against a farmer.'

X Leisure

It would appear almost anachronistic to mention leisure. It sounds an entirely modern concept, something belonging to an age where boundless possibilities exist for filling in non-working hours. We may

51

suppose that rural workers had no opportunity for leisure. It may have been true that, when they were in work, agricultural labourers had little time to do more than work and sleep; but if the employment pattern in the three Birchams was the same as that at Houghton a six-day week was the standard practice. There was time to relax on Sundays, perhaps to walk in the country, to work in the allotment or, for the Ranters, to offer one's loud and fervent praises to God.

Organized sport, such as village football and cricket teams, or bowls and darts teams, would have to wait for another era, as would annual holidays by the seaside. Rural workers might have been content simply to stroll down the country lanes. They were possibly attracted by occasional cockfights. Field sports were for the rich, and in November 1833, according to game accounts still kept at the hall, various shooting parties were active at Houghton. They shot hares and rabbits in the main. If the labourers indulged in the same activity, not necessarily with guns, they were breaking the law; nevertheless, they certainly did catch rabbits and game birds, and thus provided their families with welcome additions to their meagre diet.

A good number of working men, and not a few women, drank at Spooner's beer-house or the King's Head, and this may have led to the singing of bawdy songs and to rough and vulgar conduct. Many a person of a superior social class feared to encounter groups of young men lounging by the side of the road, as they knew that the drink and the strength of the crowd would sweep away any deference that might have prevailed in the past, and they would be assailed with ribald comments.

It is so easy to slip into the attitudes of more genteel society, and of the farmers who largely shunned the labouring population. While they were at work, the latter met the insults, and blows, of their employers, who supervised the fields on horseback lording it over them. Rarely did any farmer speak to them as fellow human beings worthy of respect. Once away from the field and liberated from their unrelenting toil, however, they could find freedom and become something more than hired hands. There was one time of the year when the old ways prevailed, and no farmer would have dared to resist. This was the 'frolic' that was regarded as a right by all who had toiled for so long in the sun in order to bring in the harvest. Another word used in Norfolk was 'largesse', and both words are met in the Houghton accounts. The workers were given a payment, which they then spent on a supper in the beer-houses or inns. We can be quite sure that Robert Spooner and George England eagerly awaited the conclusion of the grain harvest.

Harvest labourers at Great Massingham – date unknown

Another tradition was the holding of annual fairs in some towns and villages. They still continue in some fashion and their popularity is enduring, but in the 1830s they were much more raucous affairs, and frequently led to fights and rowdy behaviour of various sorts. The beer-houses naturally did good business. At Rudham Fair in 1835, for instance, James Tipple had his purse stolen after he had gone into a beer-house between three of four o'clock in the morning.[27] Great Bircham did not have a fair but there were several within walking distance of the village. There were two fairs at East Rudham (May and November), and two each at Burnham Westgate (Easter Monday and 1 August), Great Massingham (Maundy Thursday and 8 November) and Fakenham (Ash Wednesday and 11 November). For anybody who wanted to go further there was the Great Mart at King's Lynn, which began on 14 February and continued for two weeks. By the nineteenth century it had mainly lost its original commercial purpose. This evocative description from White's 1836 Directory gives us some idea of the event, and we can immediately understand its attraction to North-west Norfolk labourers and their families:

The great Mart is now more conspicuous for pleasure and amusement than business, being much resorted to by genteel company, and the young and gay of every grade from all parts of the county, and affording for their entertainment a large diversified assemblage of shows and rarities, "animals of every description, tame and wild; giants and dwarfs; tumblers, jugglers".

Candyfloss and burger vans would have to wait, but here was simple yet vibrant entertainment. Farm workers could throw for coconuts; men, women and children who had never seen anything bigger than a horse or a bull could gaze in wonder at an elephant. For a while they could forget the relentless drudgery of the farm. Yet this was a society in transition, and that theme will run deep through this study. The wilder entertainment and simple pleasures of the rural working class were later to be anaesthetized by the moralizers and by their social superiors. The harvest frolic would eventually give way to the harvest festival, and the fairs would become tamer events aimed at the whole family; yet the excitement of a modern child's first experience of a fairground ride must equal the amazement with which children of the 1830s first beheld a tumbler or a caged beast.

XI Poverty

1. The Cycle of Poverty

Seasonal variation in employment would have faced all those who were not the occupiers of Bircham farms or in trade. There was another cycle which remorselessly gnawed away at the household finances. Kay took this cycle into account when he grouped his families according to the number of children. The earnings of wives and children were crucial, but the wider life-cycle of poverty cannot be ignored. A couple would marry and both could work, but poverty would begin after the

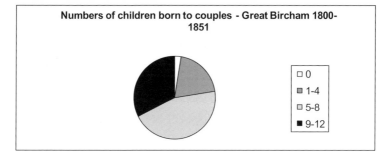

Numbers of children born to couples - Great Bircham 1800-1851

Legend:
- □ 0
- ▣ 1-4
- □ 5-8
- ■ 9-12

birth of the first child and continue with the birth of subsequent children. Things improved when the children were old enough to earn something. Soon they too would leave home and initiate a poverty-cycle of their own. The parents were able to cope, more or less, in their forties and fifties, but then earning power declined as they entered their sixties. Such a cycle is, of course, universal, but in 1835 there was no state pension, no system of welfare payments developed to the extent that it is today, and little possibility of limiting the size of a family. At the right time, a good number of children would bring in extra income; but when entirely dependent they had to be nursed, fed and clothed.

Couples had far more children than today, of course, in an age when controlling the size of a family was very difficult. *Coitus interruptus* or abstinence was possible, unreliable in the case of the first, and the second difficult to impose. It was also very likely known that pro-longing breast-feeding would provide a measure of protection against pregnancy. Nevertheless, with some couples, babies appeared with relentless frequency. Some forty couples have been identified who married between 1800 and 1835, most of them in Great Bircham. Their children were all baptized in the parish (apart from some born to one of the principal farmers and his wife), and in every case the couple appear to have stayed together at least to the end of the child-bearing years of the woman. The sample is admittedly small, but does show a clear trend. The number of children born to each couple varies between none and twelve, but the overwhelming proportion of couples had over five children.

The mean number of children per couple was just under seven. They did not all survive into adulthood: the mortality rates among infants and young children in this period were very high. Even so the large number of children living in a relatively small space imposed a great burden on many families, especially if older generations were to be accommodated in the same household. John and Susan Golding, who married in 1826, had twelve (or possibly thirteen) children. William and Jane Bell married in 1829, and they had ten. However, at the other end of the scale, Thomas and Jane Greeves (married 1826) had only three children, and John and Susan Tovell (1810) just one. With so many children clamouring for attention it should not come as any surprise to us that mothers had occasion to resort to the use of opiates. In April 1846 Elizabeth Howell of Burnham Overy, then living in the workhouse, had gone to see friends, taking her three children with her. A baby of two months did not survive the visit, and a coroner's inquest was ordered. The jury found that the child had died because of the bad weather – it is unlikely that adequate clothing had been provided – and from 'having had too much laudanum incautiously administered to it'. [28]

2. Outgoings

If it is difficult to be precise about the earnings of farm labourers then it is virtually impossible to give accurate figures for outgoings. Clearly we can list what had to be spent under various headings: food, obviously, and then rent. The latter will be dealt with in the next section. Clothing had to be bought occasionally, although evidence from early photographs strongly points to a very scruffily dressed rural population. Certain items of food could have been purchased at John Drage's or Martha Spooner's shops, and perhaps flour directly from the mill. We do not know how many cottages had pigsties, but some labourers undoubtedly kept a pig. We know that Williamson of Great Bircham had one, because Reeve's accounts record that he was paid 2s. 6d towards the cost of 'losing his pig' in April 1833. There were possibly some who had hens (the Goldings, for instance); the produce of gardens and allotments no doubt sustained others. There was always poaching, to supplement the diet.

Digby[29] gives one example of the possible weekly spending of a Norfolk family in the 1840s.

Item	Price
3 stones of flour	6s. 6d.
½ cwt of coal	6d.
1½ oz tea	4½d.
½ lb soap	3d.
¾ lb sugar	4½d.
½ lb candles	3d.
Butter and cheese	8d.
Other dry goods	1d.
Total	9s.

If we assume that not all farm labourers were earning Wanfer's 11s. a week, then it is obvious that earnings provided little more than subsistence income, despite the extra earnings of women and children.

Major items like boots or the rent had to be left to the harvest. Despite undeniably harsh circumstances, however, a man could easily drink or gamble a good proportion of his earnings away, and then go home to beat his complaining wife.

3. Diet

The diet of the labouring families was dictated by the money that was earned. A wife might often go without to feed infant children or the members of the family who were earning. If she performed weekly miracles juggling with the household income, a housewife also worked wonders with the food she provided, concocting nourishing stews from very few ingredients or serving up the famous Norfolk dumplings. Whatever the diet, it was inevitably rich in carbohydrates and lacking in fat and proteins. A great deal of bread was consumed to fill up the stomach quickly. When a labourer was in work he was outdoors in all weathers and worked long hours. Despite deficiencies of diet he generally consumed enough calories to sustain him. Meat was not unknown, but comparatively rare. After the creation of the new workhouses the disparity between the diet of inmates, which had weekly amounts of meat, and food eaten by the majority of the rural poor living outside, became apparent. Digby quotes *The Morning Chronicle* of 5 December 1849, which reported one East Anglian who declared: 'Lor, bless you, we shouldn't know ourselves if we got meat'.[30]

It is difficult for us to imagine the daily lives of the poorer sorts of people in the past. We can be sure that their tables were not piled with a surfeit of things to eat, or that they threw away a third of the food they bought, as is estimated to be quite normal for families in 2013. We have a glimpse of one family in Burnham Overy in December 1838. The visitor, who was there in an official capacity, stated:

... he visited the family on Tuesday morning and found the Man, woman and 2 sons & 2 children; at Breakfast - they were eating Bread and Butter & lb of dripping – a Tea Pot, and a very good wood fire ..[31]

Better or worse conditions might have been found, but this picture gives us some idea of the breakfast eaten by a labouring family.

Inevitably poor families hit periods when their income was insufficient for them to cover the necessities of life. In such circumstances they were compelled to seek help from members of their extended family, or from friends and neighbours. Charity could sometimes bring welcome assistance, and if need be they were able to seek relief from the parish.

XII Housing

1. Houghton Estate cottages

Despite their hardships the labourers did live in properties owned, and maintained, by their landlord, the Marquess of Cholmondeley. Overcrowding there might have been (often no different from what faced any labourers migrating to the towns), but repairs were frequently carried out. The Houghton accounts constantly refer to work done at the cottages as well as the farms. For instance, the 1836 accounts refer to Butcher, the bricklayer, being paid £21 12s. for rebuilding Carrington's cottage at Great Bircham and for repairing others, and in December 1835, 500 floor-bricks were bought for Sandford's cottage in Bircham, for £1 5s. Nevertheless, on 14 April 1836 Stephen Reeve wrote to Richard Groom:

I have had some repairs done in the village to the floors and breaches in the walls, &c. A considerable quantity of this kind of repairs is wanted upon the estate to the cottages and by finding our own materials, studs, spars, &c the expense will not be heavy.[32]

He was writing about Houghton village, but there must have been breaches in the walls throughout the whole estate. Habbakkuk Englestown also noted occasionally that some properties in the Birchams were in 'bad repair'. There was clearly always much to be done, and money was not limitless.

In the 1832 survey there were some sixty-three tenants living in cottages, often in double tenements, in Great Bircham. The 1831 census gives a total of ninety families. Even if we add the farmers, the Englands at the King's Head and the tradespeople in houses, we still cannot come close to ninety. Much depends on the census definition of a family, but it would appear that there was sub-letting, and consequently some overcrowding. There were tradesmen among the sixty-three tenants, but the majority were the labourers.

Three examples, taken from Englestown's survey, can give an idea of cottage accommodation in Great Bircham at the time of the riots. The dimensions refer to the whole building. All properties were built of brick and flint.

Tenant(s)	Roof	Size	Rooms
Thomas Marsham	Thatched with straw.	18 ft x14 ft 6 ins.	One room with pantry on the ground floor. One chamber above. Also a lean-to. In bad repair.
George Bennett; Thomas Marsters; John Golding.	Pantiles.	Three tenements. 40 ft x21 ft	Two rooms and a pantry on the ground floor. Staircase. Two chambers above. Lean-to.
Daniel Bales	Pantiles.	21 ft x16 ft	One room and a pantry; one chamber. (One storey.)

2. Rents

There might well have been improvements between 1832 and 1836, when the first rental appears. It is not completely certain that the tenants occupied exactly the same property, but they probably did. The rents were as follows, all for a cottage and allotment:

Name	Annual Rent
Thomas Marsham	£1 16s.
George Bennett	£1 16s.
Thomas Marsters	Senior - £2 6s.; junior - £1 16s.
John Golding	Junior - £1 6s.
Daniel Bales	£2 6s.

Kay, in his paper on wages, mentioned rents; he gave the average as £3 11s. 4½d, which is far above what was paid for simple cottage rents in the three Bircham parishes. Rents were due at Michaelmas, shortly after families received their harvest pay. A study of the Great Bircham rental for 1836 makes it very clear that many labouring families were struggling to pay their rents; in fact, out of the seventy-six labourers or tradespeople in the 1836 rental, only forty had no arrears at Michaelmas 1835. Thanks to the generosity of the landlord, quite considerable arrears were allowed. In the case of Thomas Carrington, who paid £2 annually for his cottage, there were arrears of £2 in 1835 and £3 14s. in 1836. Exactly the same situation appears to have applied to Richard Greaves (or Greeves): his rent was £1 16s., but he was £2 12s. in arrears in 1835, and £3 8s. in 1836.

3. Allotments

In the big ledger kept by Stephen Reeve for his accounts there is an item referring to £2 paid for 'marking out and mapping the allotments in Great Bircham, Bircham Tofts and Bircham Newton.' There is no actual date written, but the year is definitely 1835. There had been allotments in Houghton from at least a couple of years earlier. Each allotment was about a quarter of an acre. When Richard Groom wrote to Lord Cholmondeley on 8 November 1834 he must have been referring to the whole estate:

The allotment system to be placed on the best footing and some land set apart for Spade Husbandry of the able bodied pauper labourers.[33]

Groom was certainly following a movement that had gathered pace throughout agricultural districts. His wishes would have been readily accepted by Lord Cholmondeley, and soon after he had written to his noble employer most of the labourers in the Birchams had access to an allotment. Whether they would have prevented the riots of June 1835, had they been in place then, is another question. Very likely not. It is arguable that the provision of allotments was not an absolute guarantee that all the Bircham labourers would henceforth behave themselves. Nevertheless, by 1836, the rent of nearly every tenant of a cottage in Great Bircham included an allotment. Just six had gardens only.

The provision of cottages in Bircham Tofts shows a very similar situation. More cottages had clearly been built there since the 1832 survey. An 1834 bill is for 'Tovel, Carpenter's Work' on 'new cottages at Bircham Tofts - £20 14s. 4d'. In 1836 there were 14 tenants paying rent on a cottage and an allotment – typically £2 6s. – and only two had gardens.

4. Living conditions

What of living conditions inside the cottages? We can be quite sure that material possessions were far fewer than those encountered in most homes in the twenty-first century. This description of a cottage in Ringstead from April 1841 might not be typical, as the householder was described as 'not of sound mind', yet it does offer some insight into living conditions.

One Bedstead very ordinary. 1 Quilt to d° very filthy; Sheets or Blankets none; 1 Chair; 1 Broken table; 1 Boiler, 1 kettle; 2 or 3 plates, d° Basins; two knives. The floor of the House is about one third of it broken into, and in a very filthy state, no fender to prevent the fire falling about the house; the room in which they live in one corner is laid potatoes and coals, the man, woman, & children without sufficient clothing to make them appear decent.[34]

XIII A Changing World

The world was changing. The industrial revolution was gathering pace and soon many families from the rural parishes of Norfolk would be tempted to try a new life in the North of England. Of the classic three sections of the pyramid which constituted the organization of nineteenth century agriculture – the landlord, the principal tenants (farmers) and the labourers – it was the middle group that most rapidly embraced change. By the time of the Bircham Riots they were well on their way to becoming capitalist farmers employing labour when they wanted it. They kept the cost of labour down as much as they could and the relationship between them and their workers was essentially an exploitative one.

The labourers and many noble landlords (of which the Marquess of Cholmondeley was a good example) were much slower to change. The latter were still strongly wedded to philanthropy and their relations with the labouring poor were paternalistic. The labourers clung to ancient practices, and expected them to continue. These included the provision of charitable gifts, relief in case of need and the right to work.

In 1844 Bacon, in his *Report on the Agriculture of Norfolk*, charted the history of the Norfolk labourer from 1805. He plotted the social changes to which we have just alluded, and stressed the lack of progress amongst the labouring population:

Unhappily while other classes were gradually progressing, the moral and physical condition of the labourer was as gradually retrograding until at one period a complete disorganization of the rural districts of Norfolk was threatened.[35]

The causes of this regression have been well documented by historians. The enclosure of commons, which had deprived the poorer sections of agrarian society of the means of supporting themselves independently, was one cause. Another factor was the decline in farm service. At one time it had been common for young men and women to live in the farmhouse and effectively to become part of a working family. The servants ate at the same table and worked alongside the farmer and his wife. It is clear from the accounts of the Bircham Riots that farm service had not ceased in Great Bircham, but it had already been declining for years in the south and east of England. Farmers became wealthier and did not want their social inferiors in their houses.

For their social superiors it was also their labourers' improvident marriages that did much to impoverish them. It is of interest to examine the situation in Great Bircham.

Over seventy marriages taking place in Great Bircham, and of couples who stayed in the parish, have been identified between 1800 and 1835. Unfortunately the baptisms of all the grooms and brides have not been positively identified; but for thirty-two men and thirty-seven women it has been possible to calculate an age at marriage. In most cases this is a precise age, because the baptismal registers give the date of birth. Where only a baptism date has been found a suitable adjustment has been made. In a very small number of cases the closest date to the marriage is the last entry in the Banns Register. The sample is a small one but the mean age of marriage for men was twenty-three years five months, and for women just over twenty-two. These ages are below the mean age at first marriages given by Wrigley and Schofield.[36] The downward trend they identified is quite clear, however:

	1600-49	1650-99	1700-49	1750-99	1800-49
Men	28.0	27.5	27.5	26.4	25.3
Women	26.0	26.5	26.2	24.9	23.4

Brides were nearly always younger than grooms in the Great Bircham marriages, and some very young. Elizabeth Tubby, who married Downing Sampher in 1832, was just over twenty-five, older than Wrigley and Schofield's mean age. Sampher was not far off thirty, which was old for any period in the nineteenth century. However, Susan Curson, who married John Golding (1826), was way below the mean at seventeen years five months. Her spouse was twenty-four years one month.

Large numbers of young children imposed a particular burden, especially where work was so irregular. Troubles were compounded where there were illegitimate children as well. For the moral leaders of society illegitimacy was regarded as something quite shameful, and only confirmed their strong disapproval of many of those toiling in the fields. It is the views of such people that have dominated our appraisal of sexuality in the past.

Great Bircham, as any village in North-west Norfolk, had its share of illegitimate births. All births to people living in the parish between 1813-51 have been plotted, and, as the table below shows, there is clear evidence of prenuptial sexual activity. There may well have been more babies conceived before marriage, and ones where baptism occurred just after nine months following marriage could well have been in that category. Often the first child was not baptized until some time after marriage, but that cannot have been the result of any attempt to control births. There is just no way of saying whether such couples went to the altar in a virginal state or not. There is no space in this book to dwell long on this subject, but it must be stressed that sexual activity outside marriage in the past was much more common than many would care to believe.

Great Bircham			Number of illegit-
Births 1813-1851	Illegitimate children	Children conceived before marriage	imate children born in every 100 in North-west Norfolk (1845)
629	40	16	10.4

This represents a steady (but not alarming) rate of illegitimacy; and it is one that is far from untypical of Norfolk. The last column in the table represents the findings from the Registrar General's Report for 1845 and groups together four registration districts: Walsingham, Docking, Freebridge Lynn and King's Lynn. The percentage for the whole of Norfolk was in fact slightly higher. What is startling is that this figure placed Norfolk in second place in the whole of England and Wales in terms of illegitimacy. Great Bircham did not stand apart from that trend, therefore.

Whether or not their labourers had entered into improvident marriages and had many children, including illegitimate ones, to support, the farmers still needed work doing on their farms. The pattern of farming in the Birchams was typical of farms on the light soils. The principal grains were barley and wheat, with some oats for the horses. Of the latter a good many were required, and Appendix F gives some indication of the number and size of the stables. Roots were grown as break crops in a crop rotation, and by far the commonest root crops were turnips. The farms would all have had sheep. These were folded on the turnip crop, and their manure made the land strong enough for growing cereals. Obviously there was a great need for labour during the grain harvests, and it was at this time of year that labouring families could earn most. The whole family would take part. The shepherds would be particularly busy at times of lambing and shearing; ploughing was carried out in the early months of the year; the hay was cut in June (haysel); roots were drilled in April and May, hoed in June and July and harvested at the end of the year, and there was always the vital winter job of spreading muck on the land or, commonly in this part of Norfolk, marl. Such were some examples of typical jobs, but there were very often far more people looking for work than were needed.

The numbers of unemployed in the Smithdon Hundred in March 1834 have already been mentioned. Bacon gave the picture, equally bleak, for the whole of Norfolk in 1831: in 473 parishes there were 2,714 men out of work, roughly one eighth of the whole population of these parishes. The only course open to the farmers was to pay low wages, leaving the rest to be made up from the rates. This is a central theme of this book. (See Chapters 2 and 5.) Bacon described the situation of the labourer in the 1830s in these terms, not neglecting the plight of the farmers:

Broken in spirit, sunk to the depths of degradation and distress, he was compelled to have recourse to parish allowance, granted with a sparing hand, both on account of the number of applicants, and the distressed state of the tenantry themselves. [37]

The thread that binds everything together in this study is the supposed ignorant state of the labouring poor. 'Ignorance' in this context implied more than being unlettered; it had a distinct moral dimension. It suited employers of labour to keep their workforce illiterate, but later they were to be alarmed when their labourers revolted in their ignorance and poverty. We must infer from these words of Bacon, again referring to the 1830s, that the reduction of the agricultural labourer to the state of an unthinking brute roused him to revolt:

While the wealth of the landlord and the profits of the tenant had been rapidly augmented by the influence of increased practical knowledge and skill in culture, and while general education had elevated the intellectual position, and refined the habits of the higher and middle classes, the labourer had been subject to a neglect which had as rapidly sunk him in the scale of society – a neglect which recoiled on his superiors with double force at a later period. [38]

XIV Crime

We can see the recoiling of this neglect in the criminal statistics, although any researcher into nineteenth century agrarian unrest must approach them with caution. First Bacon, who plotted the rise in committals to Norfolk prisons from 1800 to 1843. A steady increase is clear, and it shows a dramatic rise in the number of prisoners that cannot be explained simply by the rise in the population. If we confine ourselves to Walsingham Bridewell, the gaol to which most prisoners in North-west Norfolk were sent, the trend is quite startling:

1807-1817	1818-1826	1827-1835	1836-1843
711	1,486	3,319	3,122

Taking the third period, it is clear that some years were particularly bad, and that the year before the Bircham Riots had the highest number of committals.[39] 1831 and 1832 were years of great unrest throughout many southern counties, and it is something dealt with in further detail in Chapter 5.

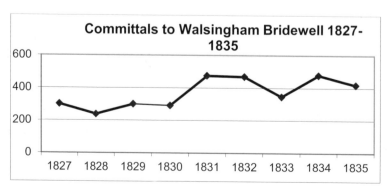

66

Next, John Weyland, Chairman of the Norfolk Quarter Sessions. At Easter 1834, addressing the Grand Jury of the County of Norfolk, he was baffled by the alarming increase in the number of trials in the courts. This was despite (in his eyes) an improvement in the condition of the labourers, thanks to a rise in their income and a lowering of the prices of 'almost every necessary of life'.

Last year we tried in this county, (exclusive of summary convictions), prisoners to the amount of one a day for the whole year, which was a great increase over preceding years. In the first three months of this year, from January 1 to March 31, 1834, there have been tried no fewer than 340 in the ninety days, or at the rate of 3½ prisoners for each day, in a population of 300,000. [40]

Weyland was quite convinced that it was all because of the Beer Act of 1830.

But what was a crime? Poaching was not felt to be criminal; at least not by the poor. Had not the Good Lord provided these animals for all to catch and eat? And if a farmer would not pay enough, then how could he complain if a turnip or two was dug up and went into the stew? Yet, poaching was sometimes highly organized, and gangs sold on vast quantities of game. Sheep-stealing too was frequently carried out by gangs, as well as by starving farm workers. Then there were the crimes of protest, such as burning stacks of barley or sticking a knife into a horse's flank. Larceny seems much easier to classify. Or is it? In January 1841, Hannah Rumbles (18) of Great Bircham was sentenced to six months imprisonment in Walsingham Bridewell for stealing a nankeen petticoat, two handkerchiefs, and other things from farmer Philip Jarrett of Bircham Newton – a crime motivated by sheer acquisitiveness, the desire to feel a luxurious fabric against her skin, or one engendered by economic necessity? Or what about Thomas Bell of Great Bircham, who was accused by John Kitton of stealing wheat? This occurred in January 1826, and Bell was sent to Swaffham Bridewell for two months, with hard labour. Presumably Bell stole from one of the barns at Church Farm. He was surely not going to sell the wheat on for gain, although that must remain a possibility. [41]

One reason for the frightening extent of criminality in country districts may have been the ease with which criminals could move about in relatively under-populated areas without detection: much criminal activity could be carried out with impunity. It was not until the 1861 census that the presence of a village policeman was recorded in Great Bircham. At the time of the Bircham Riots there was no Norfolk county police force. The best that could be done to combat crime was for the wealthier and more influential inhabitants to form associations. Thus, at this time, there existed the 'Association for the Prosecution of Felons in the Hundreds of Smithdon and Brothercross' or the 'Smithdon Association for the Prevention of Incendiarism'. The members of the latter, who were from the wealthier sort, especially farmers, had to pay £5 a year. The fund this created could be used to employ police constables and to offer rewards.

The ineffectiveness of the old parish constables is further discussed in Chapter 3, but at this point we can mention the questions sent to parishes to determine the best means of establishing constabulary forces. The replies from Great Massingham to the Home Office, submitted between 1836 and 1838, have survived. According to the Massingham Guardians there had been five felonies and twenty misdemeanours. All the felonies resulted in arrests, but only seven of the misdemeanours. It was felt that the police constables were very efficient in detecting and apprehending offenders, although the distance to be covered to reach a magistrate (six miles) was held to be a distinct disadvantage. Notwithstanding the efficiency of the constables, crime was well established in the village: generally speaking the perpetrators were native to Massingham. Two things in particular were highlighted: poaching was rife, and the large furze common was a great inducement; there were very many people in the parish without any obvious means of support, and the guardians considered that many 'must live by poaching and theft'. There had been one riot since 1829 (see Chapter 5, II) and one 'barley stack wilfully set on fire'. There had also been disturbing cases of animal maiming: a pony, belonging to 'the most active constable' had had its throat cut and two horses, belonging to one of the overseers, had been stabbed.[42]

There is no reason to believe that Massingham was more crime-ridden than other parishes. It will become apparent (Chapter 5) that a similar pattern of crime emerged from Bircham. Here, then, were crimes of protest directed at clearly identified targets. Moreover, despite the frequent attempts to ascribe crime to outsiders, such as tramps and mysterious characters in gigs intent on destroying threshing machines, it was the village population, and a largely unemployed one at that, which was to blame.

A properly constituted county police force did meet general approval, and this came into being in 1839. Inevitably complaints were made, but sometime after 1839 over two hundred and fifty people from the Docking Union (including farmers Nurse, Jarrett and Hebgin and the John Drages, junior and senior) petitioned the magistrates of Norfolk to convince them of the necessity of retaining the new force. Unfortunately the transformation which they described was a little too fanciful, but cannot have been completely untrue. The situation before the establishment of the constabulary force was one of disorder:

Previous to the establishment of the Rural Police the condition of the lower orders in many Parishes was characterised by riotous and tumultuous Meetings, the Sabbath was desecrated by the disorderly behaviour and insulting behaviour of the Idle and dissolute. Many Public Houses and Beer Houses in general were irregularly conducted and suffered to become the resort of the worst Characters – Sheep stealing prevailed to an alarming extent – Petty Thefts and Trespasses abounded everywhere and Vagrancy had become a most grievous annoyance.

What came afterwards was almost a miracle: 'order and decency have taken the place of Riot and Tumult'. [43]

The excess of tumult and of crime could always be laid at the door of the beer-houses. Another petition, in 1834, for a reduction in the number of such houses, made it quite clear:

That continued Experience has only tended more and more to convince your Petitioners that the increasing Demoralization of youth and augmentation of crime generally among the labouring classes are very much to be ascribed to the Temptations held out and the Facilities afforded to the perpetration of Offences by the Number and Character of the Houses licensed for the Retail sale of Beer to be consumed on the Premises. [44]

It may have been true that agricultural labourers did not use crime as protest in an organized way, and that they did not generally act in concert, except when seriously roused to it, but that does not imply a dull-witted and slow-moving Hodge. As A. J. Peacock, writing about radicalism in East Anglia in the first half of the nineteenth century, put it, 'he protested *all* the time, and most of the time very effectively indeed'. It is a grave mistake to think that the rural poor accepted unquestioningly their depressed state, the alarming growth of the gap between their standard of life and that of their employers. Attractive as the notion of the immutability of the different estates of man was to some Anglican clergy, it was something that the workers of the field increasingly challenged, albeit with the burning rick and ensnared hare rather than the full-blown riot. There were years of exceptional protest, but, in Peacock's words, 'no year in the first half of the nineteenth century was a quiet year in the east'. [45]

These labouring men and women were no characters in some pastoral scene, no impassive bucolic peasants receiving gratefully the crumbs of the rich man's table, or uncomplainingly the blows of their employers. The countryside was no place for the faint-hearted, sentimental idealists and those who wanted to perpetuate the arcadian myth. Such people, coming from a refined and urban milieu, might have been horrified at the depravity of the rural poor, and their uncompromising stance against what the newcomer perceived as crime and what the labourers saw as economic necessity or protest against the injustices they saw around them. Many of the poor living in the villages would not have been attractive and endearing people. Transported back to the Smithdon Hundred of the 1830s, we too should often be revolted by life in the village. Those who struck the friction match, who poached rabbits and dug up the farmer's turnips, and those who rioted, were not heroes planting the flag of freedom on the sunlit uplands. They were all criminals, however much we can find justification for their acts. For John Archer it was not a matter of a small group of criminals and a saintly majority. The following statement will give readers of this book much on which to ponder:

If there was a criminal class in East Anglia it was the entire labouring community. [46]

70

And yet, there must be light to penetrate the darkness. All those Bircham Primitive Methodists, and others who worshipped in the parish churches, knew the Ten Commandments, knew what was a sin and what was not. Archer also mentions Thomas Edwards, the father of the famous Norfolk trades union leader and MP. Even though this incident, which George Edwards described in his autobiography, occurred twenty years after the riot at Great Bircham, it is nevertheless of relevance here. Thomas Edwards and his wife both had a deep Christian faith, and were devoted parents. When his son learnt that his father had been arrested with five turnips in his bag and had to go to prison, and then the workhouse, he realized that this was a man who had been punished solely for the crime of trying to feed his children.

But was he a thief? I say no, and a thousand times no! A nation that would not allow my father sufficient income to feed his children was responsible for any breach of the law he might have committed. [47]

For many in the nineteenth century, and for not a few in the twenty-first, it was a crime to be poor; but not to provide labouring men and women with sufficient means of support was not deemed to be criminal.

XV The Noble Landlord

We have left the landlord until last, for no other reason than he played little part in the story we need to tell. The Cholmondeleys were an ancient, noble and wealthy family. Besides the Norfolk estate of over 16,000 acres the Second Marquess also owned a considerable amount of land in Cheshire. To Norfolk society he contributed little; he did not occupy the commanding heights of a Coke or a Townshend.

He had been a Member of Parliament for the old rotten borough of Castle Rising from 1817 to 1821, and later was summoned to the Upper House. He was, however, never active in politics, for which his quiet and retiring nature did not fit him. He usually voted by proxy, and gave his vote to the Conservative cause. His principal achievement seems to have been in good works, and he supported many religious societies.[48] It appears that he was sympathetic even towards poachers. There is a letter in Cheshire Record Office, written by him in

December 1827, in response to his learning of a gamekeeper's violent confrontation with a poaching gang. He could not condone the loss of life, of servants and even of the poachers themselves, simply in order to protect game. He realized the law had to take its course, but he insisted on discriminating between hardened poachers and mere boys. Treatment of the latter, in his view, required much more tolerance and leniency.[49] Perhaps this reveals an important aspect of his character, and perhaps the inhabitants of Bircham, even after rioting and causing considerable damage to his property, had much to be thankful for in 1835. A Cheshire neighbour, however, pointed out what many would have held to be a distinct lack of backbone:

If all Englishmen were like Lord Cholmondeley, they would be religious and delightful men, but the French would soon come and take London.[50]

The landlord might not have been resident in Norfolk, but that did not prevent him from bestowing charity on his poorer tenants. Obelkevich refers to the position of the gentry, in the eyes of their poorer tenants, as somewhat akin to a parochial version of the royal family.[51] The Account Books at Houghton have many references to charity payments in the estate villages. It was what the nobility did; and the dowager Lady Cholmondeley (the widow of the first Marquess) was particularly active during the 1830s. *The Bury Post* of 5 December 1827 reported that poor families in the parishes of Bircham 'received a most seasonable supply of bed clothing and wearing apparel, the joint donations of the Marchioness of Cholmondeley and her amiable daughter the Lady Charlotte Seymour, consisting of upwards of 30 pairs of good blankets, a proportionate number of thick coverlits and sheets, together with cloaks, gowns, coats, waistcoats, shirts, stockings, &c'. The same newspaper report continued:

Each member of this unostentatiously beneficent Family seems to vie in humane consideration towards the relief and comfort of the very numerous poor inhabitants on this extensive estate; the Noble Marquis himself having ordered soup to be prepared and distributed twice a week, as well as wine, porter, and other necessary comforts to the sick poor of the eight surrounding parishes, to be supplied on the discretionary recommendation of the attending medical gentleman; and Lady Charlotte Seymour has moreover directed a considerable sum to be expended for fuel during the winter season.

In the severe weather of January 1841, the inhabitants of the three Birchams were grateful to their noble benefactor for his gift of coal, which amounted to as much as six hundredweights for the larger families.[52]

Accepting charity, of course, implied social control. Anybody in receipt of hand-outs must accept a degree of control, and that was simply the way it was for the poor in the Bircham parishes. They accepted it. They would have had no reason to quarrel with their charitable landlord, so little did they see of him; yet their relationship with their employers, the small group of farmers, was of a different order. This study has much more to do with people like John Kitton or Thomas Hebgin than George Horatio, Second Marquess of Cholmondeley. Nonetheless, it is beyond doubt that all three groups (the landlord and his agents, the farmers and the labourers) needed each other. A sweetly harmonious relationship between those working in the fields and those who ran the farms was an ideal that belonged to another age, if it ever did exist. What happened over a period of less than a fortnight in the summer of 1835 demonstrated in a particularly spectacular fashion the breakdown of this relationship.

The King's Head, Great Bircham, in Hill's Survey of 1800 *(Plate XII)*

Notes

The principal sources of demographic information for the three Bircham parishes are the parish registers (NRO: PD34) and the census of 1851 (TNA: HO 107/1827). The 1811 census has also been consulted (NRO: PD 34/43). The Registrar General's Report is the 8th Annual Report (1845). Other parish registers and census returns have been consulted online using a variety of sources: FamilySearch, FreeREG and the Norfolk Family History Society Parish Register Transcripts for the former; and findmypast.co.uk for the latter.

The principal sources for the farmers and tradespeople are also the censuses, parish registers, and White's 1836 and 1845 directories. The wills of Daniel Denny (junior and senior), Thomas Hebgin (senior), John Kitton, Rebecca Kitton and James Howlett have been downloaded from Norfolk Sources; the originals are in the NRO. The sources at Houghton Hall are the rentals of 1834, 1836 and 1837; also an account book of 1836. For the descriptions of the buildings Habbakuk Englestown's *A description of the several Buildings on the Houghton Estate*, 1832 (HH: M24r) and Joseph Hill's *Survey of the Houghton Hall Estate*, 1800 (Norfolk Record Society, Vol. L, 1984; edited David Yaxley) have been used. The land tax returns (1777-1832) for the Smithdon Brothercross Division, which covers the Birchams, were searched in microform at the Millennium Library, Norwich; (NRO: C/Scd2/27).

The tithe records searched have been the maps and apportionments for Great Bircham and Bircham Tofts, again in microform at the Millennium Library, Norwich. NRO: DN/TA 155 and DN/TA 164. The two village plans in this chapter are based on the tithe maps. The NRO tithe apportionment for Great Bircham has a missing page, which covers the smaller parcels of land and the cottages. The copy of the apportionment at Houghton Hall, which must have been supplied when some properties were transferred to the Royal Estate in the 1930s, is complete.

The essential records consulted for the churches and chapels of the three parishes are the visitation records (NRO: VIS 46/6 – 1813, VIS 53/1 – 1820, VIS 64/3 – 1838); the Register of Meeting Houses 1824-1852 (NRO: DIS 4/2); the 1851 Religious Census (Norfolk Record Society Vol. LXVII, 1998 – *Religious Worship in Norfolk*, ed. Janet Ede and Norma Virgoe); King's Lynn Primitive Methodist register of members, 1838-1844 (NRO: FC54/461).

For work done at Houghton 1833-35, and some accounts, an important source is at Houghton Hall. It is a large ledger kept by Stephen Reeve, the Houghton land agent (HH: M6o).

[1] A. Armstrong, *The Population of Victorian and Edwardian Norfolk* (Norwich, 2000), p. 35.
[2] HH: M7c.

3 I am indebted to Linda Johnson, a descendant of Denny's brother, for much of the information on Daniel Denny, especially the reference to William Cobbett.

4 I can see no logical reason for the alternative spelling 'Godfery, but acknowledge that, in his history of the Norvic Shoe Company, F. W. Wheldon consistently uses this spelling. The announcement of his marriage, in 1860 (*Norfolk Chronicle*, 11 Feb.), also calls him 'John Godfery, second son of J. W. Howlett, Esq., of Bircham Tofts'; and so does his obituary (*Eastern Daily Press*, 6 May 1914), quoted by Wheldon. However, it was John Godfrey Howlett at his baptism in 1829. His memorial inscription, at the Rosary Cemetery in Norwich, is also Godfrey, at least according to the transcription appearing on the Norfolk Family History Society website. For the sake of consistency I have used Godfrey throughout, and that applies to John Godfrey, John Howlett's brother-in-law; but I concede that the Norwich shoemaker seems to have come to be known as John Godfery Howlett.

5 F. W. Wheldon, *A Norvic Century* (Norwich, 1946), p. 32.

6 *BNP*, 23 Sep. 1835.

7 *NC*, 21 Oct. 1837; 29 Sep. 1849; 25 Sep. 1852; 28 Oct. 1848.

8 *BNP*, 4 Dec.1839. On Sunday 24 February 1839 he was ordained deacon at Chester Cathedral (*BNP*, 6 Mar 1839); and at a congregation on 4 December 1839 the degree of Bachelor of Arts was conferred on John Kitton, Queen's College, Cambridge. In the census of 1851 (and later) he appears as M.A.

9 *NC*, 30 Sep. 1843.

10 *NC*, 7 Dec. 1805; *BNP*, 23 Sep. 1807; *NC*, 21 Oct. 1821; 28 Sep. 1822; Oct. 1823.

11 R. N. Bacon, *The History of the Agriculture of Norfolk* (London, 1849), pp 144-45.

12 HH: Cellar Documents, 526L.

13 HH: M17.

14 HH: M17, a bill entitled 'Ales had by the Poor in Sickness'. Some twenty people were given beer from March 1833 to January 1834. For example, between 15 March and 28 April Widow Daw had forty-three pints; and from 28 October to 10 November James Curry and his wife had twenty-eight pints.

15 J. Obelkevich, *Religion and Rural Society: South Lindsey 1825-1875* (London, 1976), p. 86.

16 *NC*, 18 Sep. 1841.

17 E. J. Hobsbawm, *Primitive Rebels* (Manchester, 1959), Chapter VIII: The Labour Sects.

18 The details of the school in Great Bircham are from White's 1845 Directory.

19 BPP: 1834, Vol. XXX (Rural Queries); answers of George Bate, Overseer, Houghton.

[20] A. Digby, *Pauper Palaces* (London, 1978), p. 24.

[21] J. P. Kay, 'Earnings of Agricultural Labourers in Norfolk and Suffolk', *Journal of the Statistical Society*, 1 (1839).

[22] Bacon, *History of Agriculture*, p. 147; J. Caird, *English Agriculture in 1850-51 (London, 1852), p. 512;* K. D. M. Snell, *Annals of the Labouring Poor: Social Change and Agrarian England 1660-1900* (Cambridge, 1985), p.130.

[23] DUGM (NRO): C/GP 4/4, 5, 7.

[24] *NC*, 24 Oct. 1836.

[25] A. Jessop, *Arcady for Better for Worse* (London, 1887), pp 41-42.

[26] G. Edwards, *From Crow-Scaring to Westminster* (The Larks Press, 2008), p. 17 & p. 19.

[27] *BNP*, 4 Nov. 1835.

[28] DUGM (NRO): C/GP 4/9.

[29] Digby, *Palaces* 1978, p. 23.

[30] A. Digby, 'The Rural Poor', in G. E. Mingay, ed., *The Victorian Countryside*, Vol. 2 (London, 1981), p. 593.

[31] DUGM (NRO): C/GP 4/5.

[32] HH: M7c.

[33] HH: M8.

[34] DUGM (NRO): C/GP 4/5.

[35] Bacon, p. 142.

[36] E. A. Wrigley and R. S. Schofield, *The Population History of England 1541-1871* (Cambridge, 1989), p. 255 and p. 302.

[37] Bacon, p. 148.

[38] ibid, p. 151.

[39] ibid, pp 154-55.

[40] J. Weyland, *Charge delivered to the Grand Jury of the County of Norfolk at the Easter Quarter Sessions 1834* (Norwich 1834), p. 4.

[41] *NC*, 23 Jan. 1841; *NC*, 21 Jan. 1826.

[42] TNA: HO 73/7 pt. 1.

[43] NRO: C/Saa 5/2.

[44] NRO: C/S 4/6.

[45] A. J. Peacock, 'Village Radicalism in East Anglia 1800-50', in Dunbabin, J. P. D., *Rural Discontent in Nineteenth Century Britain* (New York, 1974), p. 27 & p. 39.

[46] J. E. Archer, *By a Flash and a Scare* (Breviary Stuff Publications, London, 2010), p. 9.

[47] Edwards, *From Crow-scaring to Westminster*, p.16.

[48] *The Times*, 10 May 1870; *Chester Chronicle*, 14 May 1870.

[49] CRO: Cholmondeley Papers, DCH/X/11.

[50] R. G. Thorne and Margaret Escott in *The History of Parliament* (online).

[51] J. Obelkevich, *Religion and Rural Society*, p. 36.

[52] *BNP*, 5 Dec. 1827; *NC*, 21 Jan. 1841.

Chapter 2. Poor Laws Old and New

For ye have the poor always with you; but me ye have not always. Matthew 26, v 11

Laws grind the poor, and rich men rule the law. Oliver Goldsmith, *The Traveller, 1764*

Lewis Jarvis, in his letter, ascribes the cause of the Bircham Riots to the New Poor Law Bill. Before following the events of June 1835, we need to be clear about the system of poor relief that was in operation at that time, and just what changes were introduced in 1834.

I Townhouse Cottage

In Habbakuk Englestown's survey of Great Bircham properties there is a small (25 ft by 22 ft 6 ins) one-storey brick and stone cottage, consisting of a kitchen and three bedrooms. In Hill's Survey of 1800 it is called Townhouse Cottage, but Englestown called it 'poor house'. There were also town-houses in Bircham Tofts and Bircham Newton, in both cases part of a larger building let in three or four tenements.

Townhouse Cottage, Great Bircham
(Plate XVII H.9 in Hill's Survey 1800)

At one time many villages had such buildings, and they serve as a reminder that care of the aged, the infirm and the indigent was the ultimate responsibility of each parish. However, by the summer of

77

1835 momentous changes had taken place which affected the relief of the poor throughout the land. It was one particular aspect of the newly introduced legislation that sparked the Bircham Riots.

In Norfolk, as elsewhere, those in more fortunate circumstances would have always shown some degree of charity to the poorer members of the community. After the dissolution of the monasteries an important source of charity was lost, and responsibility passed to the parishes. By the reign of Elizabeth I the system was more regulated. As Anthony Brundage in *The English Poor Laws, 1700-1930*, points out, 'Tudor England grappled with frightening levels of privation and social disorder'.[1] Perhaps things were not so bad in North-west Norfolk in the 1830s, but privation and disorder certainly stalked the land. The end of Elizabeth's reign saw a Poor Law passed in 1597, which was in reality an amalgam of previous acts. One had dealt with 'vagabonds and beggars', the latter very much still with us at the beginning of the twenty-first century, although perhaps not in such great numbers. The 1597 measure brought, for the first time, a complete system of relief to the poor. It also introduced an official who still played a prominent role in the English parish in the 1830s: the Overseer of the Poor. Each parish usually had at least two of them, and often an uneasy relationship developed between the overseers and the poor whom they were to relieve. We have already seen that John Kitton was one Great Bircham overseer at the time of the riots. Thomas Hebgin was the other.

II Poor Law Relief Act, 1601

It was, however, the Act for the Relief of the Poor, 1601, that created a national structure in England and Wales. The year was the forty-third year of the reign of Elizabeth I. For the next 230 years or so the Old Poor Law provided the means by which the old, sick and impotent poor were relieved, and the 'undeserving poor' were punished in some way. For the first time the parish was established as the unit of administration for the purpose of relief of the poor, and this continued to be the case up to the period of this study, and beyond. The 'deserving poor' – the lame, impotent, old and blind, that is those who were incapable of working – were to be relieved. Relief was often in the form of money, food or clothing. Commonly it was 'outdoor' relief; in other words the poor stayed in their own homes. For those unable to be looked after at home there were the parish almshouses or poorhouses. Children were also to be helped where necessary. For instance orphans or illegitimate children were deemed to be deserving of a start in life, and many were set to work or put out as apprentices.

The able-bodied poor – a term that was to resonate throughout the ages – were to be set to work if they were not in employment. Materials such as flax and wool were to be provided, if required, to give them a means of earning a living. Moreover, a punitive element was now introduced: any pauper who refused to work was to be sent to a House of Correction or prison. Thus we see how the poor who were in dire need of help through no fault of their own, were to be split away from those who were perfectly sound in body but who either could not or would not work. Christian charity demanded that one should always help the former: nobody could watch them starve and hope to go to heaven. Different attitudes were held in relation to the second sort. To be poor was commonly believed to be the fault of the pauper. It was often regarded as a sin. It is something which has not fundamentally changed in the eyes of many, even in these supposedly more enlightened times.

Relief of the poor was to be paid for out of the poor rates. This began as a form of local income tax, but evolved into a tax based on the value of real estate. Generally the occupier, rather than the owner, paid the poor rate. Unfortunately nothing has survived for the Bircham parishes, but the Houghton Parish Accounts 1745-1835 are still kept at Houghton Hall. During the 1830s three shillings in the pound was the normal rate, although sometimes it rose to three shillings and sixpence, and at others dropped to two shillings and three pence. The rate was based on the annual rental. For example, during the period July to October 1834, when the rate was three shillings in the pound, George Bate, tenant of the Village Farm, paid £37 10s. and his annual rent was £250. There is no reason to believe things would have been greatly different in the Birchams. At Houghton, Lord Cholmondeley paid most of the rates, but the tenants of the Village Farm and of the King's Head Inn were also rated. In the Bircham parishes the farmers paid the poor rates, as must have the tradespeople, certainly those, like John Shilling and Robert Spooner, who paid quite large rents. No inhabitant of a Houghton cottage ever paid any poor rate, and this was surely the case in the Birchams too.

III Later Acts of Parliament

Further acts were passed during the following years. An important one was an Act of 1662, which came to be known as the Settlement Act. By this Act local justices had the power to remove from a parish, back to the original parish of settlement, anybody who was likely to become chargeable to the parish. Settlement was gained by children taking the same parish as their parents; or by women taking the same parish as their husbands on marriage. Illegitimate children belonged to the parishes where they were born. Later (after an act of 1691), it was possible to acquire a settlement by being hired out for a year, but often this was avoided by masters hiring a servant for 364 days; or by servants leaving a parish before the year was up. Settlement, as everything to do with the Poor Law, was a complex business, and often led to expensive court cases. There was another way of acquiring settlement according to the 1662 Act: by renting a property for at least £10 a year. We have already seen the rents paid in Great Bircham and Bircham Tofts, and even by the 1830s very few would have been able to gain a settlement in this manner. The Settlement Act did not help the poor, and all too many of them, by this time, were confined to their parishes and felt unable to move for work. As soon as they fell into poverty, and thus became chargeable to their new parish, they were liable to be shunted back to the old one.

It is the workhouse that epitomizes the Poor Law for most people. We all know about Oliver Twist, if not through the novel of 1838, then at least the musical *Oliver!* The pathetic image of the little boy asking for more has resonated through many generations, and there is something heart-rending about Christmas Day in the workhouse, an experience envied by none. Charles Dickens, and George Sims, in his 1879 monologue (*In the Workhouse – Christmas Day*) were not, of course, writing pure fantasy; yet there was more to workhouses than the few images retained by most people. Shuffling specimens of humanity close to the end of their lives there might have been, but mnay inmates of workhouses must not be compared to human wrecks. For one thing, and in Norfolk certainly, many of the buildings were quite splendid. Anne Digby, chose an apt title for her classic study of the poor laws in Norfolk: *Pauper Palaces*. The name comes from the Suffolk poet, George Crabbe, who described the workhouse as the 'pauper palace'. Norfolk workhouses were often the product of immense local pride, and built with a genuine desire to make life better for the poor. For instance, the House of Industry at Rollesby, for the East and West Flegg Hundreds, has an inscription over its entrance, which proudly proclaimed the founders' humanity and idealism to the world:

For the Instruction of Youth
The Encouragement of Industry
The Relief of Want
The Support of Old Age
And the Comfort of
Infirmity and Pain.[2]

IV Workhouses

However, we are running ahead of ourselves. The Rollesby institution was opened in 1777, but many workhouses were not built until the 1830s. In 1836 a workhouse was built in Docking, and it was precisely in the uneasy times just before its construction that our story unfolded.

There were workhouses, or houses of industry, before the late eighteenth century. We have already seen how, under the 1601 Act, able-bodied paupers were to be set to work, and so it was natural for parishes to group such people together in parish workhouses. An Act of 1722-23, known as Knatchbull's Act, enabled parishes to set up workhouses, either on their own or in combination with other parishes. Norfolk, unlike Suffolk, did not establish many workhouses in the earlier years of the eighteenth century. A Parliamentary survey of 1776 listed just twenty-four in Norfolk. One of them was in Harpley. What is important about Knatchbull's Act is that, for the first time, it put into law the workhouse test. By this the workhouse was to act as a deterrent. Relief could be had, but only if the recipient was prepared to submit to the rigours of the workhouse. The same sentiments were being voiced over a hundred years later, and would have been well known to the inhabitants of the three Bircham parishes.

East Anglia went further than individual parish workhouses, and formed 'incorporations'. The motivation to do so was financial as much as anything, as there was a perception amongst ratepayers that poor relief could be administered more efficiently and more economically in groups of parishes. Ultimately this did not prove successful; and even though splendid 'pauper palaces' were built they were very expensive. These incorporations, all rural ones (although King's Lynn and Norwich had set up their own groupings in 1701 and 1711 respectively), were formed by private Acts of Parliament between 1764 and 1806. We have already mentioned East and West Flegg, and there were six in total. The Launditch and Mitford Incorporation was formed in 1775, and its workhouse at Gressenhall will be known to many, as it now houses a museum. The other Norfolk incorporations were mainly in the east. In the western and southern parts of the county there were individual parish workhouses. Close to the Bircham parishes were Brancaster, Docking, Sedgeford, Snettisham, Flitcham, East and West Rudham, and South Creake.[3] Finally, by 1815, a workhouse had been established at Dersingham. Thus, we can be sure that the Bircham rioters had more than a passing knowledge of workhouses.

V Gilbert's Act, 1782

The next Act of Parliament, Gilbert's Act of 1782, also permitted unions of parishes for poor relief purposes to be established, but this time without the need for separate Acts of Parliament. In fact only a small number of Gilbert Unions were formed nationally. Norfolk had eleven, but none in the North-west of the county. However, Gilbert's Act was important in the history of the Old Poor Law because it stipulated that the common workhouse that could be set up by the union should be solely for the benefit of the old, the infirm and orphans. The able-bodied poor were now to be employed near to where they lived. In rural North-west Norfolk parishes this would usually mean that farmers would be expected to employ them. If their wages were too low to live on, then allowances from the poor rates would bring them up to subsistence levels. This is absolutely crucial to our story, as we shall see later.

Thus 'outdoor relief', as opposed to 'indoor relief' in the workhouse, came to be the kind of relief most often used up to 1834. According to the 'Abstract of Returns relative to the Expense and Maintenance of the Poor in England' (1803) 42,821 people in Norfolk received outdoor relief; but only 3,996 were maintained in workhouses.[4]

If Gilbert's Act allowed wages to be increased by allowances then the poor became ever more dependent on such hand-outs. They quickly became paupers, and in the eyes of many distinctly inferior sorts of human being. It was a commonly held view that such dependency only encouraged the idle and the feckless to work less, knowing full well that the ratepayers would support them. It is something that has exercised the energies of politicians over the centuries.

Gradually the system of outdoor relief was formalised. All the school textbooks dealing with eighteenth and nineteenth century social history mention the Berkshire parish of Speenhamland. Although it never formally passed into legislation, the Speenhamland system, in some form or other, became common. The amount of relief was tied to the price of bread, and in 1795 magistrates in Berkshire, meeting in Speenhamland, decreed:

When the gallon loaf of second flour weighing 8lb. 11oz. shall cost 1s., then every poor and industrious man shall have for his own support 3s. weekly, either produced by his own or his family's labour or an allowance from the poor rates, and for the support of his wife and every other of his family 1s. 6d.

The allowance would go up or down according to the price of bread.

VI Relief under the Old Poor Law

Before we pass to the New Poor Law, which is of the most relevance to the Bircham Riots, we ought to pause and examine in more detail what amount of relief was given in various North-west Norfolk parishes. As already stated, no record of allowances to individuals survives for the

Bircham parishes, but they do survive for Houghton. First, though, a look at the average weekly expenditure on poor relief in the three Bircham parishes, plus Houghton.[5] This is for the three years, ending 25 March 1835, the period just before the riots. If we reckon that most allowances were being paid to families chiefly employed in agriculture, then the figures are as below, with the last column, based on the 1831 census, showing the average amount per family, per week:

Parish	Total Average	Families employed in Agriculture (1831)	Average per Family
Great Bircham	£9 8s. 5d.	73	2s. 7d.
Bircham Newton	£1 8s. 5d.	19	1s. 6½d.
Bircham Tofts	£2 5s. 5d.	27	1s. 8d.
Houghton	£5 5s. 4d.	43	2s. 5d.

To some this would have appeared to be quite a large weekly allowance; and the farmers, who were the principal ratepayers, did have large poor-rate bills. Remember, the Houghton farmer paid £37 10s. to cover relief to the poor during the period of twelve weeks, between 12 July and 4 October 1834. It was even more from October 1834 to February 1835: £56 5s. Moreover, farmers resented paying relief to men they considered idle. If, however, we approach these figures from the viewpoint of a large labouring family, the amount of relief is far from large.

It is perhaps more instructive to look at some real figures. During that same period of twelve weeks in 1834 the total amount paid out in Houghton was £69 1s. 6d. but that includes £6 4s. paid to three men working on the roads, and a further £6 4s. in sundry payments. That leaves a total of £56 13s. 6d. paid out to support the poor. Thirty-three people were relieved, and that works out at about 2s. 10d. per person per week. Included in the thirty-three were eight widows; these mostly received 3s. per week, but one had 6s. and another 5s. 6d. The rest are nearly all men, although two girls and two boys are mentioned. There are also a man and his wife (12 weeks at 6s. 6d. per week) and a family (12 weeks at 9s.). Nearly all the rest of the payments were in the

84

form of 'allowances' (the word used in the accounts). In just two cases is illness mentioned: one man had 12s. for one week, and another 5s. for 12 weeks. Some allowances are for the whole of the twelve weeks; others are for six weeks or a shorter period. Again, amounts vary, from as little as 1s. 3d. to as much as 10s. The overseer would have had his own reasons for awarding particular allowances.

In 1833 a series of questions – they came to be known as the Rural Queries – were sent to the overseers of rural parishes throughout the land. (Urban parishes had similar questions.) The questions were certainly biased: the idea was to show how the allowance system had got out of hand and that a change in the law was needed. Nevertheless they are of some use to us. Fortunately George Bate, the Houghton farmer and overseer, answered some of the many questions. It is first of all of interest that he reckoned twenty labourers were necessary to cultivate the land, but that there were sixty-seven in the parish. Not all these labourers were agricultural: the 1831 census gives thirty-seven. Even so it shows that there was always going to be a surplus of labour. Things were no different in Bircham, and probably worse. Bate confirmed that thirty-two people had been relieved during the week prior to his replying to the questions; this fits in with the poor book kept at Houghton Hall. He also stated that there was an allowance of 1s. 6d per child in a family, which began after the third child.[6]

Of course, we cannot be completely sure that the Bircham parishes and Houghton were operating the same system of poor relief, but the figures for the three years ending Lady Day 1835 suggest they were; however, overseers, even though they worked within the same system, could vary widely in their interpretation of it. What would have been different was that there was more opportunity for work at Houghton, not just on the two farms (one of which was the home farm) but also in the garden or tree plantation. Another major advantage the Houghton tenants had over their Bircham counterparts was that their cottages were rent-free; they paid just six shillings per year for an allotment measuring one rood (a quarter of an acre). The relief payments were not huge, but they certainly brought earnings up to subsistence levels.

The Bircham labourers would undoubtedly have felt the effects of poverty more acutely than those in Houghton, and it was they who rioted. Perhaps the Houghton labourers, relatively secure financially, did not feel compelled to rise so dramatically in the summer of 1835. However, we shall never know from where all the people who rioted in Great Bircham and Bircham Tofts in June 1835 came. It would be surprising if not a single person from Houghton was among the vast crowd that assembled in Great Bircham at the end of June.

VII The Poor Law Amendment Act, 1834

The immediate reason for the Bircham Riots was the introduction of the New Poor Law, officially the Poor Law Amendment Act of 1834. David Englander, called it 'the single most important piece of social legislation ever enacted'. Keith Snell wrote that it was a law that 'had surely the most harmful and socially damaging effect on rural class relations in the south of any nineteenth-century legislation'.[7] (The south, in this context, must also include Norfolk.) It certainly had far-reaching consequences and few were unaffected. It will have been very much on the minds of the agricultural labourers and tradespeople who drank in Spooner's beer-house, or who passed through the workshops of the blacksmiths or shoemakers. It would have been perceived by the poor (the vast majority of the inhabitants of the Bircham parishes) as a great threat to their lives. It can surely be no exaggeration to say that it brought much fear.

Poor Law studies are legion, and even today there is no agreement about its effectiveness or otherwise. The popular image of the workhouse is not a positive one, and those of us used to full stomachs would find the workhouse diet very unpalatable. Nevertheless, for the truly destitute, it was better than starvation in a miserable hovel. As Anne Digby points out, the workhouses did much for the education of the children who found themselves within their walls, and she also shows how the medical care of the elderly had much to commend it.[8] By all accounts, we in the second decade of the twenty-first century have not got this aspect of hospital provision entirely right. The more positive aspects of the 1834 legislation, as well as the negative ones, are further studied in Part III.

Yet that cannot concern us here. The poor of the Birchams cannot have foreseen any advantages in the Poor Law Union which was about to come into existence. They cannot have contemplated the erection of an enormous workhouse with anything less than foreboding. Yet its advocates claimed that the Poor Law Amendment Act was designed to help them, to improve their earning power and to lift them out of poverty - unless they belonged to that despicable breed of indigent paupers afflicted with the horrible vice of idleness. Something far from pleasant was being prepared for them.

The Poor Law Amendment Act received Royal Assent on 14 August 1834. It did not meet with universal acclaim. *The Times* called it a 'tyrannical and useless' bill and it offered 'a confused mass of heterogeneous provisions - a compound of imbecility, inconsistency and short-sightedness'.[9] The labourer would, according to the *Times*, be worse off by a measure, which it considered 'a sure mode of degrading the English labourer into a miserable serf'. The newspaper certainly saw the real possibility of troubles ahead: '...the mis-calculating landlord will rejoice at the expectation of seeing his rates reduced, till he wakes some morning out of his heavy sleep of selfish ignorance, on finding his barns destroyed by an infuriated peasantry...'.

Another prominent opponent of the Poor Law Amendment Act was William Cobbett, radical Tory MP for Oldham, and champion of the poor. For him, and others of his persuasion, what was being proposed was a fundamental attack on the ancient right of the poor to be relieved if they fell on hard times. The system ushered in during the reign of Elizabeth I represented a humane means of treating the poor, and this new act threatened to sweep it all away. It had always been the case, Cobbett held, that the poor were to be relieved by the rich. This was the right of any freeborn Englishman, and those who wanted to abrogate the ancient rights were no lovers of liberty.

However, the *Times* and Cobbett represented minority views, even if not insignificant ones. Cobbett was by this time a spent force, and some of his views on the New Poor Law would hardly have been taken seriously. The bill passed easily through the House of Commons, where it was introduced on 17 April 1834; on the second reading there were three hundred and nineteen votes for and only twenty against.

There was more opposition in the House of Lords, but its eventual passage into law was never in doubt. The Poor Law Amendment Act was the work of a Whig Government in the Reform Parliament. We shall see later how a Tory Norfolk newspaper reported on the Bircham Riots at some length, but a rival Whig paper had little to say.

The Poor Law Amendment Act had emerged from the Royal Commission on the Poor Laws, which was set up in 1832. Its brief was to carry out a detailed investigation of the existing poor law and produce a report. In addition to the small group of commissioners, there were also twenty-six Assistant Commissioners. One of these was a young man called Edwin Chadwick. He was hard-working and efficient, but had a dangerous tendency towards authoritarianism. The New Poor Law was immediately seen by its critics as a highly centralized system, and Chadwick had much to do with that.

The first report of the commission, produced in some haste in 1833, painted a damning picture: the system was corrupt and was in urgent need of reform. The full Poor Law Report appeared the following year and was the work of two men: Nassau Senior, a lawyer, academic and adviser to the Whig Party, and Edwin Chadwick. Senior condemned the abuses of the existing poor laws in the first part of the report, and Chadwick set out what should be done to reform poor relief in the second part.

VIII The Reason for the New Poor Law

About the abuses of the old laws much could be written; and historians continue to present a whole range of opposing views. What is important, however, is to point to the perception amongst many people at the time, and the Bircham farmers must have been numbered amongst them, that the system was rotten and could not be allowed to continue. For one thing it was costing an enormous amount of money. For Cobbett it was money to which the labouring poor had a right, but for a classical economist like David Ricardo it meant diverting money into the welfare of the poor, and thus the money available for wages was reduced. Many would have agreed with Ricardo's views that the poor, ever more dependent on parish relief, were encouraged in their idleness and were not deterred from fathering large families, thus producing the next generation of dependants. Kitton, Hebgin and the rest would definitely have looked for legislation which reduced their poor rates. These, according to Englander, quadrupled between 1790 and 1834.[10]

The farmers, too, would have been convinced by a view in the report that indigence was not the fault of economic and social conditions but rather the impecuniousness of the individual. This flew somewhat in the face of the chronic oversupply of labour and pitifully low wages, but it was easy to become persuaded that it was all the fault of the feckless and idle labourer, and that the employer played no part in it; therefore any measures to cut down on relief, however harsh, would be eagerly adopted. Nevertheless, the farmers and overseers had to cope somehow in these dying days of the Old Poor Law. Labourers and their families could not be allowed to starve. The familiar means of support were still needed: relief, work on the parish roads (used much at Houghton) and the employment of more labourers, even if they were not needed, driving their wages ever lower.

Something had to be done. How much longer could relief be paid out indiscriminately, both to those who deserved it and to those who did not? How could it be right to go on rewarding improvident marriages that produced large families? (The Malthusian spectre of population growth outstripping the availability of food haunted much thinking on the poor laws.) How could the artificially low wages supplemented by allowances be further justified, which meant the able-bodied labourer had no more incentive to work any harder than the pauper?

What most clearly distinguished the new from the old was the infamous principle of 'less eligibility'. It was not an original idea of Chadwick's, but he set great store by it. By it the able-bodied pauper's situation must be less eligible, that is to say less comfortable, than that of the independent labourer. If the former were not willing to reach the position of the latter, then he would still be granted relief, but it would have to be in a workhouse, where the discipline would be harsh and his diet of lower quality than outside the house. To claim relief meant he had to become destitute (this state being evidently a reflection of his moral decline) and submit to the severe conditions of the workhouse.

There were those who tended to favour the complete abolition of the poor laws. Chadwick was never in that camp. For one thing the categories of the poor in need of help – the old, the infirm and the very young – would always be there, and no decent human being could ignore them. Yet the poor labourer, so Chadwick argued, would be forced to do anything rather than enter a workhouse and endure its harsh discipline. A properly administered system, however, with assistance to the indigent labourers and their families confined to indoor relief, would reduce the poor rates and restore a proper work ethic and morality. Moreover, the imposition of a greater discipline on the labourers of any parish would inevitably have been attractive to farmers, especially any who farmed on such a scale as those in the Bircham parishes.

The Poor Law Amendment Act passed into law in August 1834. There had been amendments to the Report of the Royal Commission, but essentially the legislation reflected the reforms proposed by Chadwick. At the heart of the new act was the need to establish a new system of relief of the poor throughout England and Wales. To this end a Poor Law Commission was created, consisting of three Commissioners. These were George Nicholls, John Shaw-Lefevre and Thomas Frankland Lewis. Chadwick was considerably put out at not being chosen. He became, instead, Secretary to the Commission. Lewis's name will later feature in the correspondence generated by the Bircham Riots. He was the Chairman of the Commission. Lefevre was the only Whig amongst the commissioners. Nicholls, a former sea captain, had been an Overseer of the Poor in Nottinghamshire, and had particular views on the operation of the poor laws, views owing nothing to Cobbett, but much more in tune with those expressed by Chadwick. He is famously remembered for a particularly telling remark about the parish in its relationship to the poor:

The hardest Taskmaster, the closest Paymaster and the most harsh and unkind friend that they can apply to and whose aid they cannot receive without sacrificing a large portion of their independence and self respect [11]

IX The Creation of the Docking Union

It is now time to move from Somerset House, where the Poor Law Commission sat in London, to North-west Norfolk. The first task of the Commissioners was to organize all the English and Welsh parishes into new administrative units called Poor Law Unions. To assist them in their work, Assistant Commissioners, nine of them initially, were appointed. The Poor Law Unions were to be run by an elected Board of Guardians, and the electors were the principal ratepayers. They could have up to six votes each, depending on the value of the property. It would soon become clear that in the Docking Union (in which the Birchams were situated) the farmers had many votes, and the Guardians tended to be farmers too. Norfolk was unionized quite quickly, and a start was made in the North-west, where there had previously been no incorporations or Gilbert Unions.

The means of creating a union was usually as follows: the Assistant Commissioner called a meeting of local owners and occupiers in the Hundreds where the new union was to be. He then explained the Poor Law Amendment Act and told how things would certainly improve. A resolution to form a union was drawn up and a sympathetic chairman was found for the meeting; then, all being well, a vote in favour was taken. On 22 May 1835 a meeting was held in order to establish the Docking Union and approve the eventual building of a workhouse. All went perfectly and the Assistant Commissioner was delighted to send the good news to the Poor Law Commission in London:

I have the pleasure to inform you that, at a General and well-attended Meeting of the Magistrates, Landed Proprietors and Other Rate-Payers of the Hundreds of Smithdon and Brothercross, in number of not less than 150 Persons, held this day at Docking, the enclosed Resolution was unanimously and cordially carried, expressive of their concurrence in the Formation of a Union for Workhouse Purposes.[12]

'Unanimously and cordially' might well have expressed the sentiments of those who attended the meeting at Docking – farmers like Kitton and Hebgin must surely have been there – but the Assistant

Commissioner had not bothered to consult the tradespeople and labourers of Great Bircham and Bircham Tofts.

It is of interest to point out here that the first Chairman of the Docking Union, Henry Etheridge Blyth, the nephew of John Kitton's wife, Rebecca, at first wanted nothing to do with the New Poor Law. On 9 September 1834 the Blyth family wrote to the Poor Law Commissioners asking for their property to be excluded from any new union, as they felt there could be no improvement in the way they managed the poor.[13] Lord Cholmondeley is unlikely to have been at the meeting, the Houghton Estate interest being represented by Stephen Reeve, who would have continued to consult Richard Groom.

The complete list of Docking Union parishes was:

Anmer, Bagthorpe, Barmer, Barwick, Bircham Newton, Bircham Tofts, Brancaster (2), Broomsthorpe, Burnham-Deepdale, Burnham-Norton, Burnham-Overy (2), Burnham Sutton-cum-Burnham Ulph, Burnham-Thorpe, Burnham-Westgate (3), Choseley, Dersingham, Docking, East Rudham (3), Fring, Great Bircham, Great Ringstead (2), Heacham (2), Holme-next-the-Sea, Hunstanton with Barrett-Ringstead, Ingoldisthorpe, New Houghton, North Creake (2), Sedgeford (2), Shernborne, Snettisham (3), South Creake (2), Stanhoe, Syderstone, Thornham (2), Titchwell, Waterden, West Rudham.

The number of guardians per parish was normally one, except (as indicated) in the larger parishes, which had two or even three. There were fifty-three guardians in total.

The Docking Union formally came into being in 1 August 1835, and the first meeting of the Docking Guardians took place at the Hare Inn, Docking on 12 August.[14] It was in fact the first Poor Law Union in Norfolk and it is therefore no coincidence that riots occurred in Great Bircham and Bircham Tofts in that summer.

A workhouse would not be built until the following year, but its coming was inevitable. In June 1835 everybody would know a workhouse was to be built somewhere in the Union, and rumours of its possible location would certainly have been flying around. Was it generally known, however, that it might have been built in Bircham Newton? It is just possible, and if so it would have increased the tension felt in the three parishes during the summer of 1835. Stephen Reeve wrote to Richard Groom on 13 August 1835 to say an application would be made to Lord Cholmondeley for permission to build the workhouse on Bircham Newton Common. He added: 'I think it will not be desirable to have a building of this sort upon any property, but some one must give way, it will be highly necessary to select a spot where it will inconvenience the least.' Three days later he wrote again, and referred to what he had understood from Groom: that the Marquess, having been a landowner in the district for so long, could not honourably refuse to allow the workhouse to be built on his land. The following day, Groom wrote to Reeve that their employer would not oppose his land being used, because that would be opposing the New Poor Law, something his Lordship was reluctant to do.[15] It should come as no surprise to us that what we call 'nimbyism' was as prevalent in the fourth decade of the nineteenth century, as it is today; however, there was the honourable position of the landowning class to be maintained. Without necessarily wanting to throw in his lot with any punitive behaviour to the poor – given the many philanthropic gestures expressed by the Cholmondeley family it is hard to see how the Marquess could countenance that – he nevertheless was not in opposition to the law. The owners of large Norfolk estates, like their important tenants, did not tend to oppose the introduction of the New Poor Law, although they might not have been entirely pleased by the somewhat arbitrary division of their lands. The centralizing tendencies of the Poor Law Amendment Act were not popular, either; and many resented the apparent loss of local control. In reality the individual unions – largely controlled by farmers – worked out their own ways of administering poor relief, not always consistent with the desires of the Poor Law Commissioners in Somerset House.

The workhouse was, of course, not built on Cholmondeley land, but in the parish of Docking, to the west of the village on the Heacham Road. The classical front is still there, even though the buildings have been converted for residential use, and much of the original building has gone. Its aspect is impressive even today – a pauper palace of the New Poor Law era – and it must have inspired a degree of fear in the

Docking Union Workhouse – date unknown

poor of the neighbouring parishes. To them, after all, it was nothing short of a prison, and so the workhouses remained, throughout their existence, in the eyes of the labouring classes, in spite of any positive outcomes they might have had in educating children or caring for the elderly infirm. The Docking Workhouse was designed by John Brown, Norfolk County Surveyor, to accommodate 450 inmates. It cost £9,125, the expense of its construction being borne by each parish in the union. There were certainly problems with the builders, and many defects had to be remedied before the workhouse at last was open to receive pauper inmates at the end of 1836.

However, in June 1835, there was no workhouse. Paupers could not yet suffer the punitive harshness of its regime, along with a diet poorer than perhaps they had hitherto enjoyed; families were not to endure the indignity of separate accommodation in John Brown's building on the Heacham Road. There was an active Assistant Commissioner, and it was up to him and the overseers on the ground, men like John Kitton of Great Bircham, to begin to apply the provisions of the New Poor Law as best they could in piecemeal fashion.

The coming of this momentous piece of legislation was soon to be keenly felt in the parishes of Great Bircham and Bircham Tofts.

Notes

The outline history of the various poor laws has been largely taken from *The Workhouse Encyclopedia* by Peter Higginbotham, and from Higginbotham's Workhouse website. For the Poor Law Report of 1834 the Penguin edition by S. G. and E. O. A. Checkland has been consulted.

The examples of relief awarded at Houghton are taken from the Houghton Parish Accounts: Constables' and Overseers' Records (1738-1835), kept at Houghton Hall (HH:M29).

[1] A. Brundage, *The English Poor Laws 1700-1930*, (Basingstoke, 2002), p. 9.

[2] A. Digby, *Pauper Palaces* (London, 1978), p.37.

[3] T. Ashwin & A. Davison, eds, *An Historical Atlas of Norfolk* (Phillimore, 2005), p. 147.

[4] J. Crowley & A. Reid, eds, *The Poor Law in Norfolk 1700-1850* (Ely, 1983), p. 68.

[5] TNA: MH 12/8249.

[6] BPP: 1834, Vol. XXX (Rural Queries), Answers of George Bate, Overseer, Houghton.

[7] D. Englander, *Poverty and Poor Law Reform in 19th Century Britain, 1834-1914* (London, 1998), p. 1; K. D. M. Snell, *Annals of the Labouring Poor: Social Change and Agrarian England 1660-1900* (Cambridge, 1985), p. 137.

[8] Digby, *Palaces* , 1978, chapters 9 & 10.

[9] *The Times* 16 Jun 1834 & 3 Jul. 1834.

[10] Englander, *Poverty and Poor Law Reform*, p. 3.

[11] Nicholls, Eight Letters on the Management of our Poor (1822), p. 24.

[12] TNA: MH 12/8249.

[13] Digby 1978, p. 95 & TNA: MH 12/8249.

[14] MH 12/8249.

[15] HH: M7c & M8.

Chapter 3. The Rising of the 'Ignorant'

For it really appears to be another "Rural War," and it threatens to be much more durable and mischievous than the last rural war; and there is this circumstance in addition, in this case; that is to say, that this scene of trouble, of turmoil, and of boiling blood, has been called by the Parliament itself... William Cobbett, *Political Register*, June 1835

Immense losses have been sustained in the grazing department during the present season, which, together with the ruinously low price of wheat will tend to hasten a crisis which is fast approaching - namely the pauperisation of thousands of industrious individuals with small capitals engaged in the cultivation of the soil, and the reducing of the whole of the farming tenantry to a state little short of actual bankruptcy ... From the Norfolk Agricultural Report, 30 April 1835. *The Norfolk Chronicle,* 9 May 1835.

The principal reason, of course, for Lewis Jarvis's writing to Richard Groom was to inform him of the serious destruction of Cholmondeley property. It is now essential that we detail just what happened during those ten days in June.

I Trouble expected

On 17 June 1835 John Weyland, Chairman of the Norfolk Quarter Sessions, must have felt compelled to write to Lord John Russell, Home Secretary. He pointed out that, as the Assistant Poor Law Commissioners were now busy bringing into effect the provisions of the New Poor Law, his Lordship might see the necessity of the immediate establishment of a local civil force to be ready to deal with any emergency which might arise.[1] At this time the peace was kept in the Norfolk countryside, as elsewhere, by parish constables. These men had originally been elected by the parishioners, but later were appointed by a Justice of the Peace. They were usually part-time and unpaid. As a means of maintaining law and order the system can hardly have been efficient. It was always possible to appoint special constables in an emergency, of course, and if they were deemed to be insufficient then the military would have to be called in. The

Metropolitan Police Act of 1829 had largely replaced the parish constables in London, and the agitation for county police forces was growing. Our story contains several references to Metropolitan policemen, but in North-west Norfolk in June 1835 there were only the parish constables. Weyland's letter was far from complimentary about the 'common constables', calling them notoriously 'unequal' to the duty of meeting any emergency. He did not have any more faith in special constables. The letter continued: 'but when riots and tumults are apprehended it has been found, not only that the persons so appointed have been indisposed to act, but also that it has been too late for them to do so efficiently'. The civil force he and his fellow magistrates proposed would still consist of special constables acting as a local police, but they would not be appointed except in times of emergency. They might be chosen by ballot or by parish vestries, their numbers varying according to the size of the parish. Any parish which refused to appoint constables would be heavily fined. The constables should meet regularly and thus inspire more confidence in the local population. Thus, in a sense, a forerunner of the County Police, which would eventually be introduced in Norfolk in 1839, was being proposed. Evidently the Norfolk magistrates were expecting trouble, very possibly 'riots and tumults'.

In 1835, as we discovered in Chapter 1, there were seven farmers in Great Bircham and Bircham Tofts: John Kitton, Thomas Hebgin, John Nurse, Daniel Denny, Anthony Beck, Philip Jarrett and James Howlett. The latter, who was Kitton's son-in-law, farmed in Bircham Tofts. At some point in June they, although perhaps not all of them, must have decided to pay their labourers 1s. 3d per acre for cutting the grass. This was not a good rate of pay, but the farmers knew they could probably get away with it. Besides, they had other worries: the Agricultural Reports, which regularly appeared in *The Norfolk Chronicle*, reflect the serious concerns of the farming community, especially those in May and June of 1835.[2] The cold northerly winds and frosty nights of the beginning of June were threatening to delay the wheat harvest. Moreover, they feared wet weather later, and the harvest could be a month late. There had been 'superabundant' harvests in 1833 and 1834, but a late harvest would mean a whole 'month's additional consumption to clear off the surplus stock of old wheat'. In other words, the wheat would be used for cattle-feed.

If labour was not in short supply the farmers had no need to be generous. Apparently the farmers had indeed managed to make this rate of pay stick, for on Saturday 20 June John Kitton's men, when paid, had 'appeared as well satisfied as ever'. This was reported by a local magistrate,[3] but the degree of satisfaction sensed by a labourer and that perceived by a magistrate can rarely have converged. The labourers, whilst not happy to be paid such miserable wages, would have nevertheless grudgingly accepted them, knowing full well that they would be made up – in cash – by the system of poor relief then in operation.

II Saturday 20 June

His name has not been recorded, but sometime on Saturday 20 June 1835 a labourer in Great Bircham applied to the Parish Overseer of the Poor for relief. *The Bury Post* mentions five or six labourers and states that they had been working for Lord Cholmondeley (on the roads, it emerged later), and had been paid 6s. for labour during the previous week, but had left his employment for what the overseers judged, and the newspaper called an 'insufficient' cause.[4] The labourers did not receive from the overseer an offer of relief entirely in cash, as had hitherto been the practice; instead they would have had to make do with some cash, but also with 1s. 6d. for flour, and 1s. for shop goods. Both of these could be purchased by tickets only. This offer was refused – 'determinedly' according to *The Norfolk Chronicle*[5] of Saturday 4 July – and was accompanied by a threat that the whole of the poor of the parish would resist this new method of payment of relief. The Great Bircham overseer was none other than John Kitton, the largest farmer in the parish.

III Sir Edward Parry

It is time to introduce an important person in the drama, the Assistant Poor Law Commissioner for Norfolk, Sir William Edward Parry. Several years before coming to Norfolk he had had a distinguished career as an Arctic explorer, having on more than one occasion endeavoured to find the North-west Passage; in 1822 he had even got some way over the ice floes in an attempt to reach the North Pole. *The Norfolk Chronicle* of 30 May announced his arrival in Norwich with emphasis on his previous naval career:

The celebrated Navigator, Captain Sir Edward Parry, R.N. has been visiting Norwich this week in his capacity of an Assistant Commissioner under the New Poor Laws Amendment Act.[6]

Sir Edward Parry (1790 – 1855)
Arctic explorer, and Norfolk Assistant Poor Law Commissioner
at the time of the Bircham Riots.

It is somewhat curious, therefore, to find this renowned and undoubtedly courageous explorer struggling against obstacles other than sea and ice, as he set about the task of helping to steer the Poor Law Amendment Act, the state's formidable new vessel, through the turbulent waters of Norfolk politics. In his memoirs he cites a letter he wrote to the Poor Law Commissioners that accompanied a testimony from his previous employer. He concedes that a very good polar explorer might make a very bad Poor Law Commissioner, but stresses that the testimony refers to his administrative abilities. He must have appeared to his new masters a distinguished candidate, because he was appointed, in March 1835, ahead of upwards of a thousand other candidates.[7] George Nicholls, one of the three Poor Law Commissioners, had been a sea captain, however, and could well have valued highly the strengths of a fellow seafarer.

In April he was writing that the task was an arduous one, and that he was working at it from six in the morning till eleven or twelve at night. Yet he saw the value of his work: 'Each day I see more of its importance, and take a greater personal interest in the subject, in proportion as I see with my own eyes more of the wretched system which has been tolerated so many years.' In June his wife was very conscious of the wearisome nature of his work, and the lack of repose. She said he was making satisfactory progress, although everything demanded much time and caution, given that he had to deal with so many different people. Sir Edward was no politician (he had earlier in the year declined the offer of a parliamentary seat in his native Bath) and so the 'violent party spirit' to which Lady Parry also referred in her letter must have been wearying in the extreme.[8] Nevertheless, she was convinced he was 'desirous of doing his duty according to what appeared to him right, uninfluenced by any political or party spirit'.

In the summer of 1835 he might have been much fatigued by the pressures of his new employment, but he was clearly determined to succeed against all opposition. When it was later reported to him, by a Norfolk magistrate, that the allowance offered to each one of the Bircham labourers on that Saturday in June was the equivalent of ten shillings per week, he could not resist feeling frustration at the complete absurdity of the position taken by the Bircham poor: 'To what a pass are things come! What an argument in face of the very measure which these deluded men are resisting!'[9] However, the agricultural labourers of Great Bircham and Bircham Tofts were about to show themselves less willing to submit to the discipline of their betters than the crew of a ship in Arctic waters. And there was no lash to subdue them.

The Assistant Commissioner certainly approved of Kitton's offering part of the relief in kind, instead of money. After all, there was nothing new in this; and it had been used under the Old Poor Law. More specifically, Parry pointed out to Thomas Frankland Lewis on 3 July that relief in kind had been partially adopted at Swaffham before he came into Norfolk, and at a few other places besides. In the same letter he pointed out that 'great benefit had been derived except to the Beer-shops and little Shopkeepers'.[10] Meeting the Norwich Court of Guardians on 16 June he explained at length the workings of the Poor Law Amendment Act, and he outlined his philosophy as to the giving of relief in kind: it was to be introduced gradually not suddenly; it was not, he declared, the wish of the Poor Law Commissioners to make any sudden changes. Later, in his long report on the riots of the 2 July to the Commissioners, he reiterated this approach, saying he had always recommended beginning with just 'a few of the able-bodied paupers most suspected of idleness rather than with any others, and giving at first only a proportion, say one-third, of the relief in that way, and the rest still in money'.[11] Thus Kitton was putting into operation the Parry system of relief; a textbook case. Anyway, it was not something dreamt up by Parry: his superiors in London had recommended the same in November 1834; and they were only copying a practice which had been used in many parishes before the passing of the Poor Law Amendment Act.[12]

From the standpoint of the twenty-first century all this looks eminently reasonable. After all, a labourer could not drink flour; but his hungry children could eat bread. That, however, is not the point: the labourers' wages were low and this sudden change in the system of relief was one oppression too many, one that they felt they had to resist with all the strength they could muster.

Parry reported later that there had been just two labourers, but inevitably the details of this story – given as they were in haste by several people – will not be completely consistent. It was on Tuesday 23 June at Burnham Westgate that John Kitton communicated to Parry what he had done in the payment of relief in the presence of H. E. Blythe, another magistrate and farmer (and his wife's nephew). Sir Edward was quite sure that the Bircham farmer had done nothing illegal or improper. He found the measure 'just and beneficial', and

Kitton, for his part, declared that he would not yield to the resisting labourers so long as the other farmers demonstrated the same resolution.[13]

IV The Strike

Thus began a short period of turbulence and riot, which resulted in several of the labourers of Great Bircham and Bircham Tofts receiving terms of imprisonment with hard labour, and in serious destruction of property. No lives were lost, but that was more a matter of chance than design.

There is little doubt about the level of resistance, which took the form of a general strike amongst the labourers in Great Bircham and Bircham Tofts, beginning on Monday 22 June. This points to a degree of organization. Large groups of men went to the farms in the neighbourhood and forced the labourers away from the fields and farmyards. They even obliged farm servants living in the household of the farmers to join the strike. *The Norfolk Chronicle* informed its readers that the whole of the week was spent in 'idleness, sullen discontent and complainings'. This was a period of haymaking and turnip–sowing, but these tasks were left undone throughout the parishes.

The labourers had perhaps chosen well the time to strike. The Norfolk Agricultural Report published in *The Norfolk Chronicle* of 6 June seemed to promise a good haysel, although because of the weather it may have turned out otherwise:

We do not anticipate a very heavy crop of hay; although the weather would seem to favour that supposition; nevertheless the land is well covered, the bottom thick set, the stem fine, and the quality will be excellent, if the season should turn out propitious for the harvesting.

The first labourer we can name was Richard Greeves or Greves. On the morning of Tuesday 23 June he, along with 'about twenty persons', came to the farm of Daniel Denny in Great Bircham. Clearly Greeves meant business: his purpose was to remove one John Hunt from the farm, and he declared he would have his man 'by fair means or foul'. The farmer had little choice against such odds and let Hunt go with the labourers. Hunt must have been a farm servant living in Denny's household; the overwhelming majority of the labourers in the villages were only casually employed. Later, called as a prosecution witness at the trial of Richard Greeves, he said he had gone with the men and stayed with them three or four hours, 'rather than be pulled about'. He also revealed something of the reasons for the strike: that the men would have returned to work if they had been able to receive money of the parish 'as usual'.

V The Breaking of the Strike

It was, however, on the following Monday (29 June) that the situation deteriorated. Clearly the mood was turning uglier, and the labourers were absolutely determined not to give ground to the farmers who employed them. This became apparent when John Hunter, a farmer from the neighbouring village of Barwick, sent two men to assist in getting in the turnips on the farm of Thomas Hebgin situated on the village green of Great Bircham. Their names were Collinson (probably Collison) and Simmonds (or Simmons). The latter was probably John Simmons, from Syderstone in 1841 and farm bailiff in Barwick in 1851. Hunter's two men, on leaving the farmyard on horseback alongside their master, were, in the words of *The Norfolk Chronicle*, 'immediately assailed in the most violent manner'. They were taken from their horses, and Hunter was dragged off and 'severely ill-treated'. There were some thirty men, all armed with sticks, involved in this attempt to thwart the attempt to break the strike, but inevitably some were more active than others. Particularly active was Thomas Goldon (or Golding), and another person involved was John Pilgrim. At the subsequent trial Hunter, called as a witness, said the crowd shouted 'Let us murder him' as they assailed him with stones. Hunter deposed at the Norfolk Summer Assizes of 1835:

On Saturday the 27th day of June last he was requested by Thomas Hebgin of Great Bircham, farmer, to furnish him with some labourers as his own men had struck work for the week ... On the following Monday ... he went to Bircham with two men by the names of Collinson and Simmonds who had mounted two of Mr Hebgin's horses to go to work, and were proceeding to the field to plough [when] they were attacked by several persons, to the number of 20 at least, and violently and forcibly pulled off their horses.[14]

Thomas Hebgin's farm
(Plate XXVI. 01 in Hill's Survey of 1800)

VI 'A State of Great Excitement'

John Kitton had been requested by Sir Edward Parry, when the two
met at Burnham Westgate, to let him know by letter whatever might
occur subsequent to his decision to change the method of giving relief.
Later that day Kitton wrote (apparently in some haste given the lack of
punctuation):

*I am sorry to inform you this Parish is in a state of great excitement finding
our People would not go to work we have endeavoured to get men elsewhere a
neighbouring Farmer came into the Parish with some men this morning
when we and the men were beset and driven out with stones and dreadful
imprecations and I am fully persuaded we must have military assistance and
that immediately or the act cannot be called into force.*[15]

There was thus no doubt that for one Bircham farmer the New Poor
Law must be vigorously supported if it was to come into effect in
Norfolk.

This meant arrests must be made, and on that day warrants were
granted for the arrest of four men, identified as ring-leaders: Thomas
Goldon (Golding), John Pilgrim, Thomas Bell and Thomas Marsham.

The sequence of events on the morning of Monday 29 June is not entirely clear, but very likely sometime after the events at Hebgin's farm there occurred a very violent scene at the farm of Daniel Denny. It is probably the incident which more than any other defines the Bircham Riots.

Seven labourers were identified: John Goldon (Golding), W[illiam] Hill, William (wrongly called Thomas) Wanfer (or Wanford), George Bennett, Edward Carrington, George Harrison and James Williamson. They were as determined as Thomas Goldon (Golding) and John Pilgrim to ensure that the strike of farm labourers should be complete. The labourers needed to force two servants out of Denny's farmhouse: clearly they could not be left to work if the strikers were to prevail. It was stated, when these men eventually came to trial, that about 200 people came to Denny's farm that morning.

Goldon (Golding) seized one of the servants and Wanfer (Wanford) and Hill the other. The three were 'very violent' and made Denny send a further two men out of the house. Harrison threatened to 'do for' Denny and a Mr Clarke (probably the farmer's father-in-law or brother-in-law). All the accused except Carrington, according to Denny's and Clarke's accounts at the later trials, took an active part. From these witness accounts it became clear that the events at Denny's farm had been particularly vicious. Yet, amidst all the violence, a more political appeal was heard. George Bennett declared:

Can a man live on half a stone and fifteen pence? We are bound in a bond of blood and blood will be spilt before this is finished.

The Bircham Riots were much more than an unruly mob intent on roughing up a few farmers and destroying property. Instinctively men like Bennett knew that he and his labourers had a grievance, and such grievances were deep-seated. He also feared that the already miserable condition of the Bircham labourers was about to deteriorate even further in consequence of this change in the Poor Law. The opposing forces – on a different side of an ideological line – were now squaring up. Sir Edward Parry had declared himself on Tuesday 23 June at Burnham Westgate, when he told John Kitton he was doing nothing wrong by offering relief partly in kind. Kitton had also very plainly nailed his colours to the mast when he hastily wrote to Parry and urged the use of the military in order to ensure that the New Poor Law came into force. There was more: Carrington endeavoured further to rouse the mob by charging Denny with former ill-treatment. These farmers were not popular. Twenty-first century attitudes and behaviour in the workplace must not be allowed to colour judgements in this respect: the treatment of labourers by farmers was often brutal. The labourers, who could be just as brutal, seemed intent on redressing the balance: Williamson came up with a club and threatened to 'knock Denny's brains out'. This was later confirmed by Stephen Butcher, who must have been a farm steward from Anmer. It is possible he had been called in to help during the strike. The threat of violence was increasing.

So far we have mentioned only men, but it must not be assumed that women were not involved. How active a part they played is not clear, but it seems unlikely they remained entirely passive. Now the first woman whom we can identify became involved in the disturbances. Her name was Mary Marsham. Called as a defence witness at the trial of the six men who were intent on removing the servants from Denny's farm, she denied the reference to blood but admitted she had been with the mob for three or four hours. It is improbable that there were no women among the vast crowds moving around the Birchams during the dramatic events of June 1835. After all, any decrease in poor relief would be very keenly felt by women, especially those responsible for maintaining a household with small children. Besides, why should resentment against the Bircham farmers and overseers be felt solely by the men? It is evident that virtually the whole population of the Birchams was opposed to John Kitton and the other farmers.

VII Arrests

The means of securing the arrests seem to have been planned in this manner: Money Curtis, the Governor of Walsingham Bridewell (some ten or eleven miles away), would come with caravans in which to put the prisoners. He would be accompanied by a party of constables, one of whom was William Tilney from Little Walsingham. Special constables would also be required to assist, and some of the Bircham farmers had been charged with this role.

There is a description of a prison van in the Second Report of the Inspectors of Prisons, 1837; and it is possible that Money Curtis brought something similar over from Walsingham.

They are 8ft. 4in. wide, and 5ft. 5½in. high, and will each conveniently accommodate about twenty prisoners, but upwards of thirty are occasionally conveyed. No officer is inside the van.[16]

The Inspectors were for the Home District, and perhaps things were different in Norfolk, however.

By this time, according to *The Norfolk Chronicle*, all the male inhabitants, except the very old, were armed with heavy bludgeons. Several of them are named: Luke Duffield and [George] Harrison, together with Thomas Wanfer [Wanford], [Edward] Carrington and [James] Williamson. The last three had already been active in the incidents at Denny's farm. What ensued was particularly nasty. The constables, despite receiving violent personal injuries, managed to arrest one of the men. This was John Pilgrim, and he was taken at the King's Head, Great Bircham; later he was secured in a caravan and taken away to Walsingham Bridewell.

Outside the inn a crowd of some 200 or 300 people had gathered, clearly determined to see no more arrests. Constable William Tilney seized a second man, but was knocked down. While on the ground he received many blows to the head, arms and shoulders, 'like those from a sledge hammer'. The Barwick farmer, John Hunter, also present at the scene in order to identify several of the individuals, was dragged from his horse, and was violently set upon. In self-defence, as *The Norfolk Chronicle* claimed, he produced a pistol and threatened to shoot the next man who approached.

Hunter was no stranger to gunfire. On the evening of 23 January 1834, as he was reading by his fireside at the farm in Barwick, shots were fired at his window. No doubt the shots were intended to draw him to the window so that he could present an easy target to his assailant. This did not happen, but later Hunter, along with his brother William, who was a parish constable and occupied the same farm, rode to Stanhoe, where they were able to catch a suspect. The next day another was caught, and the two men were transported for life. One of them belonged to a family notorious in the neighbourhood.

The Bury Post, which reported the incident, pointed out that three brothers from the family had been active in riots in Docking in 1831; they each earned 11s. a week on the Hunters' farm.[17] Perhaps John Hunter feared that the notorious brothers – those not transported – might return, and he ought to be prepared. Perhaps he had a dread of the mob and what they might do to him. Perhaps he was trigger-happy. Whatever his reasons for bringing a pistol, it must have increased the fury of the striking labourers.

The situation was now gathering its own momentum, and passions among the labourers were inflamed. They must have been especially incensed by the presence, among the civil forces, of Thomas Hebgin and James Howlett. They had been enrolled as special parish constables. They were both farmers and employers of many of the men. Hebgin was the other Great Bircham Overseer, and Howlett was John Kitton's son-in-law. They 'received many severe wounds'.

The mob had lost one of its leaders, but had managed to prevail. Curtis, with the rest of the civil force and his caravans, was compelled to retreat; but the unfortunate Tilney was left behind. He saw Hunter fall, and when Tilney sprang out, Harrison – or so it was alleged - struck him across the shoulder with a bludgeon. Then he received a second blow, apparently from a round hammer, and this, he said, 'cut a wound in his head four inches long'. That, together with the four or five wounds he had already received, rendered him insensible. He was carried away but recovered in a few minutes. Six or eight persons followed him into the King's Head, where they smote him to a table with their fists. He said: 'You have almost killed me, don't kill me quite.' He was able to struggle to escape, and he made his way to Kitton's farm, his assailants throwing their bludgeons after him. He was rescued 'in a dreadfully injured state', according to *The Bury Post,* and, if the account in *The Norfolk Chronicle* is to be believed, he was put to bed 'in a most dreadfully mutilated state about the head and face, having received on the head alone seven contused wounds, one of which was upwards of three inches in length down to the bone'. To the onlookers it was far from certain whether he would recover. At the scene of Tilney's foiled attempt to capture a second man, the caravan with its prisoner drove off and knocked down the wife of one of the leading rioters; *The Norfolk Chronicle* informed its readers that 'no great injury was sustained'.

Farmer Hebgin, in his role as special constable, was also active at the King's Head. He did not escape injury to himself either. One man was later indicted for assaulting him. He was Thomas Bell, the only rioter whose age, 32, appeared in a newspaper report. In the account of his trial,[18] which appeared in *The Norfolk Chronicle* of 28 November 1835, he appears as Thomas Bett and as John Bell. He was one of the four for whom a warrant of arrest had been issued. Hebgin, in his deposition at Bell's trial, was quite sure that Bell had understood for what purpose he and the other constables were there, and that is why he witnessed the prisoner 'level a stone at him, which knocked him completely off his horse, and he was afterwards senseless'. Fortunately for Hebgin he had been able to duck and the stone caught his hat, and thus he avoided much more serious injury. If he was really 'senseless', it cannot have been for long.

Once again there is mention of women. First of all there was Frances England, landlady of the King's Head. She did not emerge from the events at the inn unscathed, as she later told the court that she had received 'a violent blow on her breast'. This statement could have done the rioters no good, reinforcing the view of most readers of the Norfolk press that these despicable and vile men were capable of loathsome attacks, even upon women.

However, amongst the rioters were also two named women. There were undoubtedly more, but these two appeared as defence witnesses at the trials.

By now the mob must have been roused to even greater heights of fury. Stones were thrown at the various farmhouses in the neighbourhood, causing shutters to be raised. The Bircham Riots had reached their terrifying climax.

VIII Assistance is summoned

John Kitton had already, earlier in the day, indicated to Sir Edward Parry that a military force would be necessary if the Poor Law Amendment Act was to become effective. The need was now greater: the violent mob in Bircham threatened to inflict further damage on people and property. Accordingly, at around 7 o'clock on the same

109

evening, a messenger was sent to one of the neighbouring magistrates (the one who had signed the warrants for the arrests). According to *The Norfolk Chronicle* of 18 July 1835 the magistrate was Mr Hare. This would almost certainly have been Revd Humphrey John Hare of Docking Hall. This messenger was able to give an account of what had happened, and more importantly he urged the necessity of sending a force to ensure the safety of the property holders of the Bircham parishes. There was a great fear that 'some dreadful violence would be renewed in the night'. The magistrate had already been active, and he sent the messenger back with the news that orders to the commanders of the Yeomanry Cavalry of the Melton and Rainham troops had been dispatched, and that the Preventive Service Men from the coast had been ordered to be sent to his house by eleven o'clock to be ready to go to Bircham in case of any disturbance.

The Preventive Service Men were coastguards. There were many coastguard stations along the Norfolk coast, but the only one mentioned in any correspondence with the Home Office was Morston.[19] The principal station, however, was at Wells; the Wells District extended from Cley to Lynn, and the men must have come from various stations along the coast. According to White's Norfolk Directory of 1836 there were merely a lieutenant and seven men stationed at Morston. We know from a report of 1837 by Charles Frederick, officer in command of the Wells District, that the Preventive Men had been called in to assist in the suppression or prevention of riots on two other occasions: in November 1830 at Docking, and for twenty days at Walsingham at the end of the same year.[20]

Yeomanry was the collective name for regiments formed in the 1790s to counter the threat of French invasion. They tended to consist of farmers and were usually commanded by a member of the nobility. They were frequently deployed in the early nineteenth century in the suppression of riots. They were not always popular on account of this role, and frequently met with hostility as they entered towns and villages. The Yeomanry was active at Peterloo in 1819, where the troops gained a reputation for savagery. It is not suggested that those who entered Great Bircham at the beginning of July 1835 would have mercilessly cut down the rioters. The latter did not give them a chance, anyhow; and they rightly saw that their bludgeons were no match for the Yeomanry's guns and swords.

A satirical ballad entitled *Gentlemen Soldiers or the Exploits of the Yeomanry Cavalry* was published in Norwich not long after Peterloo, which was clearly its inspiration. It is obviously biased, but paints a very unflattering picture of the Norfolk Yeomanry. A couple of verses give the flavour:

> *For these Cavalry murd'rers are compos'd of such set,*
> *All the rakings and scrapings the Country can get,*
> *More monsters than men, a dastardly crew,*
> *Mere monkies in mischief with nothing to do.*

> *Some soapheaded farmer has a fool of a son,*
> *By nature an idiot, he is fix'd with a gun,*
> *And though he has scarce as much sense as a goose,*
> *In time perhaps the booby may find out its use.*[21]

IX The Climax of the Riots

Disturbances were expected and disturbances there were. There is a letter in the Home Office files, which was written by Ben Leak, auctioneer and surveyor of Holt, to Sir Jacob Astley on Wednesday 1 July.[22] Astley, who was M.P. for West Norfolk in 1835, had his seat in Melton Constable. Leak's account of the Bircham Riots is quite dramatic, if somewhat disjointed. He told Sir Jacob Astley that 'on Monday night at ten o'clock, strange men, out of all villages round about began to flow into the Town and continued to arrive till about 12'. He later states 'the number assembled is supposed on the spot to have amounted to 800'. The object of all these people was clear: to attack John Kitton's farmhouse (and very likely even to burn it down), and then the others. *The Norfolk Chronicle* informed its readers that between 'eleven o'clock and twelve o'clock, from the numbers of ill-disposed pouring in from the adjacent parishes, all armed with deadly clubs, it was computed that at least eight or nine hundred marched under order to the attack of Mr Kitton's house'.

Numbers in disturbances are notoriously difficult to estimate. In present-day demonstrations there is always a great discrepancy between the numbers given by the police and those given by the demonstrators themselves. It is thus impossible to confirm the accuracy of this figure, although it does seem too large. Many more people than those striking in the three parishes, however, were apparently drawn into the tumult, at least in its final stage. It was stated in a letter sent on 2 July by the local magistrates to the Home Office that an 'assemblage of several hundreds from the adjoining parishes' assisted in the attack on the farmhouses;[23] this, added to Leak's assertion and the statement in *The Norfolk Chronicle* above, confirms that the Bircham Riots had an impact far beyond Great Bircham and Bircham Tofts. The reference to marching under order is also further indicative of a certain amount of organization. What followed then was especially ugly, and it does seem that luck played its part in preventing the death of at least one person.

As we have already learned, the injured William Tilney was put into a room at the rear of John Kitton's farmhouse. Here he must have felt slightly more secure, yet it was about 11 o'clock that night when his troubles began anew. Kitton said 'he must fly'. This he did, leaving the officer alone. Soon he heard voices saying 'damn the officer' and 'many such expressions'. They already knew he was there and they declared – as Tilney deposed later at the trial of the rioters – that they would kill him.

All the doors and windows, 'even to the cills and frames', of Kitton's farmhouse were demolished, the rioters having used the upper backs of grates as battering rams. All the furniture in the two front rooms and kitchen was 'broken into ten thousand pieces, piled up in the middle of the floor on the carpet, and by means of books &c. set light to'. John Kitton and his family escaped across the fields at the back of the house, but the hapless William Tilney was apparently left to his fate. It is surely by good fortune that he had been put in the back of the house. It was even more fortunate for him, and perhaps for the whole village, that 'one, of two better disposed persons' urged the incendiaries to disperse as the military were fast approaching. This person with his companion was able to extinguish the fire.

Church Farm, Great Bircham *(Photo 2011)*

Kitton was obviously a literate man, but whether he had a well-stocked library of classical texts we are never told. It seems, nevertheless, safe to infer that he was a man of some learning, and that this was an educated household. Amongst the silverware and jugs bequeathed by his widow in 1856 there were books; presumably there had been restocking after the Riots. The Bircham farmer would certainly have had ledgers and account books, and the paper from them would have been useful kindling. Ben Leak informed Sir Jacob Astley that a relic had been brought back to Holt from the fire: 'a part of a burnt book, which had been handed round at Bircham while the yeomanry were there'.

The 'better disposed persons' were also something of a mystery. Very probably they had been part of the 800 or 900, and had seen that things were going too far. After all, if the house had been burnt down a hanging offence would have been committed. And had Tilney perished in the flames – he must have been lucky to escape death by smoke inhalation – anybody caught would certainly have hanged. Either the threat of the imminent arrival of the coastguards and yeomanry or, as Leak reported, the failure of the books, papers and broken furniture to 'burn with sufficient violence', preserved Kitton's farmhouse from total destruction, and saved Tilney's life.

The destruction of Kitton's farmhouse by fire would indeed have been a grand gesture, on a much greater scale than the burning of barley stacks. There were fire engines in the 1830s in the area, but whether one could have reached the scene in time is far from clear. We know, from correspondence kept at the Hall, that there were two engines at Houghton in 1830 but 'quite out of repair', and utterly useless. In that year there was a serious fire, certainly the work of an incendiary, at Harpley, and no engine nearer than one at Fakenham was available on that occasion. The farmer had, however, secured the assistance of some 200 men and paid them 2s. 6d. each for working throughout the night to extinguish the flames. He had also provided them with beer, gin and provisions to the value of £4.[24] These incendiary attacks could, therefore, provide the poor with the satisfaction of having struck a blow against a farmer (whose loss would be made good by the insurance company) as well as extra money and drink, all at somebody else's expense. It is possible that something similar might have transpired at Great Bircham, had the fire caught hold, but the prospect of seeing Kitton's farm burnt to the ground must have been attractive to at least some of the rioters. One hopes, however, that the Houghton engines had been repaired by 1835.

Ellen Kitton in later life (1818-1885) (the fifth daughter of John and Rebecca Kitton, one of three daughters who bcame blind)

Sir Edward Parry, in a letter to the Poor Law Commissioners in London on 2 July adds more colour to the attack on the farm of John Kitton, whom he calls 'an active, intelligent farmer'. He says that the farmer 'was driven, with his wife and family, into a wheat field, where the latter remained, almost naked, the whole night'. In the family there were a boy of eleven and three girls in their teens. All three girls were blind or at least only partially sighted.

William Tilney did, of course, recover and was able to give his account of events at the later trials. According to Leak's letter, he was unlikely to survive the night after the wounds he received, unless he was kept quiet. We know from bills kept at Houghton Hall that William Bidewell of the King's Head, Houghton provided a 'chaise to Walsingham with [the] Wounded Police Officer from [the] Bircham Riots'. His bill was £1 4s.[25]

The rioters, however, had not finished their work. Kitton's was not the only farm attacked that night. The farmhouses of Thomas Hebgin and John Nurse were also assailed, the latter only partially. Hebgin, together with his wife and infant son, managed to escape over a wall and hid for a while in the farmyard, before being taken off to Dersingham. This was to Ling House, another Houghton Estate property. Denny's farm was presumably spared, not out of any respect for the farmer, but merely because it was some distance away from the centre of the village. James Howlett had good warning of the approach of the mob, having been tipped off by 'a well disposed person'. With his wife and five children he escaped into fields at the back of the house; the children ranged in age from eighteen months to seven years, and included the future founder of the great Norwich shoe-making business. Soon afterwards, according to *The Norfolk Chronicle*, the exterior of his house was reduced to a state of ruin.

X The Riot is Quelled

It would appear that the Preventive Men were the first to arrive on the morning of Tuesday 30 June. About thirty, according to Ben Leak, were on the spot when the Yeomanry Cavalry arrived. Leak also stated, in his letter to Sir Jacob Astley, that the coastguard marched, on the evening of Wednesday 1 July, from Morston to Walsingham. However, from which coastguard stations the men came was not stated in the press or any of the correspondence held in the Home Office files.

Once again Leak is the most informative. He told Sir Jacob that the yeomanry troops arrived at Bircham about eleven on the morning of 30 June. Each man had been issued with three rounds of ball cartridge. Before they arrived, however, 'the multitude had fled'. *The Bury Post* of 8 July mentioned that 'several of the principals had fled'. Leak adds that the troops were kept about Bircham all day, and then at night were taken to Houghton. Here they found stabling at the Hall stables and those of the King's Head, which Leak calls by its former name of New Inn. They were under strict instructions to be ready to start off again at a moment's notice, and to this end they were ordered not to unsaddle, and to sleep by the side of the horses. After about three hours a messenger arrived; they turned out again and galloped back to Bircham. There they found about 150 men assembled, but they fled on the approach of the troops and 'dispersed in all directions', very many of them having disguised themselves.

The Norfolk Chronicle of 4 July stated that 'after a short time' some of the Preventive Men were drawn off to Docking to keep themselves in readiness, but whether that was on 30 June or 1 July is not clear. Part of the coastguard force and the Yeomanry stayed on duty, however, until Wednesday 1 July. Finally, also on 1 July, forty-four men, under the command of Captain Mansel, of the 6th Dragoons (Inniskillens) entered the parish, thus relieving the coastguard and the Yeomanry. The latter were ordered home, with the understanding that they were to hold themselves in readiness to march again. Three troops of Dragoons, we are informed by *The Norfolk Chronicle* of 9 May, had marched into Norwich at the beginning of May.[26] Therefore this must have been their first engagement in the county.

The Norfolk Yeomanry had been reformed in 1831.[27] There were then three troops: Rainham, Melton and Dereham. The Major-Commandant was the Right Honourable Captain George John Milles. His seat was at Elmham Hall, and in 1836 he became the fourth Lord Sondes; he had fought at Waterloo. The Yeomanry had been raised by Charles Loftus, a grandson of George Townshend, first Marquess Townshend. It was Lord Wodehouse, the Lord-Lieutenant of Norfolk, who asked Loftus to gather together the Norfolk Rangers, who had served earlier in the century. Wodehouse had been concerned about the wave of disturbances and destruction of threshing machines which was sweeping the county at that time. The Government would arm the new force as long as three troops were formed. Initially these three troops were the Dereham Troop (with Captains Lord James Townshend and Frederick Loftus), the Melton Troop (Captain Sir Jacob Astley) and the Rainham Troop. The Captain of the latter troop was Lord Charles Townshend; Charles Loftus, his cousin, was Lieutenant and the Cornet was Henry Berney Caldwell. The last of these was from Hillborough Hall, near Swaffham. He owned virtually all of Hillborough and he was the magistrate who told Sir Edward Parry that the Bircham labourers had turned down the equivalent of 10s. a week, when they refused to accept payment of relief in kind. Parry based his report of the riot to the Poor Law Commissioners on Caldwell's account, the two having met as the latter returned from Bircham. In fact it is probably true to say that much of what we know about the Bircham Riots comes originally from Caldwell.

The Melton Troop had only recently (during May 1835) been broken up; and it had been replaced by the Holt Troop (Captain: William John Brereton). This explains why the newspaper reports were wrong to write of the Rainham and Melton Troops.

Lieutenant Loftus, in the second part of his autobiography, casts himself as the hero of the day, and dramatically recounts the brief role of the Norfolk Yeomanry in the Bircham Riots. Some details do not completely accord with the newspaper reports, or with the correspondence preserved at the Home Office. He says that news had come to him of labourers meeting in the neighbourhood of Docking and showing a disposition to rioting. On the night of 29 June, at eleven o'clock a note reached him from Derick Hoste saying that labourers had attacked a farm and 'everyone was in the greatest alarm'. He was requested to assemble his troops, and he sent notice to the Major Commandant to bring up all the men he could. The place of muster was Hempton Green and Loftus worked through the night to get his Rainham men together. There was no time to lose:

I then started off myself, pistols in holster, cartridges in my pouch, in marching order. I knew where all my men lived, and called on them on my way, and they sent off messages to others, not far distant; so the news flew like the wind, and all the country side in a short time was up.

He tells us that by six-thirty in the morning fifty-five out of his troop of fifty-six were assembled at Hempton. Milles brought up the Elmham

117

and Dereham men, and about forty came from Holt. (He informs us that a farmer had sent a man and a horse with a note to the adjutant at Holt, some twenty miles away.) It was therefore quite a large force which was assembled, and all done quickly. The speed of the operation, especially given the distances which had to be covered, earned much praise. According to *The Norfolk Chronicle* of 4 July 1835 the men thoroughly deserved the refreshments which they were eventually given; and the rest 'from the extraordinary fatigue which some must have undergone owing to the distance they had come to the place of muster and scene of disturbance, and which reflects the highest possible credit and praise upon them for their alacrity'.

They then marched for Bircham, where they discovered there 'had been some attempt to riot, but that the coastguard men at Lynn, and other places, had come up in the night, and had prevented it'. Next they were requested to march to Docking, in order to show themselves. They stopped two hours by the inn, in order for the men to get refreshments. Captain John Davy RN, a magistrate from Ingoldisthorpe, was in Docking, but he had been injured by a stone 'thrown by some low and cowardly fellow'. The stone-thrower had made himself scarce, however, 'for such men invariably run away after the performance of their unmanly exploit'. The march to Docking had, he felt, been worthwhile: 'Our appearance had a good effect, for men who were standing about in groups, talking of the attempt at riot, and planning mischief, dispersed almost at once'. Loftus could well be exaggerating the effect of the cavalry, of course; although a force of probably around one hundred and fifty armed men, especially after 'refreshments' at the inn in Docking could be a terrifying prospect. What he seems to be indicating – but again we only have his perspective – is that any 'riot' might well have spread beyond the attacks on the farmhouses in Great Bircham and Bircham Tofts.

He then tells us that his troop was left at Bircham for the night, and the rest proceeded to the stables at Houghton. These were empty, so there was plenty of room. They had cold beef and sandwiches at Docking and Bircham, which would have fortified them for the night spent next to their horses. This must have brought back memories of twenty years earlier to Major Milles; he had done the same at Quatrebras, the night before Waterloo. Loftus adds that prior to that battle 'man and horse had their bed on the damp earth, many of them before the setting of the sun, to sleep the sleep of death there'. None of the Yeomanry would have to do so that night in Norfolk. In fact, if they had come ready for action they must have been disappointed. No doubt they still enjoyed their exciting night-time gallop through the Norfolk countryside.

Loftus, however, would have returned home to Rainham well satisfied:

Everything passed off quietly. The labourers who had created this disturbance were wonderfully surprised when they saw the soldiers coming, and so promptly, too, from far and wide (indeed we were much praised for our activity and zeal in assembling from all parts of the county on so short notice), and would not believe they were Yeomanry Cavalry, but the Dragoons from Norwich, our dress ... being that of heavy dragoons, and completely deceiving the yokels.

Really? They might not have known exactly what a dragoon cavalry-man looked like, but they will have quickly assessed the situation, and realized that resistance to such a force would have been lunacy. It is, however, undoubtedly true that if the coastguards and Yeomanry had not arrived more damage could have been inflicted.

Loftus finishes his account – casting doubt on the complete accuracy of it – by saying a troop of 17th Lancers from Norwich arrived at noon the next day. The day is correct, but they were from the 6th Dragoons. He might have been thinking of his brother, William, who was an officer on half-pay in the 17th Lancers.

What scene assaulted the gaze of the Honourable George John Milles, the seasoned campaigner of Waterloo and the Peninsular War, as he entered Great Bircham? Once more it is Ben Leak who paints, in his hurried letter, the most vivid picture:

There is no work going on anywhere near, The Hay Cocks are thrown out and no one to get it together, during the night, Horses, Cattle &c were turned into the standing Corn, The Wheat &c and the three Ho[use]s are now a complete wreck; not an article breakable being left whole.[28]

The Captain had served in the Peninsular War, and, according to Sir Edward Parry in his letter to the Poor Law Commissioners of 2 July, on encountering the scenes of destruction in Great Bircham and Bircham Tofts, he 'declared he had never witnessed any pillage more complete or more barbarous'.[29]

XI Aftermath of the Riot

The Norfolk Chronicle of 4 July informed its readers that 'most of the discontented requested permission of their employers yesterday [Tuesday 30 June] afternoon to resume their work, which was granted, and this morning (Wednesday) all is quiet, and the troops are marched from their bivouac for dismissal'. The same article in *The Norfolk Chronicle* concluded: 'We are happy to learn that on Thursday nearly all the labourers had returned to their employment.' The forces summoned to defend the village could not be expected to stay too long. The magistrates, in their letter to the Home Office of 2 July, stated that, though the commanding officer of the Yeomanry 'very handsomely' offered the services of his men as long as they might be required, absence from their various callings, especially at this season of the year, would be very inconvenient.[30] The officer of the coastguard, for his part, said that at least a part of his force should return to their duties on the coast. Thus only ten Preventive Men were remaining in Bircham on Wednesday 1 July, when the Dragoons arrived. Exactly when the Dragoons returned to Norwich is not clear, but a letter from magistrates, dated 13 July, to the Home Office states that they had returned to their quarters, apart from fifteen men who remained at Fakenham.[31]

Nevertheless, despite the presence of the Dragoons and the Preventive Men, the magistrates still feared further disturbances if they were to be withdrawn. They were able, in their letter of 2 July, to announce that six of the rioters had been caught and were being examined. Unfortunately they had to express their regret that 'the principals in the Riot had escaped apprehension'. They could not relax their guard: they were now taking measures to strengthen the constabulary force by swearing in special constables. They appealed to the Home Secretary for 'any assistance or Instruction' he might be able to 'afford in rendering the force more effective'. Not being able to rely on a permanent military force, special constables were about the only remedy the Norfolk magistrates could offer. Sir Edward Parry had nothing but contempt for special constables. He had already written to the Right Honourable Thomas Frankland Lewis, the Chairman of the Poor Law Commission, on 1 July. The letter was passed on to the Home Office. Parry urged the creation of a proper police force (presumably along the lines of that suggested by Weyland in his letter of 17 June) and dismissed any possibility of relying on the special constables, and – as perhaps to be expected from a former seafarer – cited an unfortunate naval parallel:

It is very unwise to wait till a tumult takes place, in which case, the Special Constables will, I expect, emulate the conduct of the Greek Fleet under Lord Cochrane, and turn their heads to every point of the compass but where they are wanted.[32]

The first few days of July saw a flurry of correspondence between Norfolk and the Home Office in London. On 2 July Parry sent a long report of the disturbances at Bircham. He must have taken some comfort from the reply from his superior, Thomas Frankland Lewis, at the Poor Law Commission. He was able to say that Lord Melbourne, the Prime Minister, and Lord Russell, the Home Secretary, sent 'the strongest assurance of their determination to enforce the operation of the Law'. However, as the force then deployed seemed quite adequate for maintaining the peace, they would sanction nothing more than the sending of two policemen.[33]

The magistrates continued to swear in local special constables. In a letter of 3 July to the Home Office they stated that they were still examining offenders, and were busy swearing in special constables 'from amongst the respectable'; these they hoped to send to the 'Several Parishes in the district'. However, there appears to have been a difference between the hopes of the magistrates in swearing in special constables and the views of Lord Wodehouse. He was the Lord Lieutenant of Norfolk and he too wrote to the Home Secretary on 3 July. The penultimate paragraph of his letter reveals the depth of the unwillingness of the Bircham inhabitants to play their part in the maintenance of the peace. 'I regret to say that the Inhabitants have formally refused to act as Special Constables, & the Farmers are afraid to give such information as may lead to the punishment of the offenders.'[34] The local magistrates, in a letter to the Home Secretary of 4 July, were quite clear that something major had occurred at Bircham, something that went beyond a strike of labourers in a couple of parishes. They too had to concede that the present system of policing was now shown up as ineffective:

... the Constabulary force as at present organized would be very ineffective for the protection against the rising of such large bodies of Labourers with the determined spirit w^h has been evinced in Bircham & most of the Parishes in this district.[35]

The magistrates, in the same letter of 4 July, urged that the civil force would be rendered more effective if 'some experienced persons belonging to the London Police should be sent into the Neighbourhood'. The sending of Metropolitan policemen into areas where there had been disturbances appears to have been a regular ploy used by magistrates to strengthen the local constabulary. How effective it really was must be questioned. For one thing, with London accents, they must have stood out a mile. All villagers instantly knew of strangers in their midst. Some might have been willing to cooperate with them, but many were not. These urbane law officers from the big city might well have seen agricultural labourers as straw-sucking yokels, but the latter were no fools. They could quite easily tell the Metropolitan men anything. Nevertheless, the magistrates in the Docking area had great faith in them. So had the Assistant Poor Law Commissioner. Sir Edward wrote to Frankland Lewis on 6 July:

I have no doubt the London Policemen will worm out all their [i.e. the rioters'] *places, and ultimately detect their Ringleaders.*[36]

For the magistrates, however, there were more than labourers behind the riots. The introduction of the New Poor Law was opposed by a wider constituency. In the 4 July letter they wrote:

A spirit of resistance against carrying into effect the provision of the poor Law amendment act is very general, & we are sorry to observe that we have reason to apprehend that the labourers are aided and abetted by the Small Tradesmen & Beer house Keepers.

X Fears not Subsided

By 29 July, when the magistrates wrote yet again to the Home Office, they reported they had sworn in about four hundred special constables in the Hundreds of Smithdon and Brothercross. Yet all was not well:

But we deem it necessary to make your Lordship acquainted with the unwillingness which prevails generally, and even amongst the respectable farmers and tradesmen to take such a lead in their respective parishes as would render such a force efficient in preserving the Peace.

Two Metropolitan policemen, officers William Wray and John Cooper, had been sent to the area under the direction of Lord John Russell, and their report confirmed the magistrates' fears:

We have visited each Parish in the Hundreds of Smithdon and Brothercross, to ascertain the practicality of establishing a Police in those districts, we find it impracticable in consequence of the refusal of the farmers and principle Tradesmen to come forward and give their aid and support towards the same.[37]

Opposition to the New Poor Law might have been expected from the labourers, but its advocates must have hoped for unequivocal support from the farmers. Support there was, but it had its limits, as the letter of 29 July made clear:

The Farmers though unanimous in favour of the Poor Law amendment act, are intimidated by the labourers, and from a fear of damage to their property by Incendiaries and otherwise, are deterred from taking an active part in the preservation of the peace.

More worrying, but, again, not entirely unexpected, was the opposition of the tradesmen: 'The Petty Tradesmen we are very sorry to observe are all opposed to the measure and desirous of throwing every obstacle in the way of its being carried into execution.' All this was in the letter sent on 29 July, and the magistrates concluded by enjoining the Home

Secretary to consider what further precautions could be taken in order for them to bring into effect 'the Rules and Regulations of the Poor Law Commissioners without incurring the risk of Disturbances which are much to be apprehended, & which we are most anxious to prevent'.

Fear of further outbreaks in the Docking area, and throughout Norfolk, was not insignificant. First, on 5 August, Walpole, Foreman of the Norfolk Grand Jury, wrote to Lord John Russell begging to impress on his Lordship 'the necessity of forthwith providing and organizing some efficient civil force to meet any emergency which may arise in carrying out the provisions of the Poor Law act into operation'.[38]

Of more immediate concern to the Docking Union was a letter (5 October 1835) from Archdeacon Henry Bathurst, North Creake, to Russell. It is scribbled in an appalling hand, but its meaning is quite clear. He insisted that the detachment of troops at Fakenham should not be withdrawn. The Home Secretary had, apparently, been mis-informed about conditions in North-west Norfolk. 'The neighbour-hood', Russell had written, 'from yr Information being perfectly quiet', there seemed no more purpose in tying troops up any longer in Fakenham. This was all a terrible mistake, said Bathurst, and his Lordship really ought to ascertain the true feelings of the Docking magistrates. Moreover, there had only the week before been a fire on the premises of Derick Hoste at Barwick House, Stanhoe. The fire had destroyed all his barley. The Archdeacon was quick to point out that much ill feeling remained; he also added that Mr Hoste was 'a most inoffensive, amiable gentleman'.[39] That he might have been, but this was not the first fire at his farm. It must not be forgotten, either, that he had sat on the magistrates' bench in Walsingham when most of the Bircham rioters were sentenced.

About a month later, there were two other fires: North Creake (8 November) and Stanhoe (9 November), and the year ended with yet more stack fires, this time at Sedgeford (28 November) and Anmer (5 December).[40] The second of the four fires was on the premises of yet another magistrate, Frederick Hare, of Stanhoe Hall. Here a large barn was destroyed which contained about thirty quarters of barley. It is interesting to note in passing that in both cases rewards were offered for the apprehension of the offenders. This was quite common, and sometimes insurance companies put up the money. Then a letter was sent to the government asking them to match the same amount, typically £100. The person claiming the reward would, if an accomplice, receive a free pardon. Unsurprisingly these rewards were virtually never claimed: to have done so would have put a certain end to living in the community.

It is interesting to note that the Home Office received notification of the £100 rewards for the naming of the persons who started both these fires from a certain Everard Kitton of Great Ringstead. He was the first cousin of John Kitton of Bircham. He served as Chief Constable of Smithdon Hundred, and he wrote in his capacity of Secretary to the Smithdon Association for the Prevention of Incendiarism. It would appear that the Government matched the £100 in relation to the fire at Hare's, and offered an extra £50 in the case of Hoste's fire.

Were these fires aftershocks of the main event in June? Possibly. Bathurst was quite right about ill feeling. Peace had not been restored entirely. Far from it.

XIII Troops Remain

The Docking magistrates followed up Bathurst's letter. They begged leave to write that Lord John was indeed correct to state that there had been no recent breach of the peace, but they were adamant that the quiet state of the neighbourhood was to be attributed in great measure to 'the presence of the Military at Fakenham'. They continued: 'If they are withdrawn we are apprehensive that Disturbances might take place, in carrying into Effect the provisions of the Poor Law Act, in which we are now so earnestly engaged. There are a great number of Labourers unemployed, the bad Effects of which we are endeavouring to obviate.'[41] Fires in stacks of barley and unemployment: things indeed had not improved in the Docking Union since George Bennett declared that nobody could live on half a stone and fifteen pence.

Finally, on 28 October Lord Wodehouse wrote to Russell that in consequence of the removal of a troop of Dragoons from Norwich to Boston and half a troop to Fakenham, there was now only a troop and a half in Norwich. During the progress of the new Poor Bill he feared a renewal of riots could be reasonably expected. This would necessitate the intervention of cavalry, and any further removal of troops from Norwich would leave the city 'almost without a soldier'.[42]

Back in Bircham life had to carry on. By the time Lewis Jarvis was writing his letter to Richard Groom repairs had already begun on the farmhouses attacked by the rioters. The farms were naturally insured, and while the farmers will have used the Norwich Union Fire Office for their crops and stock, Lord Cholmondeley insured the Houghton properties with the British Fire Office in the Strand, London. In the archives at Houghton Hall there are copies of policies on houses and buildings on the estate dated 1831, but the occupiers appear to be of an earlier date.[43] One example from Great Bircham could be relevant:

> house and offices £100
> three barns £300
> stables, granaries £180
> field barn and lean-tos £120

This appears to be the farm that John Kitton was later to occupy.

XIV Repairs

As early as Tuesday 30 June a man of Susan Tovell's was nailing up Howlett's house. On 2 July two men, also working for Susan Tovell, were doing the same thing at John Kitton's farm. Throughout the rest of July and August her carpenters had much to do, mainly replacing windows, shutters and doors. Her bills amounted to over £14. Edward Everard of Lynn supplied wood: '6 Archangel 21 ft red Deals - £3 7s. 6d'. There was much work for George Love, the glazier, and his son. Over 90 feet of New Crown Glass were supplied and fitted. Then they started painting in August and did not finish until the middle of October. Love's bill was £15 16s. 2½d. Payne, the brick-layer, put in a bill for £7 12s. 8d.; Oxley charged £6 16s. 6d. for tiles; and John Groom, blacksmith, did work – mainly on casements and window bars – which came to 16s. ½d. The total cost of work at Kitton's was £53 16s. 10½d. This was a lot of money, but there was no major rebuilding work. The rioters had caused a good deal of damage but they had not destroyed his farmhouse.[44]

The other farmers generated similar bills. The repairs were all virtually the same: windows, casements, more Archangel deals and Crown glass. In a letter dated 3 February 1836 from Stephen Reeve to Richard Groom, preserved in the Houghton Hall Archives, it appears that the Bircham tenants hoped they would not have to pay for repairs due to the riots, as they had already had to pay for new furniture. As regards the latter, Kitton, for example, had paid an estimated £79. Groom replied to Reeve on 9 February and said he needed to consult the Marquess about payment for repairs, but it cannot be assumed that the landowner footed the bill. At least one bill is shown paid by Kitton, and perhaps the tenants were never recompensed.

Kitton also applied to the Government for compensation, a claim which was fully supported by Sir Edward Parry. Kitton was a fellow campaigner in the battle to establish the New Poor Law in the Docking Union, and Parry was an ardent champion of the farmer. He claims, in a letter to the Poor Law Commissioners on 28 October, that if Kitton were not to be compensated then 'much injury would be done to our labours, as well as much injustice to himself'. The Commissioners passed the application to the Home Secretary, but it is not stated whether any compensation was ever paid. It is almost certain that none ever was. In a letter to the Poor Law Commissioners of 13 April, 1837 Kitton complains of having property destroyed, and all because he first began to pay the paupers partly in kind, to the value of £100, and had not yet received a farthing.[45]

One item in the 1836 Accounts kept at Houghton Hall is intriguing: it reads: 'At Mr. Drage's Gt Bircham after the Riot'. The summary of payments is as follows:-

		£	s.	d.
Paid	Dunger for Lime	-	6	6
	Drage for Nails	-	4	5
	Lack Carpenter	4	7	11
	Payne Bricklayer	-	14	5
	Shilling Smith	-	12	3
		£ 6	5	6

The bill was not as great as those generated by the farmers, but it was not a small one. In particular there was clearly much work for the carpenter, which suggests perhaps repairs to windows, shutters and doors. There was new brickwork required, which was also the case with the farmhouses. John Drage was a grocer and draper and had shops in East Rudham and Great Bircham. His bills are very frequently seen in the accounts at Houghton, and he regularly supplied clothing and food to the Hall and the estate villages. It was not at all unusual for him to supply items like nails. But why was he a target? His name never appeared in the newspapers. All that was mentioned was that after constable Tilney had managed to get away to Kitton's farmhouse, stones were thrown at different farmhouses and it became necessary to raise the shutters inside. The labourers did not go on an orgy of destruction around the village. They had specific targets, but everything was to be done, apparently, in order. Drage was one of the small tradesmen, one, according to the magistrates, who would have been more likely to side with the labourers than the farmers. Yet he had been singled out for some reason. Could that have been because of the payment of relief in kind? The tickets for flour and shop goods would have to be exchanged somewhere, and Drage's shop was the natural place. It appears that he had been punished for his part in the scheme which triggered the riots. Still, Lord Cholmondeley had his property repaired, and paid John Drage for nails. His shop was still in Bircham in 1845.

If Norfolk farmers, landholders and all progressive forces anxious to see the poor laws completely transformed, were still concerned about the wider picture, and had a real fear of further outbreaks, in Bircham things seemed, at least on the surface, to be better. As for the magistrates, they could report (on 3 July) to the Home Secretary that they had 'not heard of any breach of peace in the neighbourhood'.[46] To speak of calm is almost certainly wrong: the labourers might have slunk back to work with their tails between their legs as far as *The Norfolk Chronicle* was concerned, but their grievances had not been addressed.

Peace of sorts, it appeared, was restored almost as quickly as it had been so violently broken. An insubordinate and unruly mob, one capable of acting only in a brutish unthinking way, had seemingly been driven back into its rightful place. A correspondent had reported to *The Bury Post* that 'perhaps it would be impossible to find in any part of the kingdom a peasantry so ignorant and uncultivated as those at Bircham – a convincing proof that nothing is so dangerous to the peace of society as ignorance'.

According to Sir Edward Parry in a letter to Frankland Lewis of 6 July, the events at Bircham – in which, thankfully, no life had been lost – could be turned to the advantage of all supporters of the Poor Law Amendment Act. 'It will shew', he wrote, 'in its true colours, the utter unreasonableness of the labouring classes and prove the strongest possible argument for the adoption of the very measures which, in their delusion, they have been led to resist.'[47] Thus for the Assistant Commissioner and 'all sensible and judicious people' with whom he had discussed the affair, this was a necessary victory against the 'ignorant and uncultivated peasantry'.

In *The Norfolk Mercury* of 11 July it was reported that the parish of Great Bircham, and its vicinity was 'now happily restored to peace and quietness'. The newspaper informed its readers that

Mr. John Kitton, Mr. J. W. Howlett, and Mr. Thomas Hebgin, impressed with feelings of the highest respect and gratitude to those who rendered them assistance and protection during the late riotous proceedings directed against themselves, families, and property, beg leave to return their most sincere thanks to all … .

They singled out for special thanks 'Major Milles and the Yeomanry'; 'the officers and soldiers of the Inniskilling Dragoons'; and 'Captain Curry of the Preventive Service Men'. The latter, originally of Vauxhall, London, was first appointed to the station at Burnham Overy Staithe in 1828. In 1834 he was appointed to command the Wells District. In 1830, while still Lieutenant Curry, he had earned the praise and gratitude of the local magistrates for helping to suppress a riotous assembly at Docking; and it was they who recommended his promotion.[48] All were thanked 'for their obliging courtesy, and for their prompt and effective conduct in quelling the disturbance, and in defending the peaceable inhabitants from the lawless violence of an infuriated populace, and for completely restoring tranquillity and good order in the district'.

A month later (on 8 August) Parry wrote again to Lewis and was still pleased with the outcome of the Bircham Riots. The introduction of the Poor Law Amendment Act into Norfolk was not an easy matter: there were naturally going to be setbacks, and struggles along the way were to be expected; yet all was bound to be for the good. After all, the Docking Union was the first to be established in Norfolk, and it was perhaps inevitable that a fight would be needed.

I have nothing more from Great Bircham, and have every reason to believe that the effervescence has gone off in that quarter. Temperate firmness with a shew of strength sufficient to carry out our measures into effect are all that is necessary for our purpose. [49]

It is very difficult completely to absolve Sir Edward Parry, first Assistant Poor Law Commissioner of Norfolk, from blame for much of the destruction at Bircham in the summer of 1835. He can hardly have been surprised at the opposition to the change in the system of relief, however reasonable it might have seemed to him and the Great Bircham Overseer. He might have preferred not to have a riot, but he certainly knew how to turn the events in Great Bircham and Bircham Tofts to his advantage. He wrote to his superior on 2 July:

I am quite confident that the present occasion is the turning point of all our operations in the County. The Cobbettites, and the Cowards, and the Waverers, will all be anxiously looking to the conduct of the Government; and if the brute force of the idle and dissolute <u>seems</u> even to gain a victory, on this occasion, over reason, justice, and law, adieu to all our hopes of carrying into effect the provisions of the P.L. A^t Act. [50]

He was ever ready to do his duty. The Northwest Passage may not have been found, but the New Poor Law was going to be established in Norfolk. The next day he wrote again to Frankland Lewis:

I feel much flattered by your kind opinion of me. I can only promise, and that faithfully, that no exertion of body or mind shall be wanting on my part, to carry the new Measures into effect cautiously and temperately, but with firmness and decision. [51]

Thus, the Bircham Riots were over and, apparently, the mindless deeds of irrational and lawless agricultural labourers had been quelled. Seemingly this was the triumph of law and rationality. 'Ignorance' had been roundly defeated. But had it? And how 'ignorant' in reality was the peasantry of the Birchams?

The forces summoned by Reverend Hare did not arrive in time to prevent the not inconsiderable damage to the farmhouses; yet had they not arrived, the mob could well have regrouped soon after and gone on to commit further attacks on people and property.

By the time Parry was telling his superior that the effervescence had gone off, most of the principal rioters had already been brought to justice. If the Poor Law Amendment Act was to be established in Norfolk, examples had to be made; the mob could not be allowed to prevail.

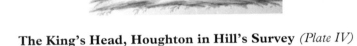

The King's Head, Houghton in Hill's Survey *(Plate IV)*

Notes

The principal source for the progress of the Bircham Riots is to be found in the press reports. These are *The Norfolk Chronicle* of 4 and 18 July 1835; and *The Bury and Norwich Post* of 8 and 15 July 1835.

[1] TNA: HO52/26, fol. 233.
[2] *NC*, 9 May & 6 Jun. 1835.
[3] TNA: MH 12/8249; Parry to PLC, 2 Jul. 1835.
[4] *BNP*, 8 Jul. 1835.
[5] *NC*, 4 Jul. 1835.
[6] *NC*, 30 May 1835.
[7] Rev. E. Parry, *Memoirs of Rear-Admiral Sir W. Edward Parry* (London, 1858), p. 248.
[8] ibid. p. 249.
[9] TNA: MH 32/60, Parry to Lewis, 2 Jul. 1835.
[10] TNA: MH 32/60, Parry to Lewis, 3 Jul. 1835.
[11] TNA: MH 12/8249.
[12] *NC*, 20 Jun. 1835. 1st Annual Report of the PLC, 1835; p. 7 & p. 73.
[13] TNA: MH/8249; Parry to PLC, 2 Jul. 1835.

[14] I am indebted to Sarah Robinson, a direct descendant of Thomas Hebgin senior, for supplying this reference. It is taken from *Violence and Crime in Nineteenth Century England* by John Carter Wood (Routledge, 2004). See also TNA: ASSI 36/2.

[15] TNA: MH 12/8249; Kitton to Parry 29 Jun. 1835.

[16] P. Priestley, *Victorian Prison Lives* (London, 1985), p.9.

[17] *BNP*, 2 Apr. 1834.

[18] *NC*, 28 Nov. 1835.

[19] TNA: HO 52/26, fol. 260.

[20] TNA: HO 73/3.

[21] NRO: Norfolk Sources (NRO).

[22] TNA: HO 52/26, fols 259-60.

[23] TNA: HO 52/26, fol. 252.

[24] HH: Cellar Documents, 768 (f) & 767 (c).

[25] HH: M17

[26] NC, 9 May 1835.

[27] Much of the account of the Norfolk Yeomanry's part in the Bircham Riots is taken from J. R. Harvey, *Records of the Norfolk Yeomanry Cavalry* (Norwich, 1908), pp 259-63; & from C. Loftus, *My Life: from 1815-1849* (London, 1877), pp 178-81.

[28] TNA: HO 52/26, fol. 259.

[29] TNA: MH 12/8249.

[30] TNA: HO 52/26, fol. 253.

[31] TNA: HO 52/26, fol. 270.

[32] TNA: HO 52/26, fol. 256.

[33] TNA: MH 12/8249.

[34] TNA: HO 52/26, fol. 264.

[35] TNA: HO 52/26, fol. 267.

[36] TNA: MH 32/60.

[37] TNA: HO 52/26, fol. 244.

[38] TNA: HO 52/26, fol. 247.

[39] TNA: HO 52/26, fol. 274.

[40] NC, 14 Nov. 1835; NC, 12 Dec 1835.

[41] TNA: HO 52/26, fol. 242.

[42] TNA: HO 52/26, fol. 241.

[43] HH: Cellar Documents, 767(f).

[44] HH: M17.

[45] HH: M7c; TNA:MH 12/8249; TNA: MH 12/8250.

[46] TNA: HO 52/26, fol. 261.

[47] TNA: MH 32/60

[48] TNA: ADM 175/77.

[49] TNA: MH 32/60.

[50] TNA: MH 32/60.

[51] TNA: MH 32/60.

Chapter 4. Trials and Punishment

I The Trials begin

The first full accounts of the events taking place in Great Bircham and Bircham Tofts at the end of June 1835 were published in *The Norfolk Chronicle* of 4 July 1835 and in *The Bury Post* of 8 July. There were reports in other newspapers; and *The Norfolk Chronicle* report is even printed in *The Times*. It was in this manner that the reading public of Norfolk and beyond were to learn of the disturbances. Names of farmers, law officers, the landowner and military commanders were given, but nowhere in these initial reports was a single rioter mentioned by name. They are, of course, a dark force throughout: at best a sullen and discontented workforce, and at worst a terrifying mob of violent incendiaries. Just the 'very old', who were not armed with heavy bludgeons, and a couple of 'better disposed persons' seem to escape the vilification of the press. As the facts became clearer, and as the trials began, all the names of the rioters were to be revealed.

The newspapers did not spell all their names correctly, but the literate population of Norfolk could read about the dreadful exploits of these 'ignorant and uncultivated peasants' in subsequent editions of the local newspapers. Full accounts of the general Quarter Sessions of the Peace for the County of Norfolk held at the Shirehall, Walsingham on Friday and Saturday, 10 and 11 July, before Lord James Townshend and a 'very full Bench of Magistrates', appeared just two weeks after the event in *The Norfolk Mercury, The Norfolk Chronicle* and *The Bury Post*. Later trials of those charged in connection with the disturbances in the Bircham parishes were also reported in the newspapers, but most of the men were tried in July.

The majority of the Bircham rioters who came to court were tried in Quarter Sessions. These courts, held, as the name indicates, four times a year at Epiphany, Easter, Midsummer and Michaelmas, dealt with cases too serious to be tried summarily at Petty Sessions (what are now called Magistrates' Courts). Outside Norwich, they met at Lynn, Holt, Swaffham and Walsingham. The last two were closely connected to bridewells, or gaols. Prisoners were tried by a bench of magistrates and their fate decided by a jury. The jurors were all men of wealth and property. It was theoretically possible for the defendants to employ a counsel, but the poor did not tend to do this. In the Quarter Sessions at which the rioters appeared the prosecution was essentially carried out by the victims, and that meant men like Tilney, Hunter and Hebgin. All the defendants could do was call sympathetic witnesses. There was no defence counsel to cross-question witnesses and address the jury.

The Georgian courtroom at the Shirehall Museum, Walsingham, where most of the rioters were tried. It contains many original features and would be instantly recognisable to the rioters today.
(Photo 2011)

II Walsingham Sessions

Before the proceedings at Walsingham began Lord Townshend was compelled to address the jury, and read to them the law in reference to the trial of the Bircham Rioters. He impressed on them 'that if they found by the evidence that the prisoners, or any of them, were present aiding and abetting, or using expressions or gestures calculated to excite the people, it would be their duty to find them guilty'. Thus, with Lady Justice's scales suitably adjusted, the trials could begin, although not before two Metropolitan police officers were sent down to the Hundreds of Smithdon and Brothercross; and not until it had been 'agreed that a small room should be erected at the Shirehall, into which the Magistrates might retire to decide on their difficulties'. Evidently there was much serious work to be done.

The first man to appear was Richard Greeves. He was indicted for rioting and forcibly taking one John Hunt away from the employment of Daniel Denny. It will be remembered he came to Denny's farm, along with others, early on the morning of 23 June, and declared he would have his man 'by fair means or foul'. The farmer had little choice against such odds and let Hunt go with the men. Hunter himself confirmed Denny's evidence.

Richard Greeves was found guilty and sentenced to three months' hard labour in Walsingham Bridewell.

Next were Thomas Goldon and John Pilgrim. (The former's name is probably more correctly written as Golding.) The two men were indicted for riot and assault. This was for their part in the incident on 29 June, when John Hunter of Barwick attempted to break the strike by bringing two of his own men to Hebgin's farm. Thomas Golding was 'very active', declared John Hunter. Thomas Hebgin was also called as a witness and confirmed Hunter's testimony, and stated that the mob threatened to murder him, too. He was able to identify John Pilgrim. A third witness was the minister of the parish, and he gave the two accused a good character, but despite that they were found guilty. Golding was sentenced to three months and Pilgrim to one month; in both cases with hard labour. The relevant Quarter Sessions Minute Book makes no mentions of John Pilgrim, although the 1835 Home Office Register of Prisoners does. Golding was to serve his sentence in the County Gaol.

Then appeared six men: Thomas (wrongly given as John in the press reports) Golding now reappeared, along with W(illiam) Hill, William (wrongly recorded as Thomas in the press) Wanfer (or Wanford), George Bennett, Edward Carrington and James Williamson. They were all indicted for riotously assembling with

135

nearly 200 other persons at Great Bircham. This was on the morning of 29 June when the farm servants were forcibly removed from Denny's farm, and when George Bennett so defiantly hurled before the farmer his declaration that the labourers could not live on fifteen pence an acre. Despite Mary Marsham's appearance as a defence witness, all the prisoners were found guilty and sentenced to be kept to hard labour: Golding and Bennett for two years; Williamson for one year; Wanfer for six months; and Hill and Carrington for three months. Hill, Carrington and Bennett were sent to Walsingham Bridewell; Wanfer to Swaffham Bridewell; and Golding and Williamson to the County Gaol. In Bennett's case it was stated he had to agree to keep the peace for six months after his release or pay £20.

Thomas Golding was able to earn a few months' remission on his sentence. A report on the prisoners in the County Gaol was presented at the Epiphany Sessions in 1837.[1] His conduct in the prison had been found 'uniformly good', and it was decided that recommendation for remission be made to the Home Secretary. John Kitton must have heard the news of Golding's possible early release with sheer dismay. On 5 October 1836, while he was serving on the Docking Board of Guardians, he declared he had heard that Golding, along with Thomas Bell (see **IV** below), was to be recommended for release, and he must have been relieved to get the Board to agree to express its 'decided opinion' that the two should remain in gaol until the expiration of their sentences.[2]

William Wanfer, (Edward) Carrington and (James) Williamson were further called to appear, along with Luke Duffield and (George) Harrison. These five were indicted for assaulting William Tilney in the execution of his duty as police constable. Tilney must have been an ideal witness: with his account of many blows and his deep head wound, then of his escape to Kitton's farm – bludgeons being thrown after him – he must have cut a pitiable figure. Then there were Thomas Hebgin, also injured, and Frances England with the 'violent blow on her breast'. The defendants hardly stood a chance. In particular, George Harrison's fate was sealed by the deposition of Money Curtis, Governor of the Walsingham Bridewell. He declared that Harrison, who had struck Tilney across the shoulder with a bludgeon, had had blood on his slop when he was taken. Harrison's sister, Bathsheba Ewen, and a certain Ann Cooper were called as defence witnesses. The former swore that she had held her brother's slop until the van had gone and that he had not had a stick when Tilney had been struck, although she admitted that he had had one earlier. The latter deposed that Harrison had stood by her until the constables' van went away. These witnesses carried no weight. Several other witnesses were called, but they 'proved nothing material'. The jury acquitted Duffield and Carrington, but found the rest guilty. Harrison was sentenced to two years' hard labour, and he was to find the same £20 sureties as Bennett. Williamson was sentenced to one year's hard labour, and Wanfer to six months.

Before the court could move on to the more familiar cases of stealing, it had just four more men to try: William Bell, William Miles, John Goldon (Golding) and William Bullock. They were all charged with riot at Bircham, but there was no prosecution against any of them.

The Bircham farmers might have taken some comfort from something which appeared on the same page of the newspaper which gave an account of the Walsingham Sessions. This was a report of the Annual Meeting of the West Norfolk Agricultural Association, held at Swaffham. The cost of labour had risen inexorably, and the price of wheat of barley had fallen:

In allusion to the distress of agriculture the Committee state their opinion that much good may arise from the judicious employment and firm treatment of the labouring classes – as proofs they mention that in Burnham the sum spent on labour has risen from 11s. 10½d per acre in 1801, to 1l 3s. 10d, in 1834; although the average price of wheat has in the last year sunk to 6l 5s. per acre being 2l 17s. less than the average of the 14 years preceding, and on barley the loss amounted to 1l 19s. 2d.[3]

All the members of the jury would have understood that only too well.

III Norfolk Assizes

The trials did not end in July, however. In the Norfolk Summer Assizes, held on 1 August, Samuel Whitely (more correctly Whitby) and John Shilling were indicted for riot at what the newspapers wrongly called Bircham Newton. Upon the advice of Counsel they pleaded guilty. Mr Evans, for the prosecution, stated that the prisoners had expressed contrition for their part in the events. Anyhow, he continued, they had not been involved at a stage when the riots became serious, and it was not the prosecution's wish to press for punishment. The judge admonished the prisoners and fined them 1s. each, and directed them to enter their own recognizances of £20 to keep the peace for two years.

At the same Assizes appeared somebody described as 'an elderly man'. He was actually forty-eight, but he must have looked a rather sorry sight, and older than his years, as he stood in the dock. This was Thomas Marsham and he was charged with riot, and also with assaulting John Hunter. Soon after the start of the trial he changed his plea to guilty. Once more, the Counsel for the Prosecution, one Palmer, said that under the circumstances, and given the prisoner's sincere contrition, they would not press for punishment. The Learned Judge did not consider Marsham's case to be quite the same as Whitby's and Shilling's, and felt he was bound to pass some sentence. Nonetheless, mindful of the 'great kindness of the prosecution' and the prisoner's state of mind when the offence was committed, he was induced to pass a lenient sentence. The Judge was grieved to learn that Marsham's conduct had brought about the subsequent death of his wife, who was lying ill at the time of the riots. He saw that the loss of a parent to a large family would be 'a source of great suffering'. Justice would be done, felt the Judge, if the prisoner received one week's imprisonment.

IV October Sessions

The final trial of the Bircham rioters took place at the Walsingham Sessions on 30 October 1835, before Lord James Townshend once more. His Lordship regretted there were 'as many as 23 prisoners, some of them for very heinous offences, and that highway robbery, sheep stealing, and other heavy crimes were greatly on the increase in the neighbourhood'.[4] Another reminder that rural criminality was rife at the time of the Bircham Riots. Here appeared Thomas Bell, charged with assault and riot. Thomas Bell (wrongly called John Bell in the newspapers) was the only one of those charged whose age appeared in the newspaper reports. He was given as thirty-two, although strictly speaking he was thirty-three. The ages of all those brought to trial at Quarter Sessions were, of course, given in the Quarter Sessions Minutes (see below). Bell was charged by Thomas Hebgin, acting at the time as special constable of Great Bircham, with assaulting him in the execution of his duty and with riot. Hebgin told the court that he went to arrest the four men identified as leaders in the attempt to prevent the strike being broken at Great Bircham on Monday 29 June. Hebgin was quite sure that Bell knew that he (Hebgin), acting as constable, was there to arrest him, and he threw his stone quite deliberately to avoid being taken. The prisoner, who had absconded after the incident, admitted his presence along with the rest, but denied having stone or stick. This did him no good: Hebgin's testimony was corroborated by constable Tilney, and the jury found him guilty. Bell was sentenced to two years' hard labour at Swaffham Bridewell.

It would appear that he was recommended for an early release from gaol. However, the Docking Guardians agreed in October 1836 that Thomas Bell, a ringleader in the Bircham Riots, should serve his full term. (See **II** above.)

V Overview of the Rioters

It might be supposed that the rioters were all young, single and illiterate. The reality is somewhat different.

Name	Age	Marital status	Read	Write	Sentence
Thomas Bell	33	Married	✗	✗	2 years
William Bell	30	Married	✓	✗	Discharged
George Bennett	58	Married	✓	✓	2 years + sureties
William Bullock	25	Single	Not stated	Not stated	Discharged
Edward Carrington	23	Single	✗	✗	3 months
Luke Duffield	47	Married	✗	✗	Discharged
John Golding	55	Widower	✗	✗	Discharged
Thomas Golding	29	Married	✗	✗	2 years

Richard Greeves	28	Married	✗	✗	3 months
George Harrison	21	Single	✓	✓	2 years + sureties
William Hill	22	not known	✓	✗	3 months
Thomas Marsham	48	Married	✗	✗	1 week
William Miles	48	Married	✓	✗	Discharged
John Pilgrim	37	Married	✓	✓	1 month
John Shilling junr	20	Single	✓	✓	1s. fine + sureties
William Wanford	21	Single	✗	✗	6 months
Samuel Whitby	20	Single	✓	✗	1s. fine + sureties
James Williamson	22	Single	✓	✗	1 year

Is it sheer coincidence that the two harshest sentences were handed out to two men who could both read and write?

The rioters do seem to divide into three distinct groups. It is impossible to say how typical this is of the crowds that gathered at the end of June in Great Bircham. Nonetheless, these men would have been prominent in the riots and were far from passive onlookers who just happened to get caught. There were undoubtedly others who played an important part in the dramatic events of the 29 June and who were not caught, but the people who appeared in court would all have been easily identified by the very few witnesses – Hebgin, Tilney, Hunter predominantly – and can be taken as representatives of the Bircham Rioters.

There are first the five older men, those aged over forty-five. Three of them could neither read nor write; and all had married. There is a further group of five men in their thirties or late twenties. They too were all married and three of them were unable to read or write; just one could do both. The young group, those aged twenty to twenty-five, was decidedly more literate: five out of the eight could read and two of those were also able to write. It has been assumed that Bullock could not write, as he signed x when he married in 1840. Just what was meant by reading and writing ability is open to question, but an apparent increase in the level of literacy amongst these younger men must reflect an increase in educational provision in Bircham from around 1820.

The young men (including most probably Hill) were all unmarried at the time of the riots; it was always such men who were the first to be dismissed from their employment and were amongst the most casualized of workers. They were the ones who had the greatest cause to be angry, and it was they who tended to fire the ricks. If we add that dangerous combination of alcohol and testosterone, something not peculiar to the present day, we can hardly be surprised by the participation of so many young men.

(For further information on the eighteen men see Appendix A.)

VI Just Deserts?

Had the rioters had a fair trial? By today's standards almost certainly not, but it is hardly sensible to make comparisons between the twenty-first century and 1835. It is very difficult not to claim that some kind of summary justice had been carried out. In a matter of weeks after the events most of the accused were beginning quite lengthy sentences. No doubt the Bircham farmers and Money Curtis wanted to take advantage of the Midsummer Sessions, so there was little delay between arrest and sentence. There was hardly any attempt to put together an adequate defence, as would be the case today; although the rioters must have tried hard to procure witnesses, which was the only real means of defence available to them. The minister from Great Bircham, called as a defence witness, might have had some influence, but he did not. Other witnesses appearing on behalf of the men were female relatives or friends, and it is doubtful if they were taken seriously. The fact is that the Norfolk magistrates needed to act quickly and nip any potential further rioting in the bud. The New Poor Law was as yet untested and it needed to be given support from the courts if it was to succeed. The riots did not escalate and the presence of the military quickly brought them to an end. For a brief period law and order had broken down, however, and if such demonstrations of popular opposition to local administration of the relief of the poor were to be thwarted, then examples had to be made. From the outset it did appear that the Norfolk magistrates were sure of securing a good number of convictions. The jury at Walsingham could have had no doubt of that.

Yet were the punishments too severe? The violence of the rioters, if the newspaper reports are to be believed, must have come close, in a couple of cases, to bringing about a death. If Thomas Hebgin had not stooped when he saw Bell's stone coming; if William Tilney's assailant (possibly not George Harrison) had struck harder and in a more sensitive place with his hammer; or if the mob had been successful in the total destruction of Kitton's farmhouse wherein lay the constable; then somebody could have been facing a much more serious charge than riotous assembly. By the same token, John Hunter's pistol could have gone off and a rioter might have been lying dead on the ground. No doubt self-defence would have been claimed and, indeed, proven. Nobody died, however, yet there must have been times when farmers and constables felt distinctly threatened. Thus two years' hard labour, at least by the standards of the time, does not seem particularly severe; especially when one considers the amount of violence used at times. This was a much harsher age than ours and, in our eyes, the penal code was brutal. Only in 1834 had the hanging of the bodies of executed criminals in chains been ended.

In 1823 the Judgement of Death Act gave English judges the discretion to pass a lesser sentence than death except in cases of treason and murder. Before then the death sentence had been mandatory for over 200 offences. Nevertheless, in 1835 people were still being sentenced to death for a range of offences, including arson. At the same Quarter Sessions (10 and 11 July), during which the majority of the rioters were brought to trial, two men were sentenced to seven years' transportation for stealing wool off the backs of sheep; although it must be said that most of those found guilty of stealing were sentenced to various terms of imprisonment, none as long as two years. Then, in the issue of *The Bury Post* which reported on the bulk of the trials of the rioters, somebody was sentenced at the Norwich Sessions to seven years' transportation for stealing two and a half bushels of barley and half a bushel of wheat; another had the same sentence for stealing a pair of sheets. At the Assizes, where Samuel Whitby and John Shilling were given their lenient sentences, three men were sentenced to death for robbery on the King's Highway.

142

Given that it is easy to oversimplify in these matters and that the harsh sentences of transportation and death were often reserved for those with a criminal past, it is probably true to say that the Bircham rioters received quite stiff sentences, but they could have been worse. Besides, we must never forget the political aspect of the trials: these sentences were intended to discourage further mass demonstrations and violent confrontations with the forces of the law. Yet very severe sentences could have provoked a serious backlash, and led to further attempts at intimidation of farmers by unemployed labourers.

VII John Shilling

The magistrates, of course, would have loved to catch those responsible for attempting to set fire to the farms. This terrible act was the culmination of the Bircham Riots. To see a man swinging from the gallows outside Norwich Castle would have given them some satisfaction, no doubt; although the creation of a martyr could well have brought about further rioting. How close they came to this is one of several unanswered questions about the events in this study. Nevertheless, they did have a name. In a letter of 4 July the Docking magistrates were able to inform the Home Secretary that they had 'only evidence to prove the presence of one Individual in Mr Kitton's house on the night of Monday the 29th of June'. What precisely was their evidence they did not reveal, and they had to admit that 'that person had absconded and hitherto escaped apprehension'. They wrote again on 8 July and were able to present a name to John Russell, the Home Secretary.

We beg leave to inform you that the person stated in our last letter to have absconded is charged with a felonious attempt to set fire to the Dwelling house of Mr Kitton of Great Bircham farmer, after having assisted in damaging and destroying the House and furniture, the name of the person so absconding is John Shilling.[5]

That would explain why he was tried later than the rest, although not as late as Thomas Bell. Did he give himself up or was he caught in a hiding place?

S. M. Phillipps, Russell's secretary, sent an immediate reply to the magistrates:

I am directed by Lord John Russell to acknowledge the receipt of your Letter of the 8th Instant, respecting the felonious attempt to set fire to the dwelling House of Mr Kitton of Great Bircham; - And I am to inform you, that in this case a Reward of One Hundred Pounds will be paid by the Gov^t to any person, who shall give such information and evidence as shall lead to the apprehension and conviction of the Incendiary – And Lord John Russell will advise the Grant of His Majestys Gracious Pardon to any accomplice not having been the person who actually attempted to set fire to the house, who shall give such evidence as shall lead to the conviction of the Principal or principals.

It is not usual to insert an Advertizement in the London Gazette, but the offer may be made known by circulation of Handbills in the neighbourhood.[6]

The magistrates wrote back to the Home Secretary on 13 July:

No time shall be lost in making known advertisement in the provincial papers and by hand bills the reward of One hundred Pounds offered by his Majesty's Government for the apprehension of the person suspected of being concerned in the attempt to set fire to Mr Kitton's house.[7]

Shilling had a counsel, and he could well have seen that pleading guilty would remove any threats brought about by his client's being under suspicion of an attempt to set fire to Kitton's farmhouse. Yet the fine of 1s., even with the need to keep the peace for two years, could have been seen as almost derisory in the eyes of the magistrates. Had there been a credible witness things might have been quite different. Tilney heard threats to kill him as he lay injured in a back room at Kitton's farm, but not being a local man he would not have recognized anybody's voice. Kitton would, but he had already fled. One thing is sure: it would have soon become generally known in the neighbourhood who had struck the lucifer, but nobody would have dreamt of betraying him, and claiming the reward of £100. To do so would have meant suffering a punishment far worse than anything encountered in a Norfolk House of Correction. The reward money represented an enormous sum for a farm labourer, but these rewards – almost routinely offered – were practically never claimed.

Of course, he could not have done everything himself. There was furniture to be broken up – everything breakable in the house, if the reports are to be believed – and books to be torn. Did the magistrates, however, have any special reason for charging John Shilling? Along with Samuel Whitby he was one of the youngest of the rioters, not yet twenty. The son of Hannah and John Shilling, blacksmith, he was baptized at the parish church of Great Bircham on 14 April 1816. John Shilling senior moved from the neighbouring parish of Houghton to Great Bircham sometime around 1808, and set up his blacksmith's business there. Blacksmiths, along with shoemakers, had something of a reputation as village radicals. They were natural leaders, and the many people who came into their shop provided them with a ready-made audience. They would have kept up with the news, and often been the first to hear of events. There is a letter in the Kimberley Papers in Norfolk Record Office which mentions a blacksmith who had made pike heads for the Chartists in 1839.[8] The Shillings might not have gone so far, but they could well have been resolutely opposed to Kitton and the other farmers. They could also have been against any change in the Poor Laws. John Shilling junior was one of four people convicted of offences at Bircham that summer who could read and write, and if he had been brought up in a radical household he would have been fully aware of what was going on. His father, however, could not sign his name on his bills.[9] It must not be forgotten, either, that Kitton would not have employed any of the Shillings as farm labourers. John Shilling senior might have repaired the farmer's machinery, but his son would never have had to scare crows or pick stones on his fields. He was an independent tradesman, and thus belonged to that group of people so much maligned by the Norfolk magistrates and Sir Edward Parry. Stephen Reeve, at Houghton, would have sent instructions for work to be done at the Cholmondeley properties, rather than farmers like John Kitton. And as long as they had enough work, which the Houghton Account Books indicate they had, the Shillings would not have needed to apply to Kitton in his capacity as overseer.

Even if Shilling junior had played a leading part in the riots, contrary to what was said in the courtroom, that would not stop the business being kept busy after the riots. Plenty of work was done, even in the summer of 1835. Some work was even done at Kitton's farm.

VIII Off to the Bridewell

What awaited the prisoners as they entered prison? In 1835 the County of Norfolk had three Houses of Correction or Bridewells at its disposal: Swaffham, Walsingham and Wymondham. There was also a County Gaol at Norwich. The Walsingham Bridewell was erected about 1797, on a plan recommended by John Howard, the prison reformer. It had been enlarged in 1822 and, according to White's 1836 Directory, had four treadmills for grinding corn, etc. It was also conducted on the 'silent system'. This, the Directory informs us, was 'found to be very beneficial, by preventing the prisoners from instructing each other in their nefarious arts'. The Swaffham House of Correction dated from about 1787, and, White's 1836 Directory tells us, had one large tread-wheel which worked a corn mill. The County Gaol, housed in Norwich Castle, had been completed in 1824, at a cost of £50,000. At the end of 1827 a rumour must have been circulating that Walsingham Bridewell was to close. A petition sent from Gallow Hundred (in which Houghton was situated) was laid before the Norwich Quarter Sessions of January 1828. The petitioners (John Drage was one) were impressed by the efficient classification of prisoners, and above all by the manner in which they were kept at work. This, they opined, had resulted from the 'superior construction of the Tread Mill' and the fact that it had never been interrupted.[10] Such a closure did not make economic sense and never came about until after the end of Quarter Sessions at Walsingham in 1861. However, even if it then closed as a house of correction, it continued to be used as a police lock-up for many years after that.

Most of the prisoners convicted in the summer and autumn of 1835 went to Walsingham Bridewell. Today the large building at the end of the car park in Little Walsingham presents a grim and forbidding aspect. It cannot have been different in 1835. In 1833 the Justices of the Peace had visited Walsingham and reported to the Quarter Sessions. The report recommended the same diet as that used

146

in Wakefield Gaol, but when the surgeon at Walsingham Bridewell had been consulted it appeared that cost dictated the diet of the prisoners. The committee of visiting justices resolved: 'it would be injurious to the Health of the Prisoners confined there to introduce the Oatmeal Diet used at Wakefield without the addition of Meat the Price of which in Walsingham and its Neighbourhood precludes its adoption when the Question of Economy is considered.'[11] Nevertheless, a report of 1835 on the gaol stated that those sentenced to more than three months' hard labour were entitled to half a pound of meat without bone per week. In addition, all prisoners committed to hard labour received two pounds six ounces 'good flour bread' each day.[12]

At the Michaelmas Sessions of 1835, Lord Townshend was able to present to the court reports on Walsingham Bridewell made by the visiting justices and the Chaplain. These reports give us a good idea of the state of the prison at the time the Walsingham rioters entered it, at least from the point of view of justices and chaplain. All seems almost too good to be true, and it very likely was. The justices reported that the cells, rooms and other buildings were in a 'proper State of Repair and Condition, and that the Duties of the Governor and the several other Officers employed therein are diligently and strictly performed'. No complaints in the management of the House of Correction had been heard, but 'on the Contrary we beg to observe that the Morals, Discipline and Employment of the Prisoners confined therein are duly and properly attended to every Respect'. There was much praise of the silent system, newly introduced at Walsingham:

We have much pleasure in reporting that during the time the same [i.e. silent system] *has been in operation it has afforded evident Proofs of the Benefits resulting therefrom inasmuch as several of the Prisoners, now in custody, have declared their Determination that they will not, upon their Liberation from Imprisonment, so offend against the Laws of their Country as to render themselves again liable to such extreme punishment as the "silent system" imposes.*[13]

Visiting justices, according to a report in the press two years later, were able to assert that 'the general conduct of the prisoners under the silent system had been exemplary'. Had that also included the Bircham rioters who had been sent there? It is difficult for us, in the twenty-first

147

century, to take seriously, however, the contention of the Chaplain, in praising the silent system, that it made 'his voice as the voice of an Angel' to the prisoners. Finally, the report attributed the reduction in prisoners (down by a staggering 188 in 1836) to the 'well-working of the silent system'.[14]

A cell in Walsingham Bridewell *(Photo 2011)*

In 1835 there were forty cells available, and one hundred and eight separate sleeping berths. The arrangement was felt particularly beneficial to the silent system, as 'that Contamination necessarily attendant upon the assembling of Prisoners together in a Day Room is considerably diminished'. The maximum number of prisoners during the previous year, according to the report, was one hundred and six (twelve females). The daily average of male prisoners had been about sixty-three. At the time of the report there were sixty-three males and three females in the Bridewell. Visits were allowed once every three months, and the prisoners could receive and send letters once every six months. The clothing provided included jacket, trousers, shirt, waistcoat, stockings, shoes (wood-bottomed) and cap. Each prisoner also had two blankets, a rug and a mat. And, as for any foolish enough to rebel against the regime in Walsingham Bridewell, there were punishments: solitary confinement (the most common), irons and whippings were for more serious cases, but minor infringements of the rules earned a reduction in food.[15]

The Chaplain reported that he performed his religious duties according to the rules and regulations laid down by Act of Parliament. Thus prayers according to the liturgy of the Church of England were read every morning, and on Sunday, Good Friday and Christmas Day there were the appointed morning and evening services (with a sermon). If there were prisoners 'disposed to receive it' the Sacrament of the Lord's Supper was administered. More importantly, the prisoners were 'separately visited and privately conversed with, their habits of Life enquired into and suitable advice and Exhortations given'. He proudly reported that all prisoners attended chapel regularly, only illness or 'some other reasonable cause' keeping them away. The literate were supplied with prayer books, Bibles and other religious works.

As for the silent system, the Chaplain was very positive in his support:

Under this system no Communication is allowed even in a whisper and every Means is resorted to, both by watchers and Monitors from among the Prisoners, to keep it in full Force both Day and Night. I have myself visited the Prison in an Evening, after the Time of the Prisoners being locked up and not a Noise has been heard in the lowest Tone. This System conduces to make those who can read more desirous of employing their leisure Hours with the religious Books provided for them.

He mentioned a man who begged for transportation rather than endure the stupefying effect of the silence. Nevertheless, he felt that discipline had been considerably improved. He concluded: 'I may remark that the Prisoners fell into the new Regulations very tractably and their Conduct upon the whole is satisfactory'.[16] Money Curtis, the Governor of Walsingham Bridewell, came in for the Chaplain's praise. He must have been particularly pleased later when his annual salary was raised to £200, the same as the Keeper of Swaffham Bridewell. He

149

was also ahead of the other houses of correction, in that he introduced the silent system before them.

Hard labour meant a mind-numbing task of Sisyphus, in which a prisoner could ascend a small mountain every day. In Walsingham, each prisoner spent eight and half hours per day on the wheel (presumably not continuously), and performed forty-eight steps per minute. (The height of the step was eight inches.) Talking was punished by solitary confinement.[17] Tread-wheels could be dangerous, and deaths from falls were not unknown. The tread-wheel had been invented by William Cubitt of Lowestoft, and had been introduced to the penal system in 1822. What could be more simple and effective for the machine age? It was an inexpensive and uncomplicated mechanical system. It never stopped and could be made to grind corn; although sometimes tread-wheels did no more than 'grind the wind'.[18]

After the introduction of the wheel, prisoners would no more laze around in idleness and plan further crimes. Their stubborn spirit could be broken. It must have seemed a frightening prospect to those outside prison walls, but we must again ask whether it did anything more to the Bircham rioters than wear them down physically?

The exterior of the surviving part of Walsingham gaol showing the windows to the cells. *(Photo 2011)*

This was a period of important reform in the prison system. It was increasingly felt that neither imposing the death penalty on a great number of crimes, nor transporting criminals, was the most efficient way of controlling the more wayward members of society. To this group the Bircham rioters would undoubtedly have belonged, certainly in the eyes of the Docking magistrates and the Bircham farmers. They needed to be taught a lesson and forced to confront their wickedness. Prison discipline was thus an important element in social control and the silent system and the rival 'separate system' were perfect instruments of prison discipline. If prisoners were to repent of their 'nefarious arts' and their insubordinate habits were to be reformed, one way was to keep them in separate cells, and another was to keep them silent. The silent system was first introduced at Wakefield prison in 1834. The following year the Select Committee of the House of Lords on Gaols and Houses of Correction in England and Wales recommended the national adoption of 'a uniform system of discipline' along 'silent' rather than 'separate' lines. The Prisons Act of the same year implemented the Committee's recommendations; and also introduced the first prison inspectors.

IX A Successful Outcome?

Governor Curtis, therefore, was in the vanguard of prison reform. Did his regime have any effect on the handful of men confined in the Walsingham Bridewell? Did George Bennett retreat from his declaration to Daniel Denny that the labourers were bound in a bond of blood? Did Carrington regret charging Denny with ill treatment? Did any of them come to admit that striking a blow against the New Poor Law by withdrawing their labour was wrong? We shall never know. These were not petty criminals; even if Thomas Bell had stolen Kitton's wheat in 1826, we can probably surmise that his crime had had as much to do with feeding his family as anything. (See Chapter 1.) In common with most labouring men, they would not have seen anything wrong in snaring rabbits to provide meat for their families, or stealing the occasional turnip to add to their meagre diets. Yet, they would have known that killing a strike-breaking farmer and a parish constable was wrong, that there was little moral justification for

151

attempting to burn down a farm house with a seriously injured law officer inside it, and that threatening the lives of young children, even if their standard of living was superior to their own children, was indefensible. Nonetheless, the pauperization of so many labouring men and forcing them to live on meagre rations had little moral justification, either.

Evidence of contrition emerged at the August Assizes: in the case of Whitby and Shilling it might have been little more than a ploy to secure a reduced sentence. Thomas Marsham was probably more genuinely contrite, especially since the death of his wife must have been on his conscience. Rebecca Marsham, aged forty-one, was buried at Great Bircham on 11 July 1835, just as the majority of those accused of riot and assault were being tried at Walsingham. Then there was Thomas Golding, who had earned a remission of part of his two-year sentence in the County Gaol, and whose conduct had been described as 'uniformly good'; Thomas Bell was also recommended for early release.

There is no reason whatsoever for judging these men as deeply corrupted and criminalized human beings. With the exception of Thomas Bell, they have not been found appearing in the courts prior to the riot; although that does not necessarily mean they had not committed serious criminal acts. Some, however, did go on to commit further offences, including Bell. (See Appendix A.) Probably many dug up a few turnips and poached rabbits; some might have fired barley stacks in the past. As young men the majority probably indulged in offensive behaviour: drinking to excess, fighting and insulting their superiors. Their behaviour in June 1835 might have been violent and terrifying. What we must not do is see them as likeable (and it is vital not to judge them through a mist of twenty-first century sentimentality); yet their crime was as much political as anything. That is not to condone them: they caused much damage and came very close to killing at least one person. Their conduct was clearly intimidatory. To Sir Edward Parry, John Kitton, the Docking magistrates, and to many of their social superiors, they were dangerous, because, for a brief moment in the summer of 1835, they appeared to pose a serious threat to the social order. Kitton and the other farmers could be grateful that the 'peaceable inhabitants' of the

Birchams had been saved from 'the lawless violence of an infuriated populace', and they had good reason to thank the forces of order 'for completely restoring tranquillity and good order in the district'.

The Bircham Riots were over. But was that the end of the matter?

Notes

The trials of most of the rioters, in July 1835, are covered by *The Norfolk Chronicle* of 18 July and *The Bury and Norwich Post* of 15 July. The same newspapers also gave a full report of the later trials: *Norfolk Chronicle* of 8 August and 28 November; *Bury Post* of 12 August and 4 November. The official accounts of the trials of 1835 are in the Sessions Books of the Quarter Sessions (NRO: C/S 1/24) and the records of the Assize Courts (TNA: ASSI 33/12). Brief details, including ages and literacy, are given in the register of persons charged with indictable offences for 1835 (TNA: HO 27/50).

[1] NRO: C/S 4/6, p. 320.
[2] DUGM (NRO): C/GP 4/2.
[3] BNP, 15 Jul. 1835.
[4] BNP, 4 Nov. 1835.
[5] TNA: HO 52/26, fol. 268; & HO 64/5.
[6] TNA: HO 43/47.
[7] TNA: HO 52/26, fol. 270.
[8] I am indebted to John Archer for this reference.
[9] HH MH/17.
[10] NRO: C/Saa 3/16.
[11] NRO: C/S 4/6, p. 52.
[12] BPP: Select Committee of the House of Lords on Gaols, 1st Report.
[13] NRO: C/S 4/6, p. 227.
[14] BNP, 1 Nov. 1837.
[15] NRO: C/S 4/6. p. 227; BPP: Select Committee of the House of Lords on Gaols, 1st Report.
[16] NRO: C/S 4/6, p. 228.
[17] BPP: Select Committee on Gaols, 1st Report.
[18] P.Priestley, *Victorian Prison Lives* (London, 1985), p. 125.

Chapter 5. A Riot from Nowhere?

53. Can you give the Commissioners any information respecting the causes and consequences of the agricultural Riots and Burning of 1830 and 1831?
- They were produced by dissatisfaction and insubordination among the Agricultural Labourers, brought about by the facility of communication at the Beer Shops, and by worthless publications; in addition to which, they were excited by itinerants. In some few cases, real necessity might be the reason; but in most cases the leaders of the riots had far the least to complain. I think the administration of the Poor Laws tends greatly to make the Labourer consider the Farmer as his oppressor, and his revenge is stack-burning. Answers to 'Rural Queries', 1834. Evidence of George Rodwell of Sculthorpe.

One plain truth I must speak, and I think it my duty to say that the great mass of operative labourers in this county are ill paid, not kindly treated, but too often neglected and insulted; and have thus been driven to commit these acts of violence, to obtain by force what they ought to have had without. Colonel John Harvey, Magistrate, 1831.

I Anti-Poor Law agitation before the Bircham Riots

The riots of 1835 inevitably raise a number of questions. Was it merely in the recently formed Docking Union that disturbances against the introduction of the New Poor Law occurred? Had there never been anything remotely similar before in the district? Did the Bircham Riots signal the end of unrest amongst local agricultural labourers? The answer to all three questions is a definite 'no'. However, the events of midsummer 1835 in these parishes in North-west Norfolk were not insignificant. There had been nothing on this scale before in the Bircham parishes, nor would rioting of that sort be seen again in the villages. It is, therefore, important to examine the Bircham Riots in a little more detail, in order to clarify just who was involved, what motivated them and to what degree they were organized.

1. Grimston

First of all, opposition to the New Poor Law in Norfolk. We can begin with an incident which, even though it occurred while the Poor Law Amendment Act was still passing through the House of Commons, has some parallels with what happened the following year in Great Bircham. This was in the parish of Grimston, where in April 1834 the overseer sent five labourers to do a job in a neighbouring village. It was reported in the press that they 'soon became dissatisfied' with this work and went 'in a body to the pay table, where they demanded to be relieved'. This was refused and soon their 'threatening language and offensive menaces' obliged the parish officers to climb down and grant them relief. What the paper called 'very uproarious' behaviour then ensued and disturbed the meeting of the officers; when the latter left the place of meeting they were greeted with offensive and threatening language. 'Run your fork through him,' said one labourer; another, 'drag him through the horse pond'. Next a large stone was hurled and struck the overseer on the back. The officers had no other choice but to flee for their safety. Short terms of imprisonment with hard labour followed.[1] This may have been very much an Old Poor Law incident, showing as it does the insolence, which quickly gave way to violence, of many poor labourers at that time, but it does indicate very strong feelings against overseers amongst the labouring poor of parishes other than Great Bircham and Bircham Tofts.

2. Hillington

The next incident, however, was in direct response to the New Poor Law. This was at Hillington in October 1834. Hillington, the seat of Sir William Ffolkes, the MP for Norfolk West at this period, was later to become part of the Freebridge Lynn Union. It was at the beginning of October when magistrates of the Freebridge Lynn Hundred met and encountered what *The Norfolk Chronicle* called 'some very unpleasant symptoms'. The paper reported that 'several parties went armed with sticks, bludgeons, &c, and though no violence took place, there was evidently a feeling of smothered discontent'. The newspaper, with its Tory leanings, could not help expressing sympathy for the magistrates who, while wishing to do their best and give the new law a fair chance, were put in the unpleasant position of becoming 'the mere instruments of Government Commissioners, in carrying into execution the New Poor Law Act'.[2]

Sir William Ffolkes was in no doubt that the New Poor Law should be given a chance. In the same edition of *The Norfolk Mercury* that reported on the trial of the Bircham Rioters at the Walsingham Quarter Sessions, there was also a report of the Swaffham Sessions of 7 and 8 July. Ffolkes, the Chairman of these Sessions, could not resist expressing his sorrow at the 'very serious riot' that had occurred 'not far from the place where he resided' to resist the operation of the New Poor Law Act. He was quite clear that the new law would now distinguish two sorts of labouring poor: the idle and the industrious. A mere comparison of the cottages of the hardworking and those of the profligate, was sufficient inducement, he felt, to all well-meaning people to promote industry amongst the labouring class. Such were the sentiments held by very many landowners and their important tenants both just before and just after the passing of the Poor Law Amendment Act.[3]

3. Elmham

Next a letter from H. E. Knatchbull, Vicar of Elmham, sent on 7 October 1834 to the Poor Law Commissioners. He writes that the countryside round about is 'in a painful state of agitation, from various interpretations given to the New Bill'. He says the local magistrates no longer know what their powers are, and 'the paupers in consequence are in a most dangerous state in several parishes'. He further complains that there have been five fires in the vicinity within the last ten days, and thefts from farms. Letters like this addressed to the new Poor Law Commission were probably common at the time. Clergymen and magistrates throughout the country must have been dismayed at the agitation stirred up by the passing of the Poor Law Amendment Act, and many would have agreed with Knatchbull's conclusion that he and his colleagues could not join in the system as long as the Commissioners' plans were unknown. Until that time 'the greatest anxiety' must prevail.[4]

4. Carbrooke

The final example, though undoubtedly others could be found, is from a letter sent to Edwin Chadwick, Secretary to the Poor Law Commissioners, by the Rector of Shipdham on December 16, 1834. He refers to the parish of Carbrooke, between Wymondham and Swaffham. Here, he explains, there are at least twenty-five able-bodied men out of work and consequently dependent on parish allowances to support their families. Nothing unusual about that: it was what the Poor Law was designed to do. He states the problem, one that will now start to become very familiar to us:

Hitherto the relief granted has been entirely in money, but this week partly in money and partly in flour or bread – this mode of administering relief has occasioned very great and general dissatisfaction and I have been applied to as Magistrate in the district to redress the grievance.

He is sure he would not want to undo the Commission's decisions, and he does not expect 'sweeping distress' throughout the parish. However, he is equally sure that the fears of the unemployed are not groundless. He explains that the labourers are in debt to the various shopkeepers. This is not so serious as long as they stay with the same shop, but as soon as they leave it the shopkeeper insists on being paid in full. If the labourer cannot pay he must hand over his goods. The Rector remains indifferent to the method of giving relief – whether entirely in money as before or partly in kind – but he is acutely aware of the miserable state of the parish. He questions whether it is really worth making what he calls 'such piddling alteration' to the system, when there is certainly the prospect of 'great dissatisfaction' and the real risk of 'considerable distress'.

The scribbled notes on the reverse made it quite evident how the Commissioners were to reply. They were adamant they would neither modify nor retract from the recommendation to relieve partly in kind. This, they stated, had been outlined in a circular dated 8 November 1834. They also pointed out that this practice had been adopted in many parishes prior to the passing of the Poor Law Amendment Act; and had since been 'much extended'. They were equally clear it was fully in keeping with the Act, and moreover had been found to be 'advantageous to the families of the paupers to whom such relief had been administered'.[5]

The Bircham Riots, therefore, were quite some time after these early reactions to the new law. Yet when the response of the labourers burst so dramatically upon the Bircham parishes in the summer of 1835 it did so with a degree of violence not demonstrated in Carbrooke or Elmham, or even Hillington and Grimston. Nevertheless, as we shall see shortly, there was an even greater degree of violence in other parts of the South of England.

II Anti-Poor Law agitation after Bircham

Anne Digby says that 'between July 1835 and March 1837 there were major popular protests against the New Poor Law in eight Norfolk unions and incorporations, and minor unrest in most of the remainder'. Thus, while the events in Bircham might have attracted the greatest number of people and caused much damage, they were far from being isolated incidents. Digby also notices something new in the manner of protesting: there were now vicious attacks against persons as well as property; something not seen in earlier disturbances.[6]

1. Freebridge Lynn Union

There was another serious incident in the Freebridge Lynn Union in February 1836. Once more we see close similarities with what had happened at Bircham the previous summer. Digby again:

... a crowd from Little Massingham assembled at Grimston where they stopped the meeting of the local board of guardians. They threatened that if the policy of relieving the poor with bread or flour was to be continued there would be violence at the next board.[7]

The disturbance was soon quelled, the crowd dispersed and arrests were made. As in the Docking Union, Metropolitan policemen were employed to keep the peace. John Beck, Vice-chairman of the Freebridge Lynn Union, wrote to Parry on 6 February 1836 and stated there was no cause for alarm, but he made it clear, just as Kitton had done at Bircham, that this was a battle that the agricultural labourers must not be allowed to win. Their best interests were to be served by their employers, now become poor law guardians, and certainly not by their supposed new friends, the shopkeepers and beer-house keepers:

... but it is absolutely necessary that they should at once be shewn that the Law is too strong for them to venture to set it at defiance, that they may settle down quietly to their work and enable us to enquire into cases that really require relief – and eventually by carefully and judiciously carrying into effect the provisions of the New Poor Law, do them essential service, and greatly improve the condition of the labourers, in spite of themselves, or rather in spite of the evil advice and interested endeavours of their greater enemies, but now pretended friends. [8]

This is an appeal which has rung out through the centuries, and is far from silent today. We shall examine in detail in the next chapter just how much the New Poor Law did improve the condition of the labourers in the Docking Union. As for settling down quietly, that remained a dream amongst the labourers' superiors.

2. Guiltcross Union

In the same month, February 1836, there was a riot in the Guiltcross Union.[9] The guardians had assembled at the White Horse in Kenning hall and a large crowd, armed with bludgeons and other weapons, came to demonstrate their opposition to the New Poor Law. Five men forced themselves into the meeting, and others attacked the doors and windows. A cry very similar to that of George Bennett's at Bircham was heard: 'We came here for bread, and bread or blood we will have.' Inevitably arrests were made and sentences passed, ranging from three to twelve months' imprisonment. Another significant detail highlighted by Digby was that one of the leaders had a good character and an excellent employment record. Likewise, at the trial of the Bircham rioters Thomas Golding and John Pilgrim were given a good character by the parish minister, and Golding earned remission on his sentence for good conduct.

3. Heckingham Workhouse

In April 1836 there was trouble at the Heckingham Workhouse.[10] This was in the Loddon and Clavering Union, an incorporation established in 1764. Here both inside and outside paupers had led an easy life. The house, in fact, had an awful reputation and the inmates were notoriously very difficult to handle. The guardians feared disturbances when the new workhouse regime was introduced, and had arranged for London policemen to support them. However, before the arrival of the police the workhouse was set on fire, and severely damaged. It was here also that Sir Edward Parry was attacked on one of his visits.

4. Erpingham Union

Shortly after the formation of the Erpingham Union on 11 April 1836 there was quite a serious disturbance, similar to what had happened in Kenninghall. There were obvious similarities with the Bircham Riots, but nothing like the violence and destruction of property were seen. Initially the Union made use of existing parish workhouses at Sheringham and Gimingham, and in the early years the Board of Guardians met at the New Inn, Cromer. The Minutes of 24 May record that there occurred 'a Disturbance and noise downstairs'. It was resolved that 'the Officer of the Preventive Station be requested to attend with the force under his command, in order to keep the Peace and protect the guardians in the execution of their duty'. It would appear, then, that the deployment of coastguard forces, especially in these coastal areas, was the natural response to a riot or the threat of one. The Yeomanry were also keen to get into action again: the guardians gave their thanks to 'Captn Girling for the promptitude displayed by him in collecting the Holt Troop of Cavalry and for his offer to march with it to the Meeting of this Board to put down a threatened riot'.[11]

The three men were brought to court for riot, and for assaulting the Relieving Officer, Timothy Murrell. It is difficult to separate any serious anti-Poor Law protest from the drunken revelry associated with the Whitsuntide Fair at Cromer. The newspaper report mentioned that ten or twelve men along with several women and children congregated, and that 'after considerable shouting and hallooing and a little dancing on the part of the women they exclaimed that what the men would not do they would'. No doubt virility had to be asserted, and it was shortly afterwards that Murrell was assaulted. He was followed into the stable of the inn, elbowed by one of the men, struck on the temple by another – 'in a state of intoxication' – and threatened by another, who was flourishing a bludgeon. Murrell, unlike William Tilney at Bircham, was later able to escape. All was calm when the coastguard arrived, 'except for a little occasional laughing on the part of the populace, who had not dispersed'.[12]

The charge of riot was dropped, and the three men were found guilty of common assault only, for which they were sentenced to three months' imprisonment, and to enter into their own recognizances of fifty pounds to keep the peace for one year. This was quite a large amount and somewhat surprising; even more surprising was the fact that each defendant had a counsel to represent him.

As we have seen, Metropolitan policemen were brought into the Docking Union following the Bircham Riots. It had been mooted by the Erpingham Union that four police officers should be procured during the time the workhouses at Sheringham and Gimingham were being altered to meet the demands of the New Poor Law. Nevertheless, despite the suggestions of Assistant Commissioner Kay, the guardians were not persuaded that the situation was sufficiently urgent to justify the heavy expense.

It would appear that Relieving Officer Murrell was about to set off with his horse and cart on his rounds of the Union's parishes in order to dispense outdoor relief to those the guardians had deemed worthy of it. The newspaper report mentioned that his horse and cart were made ready and that he then left the town. Relieving officers, along with overseers, were profoundly unpopular men. They were seen in the various communities they visited as representatives of the hated Poor Law with its miserly payments of outdoor relief. They were fair game for vicious attacks and Murrell's case was certainly not an isolated one.

5. Rollesby Workhouse

Workhouses were clearly the object of hatred and became targets of attack, and the fire at Heckingham was not the only attempt to destroy a house. In March 1837, in another of the old incorporations (and one which did not become a Poor Law Union under the new act), a fire started in the women's ward destroyed half the building, several straw beds having been set alight. This was at Rollesby in the East and West

Flegg Incorporation. The inmates were protesting at a measure under the New Poor Law that has become part of workhouse mythology: that married couples were to be separated from each other.[13]

6. Pulham Workhouse

And finally, it often proved difficult to erect a new workhouse. Night attacks, designed to pull down the walls as they were being built, were not uncommon. The classic example is the house at Pulham St Mary in the Depwade Union. As it was being built in 1836, it was found the attacks were so effective that high walls with corner sentry posts had to be built. In the sentry posts were loopholes so that armed watchmen could defend the building.[14]

III Anti-Poor Law agitation outside Norfolk

Protests against the New Poor Law, of various sorts and accompanied by varying degrees of violence, were in fact not at all uncommon at this period. They were not, of course, confined to Norfolk. Three examples, all from the southern half of England, will have to suffice. Nicholas Edsall reminds us that it was in March 1835 that Assistant Commissioners like Parry began to reorganize in a serious way. He continues:

Yet by the end of May the Poor Law authorities had had to contend with serious riots or near riots in at least half a dozen Unions widely scattered throughout the Home Counties.[15]

1. Milton Union, Kent

The Milton Union in Kent had been created in March 1835, and at first all went well. However, trouble started when the system of relief was changed. Apparently things were not quite as good as in the Docking Union. The old system involved a mixture of relief in kind and in cash – exactly what Kitton was trying to introduce, according to Parry's and the Poor Law Commissioners' principles. In Milton relief was now to be solely in the form of tickets exchangeable for goods. This quickly roused the poor to anger and soon stones were being thrown at the guardians, and a large mob had gathered to thwart the new system of relief. Nevertheless, soon the familiar ploys of swearing in special constables, summoning soldiers and bringing in London policemen were tried, and order was restored. The similarities with the much more serious Bircham Riots are obvious.

2. Ampthill Union, Bedfordshire

In May 1835 the new Ampthill Poor Law Union, in Bedfordshire, experienced severe disturbances. Once more, it was the replacement of relief purely in cash by handouts of food and clothing that provoked the poor into violence. A large crowd confronted the guardians at the Ampthill House of Industry and began stoning them. Order was eventually restored and a total of nineteen arrests made. In contrast to what happened at Bircham, the Riot Act was read, and two men were accused of continuing to create a riot after the reading. This was a capital offence, but nobody was executed. We have already seen how women were involved in the Bircham Riots, but here in Bedfordshire they were much more active. A large crowd of them pursued the new relieving officer, pinned him against a wall, and forced him to hand over all the money he had. Earlier, they had uttered a much more sinister cry than George Bennett's:

We don't want you here, and we'll have money or blood, and before you leave this we'll have either the money out of your pocket, or the blood out of your veins.

Four women were charged with riot.[16]

We can perhaps mention in passing that defiant shouts containing blood and the spilling of it were common, almost a cliché. George Bennett was not being original, but it is very interesting that it is mentioned in the newspaper reports; and it must have been a factor in his sentence of two years' hard labour plus sureties.

3. Hoxne Union, Suffolk

For our third example we can return to East Anglia, and now we are later than the summer of 1835. However, the disturbances, when they came in December, had been preceded by months of unrest. They occurred in the area around Stradbroke, in Suffolk, where the

163

Assistant Commissioner found the establishment of the Hoxne Union far from straightforward. There was strong opposition from local clergy and a shoemaker. The latter should come as no surprise, as these people, along with blacksmiths, were notorious radicals. We already know of the involvement of one of the shoe-making families of Miles in the Bircham Riots. There was also determined opposition to the New Poor Law by a Suffolk newspaper, something not encountered in Norfolk. For a while it looked as if law and order had broken down completely. The disturbance spread and there was, in Edsall's words, 'a general rising against the New Poor Law in East Suffolk with determined and sustained attacks'. The parish and special constables proved totally inadequate; and even the soldiers found it difficult to restore order at first. However, restore it they did. As in Bircham, there was no real leadership amongst the rioters. Some might have felt that the country was on the verge of revolution; but the reality was completely different.

IV The Bircham Riots - Organization

Strong leadership was apparently lacking in the Bircham Riots. It is appropriate to return to June 1835, and to speculate on what kind of organization, if any, was involved. It is equally useful to look at the motivation of the rioters and then to determine just what sort of people were involved.

For Edsall[17] it is quite clear 'there was no national anti-Poor Law organization, nor any attempt to create one'. He is equally sure that well-organized local opposition groups did not exist either. When Cobbett predicted, in his *Political Register* article in June 1835, that there would be a 'durable and mischievous rural war', he probably thought that the poor would rise spontaneously. Certainly, neither he nor any other prominent opponent of the New Poor Law provided any blueprint for physical resistance on the ground. Edsall again: 'All of these disturbances, whatever their individual peculiarities had much in common. In no case, it appears, was there what could be called proper or co-ordinated leadership.'

All these anti-Poor Law riots were, Edsall felt, perfect examples of spontaneous uprisings. They were also sporadic. He reckons, too, that 'certain men tended to turn up at every disturbance and self-appointed carriers of news and haranguers of the crowd sprang up in all these trouble spots'. There must have been all manner of types in the alleged 800 or 900 who were in Bircham on that night at the end of June: rick-burners, poachers, petty criminals, and ne'er-do-wells of many hues were undoubtedly there. But was nobody in earnest? Did nobody have a serious purpose? Surely many did; although they probably did not make up anything like a majority of the crowd. There again, Edsall does appear to point to something not entirely removed from the Bircham situation. Of the Milton Union, for example, it was reported that agricultural labourers were roaming the countryside with clubs 'forcing the peaceable labourers to quit their work,…and committing violent assaults on persons who refused to comply with their unlawful demands'. Thuggery inevitably played its part in the Bircham Riots. Without any doubt the few Bircham farm servants, John Hunt for instance, were forced out of the farmhouses, and nobody at work in the fields could have resisted the strike. The will of the principals in the strike – probably those who appeared in court – could not have been strongly resisted.

Returning to the events of the ten days commencing on Saturday 20 June 1835, let us see if any kind of organization can be detected.

1. Refusal of relief in kind

Relief partly in kind was 'determinedly' refused and a threat was made that this new system of relief would be resisted by 'the whole of the poor of the parish'. Who dared speak on behalf of most of the parish? Who was quite sure relief partly in kind would be rejected? The reports, all we have got to piece together the course of events, are completely silent here; had it possibly been expected in advance that pure cash relief would no longer be offered? The order to change the system had been made as early as November 1834. The new Assistant Commissioner had explained to the Norwich Board of Guardians on Tuesday 16 June his ideas for payment of relief partly in kind, and he was simply reiterating official policy. We know there were carriers between Norwich and Bircham, and there must have been other people whose business took them to places bigger than the Bircham parishes. It is far from fanciful to believe that news of these important changes in welfare reached, say, a shoemaker's or a blacksmith's shop,

165

or Spooner's beer-house. If Parry's address to the guardians in Norwich was not reported, it is highly unlikely that something about payment in kind rather than in cash did not reach the ears of the Bircham poor. News from Kent, Bedfordshire and elsewhere could very easily have reached somebody in Great Bircham. Perhaps, though this might be stretching things too far, somebody was merely waiting for Kitton to make his offer of relief so that resistance could begin. Taking that line of argument, it would have been the necessary trigger to start a strike. Or perhaps the whole thing was entirely spontaneous; but the choice of haysel as a time to strike was significant. We shall never know.

2. Solely a Bircham affair?

The forcing of labourers from the houses and fields has already been mentioned. To make it effective, some level of organization and control was inevitable. Nothing could have been left to chance. *The Norfolk Chronicle's* 'idleness, sullenness and complainings' could not be allowed to fester; the labourers had to be active strikers.

Was this purely a Bircham strike? Discontent amongst labourers against low wages, harsh treatment by their employers or miserly levels of relief handed out by parish officers was universal among agricultural labourers throughout the East and South of England at the time. Plenty of other labourers in the vicinity of Bircham would have felt the same disgust at the offer of 1s. 3d. per acre at the haysel; and very many of them would have had their own grievances. Yet, was there more to it than mere fellow feeling? Leak, in his letter of 1 July, told Sir Jacob Astley that there had been 'an agreement made amongst them all in the whole of the parishes to strike'. He probably, however, was referring to the three Bircham parishes alone rather than any wider grouping. (See also 6, below.)

3. A strike or anti-poor law agitation?

If the labourers thought the farmers would simply give in and increase the rate of pay they were certainly deceiving themselves. There is no doubt, however, that a strike on account of low wages was linked to an endeavour to resist the New Poor Law. It was all bound up with the perceived oppression of the poor by the rich. Very low wages and relief in kind were both methods of grinding the poor in their eyes.

Parry informed Frankland Lewis in his letter of 1 July that he had been told by the landlord of the inn where he was staying in Swaffham that the offer of 1s. 3d. per acre for cutting the hay had been the sole reason for the strike. The Assistant Commissioner was not moved to deny that, but added: 'Be that as it may, the labourers are ripe for anything.'[18]

Let us consider that price of 1s. 3d. an acre for cutting the hay. It was a major factor in the rousing of the Bircham labourers to anger. Bacon, in his *Report on the Agriculture of Norfolk,* gave prices for labour in 1843 under various headings. For mowing meadow grass he quoted from 2s. 6d. to 3s. per acre.[19] Closer to Bircham, however, in time and place, are Stephen Reeve's farm accounts for Houghton. In 1834 two men were paid 19s. for two weeks cutting the hay. A week was six ten-hour days, and thus something like 1s. 7d. a day was being paid. Grass was mowed with a scythe at this time – Alun Howkins has called haysel 'the hardest of all harvests' – and the mown grass had to be turned and raked.[20] The weather, the state of the grass and the terrain obviously varied, but we can reckon that to cut an acre of grass with a scythe would have taken a day.[21] Whichever way we look at it, then, we must conclude that George Bennett had been right to question whether a man could live on fifteen pence.

Yet the more one reads the letters the more one has the impression that Parry wrote often without much reflection, and put down whatever first came into his head. We saw (in Chapter 3) that he was telling Frankland Lewis that the Bircham events could be turned to the advantage of the Poor Law Commissioners; yet three days earlier he had written to his superior, 'this riot had been a plain strait-forward breach of the peace, with which, in real truth, the Poor Laws have nothing to do'.[22]

4. Bludgeons

We are told, in the press accounts, that on 29 June, when Curtis came from Walsingham to make his arrests, practically all the males in Bircham were armed with heavy bludgeons. This seems to present a scene both sinister and faintly absurd. This is not Phineas Finn's bludgeon, not a specially made weapon with a weighted end. It is a word which came into the language in the eighteenth century, and was commonly associated with crowds during rural disturbances during the first half of the nineteenth century. Modern English prefers the verb; the noun, along with 'cosh' and 'cudgel', now sounds dated. The 1750 definition (from the *Dictionarium Brittanicum*) in the Oxford English Dictionary, 'an oaken stick or club', must be the most relevant. Where did they all come from? Most, if not all, labourers no doubt had an oak stick, perhaps to clear a path through brambles, or to kill the odd rat. But was everybody in the village carrying one on that fateful day? If that was true then surely it was not spontaneous, but some person or persons had ordered the carrying of bludgeons in anticipation of attacks from the constables.

5. A spontaneous uprising?

We must not forget the 'ill-disposed persons pouring in from the adjacent parishes, all armed with deadly clubs'.[23] Was their appearance spontaneous? Demonstrations in our time, however organized, do often have the tendency to attract breakaway factions, intent on attacking people and property. No doubt there were such types in the 800 or 900 present on the night of 29 June. *The Norfolk Chronicle* report says that the vast crowd 'marched under order to the attack of Mr. Kitton's house'. If they really were under order then that would imply a massive feat of organization. It is difficult to imagine that this is how it happened. Parry, in his letter to Frankland Lewis of 2 July, adds an intriguing detail:

It seems that strangers did the work of demolition, not the people of the Parish. This is, of course, to escape detection.[24]

Again, a well-organized attack might have brought in complete strangers so that nobody would be able to recognize them. We have also read in Leak's account (Chapter 3) that the Yeomanry, returning to the village in the middle of the night from Houghton, caused the flight of about 150 people 'very many of them disguised'. The mention of disguise is certainly consistent with the desire to escape detection.

It is, of course, perfectly possible that strangers did cause all the damage, but there were surely Bircham labourers with a deep grudge against Kitton and Howlett. Questions can be asked, but answers remain elusive.

6. Had it been planned in advance?

Nevertheless, commentators felt compelled to assert that there was a strong degree of planning amongst the labourers. First Lord Wodehouse: he wrote to the Home Secretary on 3 July and claimed 'the Labourers appear to have acted under an organized system'. Then Parry, probably taking his cue from Caldwell, informed Frankland Lewis on 2 July:

The business seems to have had a good deal of organization about it; and it is said that a paper has been signed in several Parishes, binding to secrecy &c &c.[25]

This is the closest the whole affair comes to resembling a sinister plot. It would have needed good police intelligence, or a government spy like the notorious Oliver, to uncover such secret organization, especially one that included the signing of papers. Conspiracy theories there have always been, and if the poor could believe all sorts of rumours about what would happen to them under the New Poor Law – for instance that the bread offered them as relief was poisoned[26] – then magistrates and Assistant Commissioners were also not immune from credulity. Solidarity amongst the labourers there certainly was and whenever they came together they could have plotted against their employers. Carrying it farther than talk in the beer-house or the blacksmith's shop was entirely another matter.

Nonetheless, there is a hint of a determined effort to assemble forces from quite a wide area in the disruption of the meeting of the Freebridge Lynn Union at Grimston on 5 February 1836, and the plan to repeat the disruption the following week. (See II, 1 above.) In his letter of 6 February to Parry, Vice-chairman Beck wrote that one of the Massingham men most active in the disturbance had told the constables, who arrested him, 'that all the Parishes had been or would be written or sent to – to meet at Grimstone next Friday'. He admitted this might not have been true, but he mentioned that a guardian at West Winch 'had been told that men there had been contacted'.[27] It is not impossible that something similar had happened in the parishes surrounding Great Bircham the previous summer. Or the Massingham men had learned from the failure of the Bircham Riots to prevent the giving of relief partly in kind, and thought they could do better.

All this must not obscure the fact that at least the Bircham strike, and possibly the subsequent riots too, must have had some planning and organization; but very probably it was confined to a local level. The magistrates may have been right when they thought John Shilling junior was to blame for the planned destruction of Church Farm, but in all probability they hoped they had found the principal ringleader. As for strangers being heavily involved in the planning and execution of the events of June 1835, even perhaps being the principals, it must not be forgotten that of the eighteen men who appeared before the courts charged with riot and related offences, virtually all were Bircham residents. (See Appendix A.) The real situation was doubtless more complicated than many made it out to be; but precisely what was being planned in the summer of 1835 must remain a mystery.

V Bircham Riots – Motivation

A determined attack on the New Poor Law and all it was to bring would be one motive, but it seems far from the case that there was one simple reason for the Bircham Riots. Causing severe damage to the livelihood of hated farmers, on the one hand; or merely striking in order to gain a better payment for the haysel, on the other; certainly these were to the fore. Sir Edward Parry seemed capable of embracing both as causes. Naturally, farmers and magistrates could see no reason whatsoever for a strike. Parry had sought the opinions of 'all sensible and judicious people' and they told him that the event at Bircham had shown 'the utter unreasonableness of the labouring classes'; it had been sheer delusion on their part to attempt to resist the introduction of the New Poor Law. In his letter of 2 July he passed on Caldwell's opinion to the Poor Law Commission in London:

Mr. Caldwell says he really could not see that the people had any cause of complaint whatever, but that the labourers and the farmers have long been rather opposed to each other, and the former are ready to adopt any excuse for a row.[28]

It was rather more than a row, but Caldwell does seem to be getting close to another motive, a much more personal one. The farmers of North-west Norfolk cannot all have been bad. It remains true that all labourers were exploited and their wages, especially in times of labour surpluses, were low. These tenants of the Marquess of Cholmondeley, unlike their landlord, did not feel inclined to overdo charitable works, certainly not to the extent of giving treats to all the poor without discriminating between deserving and undeserving. Yet scores of farmers did not have their stacks burnt. It is probably true that a good number employed more labourers than they could really afford to, just to avoid giving them excuses to do mischief. Some were undoubtedly intimidated, but not all can have been objects of hatred. Some, however, suffered a large number of 'flare-ups' (the Norfolk word for setting fire to something). Several were tenants of the Houghton Estate: John Curtis of West Rudham, for example, who had as many as six fires on his farm between 25 October 1833 and 30 September 1834. No doubt, had he been an overseer who offered relief in kind instead of in money in the summer of 1835, he might have been the one who triggered a riot. But the same degree of planning and organization possibly did not exist in West Rudham, as it did in Bircham.

John Kitton and his son-in-law James Howlett seem to have provided the necessary hate figures. They were both overseers as well as farmers, and they had both seen the night sky lit up on their farms in the past. (See **V** below.) It is, of course, harsh to single out these men and ignore the excess of violence demonstrated by the labourers. One cannot escape the conclusion that many of the rioters had scant concern for the safety of the Howlett and Kitton families, but it is equally impossible not to conclude that the two men were deeply unpopular. There are several letters in the files of correspondence between the Docking Union and the Poor Law Commissioners which point plainly to the way Kitton was seen in Great Bircham, and not just by the farm labourers.

Claimed to be James Warnes Howlett (1800-1872) the tenant of Pond Farm, Bircham Tofts in 1835

Many of the farmers, especially those who were parish overseers, became guardians of the Docking Union. Kitton was no exception. On 27 March 1837 the (absentee) Rector of Great Bircham, William Pratt, wrote to the Poor Law Commissioners to inform them that Kitton's election as guardian had been improper: there had not really been an election, but Kitton had assumed the office by virtue of being the principal ratepayer of the parish. As it turned out, Pratt had no real case, and the Commissioners said so. That, however, is not the point. On 13 April, Kitton wrote to the Commission and explained that all the other ratepayers – there were only five in the parish – wished him to be guardian. He considered the office then to be an obnoxious one, and he could never go to the workhouse (where the board meetings

172

were held) without suffering personal abuse. Kitton was quite sure the Rector was against him because he (Kitton) had caused a family to be sent to the workhouse. He was also convinced that parsons were obstacles in the way of bringing the New Poor Law fully into effect.[29] Then, there was the minister of the parish (the curate, Edward Priest) who spoke in defence of Thomas Golding and John Pilgrim at their trial. He was clearly in no mood to take the side of his churchwarden. The parish clerk, Robert Miles, would certainly not have been in the Kitton camp either. It is difficult to escape the conclusion that Kitton considered himself the uncrowned King of the Birchams, and that by virtue of his social superiority.

There is admittedly not a great deal to go on, but the feelings of the parishioners of Great Bircham towards their churchwarden, overseer and guardian do seem to point unambiguously in one direction.

VI Bircham Riots - People

It was not only the agricultural labourers who were against Kitton and the rest. We have already seen (Chapter 3) from all the letters sent to the Home Office by the Docking Magistrates and by Parry, that the shopkeepers and tradespeople of Great Bircham were strongly opposed to the introduction of the New Poor Law. With them it was purely a matter of the change in the law, and had nothing to do with wage rates. Both groups, however, were united in their antagonism towards Kitton.

On 5 July John Davy, a local magistrate, wrote to Parry. He included one of those unthinking judgements of the farm labourers, calling them 'idle and disorderly', and continued:

I am sorry to say it is too evident how much they have been aided and abetted by the small tradesmen, and beer-house keepers, who are most deeply instructed in the vice of a system of indiscriminate money payment to the Pauper.[30]

The charge is quite clear: the shopkeepers would suffer because there would not be the same amount of cash coming their way. It was widely felt, and not without reason, that there were those who spent some (or indeed most) of their relief money on beer rather than on food for their families. Thus the beer-house keepers suffered. It is vital, however, not to follow the thinking of farmers and magistrates who were only too willing to judge the poor as a lump. Yes, there were those who neglected their families; there were idle, disorderly and criminal labourers; but to classify them all in those terms cannot be justified.

There is no doubt about the hostility to beer-houses felt by those in the higher strata of society. John Weyland, Chairman of the Norfolk Quarter Sessions, wrote in 1834 that the increase in crime was as much to do with the presence of beer-shops, 'in almost every remote corner of the land', as anything. He continued:

In the majority of cases brought before the Assizes and Quarter Sessions, from arson down to the lowest felony, the parties matured their plans, met at the beer-house, and thence proceeded in execution of them. It is also clear that the proceeds of the plunder are in most cases spent there, and not only those proceeds, but in many cases the money given to paupers in what is called parish relief.[31]

Obelkevich's view of the beer-house (Chapter 1) was not shared by magistrates or farmers. Many of those gathering in Great Bircham at the end of June were probably drunk, and enjoyed breaking windows. They would have been hoping for a theatrical spectacle, but sadly for them no conflagration was seen that night.

John Godfrey, James Howlett's brother-in-law, who wrote about the Bircham Riots in 1835, leaves us in no doubt that strong drink had been given on 29 June to 'promote the work of mischief'. His principal target was not Robert Spooner but George England, who kept the King's Head. We know that John Pilgrim was arrested at the King's Head, and England might not have been able to resist the prospect of turning the disturbance into profit. All those men milling around must have been thirsty.

The name England was perfect for Godfrey, and so was the fact that the terrible events of 29 June were taking place not far from the birthplace of Horatio Nelson. He began his attack by a reference to the famous signal before the Battle of Trafalgar: 'Old England expects every man to do his duty', but then continued to fire off relentless broadsides at the innkeeper. The word 'England' occurs nine times on

174

the same page, and it is quite clear what the writer is doing. For instance he writes: 'England stood and saw murder all but committed upon the head of Tilney, and did not attempt to stay the murderous hands of the assassins.'[32]

Parry joined the opponents of these low-level drinking dens. Despite his assertion that everything should be done cautiously and temperately in introducing the New Poor Law, he was frequently intemperate in his language. He told Frankland Lewis on 6 July that he hoped a detachment of thirty soldiers would be stationed at Lynn,

where there is a vile population of coal-porters and half-bred sailors, ready for a disturbance, men earning £50 in the course of 9 months, and then coming to the Parish for the other three!! They will not like a change, and will be backed up in their resistance by the influential brewers, into whose pockets the poor's rate now principally goes. [33]

Parts of Lynn may have been more disorderly than the countryside, but one has the impression that Parry, the magistrates and all the rest in rural areas felt little differently about their labouring poor.

The fear of losing their customers undoubtedly hit the beer-house keepers hard. There is more than the supplying of drink, however. Behind Davy's attack on the small tradesmen is an accusation that they were the real architects of the riots. For Godfrey, the self-styled poor man's friend, these were the false friends of the labourers. He wrote:

I am inclined to think, my misguided neighbours, that you will discover that it is not an open enemy that has led so many of you into trouble and done you so much mischief; it is not the farmers that have deceived you and misled you; but some of your near neighbours whom you have taken as your guides and own familiar friends. They are at the bottom of this mischief; some of whom are one step above the common labourers in the villages ...[34]

Surely he has the Shillings, amongst others, in his sights here.

John Beck, Vice-chairman of the Freebridge Lynn Union, wrote about disturbances in his union. He was quite clear that the beer-house keepers and tradesmen had been profiting by the parish paupers and that they were behind the contemplated disturbance at the next board meeting. (See II, 1 above.) He was equally clear that these people excited others to riot, and then left them to take the punishment. There was some truth in this, but it cannot be true that poor labourers, even if lacking in education, could not articulate their woes.

And for Assistant Commissioner Kay, there was no doubt whatsoever that in 'almost every instance of tumultuary disposition amongst the labourers in Suffolk and Norfolk' he had been able to find those ultimately responsible in 'some or more of the middle classes who had instigated this movement against the operation of the law, or had more covertly encouraged its progress and development'.[35]

This is a sinister twist to our tale. We must infer from the words of Godfrey, Beck and Kay that the labourers themselves had neither the intelligence nor the ability to organize any protest against the New Poor Law. They could be relied on to get drunk, attack people and property, but could not put their opposition into any coherent form. Inevitably arrests would be made, and it would be the labourers who would end up in Walsingham Bridewell. If the whole thing had been as simple as a beer-house keeper and an innkeeper fomenting riot, sitting back and letting the poor labourers go to gaol, then we must truly pity the latter. We cannot deny, of course, that John Shilling junior had a very light punishment at the Summer Assizes, whereas the longer sentences fell on the labourers, although the latter were not all illiterate - far from it. Everything is much less simple than that. Once more what we have is an undisguised attack on poor labouring men and women. The 'ignorant', even if their ignorance was not so great, were constantly in the sights of their social superiors. Many *were* illiterate, got drunk, poached game, pilfered and easily got into fights, but they all knew perfectly well that they were oppressed and did not need those just above them in the social scale to tell them so. However, blacksmiths and shoemakers were certainly radical voices in a community, and without any doubt people like John Shilling senior and Robert Miles played their part in the Bircham Riots. So did the Primitive Methodists. There were at least three Primitive Methodists who appear on the 1839 class-list among those appearing in court in the summer of 1835. (See, IX below.)

There was, however, another view expressed by the rich farmers, parish officers and magistrates. It held that rioters and mischief-makers were not all bad, but merely misguided. The thinking ran something like this: the labourers were like children, and had lost their way; they were a constant prey to the malign influence of others, often from outside. It was common to blame outsiders and to sing the praises of one's own labourers. For example, there had been serious incidents in Docking in November 1830. (See **V**, below.) The Docking Church-wardens wrote to *The Norfolk Chronicle* in order to defend their own men:

...although large bodies of the most disorderly men from the neighbouring villages have, at different times during the last ten days, entered our parish, and used every means to prevail upon our labouring poor to unite in their riotous proceedings, all our people (amidst a population of 1300 or 1400) have refused to co-operate, with the exception of two or three lads of marked character amongst us.[36]

It was just the few, then, misleading the 'ignorant'. Beck, in the letter mentioned above, told Parry that a few soldiers sent to the area would help:

It might possibly prevent the poor ignorant and misguided people from being induced by a few evil disposed persons to involve themselves in riots and mischief and eventually subject themselves to serious punishment and thereby cause great affliction to their families.[37]

Pure paternalism, naturally; and that is what people like Beck wanted to preserve. It was too late, however: the rise of the market economy would engulf the country just as it had started to do in the towns. We must not be carried away by this concern for the labourers' welfare. It suited farmers if their labourers were kept in some ignorance. Too much knowledge was dangerous, and could lead to treacherous radicalism. A workforce that could be called on when necessary was important to them. Far better that it knew its place than that it was able to quote Cobbett, or even parts of the Bible.

Anne Digby wrote that 'the social composition of the crowds who protested against the 1834 act cannot be determined with any accuracy; it is not even clear whether women participated as they had certainly done in the eighteenth-century Suffolk riots, and in the

Norfolk disturbances in 1816, 1822 and 1830'.[38] We have already seen how women played some part in the Bircham disturbances. As for the social composition of the Bircham rioters, the overwhelming majority of them were agricultural labourers. So much was to be expected given the demographic profile of the three parishes, and of all neighbouring communities. (Complete details of those who appeared in court are in Appendix A.)

If there are too many questions that must remain unanswered, that is unfortunate, yet we can safely say that the focus of the disturbance was Bircham. Naturally, there was 'something in the air', and after the passing of the 1834 Act it focused as much on the dread of a completely new system of managing the poor, as on low wages and under-employment. There was, too, a tradition of radical protest going back several decades. The Bircham Riots did not come from nowhere, yet what happened in midsummer 1835 was not a precursor to a revolution. A crowd of that size could easily have turned their attention to Houghton Hall if they had wanted to, but they did not. They had no reason whatsoever to hate their landlord. Their immediate targets were Kitton, Howlett, and then Hebgin, Nurse and Denny.

VII Outrages in Bircham before 1835

Anti-Poor Law protest continued in some form or other throughout the whole period of the existence of the New Poor Law. Much of the focus of opposition shifted later to the North of England, but that is way beyond the scope of this book.

It is more relevant now to examine what had occurred before the summer of 1835 in and around the Birchams. Lewis Jarvis was writing letters at the end of 1830 to Timothy Brett, Richard Groom's predecessor. On 26 November he wrote:

... I am exceedingly hurt to say that it has been this Day communicated to me that the Poor People in the Birchams have assembled in a very tumultuous way and are threatening to do Mischief – the Magistrates have been sitting for the last two Days, but I have not heard of any Damage yet committed – in haste...

A few days later, Jarvis was informing his correspondent that:

a very riotous Assembly met at the Justices Sitting on Monday last at Docking, a Parish adjoining Bircham, and threw Stones at the Magistrates & Parish Officers and very much injured Captn Davy of Ingoldisthorpe, one of the Magistrates.[39]

We are now in the period which has become known as the Swing Riots. More of that later.

1. Animal maiming, 1826

Pond Farm, Bircham Tofts
(Photo 2011)

The first recorded incident is a particularly unpleasant one. Burning stacks of barley was common; less common were attacks on animals, but such an attack occurred in Bircham Tofts in August 1826. The newspaper report, as ever, cannot refrain from using emotive language:

A most dreadful outrage was committed at Bircham Tofts, on Friday night or Saturday morning last – some inhuman brute thrust out the eye of the black mare belonging to Mr. J. W. Howlett, of that place, and also stabbed

179

it in the chest and other parts of the body. A number of clergymen and neighbouring farmers have issued a bill, as well to express their detestation of the malicious cruelty evinced by the perpetrator of this inhuman deed, as to offer a handsome reward for his apprehension, which we most sincerely hope will be speedily effected.[40]

Somebody was later charged with the offence. Howlett must have thought he had every expectation, at the Norfolk Assizes of April 1827, that justice would be done, but there was virtually no evidence against the accused. (See Appendix A.)

2. Fire at Kitton's, 1831

On 7 November 1831 Jarvis was clearly alarmed. He wrote:

The Country is in an alarming State, and God only knows what will become of us, The Fires in this County are very frequent, and yet none of the Perpetrators are discovered.

A couple of weeks later, as he reported a fire on the premises of Howlett's father-in-law, John Kitton, he expresses both dismay and bafflement:

I am extremely sorry to acquaint you that I have just received information of a Fire happening last Night at Mr Kitton's of Bircham, but I cannot say whether the Buildings are injured, and it is reported that the Produce of 45 Acres of Barley is destroy'd by the Fire – I'm vexed to say that there is a great Dissatisfaction among the Labourers in this County, altho' they are generally paid very good Wages.[41]

A press report added that the value of the stack was between £300 and £400. The report also mentioned that Lord Cholmondeley and Captain Hoste were promptly on the spot. It said, too, that exertions were being made to bring the offender or offenders to justice.[42] Many of the incendiaries, however, were never caught.

The year before (on 3 December 1830) Jarvis had expressed the hope that peace would be restored now, as the farmers were then paying 2s., 2s. 3d. or even 2s. 6d. a day.[43] If a labourer could have earned the latter sum for a whole week, he would have been doing quite well. This misunderstanding of the situation of the labourers was, unfortunately, all too frequent. People on the outside would reason: if wages were really so good, why would they need to make any protest? Often, however, the reality was different. Bad weather, a few days' sickness or simply the whim of the farmer, all were factors in reducing the earnings of the labourers.

3. Fires at Kitton's and Howlett's, 1832

Further incendiary attacks against Kitton and Howlett occurred in February 1832 and March 1833. *The Bury Post* reported that a stack of barley belonging to 'Mr. Warnes Howlett, of Bircham, was set on fire and totally consumed'. Then, the same newspaper reported in 1833:

Another diabolical act of incendiarism was perpetuated at Bircham, on Sunday se'night: a stack of barley belonging to Mr. Howlett, estimated to contain six or seven lasts, and a stack belonging to Mr. Kitton, seven or eight yards in length, were entirely consumed. [44]

'Diabolical' was a beloved word of the press at this time. For the newspapers, and no doubt many of their readers, these incendiaries had a moral standing little higher than that of the beasts of the fields. (A last was an ancient measurement and when applied to grain was 10 quarters or 80 bushels.) *The Norfolk Chronicle* also used the word diabolical, but continued in a sermonising manner:

When will these misguided wretches see that the evil they create by thus destroying the bounteous gifts of Providence cannot gratify their malignancy against the proprietors, they being protected by insurance, but ultimately, by enhancing the price, recoil upon themselves? [45]

This report must have come from the then Curate of Great Bircham, the Reverend Kirby Trimmer. On 7 April 1833 he delivered a sermon at the church and it was later published under the title of *The Folly, Sinfulness and Consequences of Stack-burning*. He was in no doubt that stack-burning was a grave sin. He cites the motives of the stack-burner as arising from envy, malice and revenge. He poses a question about the differences of wealth and power in the world, questioning whether it was chance that made some rich, and others poor. He continues,

181

laying before his readers that divine chain of being, by which certain men were clearly closer to the angels than others:

But does chance govern the world? Can I behold the various classes of society from the monarch on his throne, to him who scarcely hath where to lay his head, can I watch their way upon the earth, and not perceive that instead of blind chance, it is God that "maketh poor and maketh rich,"...[46]

Of course, the firing of stacks of barley was a crime, and, of course, it was a sin. The Ranters of Great Bircham would have thought and preached no differently. Trimmer conveniently forgets camels and eyes of needles and the Sermon on the Mount, but he was saying no more than many believed: that the poor had to accept their lot. But did they have to accept being regarded at times as inferior beings? Did they have to accept that farmers could lower their wages to barely subsistence levels?

The *Norfolk Mercury* expressed exactly the same sentiments as the other papers:

The fiend-like spirit of incendiarism is still abroad in this neighbourhood and we regret to state that the cases to which we at present allude seem to have generated from very vindictive feelings, arising we believe from some little difference between the farmers of Bircham and their labourers. The sufferers in this case were Messrs Howlett and Kitton, each of whom we understand had property destroyed to a considerable amount.[47]

The arsonist might well have acted out of sheer vindictiveness, but the assumption that there was merely 'some little difference' between the labourers and farmers must not go unchallenged. Only two years later most of the population of Bircham demonstrated dramatically that there were more than small differences between labourers and some farmers.

One thing, however, in Trimmer's sermon is not in dispute: given that the stacks were insured it would be hard to impoverish the farmers, although increased insurance premiums would have been a burden. As for the farmers' interest in the welfare of their workers or feelings of goodwill, they would hardly have been strong before any attacks. The burning of stacks could only have driven the two sides ever farther apart.

You may injure their feelings against you, till they take no interest in your welfare, you may sever every tie of goodwill, you may place a gulf of enmity between you – but you cannot, will not, make them poorer.[48]

VIII Swing

The Swing Riots took place between 1830 and 1832 (the first year seeing the greatest activity), and were often in the form of attacks on threshing machines. Agricultural labourers had every reason to hate these machines as they took away winter employment from them, and could cause much distress. There were other reasons for Swing incidents: low wages, the unfairness of the poor law, or the general condition of farm labourers, for instance. The name has always proved something of a mystery. There was certainly not one prime mover called Captain Swing, but the name did start to appear on threatening letters sent to farmers, and was first seen in *The Times* on 21 October 1830. In the classic account of the Swing Riots Eric Hobsbawm and George Rudé identified 1,475 incidents in England. More recently a team of researchers working under the direction of the Family and Community Historical Research Society pushed the number up to 3,283 incidents and extended the geographical range. The results were published in 2005 in *Swing Unmasked*. A map of Swing incidents which appears in the book shows, however, the same concentration as Hobsbawm and Rudé: essentially in the arable areas of the South and East of England, which tended to be the regions with the greatest number in receipt of poor relief. There were nearly 600 attacks on agricultural machinery, the majority involving threshing machines. *Swing Unmasked* identified no fewer than 26 types of event, but by far the largest number (1,292) involved incendiarism. The drier climate of East Anglia must also have played a part in this respect.

Norfolk was a prominent Swing County, as the map below shows. It has been produced by plotting all the Norfolk incidents recorded in *Swing Unmasked*. In some cases it is difficult to identify the precise location but it must be largely accurate. There are 142 instances of incendiarism, and included are, of course, the fires in Great Bircham

183

and Bircham Tofts. Machine-breaking was the next important offence: 129 incidents. There were 33 wages riots. The events are generally distributed evenly throughout the county.

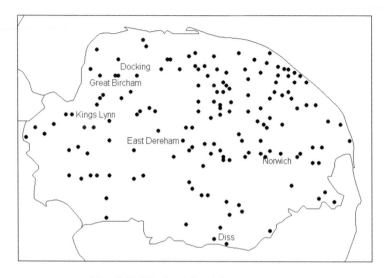

Norfolk 'Swing' Incidents 1830-32

The detailed map below of the north-western part of the county shows all the Swing incidents in places not too far away from Bircham, with the number occurring in each parish.

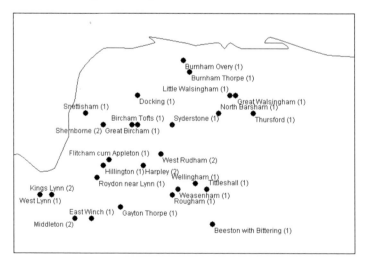

North-west Norfolk 'Swing' Incidents

The fires, of course, did not cease in 1832. The flares in the night sky around Norfolk farms continued to strike terror and to enrage farmers. Now it is perhaps more relevant to confine the plotting of Norfolk fires to the area of the Docking Union.

Between January 1833 and June 1835 there were twenty-seven incidents in the area that came to be known as the Docking Poor Law Union. Virtually all the fires were of stacks or barns. Quite a few were on Houghton Estate properties, and it is interesting to note that a couple of people were frequent victims. John Curtis of West Rudham, one of Lord Cholmondeley's tenants, was visited four times, and Frederick Hare of Stanhoe three times.

Here, then, is further evidence of the Bircham Riots fitting neatly into a local pattern of disturbances, although they remain the most serious of the Norfolk incidents.

The map below, taken from John Archer's unpublished Ph.D. thesis, shows all the fires that occurred within the area that came to be known as the Docking Union between 1833 and 1835. The Riots do not feature, as the fires – such as they were – did not catch hold and were extinguished. The Bircham fires were those of March 1833.

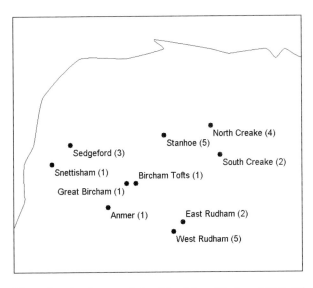

Fires in the Area of the Docking Union 1833-35

X Bircham events post 1835

The fires did not stop after the end of 1835. That would have been unlikely, as conditions for the labouring population of Norfolk villages could hardly be said to have improved. In fact the burning of ricks almost became Norfolk's trademark crime. John Archer has made a thorough study of incendiarism in East Anglia. He gives as many as 658 fires in Norfolk between 1836 and 1870. The 1840s saw a particularly high number of fires, with a peak of 76 in 1844. That is a shocking number.[49] There were fewer in the Docking Union, however.

Incendiarism in the whole of Norfolk from 1815 to 1870 (the range of dates for a study of rural crime in Archer's book) is beyond the scope of this book. Yet there are two incidents which must be mentioned, both directly related to our central theme.

1. Fire at Howlett's, 1836

On Monday week a stack of barley, the produce of 28 acres, on the farm of Mr. J. W. Howlett, of Bircham Tofts, was destroyed by fire.[50]

This was the fourth incident directed against Howlett in ten years. Why so many? It cannot really have been misfortune. There were some farmers who never had any fires on their premises, while others had several. We can only conclude that these farmers had done something to make themselves unpopular, but perhaps it was merely 'some little difference', as *The Norfolk Mercury* suggested in 1833. Maiming a horse and destroying stacks of barley (three times) do seem rather drastic ways of settling 'little differences', nonetheless.

For Archer the incendiary tended very often to be young and unemployed. Nobody was ever caught for the four attacks on Howlett's farm, so we cannot say whether that confirms his view or not as far as Bircham Tofts is concerned. Archer continues, saying the incendiaries were: '... the casual day labourers who were the lowest paid and the first to be paid and the first to be laid off in times of bad weather or falling markets'. His final point is the most telling one:

But we should not simply dismiss the incendiaries as the losers in agrarian capitalist society, for this would overlook one important feature of incendiarism. They may have acted alone under the cover of darkness but their actions were clearly supported by the labouring community as a whole before 1851. The villagers shielded them from the law and gloried in the destruction. The fires were lit on their behalf too and advertised their poverty and bitterness to rich and poor alike, though the former were, on occasions, slow to understand just who was starting up all the fires. The camouflage of deference clearly misled the landed who closed their eyes, if they were ever open, to the rural poverty which surrounded them.[51]

Some of that can be challenged here, however. Did the whole of the population – including the Primitive Methodists - really *glory* in the burning of Howlett's stacks? Very few, if any, would have had any feelings of goodwill towards him, and the majority of labouring families would have been in no doubt that the fire was a blow against an oppressive farmer, even if it was a criminal and sinful act. As for the landlord, he might have spent little time in Norfolk, but his eyes were surely not fully closed to the poverty of many who lived in his estate villages. The charitable works, which are evident in the Houghton Accounts, might have been sheer paternalism, but were surely genuinely provided.

We cannot leave James Warnes Howlett without mentioning two more things. The severe attack on his farm in 1835 obviously frightened him, although the fire of the following year suggests that his fright did not induce him to modify his behaviour towards his labourers. In the files of correspondence between the new Docking Union and the Poor Law Commission there are some hastily written notes dated 15 October 1835. They clearly refer to him, although he is not named. It says he is the only person in the parish of Bircham Tofts qualified to serve as a guardian, but as he refused to serve either as Parish Guardian or Overseer no other resident could be chosen. The note states that 'this person was one of those who suffered so severely during Riots in the summer who is quite intimidated'. However, he could not have held out much longer and he must have been persuaded to assume the two offices. By 18 March 1836 he was writing to the Poor Law Commissioners as Guardian and Overseer.[52]

The letter he wrote concerned four people who wished to emigrate to America – a man and his wife and two young men. The letter

187

further stated that all the ratepayers (there were very few of them) were 'anxious for their emigration'. On the surface this might be taken as a philanthropic gesture on Howlett's part, and we have no evidence, of course, to prove it was anything else. Yet the Docking Union Guardians as a group were also anxious for the poor to emigrate or migrate to the industrial areas of the North of England. Here was perhaps an opportunity to relieve the ratepayers of the burden of some surplus labourers.

Howlett also wrote to Richard Groom on the same day as he wrote to Somerset House, and on the 19 March Groom wrote to Stephen Reeve.[53] The cost, Howlett had told him, was £8 per person, but he had heard that other major landlords contributed two-thirds of the costs. In actual fact he had been wrongly informed, but Groom was not against the emigration. He considered it 'in all respects desirable', but he needed more precise information before he could put the case to the Marquess: whether any assistance would be provided on arrival or whether the would-be emigrants had any money of their own. A month later nothing had been decided and Groom was quite sure the Marquess would not fund the emigration unless he had been assured the emigrants were 'going out under good auspices with fair prospects of well-doing in America'. Nobody ever did emigrate, and perhaps Howlett had not really worked for the best interests of the emigrants. (See Chapter 6, IX.)

2. Demonstration in Bircham, 1852

The second incident is at the extreme end of the range of dates covered in this study.

In June 1852, Anthony Blyth, Clerk to the Magistrates of the Docking Union, wrote to the press.[54] Blyth was the brother of Henry Etheridge Blyth, who had been the first Chairman of the Docking Poor Law Union. The correspondent alluded to a speech in the House of Lords in which the Earl of Albermarle had used information gathered from a letter of H. E. Blyth, which had spoken positively of the state of the Docking Union: employment of labourers was up and applications for poor relief were down. Anthony Blyth had to point out that the letter was not recent and the situation was far from good. In the parish of Docking alone there were 40 labourers out of employment, and 150 in seven parishes. Not long before, the letter continued, 37 labourers had gone in a body, 'but in most orderly, and peaceable manner', to Docking Hall, 'as mendicants'.

There was another group of labourers mentioned in Blyth's letter. There were only twelve or fourteen of them, and they had been witnessed by the Reverend Berry parading in Bircham on Monday 30 May. They were not orderly and peaceable, because Berry had to send for the police in anticipation of a disturbance. According to the newspaper, the labourers were accompanied by instruments, which sounds like a classic example of 'rough music'. This involved extemporized and usually violent music, and often made by using such things as pots and pans; the instruments, however, might have been proper musical ones. Was it just a bit boisterous and nothing really to cause fright? Had Berry become alarmed unnecessarily? Or did Bircham labourers have a reputation? Virtually seventeen years to the day after the riots they were showing that their condition was far from improved.

XI A radical tradition

A case could be made for placing the Bircham Riots comfortably in a long tradition of Norfolk radicalism: the so-called 'Bread or Blood' Riots of 1816, on the Norfolk-Cambridgeshire border, also taking in Downham Market; the uprising of 1822, mainly in South Norfolk, which involved machine-breaking; and the frequent visits of Captain Swing and his acolytes between 1830 and 1832 are well known and undoubtedly precursors of what happened in the midsummer of 1835 at Great Bircham and Bircham Tofts. (The events of 1816 and 1822 have deliberately been omitted from this book, as to include them would overburden the narrative, and seriously over-extend the range of dates.) After the Bircham Riots, there were several incidents which allow us firmly to anchor them in a tradition of nineteenth century rural protest. The flaring Norfolk night skies of the 1840s and beyond, so comprehensively plotted by John Archer, must certainly be mentioned. Of greater importance must be Nonconformity in the first half of the nineteenth century.

In their article accompanying the map of Protestant Nonconformity in *An Historical Atlas of Norfolk*, Janet Ede and Norma

189

Virgoe conclude that 'by 1851 Methodism was the dramatic force in the county with Primitive Methodism attracting exceptional support'. The fervent emotionalism of the Love Feast and the Camp Meeting, conceived in America and then born on a North Staffordshire hillside in the first decade of the century, spread inexorably eastwards. By 1823 the Nottingham Circuit had branches in Norwich, Fakenham and Lynn. The latter place had been missioned from the Lincolnshire Circuit two years before, and in 1831 John Smith became the superintendent in Lynn. He worked tirelessly for the cause, so much so that the membership of the Lynn Circuit grew to 1170 by 1833.[55] As we saw in Chapter 1, it was his name which appeared on the registration of a house in Bircham Newton for worship in 1832. In 1836 Snettisham became the head of a new circuit, and later this became the Docking Circuit; it was in the same year that the Primitive Methodist Chapel in the village of Docking was built. Final evidence of the strength of this branch of Methodism in the North-west corner of Norfolk must be the holding of national conferences in King's Lynn in 1836 and 1844. Ede and Virgoe's map clearly shows the large number of Primitive Methodist places of worship in the north-western corner of the county in 1851, at the time of the Religious Census. We already know about the Birchams, and those class-lists of 1839 cannot be ignored, but there were several other villages in the immediate vicinity which had Ranter congregations, including Houghton.

It is known that the Second Marquess of Cholmondeley became an enthusiastic Methodist, after a youthful flirtation with Catholicism. It may not have been the Ranters towards whom he directed his enthusiasm, but the presence of Primitive Methodist within parishes on the Houghton Estate must have received his approval. [56]

It should come as no surprise that Godfrey, even if somewhat obliquely, imputes an incendiary attack to one of the Bircham Primitive Methodists. He asked, referring to an unspecified incident: 'What could be the cause of the wife of one of the persons fainting away when the alarm of fire entered the methodist meeting-house at Bircham?' Naturally, Godfrey cites scripture and is quick to point out God's punishment awaiting sinners: 'Then will they be brought down all such as work wickedness: suddenly shall they be cast down and not be able to stand.' (Psalm xxxvi)[57] George Edwards, the famous Norfolk trade union leader, and a powerful Primitive Methodist preacher, evidently did not always reach the same conclusions as Godfrey when he read scripture. He mentions in his autobiography how his study of the Bible opened his eyes to injustice:

With my study of theology, I soon began to realize that the social conditions of the people were not as God intended they should be. The gross injustices meted out to my parents and the terrible sufferings I had undergone in my boyhood burnt themselves into my soul like a hot iron. [58]

We must wonder how many Bircham Ranters in the 1830s had reached exactly the same conclusion.

If we extend our range even further and throw in the Lollards and Kett's Rebellion at one end, and the struggles of the farm workers' unions, along with the Burston School Strike, at the other, we have a much fuller picture. There definitely has been a culture of radicalism in Norfolk stretching over many centuries.

Nevertheless, radicalism or not, Edsall is surely right to say:

Nothing happened in the summer of 1835 that was calculated to raise the opponents' hopes. Unions by the dozen were put into operation; yet even the sporadic resistance which had shown itself in the spring seemed to have died away.

He added: 'There were a few disturbances during the summer, but they were scattered geographically, and of only minor importance.'[59] In the same note, he mentioned just two Poor Law Unions with disturbances: Hungerford and Docking. In a work which offers a very comprehensive coverage of anti-Poor Law protest it is easy to see why the Bircham Riots can be reduced to a mere footnote. It is sincerely to be hoped that this book has demonstrated that there was much more to them than that.

The riots did not represent an event which just came out of nowhere. They were in the tradition of Swing, only a few years earlier; and it must be remembered that not only was Norfolk a major Swing county, but there had also been Swing incidents not far from the Birchams.

191

They followed on from two incendiary attacks against Kitton and Howlett in 1832 and 1833, and they did not bring fires or boisterous demonstrations to an end. As far as anti-Poor Law agitation is concerned, they certainly must take their place (even if a minor one) amongst other incidents in Norfolk, Suffolk and in many parts of the South of England. Edsall's dismissal is unjustified, for they reached a level of violence greater than anything that had happened during the Swing Riots, or in other Norfolk agitation against the New Poor Law. There were examples of more serious attacks on property in Norfolk in the 1830s – the fire at Rollesby Workhouse, for example – but the large scale damage on the Bircham farmhouses, proved by the tradesmen's bills for repairs, is not to be downplayed. There were other places where crowds of protesters displayed violence – in the Freebridge Lynn Union in 1836, to give but one example - yet at Bircham it reached a rare level, especially on the last day. Those involved in anti-Poor Law protest were commonly to be reckoned in numbers greater than a handful; but, even if we dismiss the very large number mentioned in the press reports, the crowd assembling in Great Bircham on 29 June was certainly not small, and far from passive. Above all, what the Bircham Riots represent is a serious attempt by the powerless majority of one place to combine and use their collective strength against the ruling minority. Their voice grew stronger as it emerged from an ever greater number of throats. There was no other way of making it heard above the clamour of demands to stifle it. Nobody was going to take the slightest notice of a well-argued case enveloped in utter reasonableness. This was 1835, a profoundly undemocratic year. The attempt might have ended with little success, and it might have been easily defeated, but it truly earned more than a footnote in the history books.

Notes

1 *BNP*, 30 Apr. 1834.
2 *NC*, 11 Oct. 1834.
3 *NM*, 18 Jul. 1835.
4 TNA: MH 12/8474.
5 TNA: MH 12/8474
6 A.Digby, *Pauper Palaces* (London 1978), pp 222-23.
7 Digby, *Palaces* 1978, p. 222.

[8] TNA: MH 32/60.
[9] Digby 1978, p. 222.
[10] Digby 1978, pp. 219-20.
[11] NRO: C/GP 6/1 - Erpingham Guardians' Minutes 1836-38.
[12] *NC*, 2 Jul. 1836.
[13] *NC*, 25 Mar. 1837.
[14] Digby 1978, p. 220.
[15] N. C. Edsall, *The Anti-Poor Law Movement 1834-44* (Manchester, 1971), p.27. The incidents at Milton and Hoxne are also taken from Edsall: p. 27 & p. 34.
[16] See www.workhouses.org.uk
[17] Edsall, *Anti-Poor Law*, p. 25 & p. 31.
[18] TNA: HO 52/26, fol.256.
[19] R.N.Bacon, *The History of the Agriculture of Norfolk* (London, 1849), p. 145.
[20] A. Howkins, In the Sweat of thy Face; the Labourer and Work, in G.E.Mingay, ed. *The Victorian Countryside* Vol. 2 (London 1981), p. 515.
[21] I am indebted to Steve Tomlin and Simon Fairlie for clarifying the amount of grass that could be expected to be cut in a day with a scythe.
[22] TNA: MH 32/60.
[23] *NC*, 4 Jul. 1835.
[24] TNA: MH 32/60.
[25] TNA: HO 52/26, fol. 264; MH 32/60.
[26] J. Knott, *Popular Opposition to the 1834 Poor Law*, (London, 1986), p. 226.
[27] TNA: MH 32/60.
[28] ibid.
[29] TNA: MH 12/8250.
[30] TNA: MH 32/60.
[31] J. Weyland, *Charge delivered to the Grand Jury of the County of Norfolk at the Easter Quarter Sessions 1834* (Norwich 1834), p. 4.
[32] J. Godfrey, *The Poor Man's Friend or a Few Plain Words from a Plain Man* (Dereham 1835), p. 23.
[33] TNA: MH 32/60. 1834, p. 4.
[34] Godfrey, *Poor Man's Friend*, p. 25.
[35] Kay's Report on Norfolk and Suffolk in the 2nd Annual Report of the Poor Law Commissioners (1836), §34.
[36] *NC*, 4 Nov. 1830.
[37] TNA: MH 32/60.
[38] Digby 1978, p. 222.
[39] HH: Cellar Documents, 768L (d) & (e).
[40] *NC*, 12 Aug. 1826.
[41] HH: Cellar Documents, 768L (t) & (u).

[42] *East Anglian*, 29 Nov. 1831.

[43] HH: Cellar Documents, 768L (g).

[44] *BNP*, 22 Feb. 1832; 27 Mar. 1833.

[45] *NC*, 23 Mar. 1833.

[46] K. Trimmer, *The Folly, Sinfulness and Consequences of Stackburning* (Lynn, 1833), p. 9.

[47] *NM*, 23 Mar. 1833.

[48] Trimmer, *Folly*, p. 7.

[49] J. E. Archer, *By a Flash and a Scare* (Breviary Stuff Publications, London, 2010), p. 46.

[50] *BNP*, 23 Nov. 1836.

[51] Archer, *By a Flash*, p. 129.

[52] TNA: MH 12/8249.

[53] HH: M7c, M8.

[54] *NC*, 5 Jun. 1852.

[55] Rev. H. B. Kendall, *The Origin and History of the Primitive Methodist Church*, two vols. (London, 1906), Vol. II, pp 218-22.

[56] R. G. Thorne and Margaret Escott in *The History of Parliament* (online).

[57] Godfrey, p.19.

[58] G. Edwards, *From Crow-Scaring to Westminster* (The Larks Press, 2008), p.24

[59] Edsall, p. 34.

Chapter 6. The Imposition of Deference

I Two Dinners

There had been a very serious incident in the summer of 1835, but life in the Birchams had to carry on. Simmering resentment might have remained amongst the poor in the three parishes, but there were mouths to be fed, fields to be ploughed, turnips to be hoed and grain to be harvested. The relentless back-breaking work of the labourers continued and they and their families struggled on in the daily need to make ends meet. Yet, as far as Lord Cholmondeley was concerned, his Bircham cottagers were not to receive any punishment further than what had been determined by the courts. In March 1836, Frances England, of the King's Head, submitted a bill in connection with the Cottage Audit of 30 October 1835. This was for dinners for 103 men, and ale. The former cost £5 3s. and the latter £2 2s.11d. In the context of the nineteenth century it was quite a generous gesture. Perhaps, though, we should put this beside the bill for the Audit Dinner of 31 March 1836 at the Globe Hotel, King's Lynn. The total was £25 14s. 7d. and there were far fewer farmers throughout the Houghton Estate than labouring men in the Bircham parishes. The dinners came to £8 in total, but there were extras such as fruit (12s.), anchovies (5s.) and cigars and tobacco (6s.); the farmers were also treated to ale (12s.), sherry (£4 15s.), port (£6 15s.) and brandy (12s.), enlivening the proceedings and making their high rents, even if reduced by ten per cent, more bearable.[1]

One might have thought that the imprisoned rioters would be evicted from their cottages. After all, they had caused much damage to Cholmondeley properties. As we shall see later, the Docking Poor Law Union Guardians were urged by Assistant Commissioner James Kay not to treat the wives of transported convicts, or even women deserted by their husbands, with any degree of sympathy. Such was not the Cholmondeley way. The 1836 rental indicates that the rioters still imprisoned were having their rents paid (by his brother-in-law in Thomas Golding's case), and those already released were still in the village. There were even quite large arrears of rent, but not even that caused their eviction.

This does not imply a rejection of the New Poor Law on Cholmondeley's part. As a Tory he did not perhaps have the same commitment as the Whigs to the Poor Law Amendment Act; yet he was not an opponent, and realized that it had to be accepted as the law of the land. Nothing would diminish his philanthropy and deep religious faith, however.

II An Enemy Disarmed

Nevertheless, as of 1 August 1835, the Docking Poor Law Union formally came into being, and soon the newly elected guardians were meeting every Wednesday to enforce the new law in this part of Norfolk. Once the Docking Board of Guardians came into existence the erection of a workhouse was never in doubt. In the neighbouring Freebridge Lynn Union the same unity of purpose did not appear to exist; here, according to Assistant Commissioner Parry, a workhouse was not 'altogether palatable'. At every board meeting Anthony Hamond, an ex-officio guardian and from a powerful Norfolk family, attempted to cancel resolutions to build a workhouse. To have such a strong opponent, who could clearly command a good deal of support amongst his fellow guardians, was something that Parry could not condone. In a letter sent on 19 December 1835 he appealed to the Poor Law Commissioners to put pressure on the Freebridge Lynn Board. This 'pressure' when it appeared, on 31 December, in the form of a letter from Edwin Chadwick, was a most chilling and threatening document. The letter made it very clear where the Poor Law Commissioners stood: no proper system of administering relief to the poor could be countenanced without a workhouse. The guardians were urged to demonstrate firmness of purpose and to proceed to establish a workhouse. Chadwick was anxious to point out the positive results of the New Poor Law, even barely eighteen months after it had passed through Parliament:

Every day's experience furnishes the Commissioners additional proofs of the beneficial effects upon the character and conduct of the labouring poor which are the necessary and invariable results of the introduction of the Workhouse System.

The final threat would have left the Freebridge Lynn Board in no doubt about the Commissioners' resolute determination to implement the Poor Law Amendment Act:

No instance has as yet occurred in which the Commissioners have been forced to introduce the imperfect, expensive, and troublesome system which is the only substitute for the Workhouse, & they trust & hope that the Freebridge Lynn Union will not suffer itself to be reported to Parliament as the sole exception.[2]

A further cause of concern for Parry came in the form of a handbill written by the Revd Ambrose Goode, Vicar of Terrington St Clement. It was published in King's Lynn in November 1835 under the cumbersome title of *Substance of a Speech Prepared for the First Meeting of His Majesty's Commissioners under the New Poor Law Amendment Bill.* Goode's standing among the poor in Freebridge Marshland was high: in Terrington he, along with others, had been responsible for creating allotments for the labouring poor. In his handbill he denounced the New Poor Law as 'a violation of the fundamental laws of the realm'. All laws passed since the famous 43rd Elizabeth, the yardstick by which all opponents of the 1834 Act judged the treatment of the poor, had not been for the benefit of the needy, he argued; but nothing could have been as bad as what was introduced by the Whig Government in the Reform Parliament. The condition of the pauper was no better than that of the slave; the New Poor Law was profoundly illiberal, and he urged all lovers of liberty to resist this law, which had turned poverty into a crime, by all constitutional means. The very fact that it was subject to the interpretations of just three Poor Law Commissioners made it tyrannical, he felt; and its tyranny had the potential to touch all. For Goode it was quite clear: the poor once denied food and work would fight back. Addressing all those who, in his words, had hoisted the standard of despotism, he concluded:

Look to yourselves – Men must live – they have a right to live by labour at home, and if the legislature will not find the means, the little strife, now begun, no bigger than a man's hand, will become a torrent, which neither art nor force can control. – The voice of the people is sometimes an angry surge. – Unheeded it becomes a record of blood.[3]

His vehement opposition to the New Poor Law was evident, but that he was calling for open physical resistance can never have been the case. This was a warning like Cobbett's prediction of another rural war; but for those three Commissioners in Somerset House, and the Home Office, it was nothing less than 'seditious libel' with a 'deliberate and mischievous purpose'. On 8 December, Chadwick wrote to Parry about the handbill, and he impressed on the Assistant Commissioner that Goode did indeed encourage open resistance to the law of the land. Nonetheless, it was felt inadvisable to prosecute the Vicar of Terrington, however certain the case against him appeared to be. Instead, Parry was told to seek a personal interview with him and impress upon him the dangerous course he was pursuing. Parry was also to inform him, and this was an even more sinister threat than that contained in the letter to the Board of the Freebridge Lynn Union, that those to whom the maintenance of the peace in Norfolk was entrusted were watching him carefully.

Parry had his meeting with Goode and he reported the outcome to the Commissioners on 12 December. Goode had been 'courteous, even friendly', and had, according to Parry, expressed alarm at the possible consequences of circulating his 'mischievous publication'. Apparently he had also been told by friends in Lynn that he was pursuing a dangerous course, and so alarmed was he that he went to Lynn at 8 o'clock in the evening and stopped the publication of the handbill in pamphlet form; he also withdrew a hundred copies of the publication from Wisbech. Parry was evidently very pleased with himself and was sure that a prosecution would only have transformed Goode into a martyr. He convinced himself that he could claim a victory against the clergyman: '... if we have not made a friend, we have, I feel confident, disarmed an enemy'. Parry had to add a warning to his self-congratulatory letter that there would be tumult in the town on 26 December, Election Day. He had also been informed that the walls of the workhouse, recently erected, would be demolished at the same time, unless Metropolitan policemen or soldiers were sent.[4]

If there was one sure victor emerging from the establishment of Poor Law Unions in the various Hundreds of North-west Norfolk it was the British State; and this victory was gained, albeit not without resistance, in all English and Welsh counties. The New Poor Law won few friends amongst those members of the rural working class to whom Ambrose Goode wished to lend his sympathies, but it disarmed legions of enemies.

In reality, neither riots, nor attacks on workhouses, nor handbills nor the rearguard actions of a few backward-looking magistrates like Hamond could prevent the inevitable. The New Poor Law became a fact throughout the land, and it was to last, admittedly with changes, for over a hundred years.

III A Corrupted Poor to be Saved

Examples of protests against the New Poor Law in its several guises after the 1835 Bircham Riots were described in the last chapter. John Archer has plotted the vast number of East Anglian incendiary attacks over the twenty-five years after Bircham, and some of these were in our area. Overt protest in the form of riot might have declined in the Norfolk countryside to be replaced by more covert 'crimes' such as rick-burning, but we must not infer from this a universal acceptance of their lot by Norfolk farm labourers. This would be a serious error, but one very easy to make if we read only the contemporary accounts of farmers, magistrates and Assistant Poor Law Commissioners.

What were the gains, if any, that came to the rioters and their families once the Docking Union had been established? Who did gain from this new institution? Did everybody gain, or were there any losers?

It would not be easy to find a period in the nineteenth and twentieth centuries when Norfolk agricultural labourers could be declared winners in any true sense. The growth of their trade unions later in the nineteenth century secured higher wages and better conditions to a degree; but their industrial counterparts, many of whom had migrated to centres of manufacturing in the North of England, fared better in both respects. The passing of the Poor Law Amendment Act must have been viewed by their employers as a victory, in that it offered a reduction in their poor rates and held out the prospect of forcing their labourers into a state of deference.

It is part of the mythology surrounding English agricultural labourers, in Norfolk as elsewhere, that in former times, certainly before Speenhamland, labourers were highly prized, not only for their diligence and skill, but for their good character. For William Marshall the labourers of Norfolk were quite amazing people:

In respect to DAY-LABOURERS, two remarkable circumstances are united; namely, hard work and low wages! A Norfolk farm-labourer will do as much work for one shilling, as some two men, in many other places, will do for eighteen-pence each. There is an honesty, I almost said an honour, about them, when working by the day, which I have not been able to discover in the day-labourers of any other country.

Marshall continues by praising the agility, both mental and physical, of the Norfolk men:

... both his body and his mind become active: and if he go to mow, reap, or other employment, his habit of activity accompanies him; - and is obvious even in his air, his manner and his gait.[5]

Nathaniel Kent clearly felt the need to remind farmers of the invaluable contribution of the labourers to their success:

Every farmer I would advise, to consider the labourer not as an incumbrance on him, but as essentially necessary to carry on his business, without whom he could not live or support his own family.

He further states that no farmer would give less corn or hay to his horse, just because it has risen in price. 'Why then,' he questions, 'should the human servant be less attended to?'[6]

By the 1830s, agricultural labourers were no longer, in the eyes of men like John Kitton and Thomas Hebgin, valued servants but mere members of a rural proletariat, and as such, in the eyes of capitalist farmers, commodities to be bought as cheaply as possible. After all, if Marshall is to be believed, the labouring poor of Norfolk had been underpaid for a long time; and that should dispel any myth of a truly golden age for the eighteenth century agricultural labourer. Yet Kent is surely correct to point out the enormous value of the farm workers, many of whom possessed a range of vital skills. There was nobody to represent these men, and women, until the emergence of Joseph Arch in the 1870s. Until then a red night sky was the only way the poor had of signalling their distress.

It was a widely held view that Speenhamland had corrupted the labouring poor, and had turned their virtues into vices. One must naturally be very wary of some of the intemperate rants expressed by contemporaries. One such was John Godfrey, who had married Ann Warnes Howlett, the sister of James Howlett, in 1827. Godfrey claimed to be the poor man's friend, but his friendship was somewhat circumscribed. Nevertheless, his pamphlet of 1835 is instructive, despite the ludicrous fantasy of this passage:

I am old enough to recollect the time when the poor husbandman was rejoiced to see good crops, and glad to see the hills and valleys in his master's occupation stand so thick with corn that when the wind blew you might hear it sing, and the prospect of a plentiful harvest gladdened the peasant's heart.

That was the undiluted Golden Age. It was an age when all knew their place, and children were taught to respect the King, their masters and superiors. Yet all such meek obedience had gone by the 1830s:

But now, I am sorry to say, such good conduct is seldom witnessed; they seem to look upon the farmer with the envy, malice, and hatred against him and all connected with his family; displaying the very worst of feelings upon every occasion, ...[7]

It was, in the eyes of many commentators, the allowance system in lieu of wages which had perverted that mythical creature, the hard-working but subordinate labourer, into nothing better than a criminal. John Weyland, Chairman of the Norfolk Quarter Sessions, came at the degeneracy of the poor from a different angle. In his Chairman's address to the Grand Jury of the Sessions of Easter 1834 he made the position of all those charged with supporting the poor quite clear. Those who were genuinely in need deserved to be aided, but all those straying from the path of virtue were offensive in the eyes of God, and deserved no sympathy. Very many people today would echo these sentiments:

Now we none of us grudge that part of the payment which goes to the relief of unavoidable distress, because we believe it to be a Christian duty, and that it will be more than amply repaid to us in the blessings of Providence upon our labours. But if any part is perverted to the discouragement of industry, or in making the prudent spendthrifts, or the chaste profligate, or the sober drunken, or the honest thieves, or the well conditioned insubordinate and malicious; - such payments we do grudge and that bitterly; because we are convinced that Providence has not so constituted the laws of society, that any nation can prosper, or even long hold together, where such pernicious waste is made of the proceeds of present or of former industry.

Weyland was an intelligent and thoughtful man, and he was no enemy of the poor or of the Poor Laws. An opponent of Malthus, he believed that pauperism was not caused by any deficiency of the Poor Law, but through a lack of moral and religious education. He could not deny that the allowance system tended to corrupt. He identified the dilemma of the system in villages like Great Bircham: money was given for no work or merely a token task, and that encouraged idleness; but the money was insufficient and the labourer was tempted into crime. That is accurate as far as it goes, but it ignores the low payments given even to labourers in full employment and the distress they inevitably faced when bad weather or illness kept them out of the fields. To be fair to him, Weyland did acknowledge the weakness of the assumption that the New Poor Law could find employment for all those willing to work; and he clearly saw that, even if all the abuses of the old system were corrected, there would probably always be superfluous labourers. The new guardians of the Docking Union realized that too, and they had some solutions of their own.

Weyland hoped the New Poor Law would succeed. He saw the reasoning behind the principle of less eligibility and how it motivated able-bodied paupers to improve their situation through their own endeavours; but he predicted that success would be hampered by many difficulties and struggles. This is the eternal dilemma of welfare-reform zealots: it is one thing to force long-term dependents on benefits into employment, but another to provide the jobs, and to make those able to take them employable. It was no different in North-west Norfolk in 1835. Weyland, an evangelical Christian, hoped for the restoration of morality to the labouring poor:

... for at what price can we estimate too highly the restoration of the moral and social qualities of the English labourer to their ancient standard, and his cordial union with the other classes of society.[8]

A noble aim. For Weyland, and surely for many of his more intelligent contemporaries, including some of the Docking Guardians, it was important to raise the moral standards of the poor. Given kind but firm leadership from the landlords and gentlemen of Norfolk, at least the industrious could be restored to their 'ancient spirit of independence'. This unshakable belief in religious education and unequivocal appeal to morality seem strange to us at the start of the twenty-first century; but it is a sharp reminder that we are not to judge the events of 1835 and the formation of the Docking Poor Law Union by our own values. Yet, this evocation of a previous age of high moral standing amongst the labouring class, and of the opposing viciousness and corruption of the 1830s, is surely all too simplistic. All were not honest and upright in Marshall's time, and many who gathered in Great Bircham at the end of June 1835 were not unthinking beasts.

IV The Poor Law Union and the Elimination of Degeneracy

The writings of learned men, with time on their hands, were all well and good; but there were those in Norfolk with a task to perform. Despite the centralized control of the three Poor Law Commissioners, those newly elected guardians in the Docking Union, aided by their Assistant Poor Law Commissioner, were charged with the implementation of the new law. Part – and it cannot be too strongly emphasized it was only a part – of their work was to deal with the able-bodied poor who sought relief.

The imposition of the New Poor Law was simply a matter of the restoration of a lost morality. Parry's successor as Assistant Commissioner in East Anglia, James Kay, had no doubt about the mission to be accomplished. He must have been a man possessed of great energy and fervour, as his voluminous reports to the Poor Law Commissioners show. One missive directed at the Commissioners in

Somerset House was penned on 7 December 1835. Even though it concerns his experiences in Suffolk – he was not responsible for Norfolk at this time – it tells us much about the aims of those who sought to implement the new law in the various poor law unions. Its title is particularly revealing: *Report on certain Results of Examinations of Paupers shewing what forms of Imposture and of Physical and Moral Degeneracy Result from the Allowance System.* Cheating paupers, sunk into not only a moral degeneracy, but also a physical one (creatures that were barely human) were in Kay's sights, and they had to be restored to their true humanity if the New Poor Law was to succeed.

It is possible that things were worse in Suffolk than in Norfolk, but we have seen in the previous chapter how violence was never far below the surface when paupers and poor law officials clashed. These open and violent shows of defiance were common across the region. Kay paints a similar picture in the Cosford Union in Suffolk, where 'the paupers were accustomed to assemble in crowds and demand their allowances from the overseers with clubs in their hands'. What is of more importance is the complete transformation in the behaviour of the paupers, which, in Kay's eyes, demonstrated the power of the new system. In one parish, he informed the Commissioners:

The Paupers universally now doff their hats to the Relieving Officers when they meet them, and when receiving relief at the Pay Table bow or curtsey respectfully before they enter, and during their attendance maintain their silence and decorum in the presence of the officer.[9]

In one of his enormously lengthy communications he told the Commissioners of his success in the battle against the allowance system. We can clearly see how no paupers could escape to the privacy of their cottages and claim relief unless it were thoroughly deserved:

I have ...carefully admonished the Boards of Guardians in this county to endeavour to abate the evils of the allowance system by scrupulously exact examination of the paupers – by directing rigid inquiries to their cottages, and from their employers, – by interposing the check of distance, and by rendering the rewards of indolence and dependence less, and the condition of the paupers both less secure and in all respects less eligible than that of the independent labourer.[10]

The infamous principle of less eligibility was thus to be applied zealously and relentlessly. The administration of Poor Law Unions depended on locally elected guardians, but they were to be left in no doubt about what was required of them. And the able-bodied pauper was to be brought to a state of independence by the most rigorous means.

Turning his attention to Docking's neighbouring union, Freebridge Lynn, Kay sent to London resolutions unanimously passed by the Board on 27 January 1837, including expressions of satisfaction in the improvement in the character of the agricultural labourers. These, who were formerly 'notoriously improvident, idle and dissolute characters, were becoming industrious, steady and well-behaved workmen'. Kay added his own comments:

The vast revenue which has hitherto been expended for no labour done is now converted into the reward of industrious docility; the disbanded parochial outlaws have ceased to derive their subsistence from the reluctant authorities by threats, and open violence, but are employed in the culture of the soil, and the diligent performance of their social duties. The county is no longer affrighted by rural riots, and incendiary fires. The beershops are deserted for the domestic hearth, crime has diminished, and a greater sense of security prevails throughout the community.[11]

Things were no different in the Docking Union. The Chairman, Henry Blyth, produced a full report of the workings of the first year of the Union, which he read out at the meeting of the Board on Wednesday 16 November 1836. He detailed several aspects of the first twelve months, all in positive terms; and we shall return to some of these later. He was keen to point out that the most important benefit coming from the measures taken by the Board, and from the provisions of the Poor Law Amendment Act, was 'a decided improvement in the character of the labouring population, both as regards their desire to obtain and secure employment, and their general steadiness of behaviour'. He was quite sure that 'a great moral good had been undeniably obtained for the labouring classes of society'. He was perhaps unaware of the personal abuse suffered every week by the Great Bircham Guardian, as he made his way to board meetings in Docking. Later, in June 1838, there were reports from the police officers to the Docking Guardians of a beer-house in North Creake and of the King's Head in West Rudham remaining open during church services; and of disorderly conduct in a beer-house in Heacham. The inhabitants of the parishes in the Docking Union were not to be easily quietened.

Such sentiments as those expressed in Blyth's report were precisely what the Commissioners wanted to read. The moral degeneracy of all those labourers who assaulted parish officers, who spent their days in idleness and nights in drinking in beer-houses, and whose daughters were bearing bastards – the next generation of good-for-nothings – had at last been conquered. We have no reason to believe that the abuses of the old system – the 1834 Poor Law Report is full of them – and Kay's picture of violence and imposture at the pay table were a fabrication. Nor do we have reason to disbelieve his cap-doffing and curtseying paupers. There might have been some exaggeration to create a good effect; Blyth was undoubtedly indulging in some wishful thinking when he talked about a 'great moral good', yet the perception was that things had improved. And on the whole they had; the farmers who sat on the Docking Board of Guardians must have felt very pleased with themselves as they heard their Chairman's words. Blyth was quick to mention that, at the time of his report, the workhouse was not yet receiving inmates, and so its direct benefits could not be assessed. Nevertheless, he was confident that the mere fact of its being built was impetus enough to make many, who had hitherto relied on their parishes for relief, bestir themselves and seek work. Again, there must have been something in that. These huge buildings appearing everywhere – certainly in the western half of Norfolk, like nothing previously encountered – must have offered a frightening aspect to those who beheld them.

Kay was also right when he wrote, in January 1837, that riots and incendiary attacks had ceased. As John Archer points out, 'by 1837 guardians and magistrates were able to congratulate themselves on having weathered the storm of protest and on implementing the new law in the region'.[12] Archer has also shown that there were few fires in Norfolk and Suffolk between 1838 and 1841; although they did reappear in frightening numbers later.

V Outdoor Relief

1. Reductions in relief and rate bills

For the majority of the poor the overriding concern was to survive. They hoped to stay in employment, even if their work was rarely constant, and not to fall ill. They all needed to know that in straitened circumstances they could obtain some relief. For the able-bodied, relief outside the workhouse had supposedly been ended; the 1834 Act made that quite clear. There were, nonetheless, cases where temporary relief was given to an unemployed man and it was claimed he was ill. After all, it was the fear that relief was going to be changed for ever, and made less generous, that sparked the Bircham Riots. All those who gathered in Great Bircham at the end of June 1835 would have been anxious to know what help they could expect from the New Poor Law.

If they expected things to be better, which is extremely unlikely, they would soon have found out that in terms of relief there would be no improvement. Certainly, any hopes of relief partly in kind not being imposed must have been vain. It quickly became the norm for flour to be awarded as relief, along with money. It was a rigorous regime that the labouring poor now had to face. They would not be allowed to starve, but they were not going to be treated as generously after the Act as many believed they had been treated under the Old Poor Law. Even before the building of the workhouse (within which only a minority of the Docking Union poor would ever be confined) the guardians showed their rigour. On 19 October 1836, they voted to end the system by which women had been given money at their confinement; and on 2 November, they agreed that unemployed families would receive a mere 6d. and half a stone of flour per week until the workhouse was ready. Later, of course, it would be an offer of the house. To be able to receive this allowance they had to appear every week in front of the board. The distances that had to be covered, in some cases, were not insignificant.

Perhaps something written by Parry, who had earned the reputation of treating his men humanely in the Arctic, is of interest here. During his time spent in Norfolk as Assistant Commissioner, he wrote a long letter to the guardians of the Henstead Union. One section of the letter concerned relief in kind:

I hope you will fix your places for delivering Relief in kind, so as not, on the one hand, to let the bread and flour be brought to the door of the Pauper's, and on the other, not to make it too far for them to go. I think a couple of miles a reasonable distance.[13]

No doubt two miles was reasonable for a fit young sailor; things were rather different for many of the poor of rural Norfolk.

As for their employers, they looked for two things above all: a more disciplined workforce, and a reduction in their rate bill. Under the Old Poor Law poor rates had been particularly high in Norfolk. As we saw earlier, Henry Blyth, in his first Chairman's Report of the Docking Union (November 1836), had proudly signalled a definite improvement in the character of the labouring population. In the same report he was also able to point to a clear reduction in the amount of relief awarded. At the start of the Docking Union (in August 1835), there had been 1,670 paupers on the books, but by November 1836 the number had come down to 1,401. The reductions in the amount of relief given were, according to Blyth's report, quite startling. He showed that the average yearly expenditure for the period of three years ending 6 April 1835 was £16,840; but for the period October 1835 to October 1836 it had fallen to £10,375.

In some parishes there had been greater reductions than in others. For instance in Dersingham there was a reduction of 61%; in Thornham and Syderstone the reductions were 57% and 55% respectively; and in both Docking and Burnham Norton 47%. Great Bircham was one of the parishes where the decrease in expenditure on poor relief was slight: just 15%. For Blyth the remedy was quite clear:

The figures speak for themselves, and strongly, and it might interest perhaps some of the Guardians who are not constant at the board, to observe the difference which it has thus been found possible to make in parochial expenditures only by a close inspection of cases.

It was certainly true that attendance at board meetings varied considerably, and sometimes numbers were very low indeed. Blyth, whose attendance was exemplary, could rightly ascribe dramatic falls in relief payments to the more ardent guardians, very many of whom were also overseers of the poor. No doubt many of those in receipt of relief under the old system continued to expect something under the New Poor Law, and possibly in some cases things carried on very much as before. However, as we shall see, some parishes appeared to be more pauperized than others.

2. Houghton

Chapter 2 showed that examples of poor relief awarded in Houghton were quite generous. There is absolutely no doubt that, from the point of view of the Houghton labourers and their families, their situation deteriorated dramatically after the formation of the Docking Union. It will be useful to compare the final payments to the Houghton poor for the period between 9 February and 11 October 1835, with the early years of the Docking Union under the New Poor Law proper. Blyth's report of November 1836 signalled a reduction of 36% in the payment of relief during the year ending Michaelmas 1836 for the parish, as compared with the average of the three years ending 6 April 1836. The Houghton Poor Book for the thirty-five weeks from February to October 1835 indicates an average payment of just over £5 per week. The Parochial Ledger of the Docking Union, which covers the period October 1835 to September 1836, gives a total of £30 11s. 8d. allowed in out-relief to Houghton paupers from 21 October to 23 December 1835. This works out at £3 8s. per week.[14] Reductions in expenditure on the Houghton poor continued throughout our period. A return sent to the Poor Law Commission in London shows a large drop in the amount spent. The average for the three years up to Lady Day 1837 was £267; but the average for the three years from Lady Day 1837 to Lady Day 1840 had fallen to a little over £182.[15]

The first thing that one notices, when comparing the Docking Guardians' Minutes with the Poor Book, is that far fewer names are given. In the 1830s many of the villagers, including all the widows, were in receipt of relief. Many were for illness, and it is also difficult to escape the conclusion that several men were being paid something to tide them over during a period of unemployment. Three named examples show up the reality of the situation facing Houghton families after 1 August 1835.

The Widow Daw was getting a weekly allowance of 5s. 6d. during the whole of the period from 9 February to 11 October 1835. We come across her in the Guardians' Minutes on 14 February 1838. She appears as Phebe Daw, 53, widow with one child. She was awarded 9d. and one stone of flour per week.

Thomas Ramm received £11 8s. 9d. in sickness payment under the Old Poor Law for twenty-five weeks in 1834; and that came to around 9s. 2d. per week. The minute of 9 August 1837 indicated that Thomas Ramm had been ill, but was now back at work; and during his illness he had received 4s. 6d. per week from the Relieving Officer.

William Curry, a married labourer with six children, had received in 1834 £3 1s. 9d. for a period of seven weeks, when he was ill; this amounted to just over 9s. per week. On 14 February 1838, it was reported he had been ill, and had received 6s. 6d. from the Relieving Officer, for one week.

Were Curry and Ramm club-wielding recipients of relief under the old system, notorious for the regular intimidation of the Houghton overseer, George Bate? There is nothing to indicate that they were, although somebody called Ramm had appeared in the boardroom in November 1836 and had apparently behaved badly. Some other Houghton residents had, no doubt, behaved less than perfectly. Such was the case in all the parishes of the Docking Union. Bate became a guardian, and even acted as vice-chairman for a while. He continued to employ Houghton labourers on his farm, including Curry's son James, who later became a bailiff. Bate was caught up in the new system in the same way as everybody else, and there was no way he could give such generous relief payments as before. The widows would now have to make do with the charitable offerings from the Marquess of Cholmondeley alone to make up their allwances; indeed his Lordship's charity never dried up.

3. Outdoor relief in cases of urgency

It is well known that, according to the Poor Law Report of 1834, outdoor relief in the form that it had been administered hitherto was to be drastically altered; the workhouse was the place where the able-bodied labourer was to be sent if he found himself unemployed. The alarming words of the Report, written by Edwin Chadwick, shouted out in capital letters at all who cared to read them:

THAT EXCEPT AS TO MEDICAL ATTENDANCE, AND SUBJECT TO THE EXCEPTION RESPECTING APPRENTICESHIP HEREINAFTER STATED, ALL RELIEF WHATEVER TO ABLE-BODIED PERSONS OR TO THEIR FAMILIES, OTHERWISE THAN IN WELL-REGULATED WORKHOUSES ... SHALL BE DECLARED UNLAWFUL, ...

In practice, however, things were not so simple. The Poor Law Commission did not issue any general orders concerning outdoor relief until some years after the New Poor Law came into force. In December 1844, they issued the Outdoor Relief Prohibitory Order and it applied to a large number of unions, including Docking; but there was a more specific order issued to most East Anglian unions during the severe winter of 1840-41. Essentially, all these orders stressed the same principle outlined by Chadwick in the 1834 Report, but allowed for outdoor relief in cases of 'sudden and urgent necessity' (a phrase appearing in Clause 54 of the 1834 Act). In April 1841, the Assistant Commissioner, Edward Twistleton, wrote a report on the workings of the order in his district. He had written to all chairmen of unions, and their replies, along with his report, appeared later in print.[16] Blyth's letter to Twistleton revealed that, as far as he was concerned, the prohibitory order had been virtually in force since the completion of the workhouse (in 1836). He wrote: 'we have never knowingly offered or ordered relief to an able man, out of the house, except on account of severe illness with some of his family; if he is ill himself, we consider that he ceases to be able.'

He claimed the system of not offering outdoor relief, unless it was absolutely necessary, had the unanimous support of the board. During our period unanimity amongst the guardians was not easily won, yet it was undoubtedly true that they did not want to be too harsh on what Blyth called the 'able-bodied willing labourer'. This group, the chairman claimed, had not suffered from the operation of the order, even during the bitter winter. The one group which found no sympathy with any of the guardians comprised, in the chairman's words, 'the idler and men of loose character'. The great advantage of the prohibitory order, Blyth felt, was that the farmers had been induced to employ more labourers, having learnt that it was cheaper to employ them regularly rather than casually. This might have been an exaggerated claim, but if true the labourers of the Docking Union were indeed advantaged, even if only in a small way.

The Docking Guardians were not alone in demonstrating a degree of independence from London either. They all would have felt they knew their own poor better than any Assistant Commissioner. Everything was bound up with power: in a previous, largely paternalistic age these guardians had enjoyed virtual autonomy. From the fourth decade of the nineteenth century things changed and their power became centralized, something they found hard to swallow. What is difficult to determine is the extent to which out-relief was favoured over the giving of orders for the house. Anne Digby tells us that, by the 1840s, guardians were evading a strictly dogmatic interpretation of the orders on relief to outdoor paupers: 'A systematic use of relief ostensibly in aid of sickness as a means to relieve the able-bodied more cheaply outside the workhouse is suggested by the fact that in Norfolk, as well as in Suffolk, the rate of increase of such relief was twice as high between 1842 and 1846 as it was in England and Wales.' She supports her view that outdoor relief to able-bodied paupers was far from restricted by citing Chadwick (1846), 'who stated that in many areas of eastern England the abuses in the administration of poor relief were as great as they had been before the Poor Law Amendment Act of 1834'.[17] On the other hand, David Englander sides with Karel Williams, who amassed statistical information to show that outdoor relief to adult able-bodied men had been abolished by 1850.[18] It is beyond the scope of this book to examine the conflicting views of historians, but the view that relief was given on the grounds of spurious illness might be questioned.

It may, nevertheless, be useful at this point to refer to one of the Bircham rioters who appeared to receive outdoor relief when he was not ill. Workhouses have dominated the historical view of the nineteenth century poor, but it must never be forgotten that the majority of men who appeared at the workhouse to seek relief never saw the inside of the building. One prominent example was George Bennett. His name featured in the minute books many times between 1837 and 1847; and he almost certainly continued to appear at the workhouse thereafter; but no names appear in the online version of the guardians' minutes. Sometimes he was offered the house – and invariably so in the early period - sometimes not. Frequently he or his wife was given as ill, and he obtained relief on account of illness: typically 2s. 6d. and a stone of flour, but sometimes more. On some occasions there is no mention of illness, but he is still relieved. That was certainly no oversight by the clerk: it happened all too often.

One wonders what the guardians made of this old man and his wife; she was even older. Did they have genuine sympathy for the couple? It seems improbable, given the enormous gulf between the classes and his prominent role in the Bircham Riots. Or did they have a grudging admiration for the old rebel? He was certainly persistent: in the 1840s he often went to Docking every week. For a younger and fitter man it would have been a relatively easy walk, at least in good weather; but he was in his late sixties, late in life to be undertaking hard physical work. The concept of retirement did not exist among the labouring poor, and a labourer was frequently expected to work until an advanced age. Those whose bodies were worn out then became the sort of people who deserved help. There is no evidence that Bennett ever entered the workhouse; perhaps he accepted it as one of the rules of the game that the guardians needed, on occasions, to stand by the ideology of the New Poor Law and offer him the house. Both he and his wife Margaret lived a long life. He was apparently still working in some capacity when the 1851 census recorded him as a baker, as well as a pauper. They were living next to his daughter, son-in-law and many grandchildren; and thus, even if the Docking Guardians could not provide any relief, they were both assured of some help, however small. George Bennett was buried on 20 April 1856, aged 78. The previous entry in the Great Bircham Burial Register is for Rebecca Maria Kitton.

There are indeed other instances where it seems obvious that outdoor relief was given to various applicants, often older men, who were not ill. Further research could no doubt uncover more; but a casual perusal of the minutes also shows a relentless offering of the house to the unemployed. The last word must be with Assistant Commissioner Sir John Walsham, who wrote in his report of 21 November 1851 that 'the out-relief is, I think, unduly large in this

Union. The Guardians are, however, now employed in revising the lists'.[19]

5. Flour

From the very beginning, so Blyth informs us in his 1836 Report, flour was preferred by the paupers to bread as part of the outdoor allowance. It was extremely common for paupers in receipt of outdoor relief to be allowed a quantity of flour in proportion to the number of people in the household. One must wonder whether the pauper families were always able to find the fuel to bake bread. In the minutes there are frequent complaints about the bread delivered to the workhouse. Later, a porter was appointed who could also bake bread, but his productions were not always the best. There were also complaints that bread and flour were not delivered on time, important for a family dependent on relief. For example, on 10 July 1850 the clerk was ordered to write to Mr Humphrey of the mill at Great Bircham and to 'request him to be punctual in his delivery of Bread and Flour...a complaint having this day been made to the Board of great irregularity'.

Of greater concern was a complaint made by the guardian of South Creake in the summer of 1846. A sample of the flour provided for the paupers and bread made from it was produced at the board meeting; they were both pronounced very bad. A second sample of flour was purchased from a pauper and sent to the workhouse to be baked; the same poor quality was evident and the contractor summoned to appear before the board. It later emerged that the paupers had been in the habit of paying 1d., 2d. or even 3d. extra per stone in order to secure flour of a better quality. The flour they were supposed to receive was seconds, but that meant good seconds. It was unfortunately a common ruse of contractors to produce good samples of flour – also of meat, milk and other commodities – in order to win the contract. Thereafter the quality was reduced; but this was prevalent at a time when food was commonly adulterated and stricter laws to regulate food were not yet in operation.

6. Numbers in and out of the Workhouse

Throughout our period, the poor continued to present themselves at the Docking Workhouse and sought relief there. Some were dismissed, some were sent to the workhouse, but the overwhelming majority received outdoor relief. The workhouse was built to receive some five hundred inmates, but during the period under discussion in this chapter there were never anything like that number. Kay, when he visited Docking on 26 July 1837, expressed great surprise that so few people were in the house. He had no explanation for this reluctance. It is possible that the riots in Bircham and strong opposition to the New Poor Law had something to do with it; but that is far from clear. The winter of 1840-41 brought more into the house: there were 118 during the last quarter of 1840, and 142 during the first one of 1841. At the close of our period, from September 1850 to December 1851, numbers exceeded 100 only twice, and this during the winter. There were 109 during the week ending 15 January 1850. For most of the year, there were around sixty in the house, and twice numbers dropped to fifty-six. Few inmates were adult able-bodied males. As for outdoor paupers, there had been a drop from the 1,401 given in Blyth's 1836 report: there were around 1,150 to 1,250 in any year. The situation in the various parishes differed markedly. Some parishes like Docking, East Rudham, Stanhoe and Great Bircham were quite pauperized.

The number of outdoor paupers in the three Bircham parishes and others of similar size is given in Appendix C.

Notes

Blyth's 1836 report is to be found in MH 12/8249, as well as in C/GP 4/92.

All the references to the Docking Guardians' Minutes in this and subsequent chapters are taken from the records online at FamilySearch.org.

[1] HH: M17.
[2] TNA: MH 32/60. The alternative to a workhouse system, as far as able-bodied workers were concerned, would have been to introduce superintendence of labour.
[3] ibid.
[4] TNA: MH 32/60; A. Digby (London 1978), p. 212.

5 W. Marshall, The Rural Economy of Norfolk, (London 1787), Vol. I, p. 40; Vol. II, p. 177.

6 N. Kent, *General View of the Agriculture of the County of Norfolk* (London 1796), p. 193.

7 J. Godfrey, The Poor Man's Friedns or a Few Plain Words from a Plain Man (Dereham 18350, p. 6; p.8.

8 J. Weyland, *Charge delivered to the Grand Jury of the County of Norfolk at the Easter Quarter Sessions 1834*(Norwich 1834), p.3.p.7, p.8.

9 TNA: MH 32/48.

10 ibid.

11 TNA: MH 12/8375.

12 J.E. Archer, *By a Flash and a Scare* (Breviary Stuff Publications, London 2010), p.71

13 TNA: MH 12/8415. Quoted in Crowley and Reid,eds, *The Poor Law in Norfolk 1700-1850*, (Ely 1983).

14 NRO: C/GP 4/96.

15 TNA: MH 12/8251.

16 7th Annual Report of the Poor Law Commissioners (1841), p.213.

17 A.Digby, *Palaces*, p. 113; and A. Digby, 'The Rural Poor Law', in D Fraser, ed., *The New Poor Law in the Nineteenth Century* (London 1976), p. 158.

18 D. Englander, *Poverty and Poor Law Reform in 19th Century Britain 1834-1914*, (London 1998), p. 85.

19 TNA: MH 12/8254.

Chapter 7. The Docking Union Gets to Work

I The Beginning of the Union

Complete victory fell, then, into the laps of the ruling class of the Docking Union, at least for a while. Whether they despised the poor for their villainous behaviour, or (more commonly) whether they pitied them because of their 'ignorance', and treated them as children to be set upon the path of righteousness, all the members of this class must have had reason to feel contented. But were the poor completely subdued? Did they really mean it when they meekly came to accept relief? Would the Docking Workhouse supply Chadwick with further 'proofs of the beneficial effects upon the character and conduct of the labouring poor', which the workhouse system was designed to bring? These are difficult questions to answer, but perhaps some answers can be teased from the very detailed set of Guardians' Minutes which have survived; or from the correspondence between the Poor Law Commission and people on the ground in Norfolk.

At the Board Meeting of 7 December 1836 the Chairman, H. E. Blyth, announced, no doubt feeling a sense of history in the making, that the Poor Law Amendment Act was at last to be fully implemented in the Docking Union, and able-bodied paupers who required relief were to be given orders for the workhouse. The first admissions were to be on Friday 9 December, and it was moved by Captain Davy that police officers should be on duty on that day and the next, in order to preserve order. It had also been agreed, at the Board Meeting of 23 November, that the Masters of the Bosmere and Claydon, and of the Bulcamp Workhouses were to be invited to assist with the first admissions. Things were becoming serious.

What the paupers' families felt we can only imagine, but their views could hardly have chimed with those of Blyth and the rest of the Docking Guardians. Certainly a large amount of money had been spent on clothing: £94 for men's shirts and stockings, and an astonishing £233 for women's and girls' clothing; and then there were bills for bedsteads and chairs (£32 3s. 6d.), and for blankets and rugs (£117 7s. 5d.), and plenty more. All this was good for local business, and soon there would be regular contracts for flour, milk, meat and

217

other commodities. In all unions there was a great temptation to award these contracts to the friends or relatives of the guardians, but no blatant abuses emerged from the Docking Union. The workhouse had been built for 450 inmates, and the guardians needed to justify the expense of building it. On 7 December, the guardians had more to offer than casual relief; more even than a reprimand, which had been directed the previous week to Ramm of Houghton for failing to behave himself properly when he applied for relief. Now they at last had the notorious offer of 'the house', which was to be heard echoing with ever increasing frequency in workhouse boardrooms throughout the land. The first able-bodied man to be given an order for Docking Workhouse was probably Francis Taylor of Burnham Thorpe, a blacksmith with a wife and five children. There were ten men from Docking and two from Snettisham who also received orders, all of them married and most with children. It must have pleased the guardians when they offered Edward Hamond of East Rudham (applying on behalf of himself, his wife and two children) the house, and he refused it and said he would try to find work. That was precisely what the offer of the house was meant to achieve: only the truly destitute would enter the workhouse and suffer its uncompromising discipline; any other unemployed man would be intimidated enough by the forbidding aspect of the new bastille to escape his situation by his own efforts.

Less pleasing to the guardians, however, must have been the appearance of 'Thomas' Williamson of Great Bircham, another one given an order for the workhouse. Williamson, who was born at Appleton around 1802, was properly called Robert; Thomas was his son. An unemployed man with a wife and five children, he is first mentioned on 23 November when he was offered work at the Union House. A week later, we learn that he had been living in Harpley but had been turned out of his house for non-payment of rent. His family had been given temporary accommodation in the King's Head, Great Bircham, but he had been discharged for misbehaviour, and was detained during the day in the workhouse refractory ward. Perhaps he was the first person to be sent there. There certainly were a William and a Robert Williamson living in Great Bircham in 1841, and the rioter James (baptized in Great Bircham in 1814, and living in

Docking in 1841) was yet another Williamson. They were probably all related in some way. What emerges is a Bircham family which was no stranger to applying for relief, and one that was certainly involved in brushes with authority. However, this is not the last we hear of Robert Williamson.

The next board meeting produced more orders for the house. The Visiting Committee reported that the few people in the house – there were just four able-bodied men – all seemed content and their conduct was good; and yet again the guardians must have felt satisfied with the early progress of the union. The children had no complaints, and stated they 'were very comfortable'. The sole girl in the house must have felt rather lonely, although she was very young, as she went to her mother at night. The women were given the job of cleaning the building, and declared they had 'been very well used'. One woman was ill, but might well have been surprised at the prompt medical care she received. All the rooms occupied by the paupers – separate accommodation for men and women – were described as clean and comfortable, and there was even an extra blanket allowed to each bed in the women's room.

These were early days, and before long there would certainly be men and women whose conduct was found to be less than satisfactory. There would also be quite serious lapses in the treatment of the inmates of the workhouse. Nonetheless, it would be wrong to say that, on the whole, the workhouse was badly run and the paupers of the Docking Union were ill-treated – not according to the standards of the day, that is. Allowances might have been at little more than subsistence level, but reading the minutes from 1836 to 1851 one has the impression that Henry Blyth and his fellow guardians – men like John Kitton, Thomas Hebgin and James Howlett – generally sought the welfare of the poor of the Docking Union in accordance with the 1834 Poor Law Amendment Act, and according to their traditional paternalistic attitudes. They were not running a charity and instances of sentimentality in the Guardians' Minutes will not be found. Above all they must have felt they were doing their duty, both towards those in need and to the indolent. It would soon become apparent that it was more expensive to maintain paupers in a workhouse than outside it; and much later outdoor relief would be found to be preferable for the able-bodied. There was much wrong with the New Poor Law, but that is an appraisal based on thorough investigation of evidence built up over a hundred years. There were contemporary opponents like Ambrose Goode, and their arguments were often persuasive, but we can be quite sure that the majority of those in the Docking Union who were able to vote in parliamentary elections – a distinct minority – were broadly in support of the workhouse system, or at least its promise of disciplining their labourers. Many of the poor came to hate the workhouse and to dread entering it, but they had no voice. Nevertheless, some who gave John Wilson, the Master of the Docking Workhouse, not a little trouble, ensured a small voice was heard and recorded in the Guardians' Minutes. The poor had little choice but to go along with the whole system of relief as best they could, despite the appalling stigma they had to endure.

II Work

It is undoubtedly true that the creation of the new system was largely driven by the condition of the able-bodied rural poor in the South and East of England – the Speenhamland counties. Many believed that those paupers who abused the allowance system would be forced to find work and rediscover an independence that had been lost. For those who kept coming back for relief it was all a matter of discipline. And discipline came from regular work.

At the creation of the Docking Union, in August 1835, the guardians found they had unemployed labourers on their hands. Seasonal unemployment was well known, and farmers and labourers had learned to cope with it. What the members of the Docking Board of Guardians proposed was something quite specific, and the harshness of the winter of 1835-36 pressed them to find something for the many men thrown out of work. Because Speenhamland was now dead the guardians could not allow any form of relief to be given to the able-bodied labourers unless they worked for it. The original Guardians' Minutes before October 1836 have not survived, but copies of the minutes from 16 September 1835 to 12 April 1836 can be found in the files of correspondence from Assistant Commissioner James Kay.[1] The scheme they sanctioned was clearly felt to be of great importance, because on 16 September we read that 'the Clerk was directed to summons every Guardian to attend the Meeting next week, to take into consideration the means of employment for able-bodied paupers'. At that meeting it was resolved that it was necessary to provide the able-bodied and 'willing' labourers who were then out of work with means of employment; but that it would be 'highly improper' to send them to work on the roads, which had been a way of providing the unemployed with relief almost universally used. What they proposed was that each parish should provide land for digging. The work in the Docking Union, however, far exceeded that offered elsewhere, in that it involved not only digging, forking and trenching the land, but also the digging and carting of clay and marl. The amount paid to the labourer was proportionate to the amount of relief he would normally receive according to the size of his family. The occupier of the land that had been set aside for the purpose paid the Parish Overseer 4s. an acre, which was about the equivalent of what it would have cost to plough the land. A labourer with a family was to receive no more than 1½d. per rod, and a single man ¾ d. per rod. (The printed 1836 report of the Docking Union gave the highest payment as 2½d.) The accounts of the Overseer of South Creake confirm that digging was in fact carried out during October 1835, but that the board's rules were not strictly followed: 4d. per rod for digging on some of the farms in the parish was paid, and in September men had also worked on the roads, at rates ranging from 9d. to 1s. 6d. a day. One man with a large family earned 9s. for six days work on the parish roads.[2]

Initially the scheme was to last for three weeks and then it would be reviewed. There must have been concerns that some labourers might claim relief without working for it; to counter that the Relieving Officers (now the only people authorized to pay outdoor relief) were instructed not to pay anybody unless they produced a ticket from their parish overseer which stated they had earned their money by parish work. Inevitably, there were abuses of the system, brought about by a lack of supervision: the minute of 16 January 1836 mentioned 'the gross imposition practised at Stanhoe'.

It was decided that each of the two divisions of the Union should have a superintendent, who would serve for two months; although only one seems to have been appointed to serve any length of time. This was a man called Pickerell and he was to be paid 30s. a week by the Union. The superintendent was charged with making regular reports to the board. The name of any labourer whose work was improperly done was to be included in the reports. By February favourable reports were being made, and it was stated that during the week of 1–8 February 232 surplus labourers had been employed. By the week 4-11 March the number had dropped to 134; in April it was 109, and at the end, in May (by which time more work was available on the farms) numbers had dwindled to 56. On 23 March, the superintendent was re-elected for another month, and at this meeting it was decreed that any man who did not work as directed would not be employed at all. It was not mentioned how such people, especially those with families, were meant to provide for their families. The workhouse would not be ready to receive them until December.

The scheme had to come to an end. Kay saw to that, and in his next letter to the Poor Law Commissioners he was pleased to announce that the Docking Union had abandoned the system, and that it had now virtually disappeared from the entire county. He had attended the Docking board meeting and had been able to explain 'to what pernicious results the system tended'. He was quite sure it could not continue long as no farmers could be sure that the land had been tilled as well as when it was ploughed; or, if not better cultivated than by the plough, at least done more cheaply. Above all, though, it was completely against the spirit of the New Poor Law.

The Spirit and intention of the Poor Law Amendment Act are that the poor shall be relieved according to their necessities, but in a particular mode, indicated by the law which may render it more irksome to the labourer to be supported by the Parish than by his own industry.[3]

It must have smacked too much of the old allowance system, and Kay was quite sure that it only gave labourers the idea that they had a right to demand that labour would be found for them. It thus weakened their incentive to seek labour for themselves. It was a harsh lesson, but precisely one that was felt important for the able-bodied to grasp in the 1830s.

Blyth's 1836 report clearly shows that he did not approve of the way the Poor Law Commissioners had forced the guardians to abandon the scheme. The board did try something similar after the collapse of the digging plan: 20 acres of land next to the workhouse were hired and cultivated, but it was not felt expedient to continue. What they introduced during the winter and spring of 1835-36 was a sincere and humane attempt to deal with a pressing problem. It was only ever meant to be temporary, and market forces would certainly have shown soon enough that it was to be of limited duration and effectiveness.

III Hebert's Flour Mill

The opening of the workhouse meant that work could now be offered inside the house. In fact it was vital that it was, because no adult able-bodied paupers were to remain idle if their moral education was to be completed and they were to be turned into productive members of society. Women could be set to clean, to wash and cook, or to look after other inmates; but what was there for the men? The answer was found in Hebert's Patent Flour Mill.

HEBERT'S FLOUR-MAKER.

At the board meeting of 5 October, the Clerk was instructed to write to Mr Hebert to ascertain full details of the mill; and the next week the board decided to order a mill. It cost £78 10s. Hebert's Patent Flour-making Machine was made for those who wanted to grind their own flour, without having to rely on millers. It was particularly suited to settlers in the colonies; but it was also found very suitable for use in workhouses. *The Mechanics' Magazine* of August 6 1836 featured a version of the mill adapted for the All Saints Workhouse, Hertford. The Master of the Workhouse was full of praise for the mill, and declared it could be worked by just one man, or as many as fourteen. Even boys could be employed, and it had the great advantage of needing minimum supervision. No miller would have to be engaged. It did not use the expensive French burrstones, the grinders being entirely metallic. Naturally it was held to be reliable and to require infrequent repair, and the quality of the flour was consistently good. The Docking experience did not support the mill's claimed reliability, as it frequently was out of action; but the master must have been confident of the quality of the flour when he produced a loaf made from it at the board meeting of 15 March 1837.

It was clearly something the Docking Guardians considered an important way of keeping the men occupied. On 21 February 1838, the Visiting Committee recommended the mill be repaired, 'as there were so many able men in the house'. The following week the master had to report to the board that all was not well, and now it becomes obvious that any distinction between the use of Mr Hebert's machine to provide work or to punish had become distinctly blurred. He had to tell the guardians that five men had refused to go to work that morning. The men were then summoned, like naughty children, to the boardroom, where the chairman said that he would be prepared to overlook this refusal if they agreed to go back to work. Otherwise they would suffer a reduction in their food allowance – a common punishment. They did capitulate, although one of the men, as he left the room, complained about the state of the children's heads.

The five men had already told the master that they were not refusing to work, but objected to being locked up while at the mill. We must seriously question whether there was any fundamental difference between the hard labour on the treadmill at Walsingham Bridewell, to which most of the Bircham rioters were sentenced, and this degrading and monotonous work at the Docking Workhouse. Later, at the end of 1842, the chairman became very concerned that the mill had been worked for sixty days but there was little to show for it. It emerged that the master had been in the habit of allowing the mill to run without any corn – the equivalent of having prisoners 'grind the air'. On 7 December, the master reported that seven men could grind about one peck an hour. He was directed to see what two men could achieve, and these men were to be set to work an eight-hour day. Two weeks later the plates were broken and the master had to send for somebody immediately to repair them. The malfunction of the mill was, unsurprisingly, not always the result of wear and tear. On 11 January 1843, the Visiting Committee had to report that the mill was again broken, and said it was 'through the misconduct of John Dodman and Thomas Mendham, two of the paupers in the house'. The latter was a Bircham man. Unfortunately sufficient evidence could not be found to commit them; they were both reprimanded for their misconduct, and told that if any more complaints were received they would be committed to the Bridewell.

The mill was nonetheless obviously something that the guardians considered to be very important in their control of the able-bodied men who came into the workhouse. On 22 January 1845, the master was directed to keep it operating, and a millwright was asked to see what could be done to improve its working. This must have been successful, as the Visiting Committee reported on 12 March that the mill was working well. Over the years it cost a good deal of money in repairs and those working at it required careful supervision. It can hardly have been cost-effective, but the taming of the inmates must have been seen as more important than providing them with meaningful work and encouraging industrious habits.

The rebellion of the five men in February 1838 was easily defeated, but the minutes record later examples of refusal to work at the mill, and these earned the recalcitrant a spell in the Bridewell.

Not all able-bodied male inmates were treated unsympathetically. There is even an example of the board of guardians actively offering work. On Christmas Eve 1845, the men waiting in the yard to come and seek relief were called into the boardroom one at a time and were told where they could get work. They had to apply to a Mr Harding at the Queen's Head, Lynn. Initially they would each receive 5s. but nothing else for a fortnight, if they took the work. The able-bodied men in the workhouse were then called in and the same offer was made to them. Several of them were interested.

IV Sanfer

There are frequent references to inmates being allowed to go out and look for work. They had to conduct themselves well, of course. The board ruled on 9 November 1842 that any able man could go out to look for work as long as he had his family with him, and as long as he returned the same evening. The board did add, however, that such leave should not be granted too frequently, and on 25 January 1843 it was felt that stricter rules were needed. Several men had recently gone out on their own to look for work but had not behaved correctly. It was decided that in future men should be allowed out only with their wives and families; a notice to that effect was to be displayed in the dining hall.

Of a different order is the case of William Sanfer (Sandford) of Great Bircham. He made many appearances at the workhouse. Sometimes he received relief, sometimes offers of the house. When he appeared at the workhouse on 1 January 1845, we learn that he was thirty-eight and his wife twenty-eight, and he had four children under ten. He was out of work and consequently received an order for the house. On 22 January he applied to go out and look for somewhere to live. Permission was given and the next week he applied for a loan to enable him to get his tools together as he now had a cottage at Stanhoe. He was given 3s. and 1½ stones of flour. On 12 February, his wife was ill and he received relief of 6s. 2½d. and was allowed 3 stones of flour and medical relief. By the following week his wife had died. He was allowed expenses (23s. 3d.) for a pauper's funeral, but soon he was back in the workhouse. One presumes his work at Stanhoe did not materialize.

We next hear of him on 4 March 1846. He was an inmate of the house again and he applied to go out once more, leave his children inside and look for work. This was refused, 'as he deceived the Board last year'. The following week he tried again, and he received 2s. and

2½ stones of flour. He was granted leave to go out for work on 13 May, and this time he was given 5s. and 2 stones of flour. Going out to look for work with his family cannot have been easy. He then made regular appearances in the minutes, and was in and out of the workhouse. On 25 November, we read that he, together with James Greeves of Great Bircham (brother of the rioter) and another man from Stanhoe, applied for a week's allowance to go and look out for work. This was refused because the master had to report that all three men had behaved badly and had been confined in the refractory ward during the previous week. The board's position was quite clear: they could leave the house and take their families with them – as was the case with all inmates of the workhouse – but once outside there would be no possibility of claiming outdoor relief. By March 1847, Sanfer was ill and had 2s. 6d. and 2½ stones of flour a week, as well as medical relief. The latter was in the form of meat, and on 21 April 1847 a bill for 8s. 9d. for meat was allowed.

Was he a genuine case who was ill-used by the Docking Guardians? Or was he dishonest with no real intention of looking for work when he went out of the house? As always, we have only a one-sided view of the matter. There is no reason to believe that his claim to go out in order to get tools together and work from a house in Stanhoe was fraudulent. He had been unruly in the workhouse, but he was not alone in that; and the frustration of being cooped up in an institution with its petty rules, with nothing more productive to do other than operate Mr Hebert's Patent Flour Mill, would have been hard to bear. He had lost a wife and was left with four young children, all of which compounded his problems. The life of the children, who also were frequently in and out of the workhouse, must, too, have been particularly unpleasant. Yet such was commonly the lot of these poor labouring families.

V Migration and Emigration

The work available to the majority of the able-bodied labourers at this period was still essentially related to agriculture. Further afield the railways were being built, and there are references in the minutes to men who had obtained work, even if temporary, as railway navvies. Later in the century, many would move away and take up permanent employment in this major nineteenth century industry. The Docking Union, along with many others in rural areas, positively encouraged migration to the industrial districts, and - even more - emigration to North America and Australia. It was something encouraged by Clause 62 of the Poor Law Amendment Act, which allowed parishes to raise from the rates or borrow sums of money for the purposes of emigration. In fact the numbers leaving Docking Union parishes were high: Anne Digby tells us that, by the end of 1836, 393 people had emigrated and there had been 100 migrants; and between 1835 and 1837 emigration and migration removed three per cent of the population of the Docking Union, compared with one per cent for the county as a whole.[4]

The minutes do seem to indicate that the guardians were keen to offer migration to some of those who came to apply for relief. On 23 November 1836, the first time that the names of applicants were given, one Smith of Docking said he did not earn enough to maintain his large family, and application was made on his behalf to the migration agent. On the same day there also appeared William Andrews from Sedgeford, who had injured his hand; once more the guardians recorded their intention of contacting the agent in order to find work for his family. One must assume that the minutes that are now lost also recorded many such examples. The surviving minutes show that there were migrations to Lancashire and Cheshire as well as to the West Riding of Yorkshire. In subsequent years, those who had migrated according to the scheme were joined by others, who went on their own initiative, or with help from their parishes.

The Docking Guardians, virtually all farmers to a man, were always conscious that demand for work, in this district dominated by arable farming, was seasonal, and times of surplus labour were inevitable. Some labourers were surplus most of the time. Any scheme to remove these labourers had distinct attractions. Blyth, writing to the Manchester agent on 6 June 1837, who wanted to know if wages had changed and whether pauperism had diminished in the Docking Union, replied that there had indeed been a reduction in the number of agricultural labourers:

228

There were in this Union a great number of able hands more than were required for the proper and fair cultivation of the soil; I think there are still more than are absolutely necessary: when it appears, therefore, that in one year, ending October, 1836, 495 individuals migrated and emigrated with the assistance of their respective parishes, it is evident that the field of employment must be more beneficial to those who remained – not only by the removal of a great number of competitors from the labour market, but by the inducement given to the employer to increase the amount of labour upon his occupation in proportion as the expenses of maintaining the unemployed were diminished. Of the above number, 100 were migrants, of whom 37 were adults. I should say, therefore, ... that pauperism has been diminished to a great extent by this means alone.[5]

The expense of assisting these 495 individuals amounted to £1,726 7s. 3d., the money having come from the rates raised by the various parishes. Not all parishes assisted migrants and emigrants; but from some there were large numbers. For instance, there were ninety emigrants from North Creake and forty from Burnham Thorpe. Snettisham sent forty-seven emigrants and twenty-five migrants. None came from the Bircham parishes, but, as we have seen, four people wished to emigrate to America from Bircham Tofts in 1836, although nothing came of it. (See Chapter 5, VIII.)

Two years later, in 1838, a young man and his family from Great Bircham applied to be assisted in their passage to Australia. This was Robert Williamson, the same man who had been an early occupant of the workhouse refractory ward. The letter to the Poor Law Commission, written by the clerk of the Docking Union on 18 January 1838, stated that the parish officers had no objection to supporting the emigration, and felt that Williamson's was a worthy cause.[6]

As for Williamson, he had been a farm labourer, but latterly had worked with sheep. He was described as 'a strong healthy man', and his employers could give him 'a good character'. According to the rough draft of a reply from the Poor Law Commissioners, the passage would have cost £150 and they felt this was too much to come out of the rates. The Docking Board of Guardians was advised to apply for a free passage, and the Commissioners would then sanction raising money by the parish to cover expenses. These would include £2 a head for clothing; in addition, each person above seven years of age would be given 3d. a mile (under seven, 1½d.) to travel to the port. Francis Oakes, Clerk to the Docking Union, wrote back to the Commissioners on 1 February, saying the board would approach the emigration agent, and would consider the situation further.[7]

But who had been deceiving whom; and for what reason? The master of the workhouse appears to have had Williamson's measure. We have already seen how, in November 1836, his behaviour had been less than perfect. Worse was to come: a year later, on 1 November 1837, he received an order for the workhouse, repeated on 25 April 1838, and again on 26 September. We next come across him in the minutes on 15 May 1839. He was in the house with his family and he applied to go out and look for work, leaving his family there. The Great Bircham guardian was not present that day, and the board did not want to come to any decision until he returned. Williamson must have been allowed out, but apparently without success. On 10 July 1839, the master was seeking the board's sanction to send him to the Walsingham Bridewell for twenty days. This was because he had got drunk when out of the workhouse (he was by no means alone in that) and had been disorderly on his return. Unemployment and the need to provide for such a large family were often unbearable burdens for many of the labouring poor, and frustration could often break out into physical violence. We must, though, be cautious about dismissing the 'good character' given him by his employers. There is every chance he worked at Houghton, and Stephen Reeve knew him. His brother, William, was the Houghton shepherd. Even more intriguing is the entry in the minutes of 24 July 1839: we read that Ann Williamson applied for relief, while her husband was in the Bridewell. This was refused and she was given an order for the workhouse; yet the relieving officer reported that she had been privately relieved by the parish officer, which was an irregular procedure. The latter must have been John Kitton or Thomas Hebgin, and we can possibly detect a heart not completely devoid of sympathy for a destitute parishioner.

The application could have been made in good faith, therefore; or it could have been a way of ridding the parish of one of its less desirable inhabitants. That might well be a cynical view, but the expression 'shovelling out the poor' was used by anti-Poor Law commentators at the time. In April 1834, as the New Poor Law was making its passage through parliament, forty-five poor people from Briston set out for Canada. Whoever wrote to *The Bury Post* was quite clearly expressing a view prevalent at the time: the poor needed help but it would be best if that help were sometimes given in the form of easing them out of the country:

We trust these exertions to get rid of our superabundant poor, and to send them to a rising country, where they and their children may acquire independence, will soon be seconded by the Government. [8]

Certainly Blyth, in his letter of 6 June 1837, did not deny that the removal of surplus agricultural labourers to the northern industrial districts, or to the colonies, could work to the advantage of employers and their workers in the union. Those looking for migrants or emigrants were seeking people of good character and industrious habits; so much was a given. Yet parish officials were not bound to be scrupulously honest. They may have considered, too, the likelihood of the family becoming a burden on the rates for many years to come. There were six children, and some still very young, in Williamson's family. The week before the minutes recorded the possible migration to Australia, they also mentioned that Williamson had been given flour to the value of 4s., because of his illness. Perhaps they were prepared to give Williamson a chance. If he was strong and healthy they might well have thought he would prosper in Australia.

It was a long way to go and not something to be lightly contemplated. There is every chance, however, that Williamson had been told of the attractions of New South Wales. Still kept at Houghton Hall is a printed booklet entitled *Observations on the Advantages of Emigration to New South Wales for the information of the labouring classes in the United Kingdom.* (1836.) It paints a glowing picture of 'that healthy and prosperous colony', with 'the finest climate in the world'. Williamson had worked as a shepherd, so the claim that 'the soil is good and productive, and affords employment in the care of sheep and cattle' must have interested him. He would probably have been surprised to learn that there was no poverty:

231

The poverty, in the sense in which in parts of the United Kingdom it is bitterly felt and understood, is wholly unknown. Every husbandman is gladdened by abundance of all the necessaries, and not a few of the comforts of life. Indeed many, in the cool of the evening, after the labour of the day, have been known to give praise unto God, for His exceeding goodness, and to wish, that distant friends were amongst them to partake of their happy lot.

That was far removed from the daily experience of a Bircham labourer – or, no doubt, of many an Australian one.

We do not know the complete story, and can do no more than speculate. Robert Williamson never tended a flock of merino sheep and his children never got to see a kangaroo. He stayed in the area, and died in Dersingham in 1868.

Gary Howells, in a study of emigration from Norfolk in 1836, sees it essentially as a positive move and far from 'shovelling out the poor'.[9] We must surely see the embracing of Clause 62 in the same light as the digging scheme. They were both enthusiastically pursued by Blyth and the Docking Guardians, and were both intended to provide genuine help to the poor – always within the strict and unsentimental limits of men far removed socially and empathetically from their social inferiors. There is no reason to dismiss outright Blyth's statement in his 1836 report, that 'any number of families may do well out of emigration', and that the Docking Board 'have every reason to believe that they have been [the] means of contributing to the independent and permanent comfort of their poorer neighbours'. Nonetheless, all was not perfect in the colonies, and some emigrants failed.

One view of emigration was expressed by the Holkham agent in a letter to his Houghton counterpart in 1836, and this also hinted at the ridding by parishes of the less desirable sort of people. The letter had been sent in reply to a question as to the amount of money Thomas Coke provided for emigration. It was, in fact, never more than half the cost. The correspondent (William Barker) felt that too strong support for emigration might be harmful:

As to the consequences of Emigration I have my fears that it may be carried too far, particularly as you cannot choose your Emigrant, and it is beyond a doubt, that the best Labourers and most industrious persons are the people now leaving the Country.

It was quite clear that the New Poor Law had sent feelings of panic through the labouring population of North-west Norfolk:

We have not been affected with the emigrating mania until this season, and now they are leaving this neighbourhood to a very great extent, which I believe the operation of the New Poor Law Bill has been the principal cause of the lower class of people having absolutely taken fright at it.[10]

Notes

[1] TNA: MH 32/48, 7 May 1836.

[2] B. Allen, 'Perspectives on Poverty: The Divergent Approaches to the Poor Law Amendment Act 1834 with ParticulaReference to its impact in the Docking Union', Third Year Dissertation (Cambrudge University Board of Extra-mural Studies, 1990), p. 28.

[3] TNA: MH 32/48, 12 May 1836.

[4] A. Digby, Pauper Palaces (London), 1978, p.103.

[5] 3rd Annual Report of the PLC (1837), Appendix B, p.163

[6] TNA: MH 12/8250.

[7] ibid.

[8] BNP, 30 Apr. 1834.

[9] G. Howells, 'Emigration and the New Poor Law: The Norfolk Emigration Fever of 1836', *Rural History* (2000).

[10] HH: M8.

Chapter 8. The 'Ignorant' are to Know their Place

I. Discipline

Some families found employment beyond Norfolk; some were relieved on account of age or infirmity; and a small number went into the workhouse. Some of these went there to die, others were too young to do other than follow their parents. We shall return to these groups later, but we must remain a little while longer with the able-bodied men who entered the Docking Workhouse.

Grinding corn was their principal occupation, and we saw that the flour-mill was one of the early purchases for the house. Just after the opening of the house in December 1836, all seemed perfect, but there were inmates whose behaviour was far from docile. This book is about a violent reaction to the introduction of the New Poor Law, and now let us see how much that resistance was carried into the workhouse itself.

Pre-eminently a workhouse was about control and discipline. After all, so contemporary thinking went, the indigent pauper needed to be taught habits of industry, and was to be restored to the mythical moral state of the past. One almost insignificant entry in the guardians' minutes, made before the workhouse opened, reveals much about the scrupulous adherence to the rules. On 2 November 1836, the Visiting Committee reported at length on the state of the building, and one deficiency, they felt, was that the dining hall windows allowed an uninterrupted view from one yard to another. This was 'thought a great objection', and it was promptly ordered that the lower parts of the windows be covered up. The offence here was to do with the separation of the different categories of inmates, even if contact was purely visual; this was a fundamental tenet in the proper management of any workhouse. The guardians and workhouse masters had their rulebook, but for the poor such punctiliousness was not only petty, it was also heartless.

Yet discipline had to be maintained at all times. In the early days of the workhouse at least, the master sent off weekly returns to the Assistant Commissioner, and he must have been satisfied to report

234

that discipline was 'very strictly attended to'.[1] That cannot have been difficult, as there were only twelve inmates in the house. If the guardians were the officer class, the workhouse master was more akin to a sergeant major. It was to him that the former entrusted the efficient running of the establishment. The Docking Guardians were not above reprimanding the master, John Wilson, where necessary – their social standing was well above his – but only he could attend to the day-to-day running of the workhouse, and he had his rulebook to guide him at all times. The essence of his function within the operation of the New Poor Law can be stated thus:

To enforce industry, order, punctuality, cleanliness, and the observance of the several regulations herein contained, by the paupers in the workhouse, and by the several officers, assistants, and servants therein employed.[2]

How different from those noble sentiments on the inscription outside the Rollesby House of Industry! John Wilson, therefore, had much power. It cannot be said he misused it to any serious degree. He, in common with virtually every workhouse master, made mistakes, and he certainly clashed with other paid officers under his control; but in no way can he be judged to have been a cruel tyrant or abuser of the poor. Whether all paupers saw him in such light is far from certain. He had a job to do and his control, as in all workhouses, was essentially psychological. Was it so very different from the silent system which the Bircham rioters encountered in Walsingham Bridewell? That, too, was designed to change behaviour and attitude. Escape from the Bridewell was not easy, but workhouse inmates could manage to get away if they were careful. James George of East Rudham, a young man of twenty-two in the workhouse with his family, escaped in November 1838; but the master went after him and brought him back. He was brought before a magistrate and sent to the Bridewell (a real prison) for a month. For a brief period in 1839 it was even possible for the police officers to lodge a prisoner in the refractory ward of the workhouse overnight, before taking them before a magistrate; but on 11 August that practice was ended.

Wilson's rulebook outlined two categories of misbehaving pauper: (1) disorderly, (2) refractory. Behaviour distinguishing the first was less serious than the second, and included such offences as trying to enter the ward or yard of another class of pauper, not keeping clean, using obscene language or misbehaving when out of the workhouse. Any repeat of such offences within seven days would be deemed refractory behaviour; and so would violence against any person, insulting any workhouse officer, wilful or malicious damage, or being drunk. Sanctions for disorderly paupers – children under twelve, those over sixty, pregnant women and those still breast-feeding were normally exempted, unless the medical officer decided otherwise – usually took the form of a reduction in diet. For the refractory there was a special room, the refractory ward, and we know this was there right from the start, because Robert Williamson was confined in it. The Visiting Committee, at the board meeting of 20 December 1837, recommended an alteration to the refractory ward (called by them the 'penitentiary ward'), 'as it was considered too small for the number of inmates who at present occupied it'. There could also be a reduced diet, but confinement was not supposed to be longer than twenty-four hours. Corporal punishment with a rod was reserved for boys under fourteen. There was no lower age limit.[3]

All rules, as well as the dietaries, were displayed in the various rooms in the workhouse used by the inmates. Everything had to be above board and nobody was to be dealt with except according to the regulations. Henry Blyth was meticulous in ensuring that there was thorough observance of all procedures set out by the Poor Law Commission.

Besides the punishments described above, there were also reprimands from the chairman, who had to take on this headmaster's role when occasion demanded it. When Thomas Rhodes of North Creake appeared before the board on 28 November 1838, the scene, as described in the minutes, is pure naughty boy and admonishing head. He had falsified his register of age, signed by a clergyman, to make himself appear older than he was. A severe reprimand was delivered, but Rhodes was rather more than a low-level impostor: he was in the Bridewell when his wife had been given an order for the house in April 1838.

The outside of the former Walsingham Bridewell and the nineteenth century mill chimney. *(Photo 2011)*

Whether they received reprimands, were deemed disorderly and had their diet reduced, were held to be refractory, or were sent straight to prison, there were quite a few inmates – often men, but sometimes boys, girls and women – whose cases came before the Docking Board of Guardians between 1836 and 1851. To what extent breaches of the rules and abusive or violent behaviour were the result of being in an institution with a discipline that was alien to the inmates, or whether the offenders were simply of bad character, must remain an open question. The vast crowd that assembled at Great Bircham at the end of June 1835 must have included people whose conduct was far from admirable, even by the standards of the 1830s. We have also seen how threatening in their behaviour recipients of poor relief could be. Since many of these men (they were nearly always men) had frequently fallen foul of under-employment in this agricultural district and had suffered low wages over the years, it was hardly surprising that they were amongst those who were sent to the workhouse.

For most of their contemporaries, at least those of a higher social class, all those becoming so pauperized as to need to seek the refuge of the workhouse, were morally, even physically, degenerate. Their dissolute habits of idleness, drunkenness, filthiness and indecency, along with lesser ones such as enjoying a pipe of tobacco, were to be expunged, and they were to be made whole. The 'ignorant' had revolted at Great Bircham, but at least in the well-regulated workhouse a victory against ignorance might be achieved. They were to be tamed. The paupers, on the other hand, did not see their time spent in a workhouse as an opportunity to rid themselves of their degenerative vices, but as a punishment for being poor and out of work.

II. The Punishment of the Able-bodied

What kind of offences came most frequently before the Docking Board of Guardians? It cannot be denied some deeds committed in Docking Workhouse were nothing less than malicious acts of violence against persons or property. Such, for example, was the violent behaviour of Michael Mitchell, who, in March 1844, broke up the brick floor, smashed the door and made a great hole in the wall of the refractory ward. All could be explained, but not justified, by the sheer frustration of being shut up and regulated in the house; yet there were also incidents where our sympathies might be with the offending paupers. As already noted, it became quite common for men to ask to go out and look for work. Some took advantage of their freedom – perhaps

The punishment cell at Gressenhall Workhouse

238

they had no real intention of looking for work – and came back drunk. An early case was that of Thomas James (27) an unemployed man from Docking, with a wife and two children, who appeared before the board on 27 June 1838. The master reported that he had given him permission to leave the house in order to find work two days earlier, but that when he returned in the evening he was drunk. Moreover, his behaviour was very disorderly as he resisted being searched. A search discovered nearly 8 oz. of tobacco concealed about his person. Another example is of Thomas Wacey of South Creake, who had left the house in May 1839 and had come back very drunk. For that, he was put to bed naked and confined in the refractory ward. Isaac Everitt, South Creake guardian, questioned the master's treatment of Wacey, but was assured that he had not exceeded his authority. Here, then, was just what the morally deficient pauper did: he got drunk and smoked. The Metropolitan policemen charged with preserving order in the Docking Union, and the work-house schoolmaster responsible for the expulsion of vice and ignorance amongst his young charges, might both have over-indulged in alcohol, but that did not concern the guardians when they examined James. They decreed that his allowances should be reduced by a quarter, and that he should be refused leave to go out again.

Bringing tobacco back into workhouses must have been common. If they were to be able to find a quiet corner to enjoy a smoke the paupers returning from a search for work would first have to get past the porter. Being searched was something they bitterly resented. The two Mendham brothers from Bircham Newton – James (23) and Thomas (25) – were no strangers to the workhouse in the 1840s. On 25 July 1843 they, together with a third man, were ordered into the boardroom to answer the master's complaint that they had returned with concealed tobacco. Furthermore, James Mendham had refused to be searched and he threatened to strike the porter. For that, he was ordered to eat bread and potatoes only for his dinner for two days.

However, perhaps the defiance of the more desperate inmates gradually brought about an improvement in the treatment of the paupers by the porter. It is certainly true that the guardians came to show a little more fairness towards the former. At the board meeting of 10 December 1844, it was reported that an able-bodied man had gone out and returned with tobacco concealed in his neckerchief. The board felt the need to stress that the regulations did not forbid the possession of tobacco to chew. The master was told at the same meeting not to refuse permission to men wanting to leave the house to look for work or to go to church. A small shift in favour of the workhouse inmates, but progress of sorts; but all those who on their return behaved improperly were to be reported to the board.

In August 1846, an aged inmate called Robert Twiss of Dersingham started to give trouble; he was removed to the able men's ward and had his allowance of tea, sugar and tobacco stopped. It appeared that he was heading for a punishment. Soon his quarrelsome behaviour during meals led him into conflict with the porter. Twiss kicked the porter and the latter retaliated by knocking him down. The board considered the porter had been wrong to take the law into his own hands, and ordered him to inform them first if he wished to complain about any of the inmates. Twiss died in the workhouse in the December of that year aged 68. Old people behaving badly were a category of inmates the workhouse staff found difficult to handle, but that was also the case with women and children. Amongst workhouse staff in this period there was very little experience of dealing with the more challenging sections of humanity.

III Eventual Victory for the Non-conformists

Going to look for work was one reason to leave the house, and going to church was another. Inevitably that also led to conflict. The workhouse regulations drawn up by the Poor Law Commissioners made it quite clear that daily prayers should be said before breakfast and after supper, and that every Sunday all paupers, except the sick, the infirm, those of unsound mind and young children, must attend divine service. Naturally this was provided by the Established Church, although there were special arrangements for dissenters. Workhouse regulations also made it clear that dissenting ministers were allowed into a workhouse to see any pauper of the same religious persuasion. Nevertheless the guardians, on 8 March 1837, decided that no gentleman or clergyman could be admitted into the house to visit the paupers without an order from a guardian. Clause 43 of the Poor Law Amendment Act was invoked: it permitted a J.P., a medical man or the

'Officiating Clergyman of any Parish' to enter the workhouse without an order. The guardians were quite happy to restrict visitors to this narrow group, thereby severely limiting the visiting rights of dissenting ministers. The paupers in the workhouse were to be constrained within an Anglican box, as far as possible. All workhouses had a chaplain, and the first one to be appointed in Docking (at a salary of £50) was the Revd Edmund Senkler, a Docking resident, and the Perpetual Curate of Barmer.

Yet, it was to prove impossible to restrict the inmates of the Docking Workhouse to the Anglican path. Nonconformity was just too strong in the area and sooner or later paupers were going to ask to leave the workhouse on Sundays and go to their own places of worship. However, we must not be so naïve as to believe that requests to leave the house on Sundays were always for the purpose of worshipping God in a different setting from the workhouse chapel. On 26 February 1845, the master reported that Nathaniel Rennie, 45, and a single man from East Rudham, had had leave to go to church the previous Sunday, but had returned drunk. On the same day the board learned that paupers, who had gone out to church, had left as soon as the mid-service prayers were over. Several of the men were called in and admonished for their conduct, and were told permission to leave the house the following Sunday would be refused. Going to church or chapel, like going to look for work or simply leaving the house for a walk, must have been attractive to many inmates – if only to escape the stifling monotony of a life regulated by petty rules from morning till night. Here was an opportunity to return, if only briefly, to a former existence. The workhouse system, however, was not going to relinquish its grip on them. If depravity and ignorance were to be eliminated religion – the religion of the state – would need to be a major component in the guardians' armoury.

Sometimes paupers were bold enough to reject the doctrines of the Church of England, in the same way as some refused to work. On 22 January 1845, the master had to report to the board, and it was confirmed by the chaplain, that the able-bodied men had refused to go to the workhouse chapel the previous Sunday. The men were called in to the boardroom, and the chairman 'at considerable length addressed them on the impropriety of their conduct'. They were left in no doubt that a very severe punishment would follow any further defiance of the rules and regulations of the workhouse.

How typical such rebellion was is not clear, but it was a serious challenge to the regulations. Some paupers, probably a good number, did not object to going to services in the chapel; after all it was the one occasion in the week when families and separated couples could meet, even if the obligatory division of paupers into classes kept them at a distance. When there was no service in the workhouse chapel some inmates wanted still to worship, and then it was possible to ask to attend a service in more congenial surroundings. By February 1843, there was clearly a more tolerant attitude. John and Catherine Wagg, an aged couple from Great Bircham, sought permission to attend church or chapel outside the workhouse and this was granted. On 27 December 1843, they and Thomas Rhodes of North Creake (the same one who had attempted to falsify his age in 1838) had applied to go to the Wesleyan Chapel in Docking on a Sunday when there was no service in the workhouse, and their application found favour; but they had to return immediately the service was over.

The Primitive Methodists, who were invariably called Ranters in the minutes, were not as lucky as the Wesleyans. That revolutionary sect with its millennarian dreams, so strongly supported in the Bircham parishes, was obviously not to be encouraged amongst the paupers of Docking Workhouse, hostility even extending to an old couple in their seventies. On 8 May 1844, John Sheldram and his wife were allowed to go to the Wesleyan Chapel, but Charles Claxton (78) and his wife (75) of East Rudham, were refused permission to go to the Primitive Methodist Chapel. The next request to attend a Ranters' service came on 30 October 1844 from James Francis (39, Docking), Robert Rose (31, West Rudham) and Thomas Ayton (34, Syderstone). They too were refused, but on 5 February 1845 permission was finally given. Edward Townsend (22, Bircham Newton), Robert Wacey (40, South Creake) and William Lack (34, South Creake) were among a group of six who successfully applied to go either to the Ranters or the Independents.

IV Separation of Men and Women

Seeking permission to go out of the workhouse was not the only source of conflict between master and pauper. There was also the question of separation of classes. There were actually seven of these: able-bodied men, able-bodied women, boys aged seven to fourteen, girls aged seven to fourteen, children under seven, infirm and aged men, infirm and aged women. Strictly speaking they should have been totally separated and given their own wards, but in practice young children often stayed with their mothers. The separation which is best known and, like gruel, pauper uniform and eating in silence, has become an enduring aspect of workhouse mythology, is that of married couples. Poor Law Commissioner George Nicholls, a former navy man, had no truck with anybody objecting to this, as it was normal in the navy for men to be apart from their wives, sometimes for several years.[4] The labourers of Norfolk, like virtually all English paupers, did not share his view, and their hatred of this totally unnatural state of affairs was almost universal. Nonetheless, certainly as far as the older inmates were concerned, we must concede that the Docking Guardians were sympathetic towards aged couples. As early as 9 August 1837, they reported that a man and his wife, both aged seventy, had been admitted into the house, but had not been separated. And on 14 February 1838, we read that the women Nichols and Williamson applied to the board to stay with their husbands, and that the master had found a separate ward for them. The guardians were entering difficult territory here, however: the previous week they had had to order the separation of two couples they had permitted to be together, as they were always quarrelling and annoying other inmates.

When it came to younger couples the situation was different, and in keeping with the harshness of the Poor Law Amendment Act. On 31 July 1844 three men made a spirited challenge against the law. James Doughty (24, with a wife and one child) from South Creake, came to ask for relief, but when an order for the house was made out he said he would not be parted quietly from his wife. In consequence relief was refused him and he was dismissed. John (or Thomas) Covell, 25, of Ingoldisthorpe next entered the room. He was already an inmate of the house, the order having been made on 17 January, and his wife and three children were also in the workhouse. He wanted to know whether it was lawful to part man and wife, and requested to have his wife with him. The board ordered the whole family to be discharged. It was indeed the law of the land, and now these two families had to cope as best they could without any assistance from the Docking Union.

At this point it is worthwhile to introduce the comments of one contemporary who was not a poor law union guardian, a member of the gentry, or a farmer. The voices of the poor were largely unrecorded, and here is someone, albeit a Roman Catholic Irishman, a gentleman's gamekeeper and not a mere farm labourer, who could speak with real conviction and from personal observation. Larry Banville, gamekeeper to Lord Buxton of Cromer from 1823 to 1869, visited the Sheringham Workhouse in October 1836, and witnessed the separation of the different classes in the workhouse chapel. His account of what he saw shows graphically the sheer absurdity of much that went on under the New Poor Law:

What a disgraceful system is used there by the clergymen that is to preach for the poor. There is 2 rooms, or otherwise one large one and boards put in the middle of it. The parson is to stand so as to see into the two apartments, then the poor men is to be in one part, the women in the other and not to see each other ... although been joined together by the same creed that they are under at this time.

Then later in his diary, he wrote about an incident at Gimingham Workhouse, and expressed sentiments that must have been universal amongst the poor:

At Gimingham the other night the men got each of them to their own wives and there is a great row about it. What a cursed law to take a man's wife away from them on account of being poor in this blessed country ...[5]

V. Food

The separation of married couples is one aspect of workhouse life known by many; another was what pauper inmates had to eat.

It was true that many paupers had not always been able to eat regularly and adequately outside the house. Working under the principle of less eligibility, the Poor Law Commissioners had decreed in 1835 that a workhouse diet should never be 'superior or equal to the ordinary mode of subsistence of the labouring classes of the neighbourhood'. By the same token, though, it should have been more than required merely to keep a person alive. The labourers of the area certainly could, and sometimes did, eat quite well; but not all of them. Within a family the male adults were often able to eat enough for them to earn a living at the expense of wives and children. It all depended on the regularity of work; and outside the workhouse it was frequently possible to supplement one's diet by the occasional rabbit caught in a trap. There was always charity, of course; and the Cholmondeleys provided many a treat for the poor of the parishes on the Houghton Estate. When times were hard, and work was lacking, a family's food was often inadequate. Within the workhouse at least there were regular meals.

From the end of 1835, the various poor law unions had a series of model dietaries from which to choose. It was never expected that there should be complete unanimity across England and Wales, as regional differences would always prevail. There was scope for even some small variation from the published dietaries. Just before the Docking Workhouse opened its doors to the first inmates in December 1836 the guardians decided on their dietary, which had been slightly adapted from that of the Bosmere and Claydon Union. They submitted it to the Commissioners in London, who found it 'in every respect unobjectionable'.[6] (See Appendix D.)

But was it adequate? In the fourth decade of the nineteenth century, knowledge of the true nutritional value of food was not as advanced as it is today; yet even in 2013 there are so many opposing views on what is good or bad to eat that many people in the developed world remain confused. In the Norfolk of the period covered in this book, it was quite clear that an adult male agricultural labourer needed a daily calorific intake sufficient to allow him to perform the physically demanding tasks on the farm. What did Sir Edward Parry have to say?

Parry, in common with all others who had given some thought to the subject, was concerned essentially with the weight of food consumed. Naturally for his expeditions a vessel was limited in the amount of weight it could carry, and there were arduous tasks to be performed, such as pulling boats across the ice. The extreme cold influenced the daily intake of food, and it was found that twenty-seven or twenty-eight ounces of food per day (which yielded twenty-two or twenty-three ounces of nutritive value) were sufficient. Far less – something like ten ounces of nutritive value - was required by an agricultural labourer undertaking normal farm tasks. These findings of Parry strongly influenced Assistant Commissioner Charles Mott, who published the 1836 dietaries.[7] The daily average intake of food provided for an able-bodied man by the Docking 1836 dietary was twenty-three ounces; for Mott this would have been nutritious enough. There were, however, other dietaries which provided a greater intake.

Peter Higginbotham cites the 1991 daily recommended Dietary Reference Values (DRV) for males aged nineteen to fifty-nine years, and he assessed the adequacy of the six model workhouse dietaries according to these values. He found an overall deficit in energy of about 25%. Workhouse meals consisted largely of bread, and there were sometime potatoes (grown on the workhouse premises in Docking); even so the carbohydrate intake was less than the DRV. Even worse was the vast difference between the dietaries and the DRV for fat. There was a daily allowance of cheese, and the meat contained fat; but it was seriously inadequate.[8] As for vitamins and the value of fruit and vegetables, that had to wait for many years.

The Guardians' Minutes contain some examples of paupers complaining about their food. There is a minor complaint in the report of the Visiting Committee of 14 December 1836: the able-bodied men said there were not enough potatoes on Sunday, although the meat was quite sufficient. More serious was the complaint made by Christmas Callaby, of Docking, on 1 November 1837. He came as a spokesman for the other men, and stated they had not got sufficient to eat; he hoped the board would give them more. Both the chairman and Captain Davy were able to hide behind the Poor Law Commissioners' regulations, which could not be altered; however, the following week it was decided to adopt another of the model dietaries.

Now, it was part of the workhouse regulations that the amount of food allowed should be clearly displayed, and that there should be scales in the dining areas in order that anybody who so wished could verify they were not being cheated. On 20 December 1843, Robert Boulton, a pauper from Sedgeford, complained that the provisions were short of weight. He also used his appearance before the board to make more complaints. The chairman declared he would 'proceed immediately to the able-bodied men's wards and caution them against the ill spirit or feeling that they now evinced to the Orders and Regulations of the House, and that they certainly would be punished if they continued in the same state of insubordination, as they were in at present'. Boulton would not be the first pauper to be cowed in front of the board; however, the chairman did admit the short weight would be remedied.

There were other modifications to the dietaries, and the master was able to report on occasion that there was general satisfaction. This did not reach Thomas Ayton and Samuel Rush of Sedgeford. On 8 January 1845, they also said the food was not adequate. They were quite content that the master had weighed the quantities correctly, but there was simply not enough food. Inevitably the board could do nothing, as they said they had remodelled the dietaries at the request of the paupers themselves.

It would appear that, at least for the adult males, the food was not always considered to be sufficient. Again, in 1849, a further change was made, and the amount of bread increased. As for quality, that too must have been in doubt. A month after the complaint of the Sedgeford men, the Visiting Committee reported that some of the able-bodied men had also complained of the quality of the food. Considering the frequent complaints appearing in the minutes about food supplied to the workhouse, this was hardly surprising, but the complaint was considered to be 'entirely groundless'. Finally, during a cholera epidemic, a more liberal diet was ordered by the medical officer of the house; but in July 1849 it was reported that several paupers under the present dietary had scurvy; three had died and some others were severely affected.[9]

VI. The Paupers become more Disorderly

It is evident from the minutes that the mood of the mid-1840s was quite different from the artificial optimism of December 1836, when the Visiting Committee reported so optimistically to the full board.

Ten years on, with more people in the house (although it was nowhere near filled to its capacity), things had changed and there was a definite sense of unease. There were more violent attacks against the officers, more punishments given, even to children. For instance on 17 January 1844, James Eke of South Creake, let out of the workhouse the previous week, returned later than he should have done and his insolence to the master earned him forty-eight hours in the refractory ward. On 20 March 1844, it is recorded that John Smith of Docking had received the same punishment for assaulting the schoolmaster and threatening the porter. Moreover, the master said he must be further confined when he applied to leave the house with his wife and family. Things were no better a year later, as on 5 March 1845 there is this short entry: 'The able-bodied paupers were reported to be in a state of insubordination, and one man is in custody.' The following week, the master's report stated that 'several of the paupers who left the house during the past week were very disorderly'. It did look as if Wilson was finding some of the pauper inmates increasingly difficult to subdue. The same names kept appearing in the minutes, as they presented themselves at the workhouse and asked for relief; and the same inmates reappeared among those punished. Agriculture was in a depressed state in the 1840s, and work was hard to find. The workhouse regime was now becoming well known and the master and porter were the officers who had to deal directly with these disorderly and refractory paupers. They must have been the first targets of desperate men.

The master had the twin sanctions of a temporary reduction in diet or the refractory ward. In December 1844, the board had to remind him that he had exceeded his authority and gone beyond the rules and regulations laid down by the Poor Law Commission. This is an important moment in the life of the workhouse in the 1840s, and we shall return to it later.

VII. Troublesome Boys in the Workhouse

Boys were the only ones to whom corporal punishment could be administered. This was supposed to be by a rod or cane on the bottom and was not given to any male above the age of fourteen. Only the schoolmaster or master of the workhouse could carry out the punishment. Twenty-first century values have no place here, because physical chastisement in the first half of the nineteenth century was very common. Children of Docking Union families who went to northern mill towns in the 1830s, and who were not nimble enough around the looms, could expect to be hit with leather straps. Victorian society grew to be very sentimental about children, but many working-class fathers were quick to beat their children – and their wives. The Bircham Riots need to be firmly set within the context of an often violent and brutal society.

On 12 June 1839, the schoolmaster complained that the boy Wright and the boy Langley had been fighting. They were called into the boardroom and reprimanded, and 'half their dinners to be stopped'. This serious reduction in diet should have been for a short time only, as was stipulated by the regulations. Nevertheless it was no hardship for the boys, since a boy on reduced rations could always find a way of being fed. On 15 February 1843, George Allen of Sedgeford was brought to the attention of the guardians, because he had been several times reported as being disorderly. Both schoolmaster and master declared they could do nothing with him. The master also stated that punishing the boys 'by stopping their dinners was of no use; as the other boys always took something away with them in their pockets for them'. In March 1839, the minutes had made reference to the 'irregularity' of the children at meal times; evidently discipline in the house was not all it should have been, and food could easily be secreted in pockets. The master was directed to flog Allen that afternoon, and the following week John Wilson 'reported that the Boy George Allen was flogged on Wednesday last, as directed by the Board and received one dozen strokes with a Cane across his Bottom with his clothes on; which had made him, and others in the school to behave much better'. Even so it was quite a severe punishment for a boy of twelve or thirteen.

Fighting between boys (and girls) was not uncommon, as would always be the case in any institution. These disturbed adolescents found themselves shut up in a totally alien environment, and they were forced to abide by a relentless daily routine. They were allowed out, under supervision, to gain a little exercise, and there are instances of the schoolmaster taking them out for a walk, which cannot have been an easy duty for him. One type of behaviour deemed disorderly was not to keep oneself clean. Many inmates had come from very poor homes where washing the person was not routinely done. The New Poor Law wanted to cleanse the body and thereby to swill off the accretions of licentiousness and vice. It will come as no surprise to anyone who has brought up boys to learn that, on 5 February 1840, the Visiting Committee reported the girls were clean, but that the boys were very dirty. One specific example is that of a young boy called Charles Bridges.

His mother, Jane Bridges of Snettisham, presented herself and three children at the workhouse on 15 April 1840. She had been deserted by her husband, and all she was granted was an order for the house. The following week out-relief was refused. On 20 May 1840, Margaret, Charles and Elizabeth Bridges (9, 6, and 4 years of age) were brought by their grandmother to the workhouse, as they had now been deserted by both parents. There was nowhere else for them to go, but before the grandmother departed, she was informed that the parish would be applying to her husband for the children's maintenance. Here, then, was a family barely functioning, and three young children shut away from any hope of a stable environment outside the house. The temple of cleanliness had nonetheless to be honoured. The Visiting Committee reported, on 19 May 1841, that Charles Bridges was an extremely filthy boy. He would have been aged seven but he was called into the boardroom, and received, in the beloved phrase of the clerk, 'a severe reprimand'. Worse than that, the master was directed 'to punish him at his discretion by stopping his dinner or supper two or three times a week, till he left off his dirty habits'.

This stoppage of food, provided it could be done, seems to us particularly inhuman, and no doubt many opponents of the workhouse system thought the same. In November 1842 Charles Wright (13) had his meat stopped at dinner for a week following misconduct. The following week the master reported this had been done, and the same punishment had been meted out to two other boys for 'behaving improperly'.

Degrading and vicious the punishments might have been, but they continued through the 1840s, and, if anything, grew harsher and more frequent. This reflected the growing insubordination of the house and the increasing number of difficult paupers there. The New Poor Law was undoubtedly underpinned by idealism, but it is extremely doubtful whether this touched many of the families who were forced to enter the Docking Workhouse. Even a casual reading of the minutes quickly shows the same names cropping up over several years. Charles Wright was typical, although in fairness to the board they did try to encourage him go to sea in 1845, when he was sixteen, and allowed him new clothes. Yet he must have sorely tested the patience of various schoolmasters and the master. In October 1843 a young boy, John Bullock (7) stole the schoolmaster's watch from his private room. Wright (14) must have put him up to it, and the two of them then 'did wilfully break it to pieces and throw it away'. Wilson must have been at his wit's end and took the boys before the magistrates, who recommended his keeping the boys in the refractory ward until the next board meeting. At this meeting, the magistrates on the board first considered sending them off to Walsingham Bridewell and then to be tried at the Quarter Sessions of 27 October. They reconsidered their decision later, and directed that the boys be kept in the refractory ward for another week. Such punishment was very harsh, especially when one boy was so very young. Furthermore, we are hard put to see a distinction between a workhouse and a prison. The length of the first period in the refractory ward could just about be deemed within the regulations, which decreed that paupers could be detained in a refractory ward longer than twenty-four hours only if they were to be later taken before a magistrate. The second period was nothing but another form of imprisonment, and that without a trial. It was also completely against the rules.

The minutes of 1 November 1843 make for rather chilling reading, and the clerk had to find something stronger than 'severe reprimand' this time:

The Boys Bullock and Wright, who took the schoolmaster's watch out of his private room, and broke it to pieces were again brought before the Board – the Schoolmaster with the remainder of the Boys attended when the

Chairman in a very impressive manner, addressed the Boys on the enormity of their crime and directed the master at the suggestion of the Board that he should well flog with a rod, in the presence of the other boys - the Boy Chas Wright twice during the present week, and the Boy Jno Bullock once – and all their meat dinners to be stopped for a fortnight - to have only bread instead of meat ...

John Bullock was obviously not chastened by this experience, since five years later, on 7 February 1848, he and another boy absconded when out walking with the schoolmaster. They got as far as Walsoken, and were brought back from there by a police officer. On 23 February, the master was ordered to flog Bullock 'with a rod for absconding with Clothes belonging to Docking Union, he being an old offender'.

This is all very depressing and reminds us that some sort of progress has been made since the 1840s, although the beating of young boys sadly lasted well into a period within living memory. There were probably few guardians, if any, who blanched at the physical chastisement of a seven-year-old. They had a duty to perform and that was to arrest the moral decline of a section of the rural working class; and if that involved flogging young children, feeding them on bread instead of meat and confining them within a workhouse prison, then that is what they had to do.

Notes

[1] TNA: MH 12/8250.
[2] 8th Report of PLC (1842), p.92
[3] ibid. p.55-58
[4] G. Nicholls, *A History of the English Poor Law* (London 1898), p.302.
[5] N.Virgoe and S.Yaxley, *The Banville Diaries, Journals of a Norfolk Gamekeeper 1822-44*, (London 1986), pp. 163-64.
[6] TNA: MH 12/8249.
[7] 2nd Annual Report of the PLC (1836), Appendix A. pp.63-68
[8] P. Higginbotham, *The Workhouse Cookbook* (Stroud 2008), p. 56.
[9] TNA: MH12/8253.

Chapter 9. Women

I The Punishment of Women

In the minutes of 28 February 1838, there is mention of a letter from James Kay about the punishment of refractory women. Kay was replying to a letter from the Docking Union Chairman. The previous week, some women had left the house saying they were frightened by noises. The women had been put in the refractory ward and it would appear that Blyth did not know what to do with such women. Kay's recommended punishment was to make them wear a 'different and marked dress', and to change and decrease their allowances. After a discussion, the guardians decided to put all the women on a bread and flour diet instead of meat. Perhaps we can be charitable to Blyth and his colleagues: they did have the right 'to direct that a dress different from that of the other inmates shall be worn by disorderly and refractory paupers, during a period of not more than forty-eighty hours, jointly with or in lieu of the alteration of diet to which any such pauper might be subjected'. What was unlawful was for them 'to cause any penal dress or distinguishing mark of disgrace to be worn by any adult pauper or class of adult paupers, unless such pauper or paupers shall be disorderly or refractory'.[1] Disorderly or refractory conduct was subject to precise definition, and the guardians wanted to be quite sure about the exact nature of the punishment they could inflict on these women. The question of special dress for women will reappear later.

Just what had they done wrong? Clearly running off was a serious offence, and it was quite easy to bring a charge of theft, as their uniform was the property of the poor law union. This seems rather different because they had complained of hearing noises. Unfortunately, as no names appeared in the minutes, we do not know who these women were, or even how many there were. In the weeks before the incident there had been the usual crop of offers of the house. Several were for whole families, and others were for single women, usually with children. Some of the women may have taken their children with them, but that would have been possible only if the children were young enough to be in the same ward. No doubt they had genuinely given the 'noises' as their reason for leaving the house, but that might have been purely frivolous, and they too merely wanted to enjoy some freedom outside the grim walls of the Docking Workhouse. Yet, a short minute of 14 February mentioned a letter from Assistant Commissioner Kay about the master's ability to have communication at night with any of the wards. Is it not possible that they felt insecure in this great building and their fear of others entering their ward was perfectly genuine? The guardians, of course, would not have seen the matter through the eyes of pauper women, some of whom they probably considered as little better than whores.

The New Poor Law set itself the lofty, and impossible, aim of eradicating the immorality which transformed the poor into paupers. In the case of men, moral degeneracy – thus believed many observers in the 1830s - manifested itself in idleness and intemperance of various kinds. As for their women, they had strayed far from their dutiful path of servitude and motherhood and had shown no shame in bearing illegitimate children. Some of the views of contemporary Norfolk pamphleteers are perhaps instructive. In 1836, the Revd John Fellowes, Rector of Shotesham (in the Henstead Union) published a pamphlet, in which he outlined and supported the principal clauses of the Poor Law Amendment Act. His pamphlet was an attempt to persuade the poor that much good could come of it. The 1834 Act made it very much harder for mothers of illegitimate children to obtain affiliation orders, as had been the practice in the past, and effectively shifted the responsibility of raising illegitimate children onto the mothers. Naturally any of them unable to fulfil their maternal obligations had to enter the workhouse. For Fellowes, and no doubt for many of the Docking Guardians too, it was simply a crime to bear a bastard child:

The object and intention of the legislature in this enactment is to put, as far as possible, the most effectual check upon a crime which in former days was attended with such deep and lasting disgrace, but which unhappily of late years has been too commonly spoken of by the offending party and later connections, merely as an accident or misfortune, and hardly considered any crime at all, or any serious blot upon the woman's character.[2]

Another pamphlet of 1839, *The Nature and Design of the New Poor Law, explained in an address to the labouring classes by a Norfolk Clergyman*, had more telling observations on the infamous Bastardy Clauses of the 1834 Act. The author, Samuel Hobson, concedes that the clause by which a woman is compelled to support her illegitimate offspring is a harsh one, and he does admit that a woman can be seduced, but even so her own credulity stands condemned: ' "Weaker vessel" though she may be, she cannot fall without her own consent.' He is adamant that unchaste women should be punished. For him they had all departed from the path of virtue, and unchastity must be seen as a stigma. As for 'those abandoned females, who not only do not check, but absolutely invite, the approaches of licentious men', they were far worse than the fathers of their children. For them a severe punishment was essential, otherwise the whole of womankind stood in danger of being irretrievably corrupted. The only treatment for such lewd and degenerate women was to send them to a workhouse. Hobson concludes: 'but let me again remind you, that she is put into this painful and humiliating situation, not from a vindictive desire of punishing and disgracing her, but that thousands of other females may be saved from infamy and wretchedness.'[3] As we shall see shortly, this was precisely the attitude that prevailed among the guardians of the Docking Poor Law Union when they decided to make an example of some of their female inmates.

II. Deserted Women

The onslaught on women in the Docking Union did not stop at those with illegitimate offspring. It was at a meeting of the guardians on 8 November 1837, attended by Kay, that the Assistant Commissioner outlined at some length the policy of awarding outdoor relief. He stated that 'all out relief ought to be denied to the wives and families of men who have absconded, or are in prison for any offence'. Twenty-first century sensibilities are revolted by this cruel treatment of innocent women and children, but the entire armoury of the New Poor Law system was directed against a whole group: the supposedly morally rotten section of the labouring poor.

Indications of a sympathetic attitude towards deserted women paupers did become clear later, but not in the early years of the union, where wives of those convicted of serious offences were concerned. Take three examples from the Rudhams from the minutes of 25 January 1837: Sarah Hamond (with three children), and Ann Hamond (also three children) from East Rudham, both with husbands transported for sheep-stealing, received orders for the workhouse. On the same day the master had to report that he had been obliged to take Susan Pile, of West Rudham, before the magistrates for misconduct and ill behaviour, and that she had subsequently been committed to Walsingham Bridewell for fourteen days. Here is an example of a woman inmate apparently capable of the same level of disorder as some of the men we have already encountered; but Pile's case was not a simple one.

Susan Pile, with four children, appeared before the board on 14 December 1836. It had been supposed that her father could maintain the family, but he was not able to do so; the guardians allowed her 1s. 4d. and 1½ stones of flour for one week. If they thought she was worth a chance, it did not work, because on 4 January 1837 she received an order for the house. We can only surmise what pressures brought her before the magistrates within the next two weeks. It must have seemed to her that not only was her husband to be punished with transportation for life to Australia, but that she and her children were to receive a similar punishment and to be incarcerated in Docking Workhouse. She might have been a violent woman, but she did not cease to care for her children after they had all been sent to the workhouse. On 18 October 1837, she applied for clothing for her daughter of thirteen, who had gone into service. She was given 10s. on this occasion, although two years later, when she tried to obtain clothing for her son of fourteen, the case was dismissed. Similarly, in August 1841, she failed to remove her two younger children, aged eleven and eight, in order that they might be relieved at home. There were other concerns, too: it was reported of her daughter Martha on 21 August 1839 that 'the Girl Pile is again showing symptoms of scrofula'. Martha Pile gave the medical staff and the guardians not a little trouble, and appeared several times before the board to have her head examined for further signs of eruption.

The cases of Pile and the two Hamonds were from a period when Blyth and his fellow guardians were still feeling their way. They were possibly a little too zealous in the implementation of the Poor Law Amendment Act; moreover, in James Kay, they had an Assistant Commissioner of great energy and determination. By 11 March 1840, there was a new Assistant Commissioner, and he was present at the weekly board meeting. He stated that any woman whose husband had deserted her could claim outdoor relief on behalf of any children under seven. Although he was personally against it, he assured the guardians it was within the meaning of the act

III The Marshams of Great Bircham

There was one deserted Great Bircham family for whom the outcome was favourable. Moreover it involved one of the convicted rioters. This was Thomas Marsham, who had received a very short penal sentence of one week. The judge had no doubt taken pity on him because his wife had died soon after the end of the riots, and his 'sincere contrition' was useful to his cause. The judge recognized that the loss of Rebecca Marsham, the mother of his six children, was a blow, and he must have hoped that Marsham would redouble his efforts to stand by them. A baby had been baptized on 7 June 1835, and that may have influenced the judge too. Marsham might well have tried to support his family, but if he did it was not to last. On 5 May 1839, now out of work, he received an order for the workhouse; and there was another order on 16 October. By the following week, Marsham had deserted the family and the children (four of them under sixteen) were also given an order for the house. Marsham's subsequent life can be seen, at least in outline, from the censuses. He went into Lincolnshire and continued as an agricultural labourer. In 1871 he was in Spalding Workhouse, and it was here he probably died in 1874, aged 88. His eldest child, also called Thomas, stayed in the village until his death, at the age of 68 in 1884. In 1861 he was enumerated as a teamsman. He married Mary Ewer, niece of the rioter John Pilgrim. It is, however, with Marsham's daughters that we see the real change of fortune.

On 27 November 1839, his daughter Hannah, aged 20, appeared in the workhouse boardroom and asked for some assistance towards the maintenance of the family. She was given 1s. and 2 stones of flour. On 18 December, the relief was increased by an extra shilling a week.

We next hear of Hannah with her brothers and sisters on 14 April 1841. Hannah was a schoolmistress and earned 3s. 10d. a week; some of the children earned 1s. 6d. She asked for clothing for the children and was give £2. The following month she was ill and had 2s. 3d. extra by medical order. There was further relief in March 1843, April 1845, April 1846 and September 1847. The siblings were fewer by then but Hannah clearly took on the role of mother and saw to it that some relief was made available to them.

We must, therefore, claim the Marsham family as a success. Hannah, in particular, did well for herself. As a schoolmistress, she was undoubtedly further up the social tree than others in her family. She and her sisters, Catherine and Rebecca, were Primitive Methodists, so we must presume that Hannah did not teach in the Church of England school. By the time of the 1851 census, Hannah had abandoned the fight against ignorance amongst the children of Great Bircham in favour of clothing the bodies of their mothers. She and her sisters Rebecca and Maria were enumerated as milliners and dressmakers; in addition, Hannah was employing six apprentices.

We cannot tell how successful the three Marsham sisters would have been, as they all died at a comparatively young age – Hannah in 1859; Rebecca (who had married a tailor and draper) and Maria in 1860. Mary Marsham, the fourth daughter (born 1828), did achieve a measure of success in her life. She too became a teacher, and on 26 September 1849 was appointed schoolmistress in the Docking Workhouse. On 9 January, the clerk was able to inform the Poor Law Board (the successor of the Poor Law Commission) that 'Mary Marsham the Schoolmistress has discharged the duties of her Office since her appointment to the satisfaction of the Board'. There was more to come: she later became matron of the workhouse, following the death of John Wilson's wife in 1855. She was still there in 1861.

In the eyes of many in Great Bircham the Marsham girls might have been seen as class traitors. Running a small business and employing apprentices was a distinct move up the social ladder. The work was very demanding, especially on the eyes. We cannot discount the help, however modest, they received from the Docking Guardians; and it is surely not fanciful to state that Kitton and Hebgin were not hostile to assisting the children of a rioter. Further research can possibly reveal more about Mary Marsham at the workhouse. She might have been a martinet and the women and children inmates might have walked in fear of her. Yet, there is absolutely no reason for believing that, and all we can say with certainty is that her rise represents genuine success. For one thing it was a sign of enlightened progress that a non-conformist became a teacher in the workhouse. It would be a long time before working-class guardians were elected, but right from the start men and women from labouring families occupied positions such as nurse or porter in the workhouses. Mary Marsham would have known what poverty was and understood the troubles of her female charges. Her role as schoolmistress was a vital one: helping to dispel the 'ignorance' that was rife among the children of pauper families.

IV The Punishment of Girls

This task cannot have been an easy one in Docking Workhouse. As we have seen, some of the women inmates could be difficult. Troubles often started with the girls in the school, and a couple of examples are illustrative here; in one case a positive move forward, not just for girls and women, but also for able-bodied men can be seen.

First the case of Charlotte Wright of Burnham Overy. She was aged fourteen when she was given an order for the house, with her eight-year-old brother Charles, on 6 December 1837. They were both orphans. It is obvious that many inmates of the workhouse, as in all institutions, were difficult to handle, and the Wright children were no exception. A year later, on 12 December 1838, the guardians had to consider a letter from the Poor Law Commission, which required them to conduct an inquiry into the alleged mistreatment of the girl Wright by the officers of the workhouse. The master was summoned and he recounted the habits of this problematic adolescent: '... the Girl on the entrance into the House had used herself to such filthy and disgusting habits by indecently exposing her person, and dirtying the House at any time and place most convenient, in the presence of other children'. It is clear that she was an extremely disturbed child, and even today such a girl would present her carers with a serious challenge. John Wilson was out of his depth. He had first tried to reason with her, but had soon given in to his frustration, and had applied a cane across her shoulders, and once or twice he had rubbed her nose in the dirt. In the former he had sailed very close to the wind, because any physical chastisement of female inmates was strictly against regulations. As for the latter, it cannot be many years since that has ceased to happen in various institutions. He had finally achieved some kind of victory by correcting her in front of the other children in the dining room, but the nature of the correction was not revealed.

The girl was brought before the board, and faced with nine stern and articulate men she stood no chance whatsoever; but that was the case with virtually all the paupers who were forced to place themselves in the intimidating situation of the boardroom, no matter how just their cases were. Charlotte Wright confirmed that all the master had said was correct, that she had also been punished by the schoolmistress for not knowing her lessons. She denied that her punishment had ever been severe and that she had indeed deserved it. She said her dirty habits had now stopped and that she perfectly understood that she would be kindly treated as long as she behaved properly.

It was too much to expect that her behaviour would improve. In March 1839, she, together with two other girls, was brought before the board by the schoolmistress for fighting and swearing. They all promised better behaviour, but still had half their food stopped for two days. A further complaint would put them in the refractory ward, and that was precisely where Wright ended up – 'shut up by herself' – at the end of May. This time it had been because of not speaking in class and neglecting her duties. In June, again on the complaint of the schoolmistress, she had a day in the refractory ward; and the inevitable occurred on 10 July 1839, when she was sent to the Bridewell for fourteen days for unspecified 'disobedience and misconduct'. The downward slope was now too slippery for anybody to hold her. Hardly had she been released when the minutes (7 August 1839) record, in words that betray the utter futility of the master's position, that she was being 'directed to behave properly'. By this time she had been transferred to the able-bodied women's ward, but that brought about no improvement. The familiar pattern of leaving the house and then being given an order to return soon afterwards continued. On 5 May 1841, she was severely reprimanded by the board for gross misconduct and once more threatened with the Bridewell. One can barely imagine how she was living when outside the workhouse; on 22 September 1841, she was reported by the master to have been in a 'very filthy state' when she returned to the house. The system clearly could do nothing for her. When she came on 8 February 1843 to apply for some clothing, she was described as 'not of good character'. She was given no clothing but received an order for the house, which she refused. Her life outside the workhouse must have been a desperate one. In 1846 she was admitted yet again into the house, having been found destitute in Bircham Tofts.

The master also used physical restraint in the case of an aged woman pauper, Margaret Gay. On 19 December, he was compelled to attend the board because somebody had written to the Assistant Commissioner to say that Gay had been strapped to the bed by the master. We can probably just about excuse Wilson, assuming his explanation was correct. The pauper had been very noisy and quarrelsome and refused to go to her bed quietly. He stated that he had strapped her to the bed for a few minutes only, and the porter and other aged inmates had been present. It is also possible that one of the schoolmasters 'several times' used corporal punishment against one Sarah Chapman, in August 1842. He denied the accusation, and it is equally possible that the workhouse master was trying to discredit him.

The other case involves two or three girls called Willoughby from Hunstanton. They were also orphans. There is every indication of the same waywardness that afflicted Charlotte Wright: the minutes of 19 January 1842 record that when the Girl Willoughby had recently been out of the house 'she went about begging in the neighbouring villages'. On her return her conduct earned her a severe reprimand (that favourite phrase of the clerk) from the chairman, and a threat of the Bridewell for any repetition of such behaviour. Then, in February 1844, we learn that a Girl Willoughby had been in service with the Whartons of Great Ringstead (the position having been found for her by the board) but that the Whartons had been unable to do anything with her, and when the master of the workhouse had been summoned he had similarly failed to change her ways. She was summoned before the board and once more a severe reprimand was delivered, this time for rejecting the Whartons' kindness and their endeavour 'to make her a useful member of society'. On 11 December 1844, the minutes report that the Girl Willoughby had beaten another girl. On this occasion, however, her punishment was far more than a reprimand, severe or otherwise; rather she had been punished by 'confining her 48 hours in the refractory ward, and by altering her dinner according to the rules and regulations of the Poor Law Commissioners'.

However, the following week this particular punishment was questioned by one of the guardians and after a careful examination of the regulations it was discovered that the master had seriously contravened them. The longest time he was sanctioned to keep a pauper in the refractory ward was twelve hours, along with a change of diet. At least that is how the guardians interpreted the regulations. An enormous amount of paper emanated from Somerset House, and for workhouse officials and guardians to keep up with it must have been nigh on impossible. *The Annual Report of the Poor Law Commissioners* for 1842 makes it clear that in the case of disorderly paupers a workhouse master, without direction from the guardians, could substitute for a period not exceeding forty-eight hours the pauper's normal meal for one consisting of eight ounces of bread or one pound of potatoes; and all tea, sugar, cheese, cheese, butter or broth could be withheld for the same period. Confining a refractory pauper in a special room, with or without alteration of diet, required a special direction from the board of guardians, and the regulations stipulated that no pauper should be confined longer than twenty-four hours, the only reason for imposing a longer period in a refractory ward being occasioned by the necessity of waiting to see a magistrate. If we put to one side the period of detention – whether the Commissioners' twenty-four hours or the guardians' twelve – it is obvious that John Wilson had been going beyond his powers for some time. The Willoughby girl's offence, beating another inmate, was serious and merited an appropriate punishment, but to keep her confined for two days was quite improper. What is more serious is that the guardians had been allowing him to get away with his punishment regime for far too long, either through deliberate disregard of the regulations or – more likely – by contentedly leaving the discipline of the workhouse to him. They were now confronted by the unpleasant fact that they, too, had sanctioned illegal punishments.

Perhaps it was because the punishment involved an orphan girl in her teens – one of those whom they desired to transform into 'a useful member of society' – that the guardians were so concerned. Whatever the reason, it probably curbed the master's powers of dealing with difficult paupers. Clearly it did not have much effect on discipline. As we have already seen, there was a spirit of insubordination in March 1845, and Wilson, in common with most workhouse masters, must have struggled to maintain order. Nevertheless, this mild admonishment of the master in December 1844 – he was merely told to be more attentive to the regulations in the future – can be seen as a move slightly in favour of the inmates.

V Help for Girls in Service

We must not, however, be too pessimistic. The Whartons' gesture in giving a position to the Willoughby girl, even though it failed, was not an isolated incident, and showed something very positive on behalf of the Docking Guardians.

From the beginning of the workhouse, there are references to assisting girls going into service by equipping them with new clothes. Many families hoped their girls, once they reached the age of thirteen or fourteen, would go into the household of a local farmer or gentleman as a servant. It was perfectly natural, therefore, for the guardians to want to help in deserving cases. In 1840 they turned their attention to girls in the workhouse. On 26 February, the chairman gave notice of a resolution to the effect that anybody willing to take girls in the workhouse into service, and to teach them the habits of industry, should be given a premium. The following week, he reported on the practice in other unions, and told the board that the Mitford and Launditch Union gave £2 for clothing, Swaffham from 5s. to £1, and Freebridge Lynn nothing. It was agreed that a sum no greater than £2 for clothing should be provided for each girl who had been in the workhouse for twelve months, and who wished to go into service; the parish to which the girl belonged would pay. On 1 April, it was further agreed that the girl should be engaged for one year, but should be first put on trial for a week or two.

The guardians must have been proud of this scheme, and rightly so. In 1845 the Poor Law Commissioners had challenged them to explain the frequency of the payments given to girls sent into service. The chairman read out his letter to the Commission, and in it he stressed the depressed state of agriculture in the Docking Union. Wages were of necessity low, and men, when in employment, usually earned ten or eleven shillings per week. Where there was an older, unemployed girl she was rarely able to contribute to the family income. Previously, field-work for girls had been more readily available, but by this time men were more usually employed. Blyth did not raise the moral objection to girls working in the fields alongside young men, which – especially after the 1843 *Report on the Employment of Women and Children in Agriculture* – was of particular concern. The Report highlighted the fact that in Docking girls of fifteen and above much preferred outdoor to indoor work, and that this was 'attended often with the worst results as regards manners and morals'.[4] He and his fellow guardians were anxious to get girls into what they perceived to be much more respectable situations. In order to do that, they were perfectly aware that the only chance the daughters of poor labouring men had was to make a decent appearance. They also knew they could face the charge of interfering with the labour market, although they did not find that to be so. They felt they had been able to help many girls to find work who otherwise had been unable to do so.

VI The Dress of Shame

We must not, however, be deceived by the reaction against the case of an orphan having to endure forty-eight hours in the refractory ward or the desire to assist girls in the workhouse to find a situation as servants. The workhouse was a man's world and there were few female officials. Whatever influence the matron (Wilson's wife), the schoolmistress or nurse had was severely limited. Before we leave the situation of women, we must now consider something which carved an ugly scar on the face of the Docking Union in the period under consideration in this book.

On 3 April 1839 the master drew the attention of the board to the number of women with illegitimate children in the house. There were ten women and thirteen children. He continued: 'I beg leave to suggest that they might be distinguished in dress or diet, as they think very little of being in the house as they appear to make the house their home.' This shameless behaviour was not at all what the New Poor Law was designed to encourage. If a woman, either through careless-ness or lewdness, had borne an illegitimate child and she could not provide for it herself, she was supposed to endure the stigma and shame of the workhouse. After 1834 many young women entered workhouses with their illegitimate children. Docking was no exception, and they soon became one of the largest classes in the house. (See Appendix B.)

The chairman and sixteen guardians discussed the matter and ordered that sufficient yellow serge be ordered to make ten dresses. This distinctive style of dress was not unique to Docking, but the Poor Law Commissioners did not approve of it. *The Sixth Annual Report of the Poor Law Commissioners* (1840) contains a minute, dated 5 March 1839, entitled 'Ignominious Dress for Unchaste Women in Work-houses'.[5] However convinced a pauper in the Docking Workhouse in 1839 might have been that it was a place of punishment, little different from a prison, that was not what the Poor Law Commissioners wanted. A workhouse existed to relieve the destitute in their various classes. There was a strong hope that able-bodied paupers would learn the habits of industry and become useful members of society. The house sought neither to reward nor to punish: in the words of the 1839 Minute, 'the workhouse is not intended to serve any penal or remuneratory purpose; and it ought not to be used for punishing the dissolute, or rewarding the well-conducted pauper'. It is important to clarify the notion of punishment in the workhouse.

A workhouse did indeed punish, but the Commissioners would have felt the need to distinguish between present and past misconduct. The 1839 Minute makes it quite clear: '... it was not the intention of the legislature to constitute the Board of Guardians a tribunal for the punishment of past profligacy by any varieties in the mode of administering in-door relief.' They knew that boards of guardians wanted to repress vice, and they did not want to come down too hard on unions that forced some women to wear a certain dress as a mark of disgrace. Yet their opposition to these yellow dresses was unequivocal, and the Commissioners could not ignore it. The 1839 Minute acknowledged that the 1834 Act had brought in a change: no longer was it a crime to bear a bastard, but the child was now to be a burden to the mother. Such was to be the consequence of her behaviour, yet the Commissioners were clear that this should not affect her treatment in the workhouse:

Any attempt to inflict disgrace or punishment on the mother of a bastard, as such, appears to be in opposition to the principles which guided the legislature in the alteration of the law on the subject.

The Poor Law Commissioners' case was first presented politely and not particularly firmly. On 11 September 1839, the Assistant Commissioner, Twistleton, was present at a board meeting, and was pleased to remark on the cleanliness and good order of the workhouse; but he 'recommended the discontinuance of the dress to the women who had illegitimate children which was worn, as it was not sanctioned by the Poor Law Commissioners'. A letter written by a clergyman on 29 September 1841 to Prime Minister Robert Peel, however, could not be ignored. The writer was Stephen Reed Catley, who lived in Fulham. He was the absentee Rector of Bagthorpe, and his curate was the Chaplain of Docking Workhouse, Revd Edmund John Senkler. It was, in fact, through Senkler that Catley had gained the information, in confidence, 'that the females who are sheltered there having had illegitimate children wear a badge of disgrace, betokening their past irregularities'. Senkler was of the opinion that the practice had no salutary effect whatsoever upon the women, and had expressed his surprise to his rector that anybody could have thought otherwise. [6]

The Docking Guardians certainly did think otherwise, as the Poor Law Commissioners were soon to discover. Twistleton first wrote to his superiors on 7 October 1841, in response to their enquiry about Catley's letter, which had naturally been passed on to them. He was able to tell them that things had, if anything, got worse since April 1839. Now the dress, of blue and yellow, had red stripes on one of the sleeves, to indicate the number of illegitimate children the woman had borne. Twistleton repeated that he had made strong objections to the practice in 1839, even recording in the Visitors' Book the reasons which made it so objectionable. He reported that the Docking Guardians had not been in any mood to change their minds. In particular, he reminded the Commissioners of the way that the

Chairman of the Docking Board of Guardians, Henry Blyth, had filled his office since the union had been formed 'with remarkable zeal and ability'. Twistleton had quickly realized that, given such determined chairman and guardians, no call for discontinuance of the practice could be effected unless a formal prohibition were to be issued from the Commissioners. Such a move, Twistleton was quite sure, would have brought about 'a disagreeable collision with the guardians'. All he had felt able to do, he told the Commissioners, was to remind the board, from time to time, of his disapproval of the blue and yellow dresses and their stripes of dishonour.[7]

This was a boat not to be rocked, not unless the whole of the Docking Board of Guardians were to be tipped into the water. That was something Twistleton could never have contemplated, given his strong approval of the performance of the board and its chairman in every other respect. However, this independent approach by the clergy to the Poor Law Commission had emboldened him somewhat in his desire to rock the boat again. He was prepared, if necessary, to ask the clerk to convene a special meeting; he would then make every effort to induce the guardians 'to consent to a discontinuance of the objectionable dress'. He added that this practice existed in no union in his district. That might have been true, but certainly, as early as 1837 in the Mitford and Launditch Union, there were the so-called Jacket Women, also mothers of illegitimate children.[8]

The Commissioners had also written to the Docking Union on 4 October, enquiring whether a distinctive dress existed for female inmates who were mothers of illegitimate children. The board discussed the issue at some length on 20 October and 'almost unanimously' passed these two resolutions:

1st. That it appears to this Board that the adoption of the dress for distinguishing unchaste women in this House has been of great service for the following reasons – That previous to and at the time of the first adoption of the dress there were eleven women in the House (with from one to three Children each) that in the first week after, seven left, & the four that remained soon after; and that only four out of the eleven have since returned, and that these were the most dissolute. That there are none now, and have not been for more than a month, that there has never been more than five at one time since the adoption of the dress.

2. That this Board with all due deference therefore think the use of the dress of the greatest service in every point of view, & earnestly request the Poor Law Comm^{rs} to sanction the continuance of it.

The might of the Assistant Commissioner and of the three London Commissioners was being applied, but the Docking Guardians were not going to permit any rocking of their sacred boat. On 24 October, in a letter to the Poor Law Commission, Twistleton claimed, presumably from his reading of the second resolution, that he detected a chink in their armour; he felt that the board would be prepared to abandon the practice if the Commissioners withheld their sanction from it. They certainly had the power to issue a legally binding prohibition, but Twistleton believed this was too severe a move, and that a letter prohibiting the dress would be sufficient. He suggested the way the Commissioners could couch their objection. They needed to stress that they had no doubt that the dress had been effective in keeping mothers of illegitimate children out of the workhouse, but to impress upon the board that the practice was contrary to the principle of the Poor Law Amendment Act of 1834. The letter, Twistleton felt, should refer to the Minute of 5 March 1839 and stress that this had gained general acquiescence, and that the use of a particular form of dress was retained in no workhouse other than in Docking. That last statement alone was open to challenge, and in fact Twistleton invited the Commissioners to do so. He then stressed that any letter coming from London should acknowledge that the dress in the Docking Workhouse had never 'proceeded from any feelings of severity and hardness to an unfortunate class of persons but had proceeded from a desire to suppress vice'.[9]

No communication of that nature was apparently ever sent. At the board meeting of 10 November, Blyth stated he had received a letter from the Commissioners, which had acknowledged the receipt of the resolutions of 20 October. They had asked the board to reconsider the matter. This they did on 1 December after a special order had been issued to summon the guardians to attend. A good number were present, and so was the Assistant Commissioner. The latter went into considerable detail as to the legality of the subject, and trusted that the board would discontinue the special dress. When the vote was taken, it emerged there were eleven members (including Thomas Hebgin) who had taken Twistleton's arguments to heart and wanted to end the imposition of the dress; but thirteen members (amongst them James Howlett) voted for its continuation. In a memorandum to the Commissioners, received in London on 6 December, Twistleton had to admit that the Docking Chairman had been so decided in his defence of the dress that it had been impossible to counteract his influence.[10] There was no doubt, however, that if a legal order of prohibition had been issued Henry Blyth would have immediately submitted; but as long as the matter was left to the discretion of the guardians the chairman would never act contrary to his deeply held convictions. Moreover, Twistleton had to concede that Blyth had the numerical evidence on his side, showing a clear decline in the number of mothers of illegitimate children in the house. (There had, nevertheless, been no fewer requests for relief from such women.) In the guardians' eyes another effect of the dress, given that it tended to keep a mother of an illegitimate child out of the house, was that her parents were compelled to provide for both daughter and grandchild. The chairman was quite sure that whenever young women were unchaste their mothers were seldom free from blame.

Twistleton's blood was now up, and his feelings were exacerbated by the fact that some guardians were suggesting that, because no formal prohibition had been delivered, the Commissioners themselves doubted whether it was expedient to ban the dress. He earnestly requested that there should be no more delay in prohibiting the dress, the legality of which he doubted. He was quite sure – and we, 170 years later, can have no doubt - that the dress blunted the feelings and hardened the hearts of young women. The time for tipping the crew out of the boat had arrived.

A prohibition order was drafted, which rehearsed the familiar arguments. There also survives the draft of a reply to Blyth's letter sent after the meeting at which the guardians decided to continue with the dress. The Commissioners acknowledged that the dress must indeed have had the effect of keeping mothers of illegitimate children out of the workhouse, but were not entirely convinced that a good moral effect was transmitted into the woman's family, even if she had younger sisters. Where they were on strongest ground was when they invoked the spirit of the Poor Law Amendment Act, and the Minute of 1839. Twistleton had also conveyed to his superiors another argument from Docking: that, if it was quite proper to punish paupers who had been disorderly in the house, then it was surely permissible to impose a special dress in order to maintain order. This argument was countered by informing the guardians that, whereas a special dress might be allowed as a temporary punishment for misconduct in the house (and this could apply to the unchaste women), it must then have been understood that such women were not being punished for past immoral behaviour outside the house, but for infringements of the regulations within it.[11]

And there the matter stood. The boat had been rocked, but it was still afloat and the guardians of the Docking Union remained in control. For the most part they probably felt they were not treating these women badly; on the contrary, they would have been conscious of their stand against vice. If eleven voted to discontinue the dress, it was more likely to have been out of respect for the law of the land. They had not been defeated by three Commissioners in Somerset House or by the Assistant Commissioner in East Anglia, but had maintained their position. They had also saved themselves some money: mothers and their illegitimate offspring were notoriously expensive to maintain in workhouses. Henry Blyth emerged as a clear victor from this particular conflict; but the same cannot be said for a small group of women in the Docking Union.

At least one of the Docking guardians must have followed the debates on the dress of these unfortunate women with a particular interest. Anybody searching through the baptism records of any parish church will inevitably come across references to illegitimate children. There were a good number in the Great Bircham Parish Registers, as we noted in Chapter 1. One such entry recorded the baptism of Mary Anne Spanton on 11 February 1827, the daughter of Susanna Spanton. Many registers would have given no more information than this, but the curate, John Spurgeon, added the name of the father: 'T. Hebgin', and also gave his Quality, Trade or Profession as 'Farmer'. Susanna Spanton was barely seventeen years old in February 1827. By what moral authority did this man presume to decide on the need to provide a special dress of yellow serge, with red stripes on the sleeve, for any woman in the Docking Union bearing an illegitimate child? (See also Appendix D.)

Nevertheless, for nearly all their social betters, and not a few of their equals, women who had illegitimate children were regarded as totally dissolute. Walking down the aisle when several months pregnant was one thing and marrying shortly after a birth was just about tolerated; but to bear a child and to bring it up without the support of a husband was not remotely considered as an option by the moral guardians of society. However, as Barry Reay has pointed out, it is necessary to have regard for the concept of a 'bastardy-prone sub-society'. For Reay it is quite clear that in rural working-class communities 'bearing children outside marriage should not be seen as a form of deviancy but rather part of normal sexual culture'.[12] This whole episode of the 'badge of disgrace' in the Docking Union must not be viewed solely through the eyes of clergymen, poor law guardians and commissioners. Unfortunately, the mass of surviving material from the period forces us to see things in one particular way. That is why the conscientiousness (but it was surely more than that) of John Spurgeon is so helpful to us; and although the information written in the baptismal register is minimal, it is enough to tell us that men might condemn the immorality of their female servants, in order to disguise their lust.

Notes

[1] 8th Annual Report of the PLC (1842).

[2] J. Fellowes, *Short and Plain Adress from a clergyman to his Parishioners on some of the Chief Provisions of the Poor Law Amendment Act.* (Norwich 1836), p. 17.

[3] S. Hobson, *The Nature and Design of the New Poor Law Explained,* (London 1839), pp 29-37.

[4] Report, p. 244.

[5] TNA: MH 12/8251.

[6] ibid.

[7] S.Pope, Gressenhall Farm and Workhouse (Cromer 2006), p. 30.

[8] TNA: MH 12/8251.

[9] ibid.

[10] ibid.

[11] ibid.

[12] B. Reay, *Microhistories: Demography, Society and Culture in Rural England, 1800 – 1930* (Cambridge 1996), p. 180.

A woman carrying her child in front of Thomas Lowe's house in Bircham Tofts – Hill's Survey of 1800 *(Plate XXXII)*

Chapter 10. Good Intentions

I. Educating the Poor

> *There are who even in these latter days,*
> *Against instruction, vain objections raise,*
> *On all attempts this hackneyed adage fling,*
> *"A little knowledge is a dangerous thing",*
> *'Once educate the children of the poor,*
> *And willing service they will yield no more.'*
> *Such gravely argue 'if they're never taught*
> *Their duties they'll perform them as they ought.'*

The Village Paupers. G. W. Fulcher, 1840-44

1. Kay and Pauper Education

We know there were several schools in Great Bircham at the time of the riots, and in each Houghton Estate village there was always a school. The other villages in the Docking Union also had schools, usually run along Church of England lines. Yet not all children attended, or if they did it was irregularly. Schooling was not free and often children were needed at home, or had to earn some money for the family. In workhouses it was different, as they all had schoolrooms. The school population was inevitably transitory, as families moved in and out of the house. Yet for some children this was a free school, if only for a few hours a day, something they did not have outside. East Anglia was indeed fortunate for a period in the 1830s to have James Kay as the Assistant Poor Law Commissioner. He firmly believed in education for all, and for him the principle of less eligibility did not apply to children. Their parents might have had to endure a harsher regime in a workhouse than that of an independent labourer, but their children, if they came into the workhouse, were to be given every opportunity to dispel their 'ignorance'.

He set out his educational principles at some length in his *Report on the Training of Pauper Children* (1838).[1] When it came to matters of education he was adamant the workhouse could improve on the standard of religious and cultural upbringing seen in many labouring families. Only through education could pauperism be eliminated – and property protected:

...education is to be regarded as one of the most important means of eradicating the germs of pauperism from the rising generation, and of securing in the minds and morals of the people the best protection for the institutions of society.

It is important to acknowledge how far ignorance is the source of pauperism, and to show how important an aspect for the removal of pauperism is a careful training in religion and industry. Of the ignorance which prevails among the pauper classes the proofs are abundant.

It was not a given amongst farmers, in Norfolk and elsewhere, that educating the children of their labourers would bring good, however. One of the Kitton guardians (whether Everard or John is not clear, but probably the latter) was quick to move, in April 1837, that as there were a mere six children in the house there was no need for a school-master or a schoolmistress. The opposition to raising the aspirations of these children and giving them ideas above their station is well known, and we can detect echoes of it amongst the Docking Guardians. They were all for discipline and teaching the poor their place, but they knew that they needed young hands to help with the harvest, to scare the crows or to lead the horses, before they needed boys and girls who could read and write

In his 1838 report Kay cited, as a proof of pauper ignorance, the result of a survey of adult paupers in twenty-two unions and five incorporations in Norfolk and Suffolk, taken on 12 June 1837. There were 1,675 paupers, but a mere ten of these could read and write well; 281 could both read and write in some fashion; and 928 were totally illiterate. It is inevitable that a workhouse must have included a high proportion of the poorly educated. 17.37% were able to read; and this compares very unfavourably with the 50% of the Bircham rioters appearing in court who could read. Things looked somewhat better amongst the children, and he gave the results below, taken from all Norfolk and Suffolk workhouses during the week ending 9 December

1837. He was bold enough to claim that each passing week would bring steady improvements

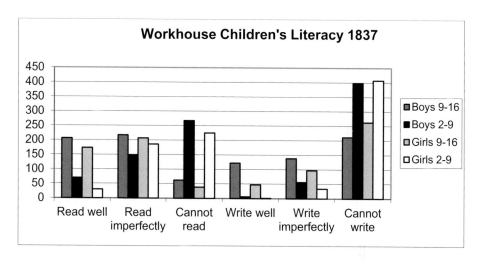

Kay's goal was no less than the eradication of hereditary pauperism. The key to success was in a 'well-devised system of education', one which would 'render their future dependence on the rate-payers improbable'. Above all, children were to be kept away from the corrupting influence of adults, and placed under the care of diligent teachers.

It is easy for us to dismiss Kay's views as narrow and as anchoring children firmly within their class. He seemed to offer these Norfolk young people little more than farm work or domestic service. That was the reality for the majority of them, after all. The decennial censuses in Great Bircham might show an increasing variety of occupations as the nineteenth century progressed, but most men worked as agricultural labourers. As ever, we must guard against seeing everything through modern eyes. What is undeniable is that he had, according to his own judgements, the best interests of the child at heart; and some Docking Guardians, including Henry Blyth, shared this sentiment. The old apprentice system was something Kay despised, and it could never, in his eyes, lift the child out of a despised dependency:

A child should not be degraded in his own estimation by being a member of a despised class. A child cannot be a pauper in the sense in which that term is

commonly understood – that is, he cannot be indigent as the consequence of his own want of industry, skill, frugality, or forethought, and he ought not therefore to be taught to despise himself. The pauper apprentice and the juvenile vagrant were, under the old system, brethren of the same class – outcasts, neither trained by frugal and industrious parents, nor by a well-devised system of public industrial instruction.

2. The habits of usefulness

Good work habits for Kay were important. Merely concentrating on the Three Rs was not sufficient, and would not fit a boy for earning his living by labour, but make him effeminate. Industry in workhouses meant, say, repairing clothes or shoes for boys; and, depressingly, the usual domestic tasks for girls. Above all, a schoolmaster earning no less that £35 was essential; and the schoolmistress ought to earn at least £20. In our period, the Docking Union did not pay those salaries, but they did employ a shoemaker. The schoolmaster should not be distracted from his duties by demands made on him connected with the internal running of the workhouse, and he should be allowed to eat his meals in private or with superior officers of the house. Unfortunately, neither schoolmaster nor schoolmistress was treated with anything like that level of respect at Docking. Invariably, when a new schoolmaster was appointed, he was summoned to appear in front of the board and told he had to obey the directions of the workhouse master and chaplain, and attend in the dining hall at meals.

The first schoolmaster and mistress of the Docking Union were Mr and Mrs Bennett, and they were appointed on 30 November 1836. An application from John Salmon and his wife was dismissed as he was a dissenter. Books were ordered from the National Society, and by December it was reported that the chaplain had begun catechising the children. All very routine, and what also became routine for the Docking Workhouse was that complaints were heard, and schoolmasters forced to resign. This was hardly surprising, and typical of many unions at this time. Teaching in a workhouse school was hardly an attractive career, especially with the low salary. Guardians had little idea of the sort of person they needed, and there were not great numbers of experienced teachers to draw on. The Bennetts were soon declared to be inefficient. The next schoolmaster was James Bilby (30), a former tailor, although his wife had kept a school. He was the brother-in-law of the master, and the Bilbys took up their posts in the summer of 1837.

By November, Kay was agitating for a new system of keeping the school, and to that end he requested that the guardians should send the schoolmaster to Lynn, in order to observe how things were done there. The attraction of the King's Lynn workhouse school was that a Scottish schoolmaster taught there and used books that were to be found in the Sessional Schools of the Church of Scotland. In the event, it was the Lynn schoolmaster, Ross, who came to Docking on 1 December 1837.

For Kay there was much to be done in Docking. It was clear to him that the increased number of children in the house demanded that their instruction should be seen as a matter of importance. The board formed its own education committee, comprising the clergymen guardians and others, including John Kitton. When Kay addressed the board on 13 December, a letter he had written on 2 December was read, and in it he stressed that there should be three hours set aside each day for instructing the children in 'reading, writing and the Christian religion'; and he added 'that such other instruction shall be imparted to them as may be calculated to train them to habits of usefulness, industry and virtue'.

More precisely, Kay wanted religious teaching to be entrusted to the Revd Senkler, the workhouse chaplain, but not to overlook the law permitting any licensed dissenting minister to instruct children of their own persuasion. The guardians at Docking, however, were reluctant in the early years of the workhouse to show tolerance towards nonconformist paupers. The 'habits of industry' were to be inculcated every day and the children were to be 'set to work at some useful employment by which they should be enabled to acquire skill, rendering the boys desirable servants as Agricultural Labourers, and the girls as domestic servants'. They should also become proficient in reading and writing, but always their lowly status was to the fore: the Assistant Commissioner insisted that the children should acquire 'such a knowledge of their duties in their station in life, as would fit them to become useful members of society'.

3. The Scottish system

The farmer guardians could not have objected to turning the children of the labouring poor into 'useful members of society' – that, after all, was what they had hoped to make of the orphan Willoughby girl by sending her into service – as long as their station in life was firmly to be maintained. The difficulty arose with the nature of the Scottish reading books. Kay set great store by them; the Bishop of London was an ardent supporter; and Senkler was full of praise and had seen them in use, to great benefit to the children, at the Gressenhall Workhouse. Not so the guardians who formed the education committee, however. At the board meeting of 13 December their report was also heard.

Taking his lead from objections already circulating in the area, that the books tended towards Unitarianism, Frederick Hare had proposed that the board should continue to use the Bible, the church catechism and books of the National Society. Chairman Blyth had proposed an amendment that the Scottish Sessional books should be used for another week, and eventually used in conjunction with the books of the National Society and the S.P.C.K. Summoned before the committee, Ross had stated that there was no tendency towards Unitarianism, and that John Wood, the compiler of the books, stood high as an Episcopalian and churchman.

There was no doubt about the strength of feeling against these books amongst certain sections of the Anglican clergy in North-west Norfolk. The Revd Kirby Trimmer, whose views we have already encountered in conjunction with the folly of stack-burning (see Chapter 5), published a pamphlet in which he attempted to justify the protest against the use of the second books of the Edinburgh Sessional School in the Docking Union. John Wood published his reply on 22 May 1838.[2] The doctrinal debate need not concern us, but one of his arguments is of interest and is a vigorous assault on 'ignorance' amongst the children of the poor. Trimmer had raised the absurdity of teaching children in agricultural districts a rather refined vocabulary. The actual charge against the use of the second book was:

Because it is <u>absurd</u> to teach pauper children <u>in an agricultural district</u>, and whose occupations are for the most part those of CROW-KEEPING, PIG-MINDING and TURNIP-PULLING; that minerals are, as the case may be, brilliant, opaque, malleable, ductile or fusible; and because such a system is <u>not suited to the station</u> in which it has pleased Providence to place <u>the agricultural poor</u>.

For Wood it was equally absurd that any Anglican clergyman should express such sentiments:

How melancholy to think that there are human beings whom, he considers so astricted to the soil, or rather to its "pigs," its "crows," and its "turnips," that their minds and intellects (so far as his influence extends), being for ever chained down to these, to the exclusion of every other earthly object, are not to be permitted to wander to any thing beyond their own "agricultural district," or, as I presume, to be permitted to know that any thing beyond its limits under heaven exists.

The teaching of words like 'malleable' and 'fusible' to young children may well strike us as somewhat odd, given that there was a more basic vocabulary to be acquired first. Nevertheless, any true educator cannot but praise the endeavour to allow young minds to soar beyond their narrow environment. Wood knew that there had to be pig-keepers and turnip-pullers, but that did not mean their minds had to be forever dulled. He quoted the Bishop of London, just as Kay had done in his 1838 report:

I see no reason, why the education given to the poor should differ from the education of their superiors, more widely than the different circumstances and duties of their respective conditions in life render absolutely necessary. One thing is certain, and it is a very important consideration; that if we teach them the methods of acquiring one kind of knowledge, they will apply them to the acquisition of other kinds; if we sharpen their faculties for one purpose, they will be sure to use them for others.

Lofty and laudable these aims might have been, but the man sent to Docking Workhouse from King's Lynn received nothing but rejection from the Docking schoolmaster, James Bilby, and his father-in-law, the

279

master of the house. When Ross appeared before the committee on 13 December, he had to inform them that he had encountered so much hindrance on the part of Bilby that he felt he could do no good in the school. Nowhere else had he been treated so badly, and he had no other option than to seek permission to leave Docking. The committee had to accede to this demand. On 13 December, the chairman had to inform Wilson and Bilby that they had treated Ross badly, and that in future they should pay more attention to their orders. Undeniably they had ignored the fact that Ross had come with the sanction of the board; but for the sake of maintaining the smooth running of the house their reprimand could not have been too strong.

Nothing more could be done in December, and in the first meeting in January the committee recommended that the use of the books should be suspended. On 18 January 1838, on Blyth's recommendation, the board closed ranks and resolved not to re-open the arguments. After all, Parliament was debating a national system of education for the poor, and waiting for the end of the present parliamentary session was always a means of deferring difficult decisions. The harmony of the board was paramount. A few representatives of Norfolk Anglicanism might have prevailed, but what was vital was to maintain the integrity of the Docking Union.

The board asked Wilson to pursue Kay's other requirement: that a system of industry should be introduced. On 31 January 1838, he reported that he had previously been able to set some of the paupers mending clothes; and now he had prepared six seats in order that a man might be employed to teach the boys how to make or mend shoes. On 7 February, John Playford was appointed at 15s. a week, and he declared he could work from 6 a.m. to 6 p.m., if required. Wilson considered it best if the orphan boys were first entrusted to the shoemaker, and Senkler agreed.

The Bilbys did not remain long in post. On 14 February 1838, it was reported to the board that they had repeatedly refused to take orders from the master and matron. The schoolmaster was further accused of 'having taken improper liberties with one of the females by the name of Ireson belonging to the establishment; and also with having instilled into the minds of the paupers to resist the authority of the Governor'. There were countercharges from Bilby, but he and his wife were forced to resign.

4. Teachers in the workhouse

The Docking Workhouse School never properly settled to deliver valuable education to pauper children, although even the meagre and ineffective instruction they received was often better than anything available outside. The guardians might have resolved to pay a salary of £35 per annum to the schoolmaster, and £15 to the mistress (or £50 to a married couple) in 1838, but they were never generous during the period under consideration in this book. A succession of teachers, with varying degrees of competence, some even trained in Scotland, appeared before the children of the workhouse. In the summer of 1838, the schoolmaster was sent to the workhouse school in King's Lynn and returned impressed by the system there; but he considered it would not be practicable in Docking, where one hour only could be spared for education from the time devoted to industry. Six hours were allocated in Lynn.

The complaints against the teachers continued with depressing regularity. The schoolroom, the wards, and the children (certainly the boys) were dirty. The schoolmaster was reported drunk, or had neglected his appearance. There were accusations of insolence and disorderly conduct, and of insulting the chaplain. As we have already seen, one was accused of giving corporal punishment to a girl. There was a brief period, however, when the pauper children were in the hands of competent staff. Jane Wilson, the daughter of the master and matron, had already been managing the girls' school for nearly nine months when she was appointed in March 1841. She was only thirteen, and must have worked closely with her mother. For the first year she had no salary, but then earned £10. On 1 April 1846, it was reported: 'The Board agreed that the School was greatly improved under her superintendence.' Her salary was then increased to £15. She must have satisfied the requirement to employ an 'excellent sempstress', as, on 5 August 1846, the Visiting Committee recommended that the board examine some needlework done by the girls in the school under her supervision.

5. Richard Little

A perhaps more significant appointment, in August 1843, was that of Richard Little, aged 23, who had some teaching experience. He had to suffer the indignity of having his watch stolen and broken soon after he had commenced his duties, but he must have brought about genuine improvements. We have to rely solely on the Guardians' Minutes for our evidence, but on 23 April 1845, the chaplain reported that five boys and five girls had been confirmed, and that the Bishop of Norwich had been 'greatly pleased with their behaviour, appearance, and the knowledge they had acquired in the School at the Union Workhouse'. On 3 December 1845, the Assistant Commissioner's report was read to the guardians: he had visited the house the previous week and he 'expressed his entire satisfaction with the whole of the Establishment, particularly the Schools'. Then, on 15 January 1845, the Revd E. G. Blyth (brother of H. E. Blyth) examined the school-children, and reported to the board. He told the guardians that 'the School was progressing very fast and that there was a great deal of credit due to Mr Little the Schoolmaster for the manner in which he conducted himself.'

But it was not to continue. There were women still entering the house with illegitimate children at this time, and there were women in the Docking Union, as elsewhere, who went up the aisle heavily pregnant. It must have been a great embarrassment to the master and matron of the workhouse when their own unmarried daughter, Jane, announced she was carrying Little's child. The young lovers had to resign, and they married at Docking Parish Church on 20 June 1846. Amongst the labouring families of Norfolk, as we have seen, such behaviour was frequently dismissed as dissolute, the woman often classed as little better than a harlot. The then Assistant Poor Law Commissioner described what Richard Little and Jane Wilson had done in somewhat different terms, although for all those who knew their Old Testament the condemnation was no less strong: 'The Schoolmaster and Schoolmistress who have been long engaged to be married have chosen to anticipate the nuptial ceremony and wrought folly in Israel.'[3]

It should come as no surprise to us that the schools soon deteriorated again, and complaints were made once more. There was a brief improvement under the schoolmaster Fisher in 1847, but the master complained that the boys spent too long in the school, and did not devote enough time to industry. In December 1848, John Crittenden was appointed schoolmaster, and cannot have proved a failure as he was still there in 1851. We have already seen the apparent success of Mary Marsham.

A mixed picture, then, but what emerges is a largely unsatisfactory educational experience for the children of the Docking Union workhouse school through the first fifteen years of its existence, despite the good intentions of Kay and others.

II Curing the Sick

Now we need to discover if the population of the union, especially those of limited means, fared any better in terms of health. Sickness often proved calamitous for the poor: a great many of them slid into pauperism through illness or injury, which drained the family's resources and rendered the breadwinners incapable of earning enough to support their dependents. Treatment was available for the rural poor, but it was frequently beyond their means. There were medical clubs, but even these were too expensive for some. Indeed, the Docking Union was active in promoting these clubs throughout its parishes soon after it came into existence. There was always charity, of course. Houghton Estate inhabitants certainly had free medical treatment available to them before and after the introduction of the New Poor Law. Despite the virtual absence of any reference to medical relief in either the Report or the Act of 1834, what happened after the introduction of the New Poor Law was quite remarkable. Boards of guardians divided their unions into medical districts under the care of a medical officer, and workhouses provided sick wards. During our period, we can see a genuine concern for the health and sanitary conditions of a whole area. In many ways these developments represented an embryonic national health service.

The Docking Union was no exception. A long report in the minutes of 2 November 1836 (before the workhouse was open) mentions the attendance of surgeons at a meeting to arrange for the requisite fitting out of the surgery. Later, on 14 December, in the report of the Visiting Committee on the state of the house, we learn that Mr Church, medical officer, had been in attendance since the house was occupied. The minutes do not survive before October 1836, but clearly there were medical officers appointed before then. The union was divided into large medical districts, and one medical officer was made responsible for the workhouse. In December 1836, the minutes recorded that the three officers had been paid £17 10s. for the quarter, less than the master, who had been paid £20. We have already seen there were many flaws in the running of the workhouse; things were no different with medical provision for the poor in the Docking Union. There was no proper ward for ill paupers in our period, although there was a ward for contagious diseases.

Nursing care, too, was often lacking and of poor quality. Just as some schoolmasters and schoolmistresses proved inadequate for their office, so it was with some medical men. Salaries of medical officers were not high, and so the best men were not attracted. For David Englander the workhouse medical officer was generally regarded as no better than 'a struggling tradesman'.[4] The districts of the union medical officers, especially in a rural union like Docking, were large and unwieldy. Agricultural labourers were never going to receive the same level of care as their employers or their better-off contemporaries. Even so, after the passing of the Poor Law Amendment Act, there was provision made by the guardians for their health needs. Medical knowledge in the 1830s was nothing like it is today, and doctors were often of little use in treating sickness, but that should not detract from what the guardians of the Docking Union strove to achieve.

1. Wingfield Dutton

As Anne Digby has pointed out, the majority of accusations of negligence against Norfolk medical officers proved to be groundless.[5] However, we cannot avoid the failures. Such possibly was the case with Wingfield Dutton (19). Here we see the influence of yet another clergyman, a more fanatical one than Ambrose Goode. He was the Revd Henry Holloway, patron and curate of Brancaster, and, during the early period of the Docking Union, a deeply penetrating thorn in the flesh of the Docking Guardians. The accusation was that Church, the medical officer, had neglected the pauper Dutton of Brancaster from 20 January to 6 February 1837. A committee was formed and went to visit Dutton and his sister who both insisted he had not been visited by Church during that period. Church, of course, could show from his returns that he had in fact visited the man twice. Nevertheless, his health soon deteriorated, and he died in May.

Holloway did not remain inactive and pursued the matter as far as the House of Lords. Kay later declared that the clergyman was 'an evil and malignant spirit', and by the end of January 1839 Blyth declared he would no longer open any of his letters. His was undoubtedly an obsessive character, but he was dogged in defence of the poor and in his attacks on perceived failings of the medical men in the Docking Union.

2. Anne Ireson

Anne Ireson, of South Creake was, no doubt, held to be one of the more dissolute female paupers. She was unmarried and had two illegitimate children; she received an order for the workhouse on 29 November 1837, when her age was given as twenty-seven. Quite when she entered the house for the last time we do not know. We know that she was there by 14 February 1838, because the minutes of that day recorded that the schoolmaster had been too familiar with her. Before another two weeks had passed she was dead. Holloway had also been very active in this case, constantly badgering the board.

She died in the workhouse on 25 February. Letters from Mr Shaul (a medical man from Docking) and from Mr Senkler relating to her death were sent to the board, and consequently a coroner's inquest was held on 27 February, the jury returning the verdict of natural death from typhus fever. Her son James (2½) was allowed to go out of the house to his grandmother, Jane Ireson of Stanhoe. A little later, in the minutes of 28 February, it was recorded that one of the guardians, Mr Joseph Wright, had moved that 'Jane Ireson should not be allowed any longer Relief out of the house'. Now, after her daughter's death, she had two grandchildren to raise, one only a few months old.

The matter came before the board on 28 February. The workhouse doctor, Mr Wells, was deemed to have been neglectful, and the chairman stated that the patient should have been seen daily. Such admonitions, however, were not enough to prevent his salary being raised from £40 to £50. The matter was not going to rest there. There were strong rumours circulating that the master had been responsible for Anne Ireson's death, because he had not properly administered the powders prescribed by Wells. Wilson wanted the whole matter to be thoroughly investigated. On 21 March the board came to the conclusion that they had been 'remiss in not attending more particularly to the orders of the Medical Officer'. The guardians were clear that there had been 'an attempt to injure the Character of Mr Wells, & to prejudice the interests of the Board by exaggerating imperfect Information and inventing false statements'. It was a serious charge, but the guardians were in no mood to dismiss the Wilsons. They were too important in the day-to-day running of the workhouse.

Amidst all this, the sufferings of a young mother were largely forgotten. The guardians felt that they had done their duty by offering both Anne Ireson and her mother the house in the first place, and that they had done the right thing for Anne's orphaned children by allowing them, on 14 March, 1s. and 1 stone of flour per week while they lived with their grandmother, thus countermanding Wright's refusal to give more outdoor relief two weeks earlier. However, on 23 May 1838, when Jane Ireson asked for more relief, her case was dismissed. The reason given was that 'she stated that her daughter had been smothered out of her life'. It was a time when the poor imagined all sorts of things happened in workhouses, therefore the guardians scoffed at this statement. Yet she too was a desperate mother, and wanted her daughter to survive. She probably knew things that never reached the guardians' ears, but nobody was going to believe her. A mere four days before Anne died, her mother was detected taking 'bread, meat, wine and other things' to her daughter in the house. The board summoned her. She did not receive the familiar reprimand, but it was made quite clear that such things were not allowed and that she must not repeat the attempt. The gathering together of the food and drink would not have been easy (or cheap). They, like the powders, would very likely have been too late. It hardly mattered to the guardians; the visiting of paupers was allowed, but only on their terms. The management of life - and death - in the workhouse was under the control of guardians and poor law officers. Two women belonging to the working-class poor, one of them of that degenerate sort which littered the world with bastards, could never penetrate the defences of the Docking Union, any more than the obsessive Holloway could achieve anything other than an irritating soreness of the flesh with his letters.

3. Richard Rix

The lack of communication between the various officers of the union meant that the sick poor were often badly served. An example was Richard Rix of East Rudham. Frederick Manby, a medical man, but not attached to the union, wrote to Joshua Freeman, East Rudham guardian, and pointed out the failure to give proper medical attendance to Rix. Manby's note was raised at the board meeting on 29 May 1839, and the guardians had no option but to discuss the matter the following week. Rix's widow was called into the room and she explained that, on Thursday 23 May, she had asked Mr Stedman, another guardian, to let her have a doctor for her husband, now taken very ill. Stedman sent her to the district medical officer, who was none other than Wells, the same man whom the Wilsons had tried to malign the year before. Mrs Rix called twice on Wells, but he wanted a note from the overseer. She naturally assumed that an instruction from a guardian was sufficient, but Wells declared that Stedman had no right to give her a medical order. When she asked who the overseer was, his reply must have shocked her: 'Mr Wells said "I neither know nor care, find out as you can".' It was eleven o'clock at night by the time she got the note, and Wells came to her husband about midnight. Now Wells wanted to know how much her husband earned, and when he learned that it was 9s. a week, he said he did not consider Rix to be a pauper. Nevertheless a powder was given, and Wells promised to visit the following morning. Wells was wet and cold, and had eaten nothing all day; he was not willing to turn out again that night.

Rix's wife then asked Freeman, guardian and overseer, to give her money so that she could get her own doctor. Freeman was quite sure that Wells should attend, but he did not do so on the Friday or the Saturday. She went to get him, but on learning that he was not at home she procured the services of Manby. It was obvious to the latter that Rix was dying. Wells finally came round about nine o'clock in the evening of Saturday, and left some powders, even though he said they would do no good. He came again twice on the Sunday, and Rix died that afternoon. His widow had had no complaints against Wells prior to this incident (he had attended her husband before), but had been appalled by the way he had spoken to her on this occasion.

This proved to be one incident of neglect too many for Wells, as soon afterwards he was dismissed, on the recommendation of the Poor Law Commission.

It is likely that Rix would not have survived even if he had been properly attended. We have no reason to doubt Wells when he told Mrs Rix that he had been busy all day on Thursday. What is particularly interesting is that the guardians were prepared to allow the wife of a labourer earning 9s. a week to address them so freely. They might have been waiting for such an incident in order to get rid of their medical officer, but this example of neglect and contemptuous treatment of a poor woman goes to show how labouring families were at the mercy of inefficient and negligent medical men. In this instance at least, the Docking guardians were prepared to make a stand in favour of the medical needs of the poor.

4. Mendham's child

Other examples of neglect mentioned in the minutes could be cited, although it must not be denied that the medical men also did much good, and brought treatments to a class of people who had been much neglected in the past.

The case of James Mendham's child was somewhat different, although potentially serious. James (23) and Thomas Mendham (25), two unemployed brothers belonging to the parish of Bircham Newton, had both been given orders for the house on 30 November 1842. James's order for the house was delayed for three days, as one of his children was ill. The child, his elder daughter Susanna, who had been baptized in Great Bircham Parish Church on 9 August 1840, was to have relief by medical order. She survived only one more week

The death of the little girl caused Thomas Booth, the curate, to attach great blame to the medical officer in a letter he wrote to the board. The board held an enquiry into the death on 14 December, when Booth's letter was read and when the medical officer, Mr Upjohn, was summoned to attend. The decision of the board to give medical relief for three days, rather than send her straight to the workhouse with her parents, had come about because they feared the child might have scarlatina, then very prevalent in the Docking Union. The order for the house was conditional on Upjohn's judgement of the child's condition. If he thought she could not have been removed to the workhouse after three days, out-relief should have been given for a whole week. Upjohn had seen Susanna the following day (1 December) and had advised her parents 'that with precaution and care the child might be removed to the workhouse about three Miles'. He had given no medical relief, however. The mother went immediately to the curate, who, on seeing her daughter, thought the child much too ill to be moved. The parents, acting on this advice, neither went into the workhouse nor applied for further relief; Susanna Mendham died four days later.

Upjohn was candid in his report of 7 December, stated that the child had died from want of attendance, and admitted that there had been 'incipient symptoms of croup'. However, he was clear in his own mind, that when he advised the parents that their daughter could have been moved, with care, he thought they would have gone immediately to the workhouse, where the girl would receive proper attention. The Great Bircham guardian had been present when he saw the child, and it was he who gave the order for admission into the house. Upjohn declared he had never heard anything further from the parish officer or parents until the death of the child was reported.

Nothing really came of the incident, although both board and Poor Law Commission were compelled to declare that Upjohn had acted 'injudiciously'. Yet again this was a patient who probably stood little chance of survival, given the living conditions of the poor, (especially those only irregularly employed like the two Mendham brothers), and given the inadequacy of medical knowledge in the 1840s. A serious misjudgement, however, cannot be denied. The problem was with the system. The New Poor Law's obsession with the workhouse test, especially when men like James Mendham were involved, was all embracing, and the needs of a seriously ill young child were secondary to the moral reform of her father. The innocent –

the very young and the old – deserved a different regime, but unfortunately all were lumped together.

III The Itch

Infections must have spread rapidly in workhouses, as they would in any institution. One particular infection was what was generally known as 'the itch'. This was a general term for serious skin infections, and was most often scabies. A very tiny mite, *sarcoptes scabiei*, burrowed into the skin and caused intense itching. It was highly contagious and generally transmitted by skin-to-skin contact; but factors such as dirty bedding – occurring several times in the minute books – were also important. There is also mention of 'scald head' (or scalthead), which was ringworm of the scalp. We have already met Martha Pile, whose head was examined several times in the boardroom; she must have been suffering from this complaint. Medical officer Church, not always one to be cautious in his reports, had written that he had attended Richard Ayres's family of Burnham Thorpe. They all had the itch, and his report stated that it had been caught in the Docking Workhouse. He continued: 'truly this Establishment is likely to be renowned as the disseminator of every loathsome disease that human flesh is heir to.'

Church's report on the Ayres family was made in March 1839. In the minutes of 2 January of that year the Visiting Committee had reported that 'the aged paupers, and children are not properly attended to by the Medical Officer, the children in particular with bad heads, & the Itch'. In all workhouses it must have been a constant struggle to combat these infections, and despite assurances made to the guardians that all was in hand, the battle was never entirely won. A particularly serious incident, which involved children in the workhouse and led to the dismissal of a medical officer, occurred in the summer of 1845.

The medical officer was Mr Paul and a former instance of his outrageous negligence is mentioned in the minutes of the previous year. On 8 May 1844, he was called into the boardroom and was required to answer the charge of not attending to paupers when sent for; he was even accused of 'passing frequently the very doors of the parties he was called upon to attend'. It was to such medical men that a few of the poor of the Docking Union were entrusted.

In the minutes of 25 June 1845 the master reported an 'eruption' in the house affecting several children. He considered it contagious, although Paul, the medical officer of the house, disagreed. The master said the contagion had been in the house for nine months, and had much increased. In October 1844, Paul had asked another medical officer, Davies, to examine the children. He pronounced the eruption not to be the itch, and recommended 'warm baths two or three times a week, and rather better diet'.

The board took the matter more seriously in June 1845, and brought over a medical officer from King's Lynn, Mr J. B. Whiting, to examine the children with Paul. He examined the children for several hours and 'pronounced it to be decidedly the Itch'. He also found that some children had other cutaneous diseases. The board of guardians, at their meeting of 2 July, discussed the situation at length, and found Paul negligent in not discovering the itch; they also agreed to withhold his quarterly salary in order to cover the costs of employing Mr Whiting and the treatment he prescribed. As was usual in serious cases, they signalled their intention of informing the Poor Law Commission.

When Whiting returned on 17 July, he found all the affected children and adults convalescent, and some 'quite cured'. He recommended that the workhouse medical officer should exercise great care in regularly inspecting the children. The Poor Law Commissioners wanted more information and at the board meeting of 6 August a detailed account was presented. Paul had also written to Somerset House, claiming that he had not neglected his duty. The report of October 1844 had been signed by Davies and Paul, and both had been quite sure it was not the itch. The warm baths and altered diet had in fact been put into operation, which cannot have pleased the penny-pinching guardians, and some children had been given ointment. Yet the master had become increasingly alarmed as the number of cases increased, and cures had not been effected. He had repeatedly called the attention of Paul to this fact, but the latter had assured him that the eruption was 'of no consequence and would soon go away'. As the year advanced, the sufferings of those affected, mainly children but some adults, had become greater. In June, the master had been obliged to put ten children into the infirmary. The meeting of 6

August also detailed how Mr Whiting, on 25 June, had found thirty-seven cases of the itch. Most of them were children, and all cases had been seen by the guardians, who found their 'appearance most disgusting and pitiable'. These cases had not been new ones.

The guardians concluded there had been gross neglect, and now submitted their findings to the Poor Law Commissioners. Their reason for so doing was clear: they wanted to assure the inmates of the workhouse, and the public in general, that they were 'not wilfully indifferent to or negligent of the health and comfort of those who were under the necessity of accepting relief in the workhouse'. Once more we see how they presented a united front to the people of the Docking Union. If the latter were to believe in the New Poor Law it was vital the guardians made it work, and were scrupulous in their conduct. As a postscript, it was also reported on 6 August that the master had found twelve fresh cases: six children and six adults previously unaffected. He said he had had some difficulty in obtaining the necessary ointment from the medical officer and had not even received all he needed. The board then took the rather drastic decision not to admit any paupers into the house for two months. It being harvest they calculated that few of the able-bodied would seek admission.

Paul's fate was irrevocably sealed. The Commissioners wrote to say that they had fully considered the matter, and had come to the conclusion that Paul must be required to resign. We must, however, exercise caution. The minute books present entirely the guardians' version of events, and the guardians never appear in a bad light. We do not really know Paul's full explanation. He was very probably at fault, but he was overworked and not well paid. Ultimately it was a question of money: the guardians were elected and they needed to appease their electorate, the ratepayers. It was imperative to drive down costs, and the Docking Union was no different from other poor law unions; there were plenty far worse.

IV A Slowly Improving Situation

Negligence and incompetence were certainly evident in the behaviour of some medical men, as was the case with other workhouse officers. This was inevitable and the situation probably obtained in every poor law union to some extent. There was still neglect at the end of our period, but this must not detract from what was an improvement in medical aid to the poor, however imperfect. The doctors had to be properly qualified after 1842, although it was rarely the case that the best doctors worked for poor law unions. They also had to supply their own medicines, which might well explain the inadequacy of some treatments. And yet the poor were probably obtaining better treatment than before. A nurse was frequently assigned to the sick as the years passed, or more food was granted to the sick poor. In the 1840s we can see from the minutes that, where medical aid was given, it included meat, something not always a regular part of the diet of the poor. Naturally, we can merely speculate on the quality of the meat, but we can be sure the best cuts were not provided. At the board meeting of 20 February 1839, the chairman referred to a complaint from the auditor, that as much as one third of the meat supplied to the Docking Union was waste, a greater proportion than in any other union. The clerk was told to advertise for meat free from bone.

Where we can discern a definite move forward was in response to a serious outbreak of cholera in 1848. At the board meeting of 1 November 1848, the chairman (now C. F. N. Rolfe, Esq.) wished to call the attention of the guardians to 'the adoption of such means as should appear most advisable to reinforce cleanliness in the several Parishes, as one means of preventing the spreading of Cholera which had made its appearance in different parts of the Country'. Handbills informed the inhabitants of the parishes in the union that the guardians had the power to 'compel the removal of accumulated filth and all similar nuisances'. Several resolutions were passed unanimously: the board was to become a sanitary committee, and would appoint the guardians of the different parishes a sub-committee, to work together with the clergy and other persons. Their duties were far-reaching: they were to provide lime or other disinfectants where necessary; relieving officers were to report any nuisances to the sub-committee, and any failure to remedy them was to be reported to the full board; medical officers were also requested to assist the sub-committee and to arrange the best means of storing medicines. The final resolution was:

That the Board request the attention of the Poor Law Board [which replaced the Commission in 1847] *to the fact that many Houses in the District are so crowded together, having no proper drainage or conveniences that no sooner is the filth removed than a fresh accumulation commences.*

By this positive development, prompted by national legislation and the severity of the cholera outbreak, but efficiently managed by the Docking Guardians, the poor were to gain much. It took a long time for sanitary conditions in both urban and rural settings to be more like those of the present day. Yet, the board of the Docking Union, spurred on by their more diligent members, made genuine moves to eradicate the filthy conditions of several of the parishes under their jurisdiction.

The outbreak of cholera, which had begun in the summer of 1848, was particularly severe in East and West Rudham in February 1849; there were twenty-four deaths in the two parishes.[6] Frederick Manby, who had been the Rudham District medical officer only since 18 October, turned out to be something of a hero. On 10 January 1849 he reported a death in West Rudham and the appearance of other cases. He could see that things had to move quickly if the disease was not to spread. He recommended the inspection of the Rudhams, and of neighbouring parishes such as Syderstone, by an outside inspector from the Board of Health. He alluded to a house in West Rudham, occupied by a family called Rose. He left the board in no doubt as to its state: 'The squalid wretchedness of this House (Rose's) is scarcely to be exceeded by Ireland.' The guardians were then urged to abide by the resolutions of 1 November 1848, and report to the board what steps had been taken to carry them out in the various parishes. There was evidently some tardiness in this matter, as the clerk was instructed at the meeting of 17 January to write to those parishes that had not reported to the board.

At the same meeting, Manby presented a second report informing the guardians that there had been twenty-two cases in the two parishes. He had still not heard from the Board of Health, or seen any inspector. He reminded the board that it was obvious that, where the cases had been most virulent, there were always 'stagnant pools or other filth' near the dwellings. He had ordered brandy, rice, sugar, chloride, and other items to be procured, and given out as needed by the poor.

The board then formed a committee to act on the reports from the parishes and to ascertain what steps had been taken since 1 November. The guardians learned that in the majority of parishes visits had been made to the cottages, and recommendations carried out. However, from some parishes the reports were unsatisfactory as regards both the state of the cottages and the adjacent heaps of manure and filth. The minutes continued: 'but it appears from the perusal of the whole that there is a lamentable want of privies and other accommodation necessary for the maintenance of healthy and cleanly habits.' It was noted that in about a dozen parishes, Great Bircham and Bircham Tofts among them, 'whole rows of Houses have been built without these conveniences'. In particular it was felt that the heaps of filth close to the doors of cottages, and even in yards or gardens, presented an intractable problem.

The board again discussed the matter on 14 February, and now their tireless resolve to bring about improvements was unmistakable. Where there were no privies, or they were in disrepair, the owners of the properties (or their agents) were now informed that a complaint had been made to the guardians. The latter sent a petition to the Board of Health. They wanted any parishes not taking public health seriously to be compelled to do so:

The Guardians wish to suggest that although the general regulations issued by the Board of Health must if only partially carried out be of great service; that it is still highly necessary that some measure of a public and compulsory nature should be adopted to regulate the Building of Houses with ground attached sufficient to provide healthy accommodation and efficient drainage.

The Docking Guardians seemed unwavering in their determination to eradicate dirty habits not only in the workhouse but also throughout the union. It was something that exercised Victorian health reformers a great deal.

Notes

[1] 4th Report of the Poor Law Commissioners (1838), pp 228-65.

[2] J. Wood, *Letter to the Rev. George M. Musgrave containing strictures on a protest and a pamphlet by the Rev. Kirby Trimmer* (1838), pp 36-40.

[3] TNA: MH 12/8252

[4] D. Englander, *Poverty and Poor Law Reform in 19th Century Britain, 1834-1914* (London, 1998), p. 36.

[5] A. Digby, *Pauper Palaces* (London, 1978), p.167.

[6] C. Mackie, *Norfolk Annals*, Vol. 1 (Norwich, 1901), p. 475.

Chapter 11. Tamed at Last?

I. The inevitability of the New Poor Law

This book has at its core a riot involving many people. The over-whelming majority of those who thronged the narrow streets of Great Bircham were poor labouring men and women, employed (but rarely on a permanent basis) on the farms in the locality. Their protest was triggered by a change in relief awarded in addition to meagre wages, a change brought about by the passing of the Poor Law Amendment Act in August 1834. There were inevitably local factors. Besides the low offer of wages for cutting grass, there was the unpopularity of some farmers, and the fermenting of unrest by the tradespeople; but the riot had much in common with other forms of anti-Poor Law protest. In no way did the Bircham Riots prevent the formation of a poor law union centred on Docking; and the workhouse, built by the road from Docking to Sedgeford, remained in use for a great many years thereafter.

Only a very small fraction of the population of the Docking Union had occasion to enter the gates of the workhouse, and it was a minority of the union's population who had need of relief. In 1851, the period with the greatest number of outdoor paupers was the second week in December, when there were 1,245 on the books. The total population of the Docking Registration District, according to the census of that year, stood at 18,149. Naturally, there would have been more than 1,245 people receiving outdoor relief throughout the year, including payments for pauper funerals, but even so it must not be forgotten that, for many agricultural labourers, there was never a question of having to rely on doles from a relieving officer. Nevertheless, the system was in place and soon all the working-men and women of the various parishes in North-west Norfolk knew what it could or could not do for them. The workhouse cast its intimidatory shadow over the whole region. It was Kay who said that a workhouse should be 'as prison-like as possible',[1] and that would have been the effect it had on all who encountered it.

The New Poor Law was not to be ignored, and more often than not it was seen as a threat. We have seen some of its unpleasant effects such as its punitive regime towards able-bodied, children and women; its often inadequate medical treatment and unsatisfactory education in the workhouse school; flour given to the poor that was frequently of a substandard quality; and, something that quickly became obvious to all, its considerable reduction in relief payments. On the other hand there were distinct gains. These must include the help with migration and emigration, a concern to help young people (not always girls) into service, some genuine educational progress, an overall improvement in health care, and a real determination to tackle the poor sanitary condition of many villages.

II. Deference

There is one thing that strikes anyone reading the official reports or spoken words of guardians and clergymen, and that is the marked improvement in the relations between master and man. A year or so after the passing of the 1834 Poor Law Amendment Act, the Poor Law Commissioners were apparently likening its effects to nothing short of a miracle:

I have seen the effect on the poor-rates, the character of the population, the improvement of the land – such a change! I have talked with all sorts of persons, of all sorts of opinion on other subjects, and have heard but one opinion on this – that the measure has saved the country.

I am sick of the pitiful cry attempted to be raised against the measure, and especially at the supposed inhumanity of it. Let any man see the straightforward walk, the upright look of the labourer, as contrasted with what was before seen at every step in those counties. The sturdy and idle nuisance has already become the useful industrious member of society. No man who has not looked well into human nature, and the practical working of the wretched system of pauperism, can form an idea how different is sixpence earned by honest industry, and sixpence wrung from the pay-table of a parish officer.[2]

We have already read (Chapter 6) what Kay and Blyth wrote at the start of the Freebridge Lynn and Docking Unions. It is tempting to believe there must have been something in the sentiments expressed and that there was a real improvement throughout the labouring population. But that surely cannot have been the case, and as the New Poor Law became more established it became apparent that the poor had not embraced its provisions with universal accord. It might have been true that wages were higher in the west of Norfolk, but even so we cannot accept that the labourers had undergone a complete reversal in the assessment of their employers. Keith Snell quotes from a *Select Committee on Settlement and Poor Removal* (1847):

... the farmers were under a delusion; they think there is that tie existing between them and their labourers, but when you come to analyse it, you find there is no such thing in the present day, though there was formerly.[3]

Assistant Poor Law Commissioners, chairmen of boards of guardians and all who had been true supporters of the 1834 Act might have been deluding themselves, especially when it was important to sing the praises of the New Poor Law to the three Commissioners sitting in Somerset House; but it is doubtful if farmers truly saw an improvement in the relations between employer and employed. In rural unions like Docking the farmers were firmly in control. They had roundly defeated Speenhamland and all it stood for. No more would they need to use the rates to supplement wages with allowances. They might have had to box clever and manipulate the awarding of relief, particularly by not sending whole families into the workhouse when it was cheaper to give out-relief. Above all, they needed a deferential workforce, and the New Poor Law, with its grim prison-like workhouses, gave them that. So did the bullying conduct of relieving officers. The 1834 Act was supposed to favour the independent labourer; but that was the last thing the farmers wished to see. They wanted a tame labourer, with a deep psychological dread of the workhouse, one who would accept low wages and inadequate relief rather than be confined in one of those dreadful bastilles. If that meant a curtsey or a doffed cap, then that was how it had to be; but as long as farm labourers were oppressed any deeper transformation was impossible. Labourers were not deceived by the attractions of this much-vaunted independence either, especially as that came increasingly to underline the failure of their wages to rise to anything like adequate levels. Fifteen years after the passing of the Poor Law Amendment Act, these words from *The Morning Chronicle* are stark but telling:

As regards shelter and food, an industrious man is much better off if he pauperises himself ... To him independence is privation, whereas pauperism would be comfort.[4]

We must, nevertheless, accept that, at least for those we have come to regard as the 'deserving poor', the guardians of the Docking Union aimed to do their best. In common with what happened in many agricultural districts, Docking saw the creation, by the Docking Guardians in 1840, of the Docking Union Association. This replaced an earlier Smithdon and Brothercross Friendly Society. The full title of the association was *The Docking Union Association for Promoting & Rewarding Good Conduct and for the Encouragement of Industry & Frugality amongst Labourers, Servants, and Cottagers.* The president was Lord Cholmondeley and amongst the subscribers were Henry Blyth, Captain Davy, George Bate, John Drage, Thomas Hebgin, James Howlett, John Kitton and John Nurse. There were annual prizes, which must have been very welcome. Some were for farming skills: building corn stacks, thatching and hedging for instance; some still feature in competitions today. The most interesting prizes, however, were awarded for maintaining a large family without receiving parish relief, for being loyal servants, or keeping a tidy cottage. One wonders who these paragons were, but there were winners from the Birchams:

1840. Dennis Toll, of Bircham Tofts, labourer for James Howlett. 46 years on the same farm. He had received 12s. in relief, but still won a prize of £2.

1841 and 1842. Thomas Bowman of Great Bircham, a labourer with John Kitton, for supporting a family of eight children, seven of them under twelve, and had never received any parish relief. 2nd premium - £1 10s. 1st premium - £1 10s. His marrying a heavily pregnant bride in 1828 obviously did him no harm. (See Chapter 1.)

1842. William Osborne, shepherd to Thomas Hebgin of Great Bircham, had lived thirty-seven years in that capacity on the same farm.

1842 and 1844. Robert Marsham (a relative of the rioter), drillman to John Kitton. 1st premium - £2.

1847. Mary Lown, hired servant under twenty; three years, from the age of fourteen, with Thomas Hebgin of Great Bircham. 15s.

The association also encouraged clothing clubs, and these vied with each other to enrol the greatest number of members. In 1842 in Houghton, there were 111 members, paying 3d. each; and seventy-five in Bircham Newton and Bircham Tofts in 1843. Marquess Cholmondeley encouraged these clothing clubs, as well as benefit clubs. Anybody in the latter always received less relief if they applied to the Docking Guardians.[5]

Family historians would be pleased to come across these prize-winners, rather than to know their ancestors were drunkards, wife-beaters or complete idlers. Yet the working population was clearly subject to a strong degree of social control. To earn the prizes mentioned above demanded complete deference from the recipient. Ultimately, the whole system was degrading and did not help the labouring population in any way. What they needed above all – and this was very much in the minds of many rioters in Great Bircham in June 1835 – was an adequate wage. If paternalism had been overwhelmed by the market economy then both employers and employees needed equal treatment, and the freedom to bargain for wages and working conditions. It would be a long time before agricultural labourers were to become active in trade unions, and the struggle was to be long and hard. It would be longer still before they had the vote.

III. Paternalism in Bircham

Ten years after the momentous event of the summer of 1835, the farmers of the Bircham parishes were evidently pleased to display their charitable works to the world, or at least to those reading the Norfolk press. Perhaps they had been chastened by the riots, and felt a great need to do their duty by the poor. We have no reason to doubt the Christianity of the Kitton daughters and others, but to what extent they desired the material improvement of some of the Marquess of Cholmondeley's lesser tenants we must question. Nonetheless, the representatives of the Bircham ruling class could enjoy the happiness they engendered and start to believe that the bad old days had gone. It was, however, best to keep an eye on the ricks.

In July 1846, some 140 children belonging to the Great Bircham National and Church Sunday Schools were regaled with a sumptuous feast of plum pudding, roast beef and ale prepared by Rebecca Kitton and one of her daughters; the same feast, incidentally, would have been offered to any of the villagers of Bircham who happened to find themselves in Docking Workhouse on Christmas Day. 'Animating sports' were then on offer on a pasture made available by Charles Kitton, and before the children went home their stomachs were filled with more good things: cake, ale and nuts.

A similar entertainment, including 'jumping in sacks', was provided in 1847, and this time Thomas Hebgin made a pasture available and Mrs Hebgin supervised the tea and the plum pudding after the frolics. This was an occasion in praise of the noble landlord, and his wife. The incumbent of Great Bircham was of course there in both years with the headmaster of the school, and all the farmers and their wives. These entertainments were *not* Ranter celebrations, which the teachers, farmers and clergy present would have been most anxious to emphasise. In 1846, the children were praised by the Marchioness of Cholmondeley, who expressed herself most gratified by their 'decorous conduct and good order'. John Livock, the schoolteacher, was playing his part to perfection, and shaping the morals of the next generation of working men and women.[6] As early as 1838, at the time of the visitation, the incumbent, William Pratt, had considered that Sunday was being observed 'rather better than formerly'.[7] Perhaps relations between the classes had truly improved in the three Bircham parishes since 1835.

It is interesting to speculate how many of the children present were the offspring of 1835 rioters. Probably a good number; yet any thoughts of previous unrest or future hardships would have been far from the minds of the young villagers. Replete with good things to eat and drink, they could enjoy themselves, and their parents would not have to feed them that day. A few loud cheers for the Marquess and his good lady, would have completed the day; little did they need to care about the lifetime of deference ahead of them as domestic servants, farm labourers and dutiful inhabitants of the three villages.

IV. The final verdict on the Docking Union

Blyth, Davy and their fellow guardians tried to serve the poor of the Docking Union according to their lights, and according to the spirit of the age in which they lived. They operated in a framework of prejudice, paternalism and subordination; but they were not unfeeling brutes. There were certainly worse poor law unions than Docking. In October 1836, Kay had classed Docking as one of a number of 'very loyal Boards' in Norfolk.[8] It was a board which stayed loyal, as far as it could, to the state, but one which tried to do its best for the poor, or at least some of them. Frequently it did not succeed.

The Docking Guardians must have been pleased to hear the report of the Visiting Committee on 8 July 1845 to the effect that the old people were perfectly satisfied with their dormitory, and did not wish to have any alterations made. Or again, on 5 December 1849, we see another of those instances of the board asserting its right to go its own way. The Assistant Commissioner, Sir John Walsham, had complained that the aged and infirm inmates had been allowed to take their meals in their own wards. The board, however, felt they were perfectly satisfied with the arrangements, and the chairman was requested to write to say they could find no reason to alter them.

Yet, what do we make of this minute of 17 November 1841?

James Keeley, alias Bullock applied to have a pair of drawers, as he was very cold, which was not allowed.

Amongst the enormous amount of information in the minute books, it is very easily missed, and it seems a most insignificant entry. James Keeley of East Rudham was aged forty-five and out of work and had received, with his wife and five young children, an order for the house in October. He might have been a thorough nuisance who was just trying to annoy the master. He might, on the other hand, have really been feeling the cold. Whatever the circumstances he was a victim of the petty rules of an institution. The master and the porter, during a brief period in the 1840s, were indulging in equally petty squabbles about making bread, and showing their utter childishness. Sheer monotony and mind-numbing pettiness were ever present in the Docking Workhouse. The age of bureaucracy had arrived and many a poor labourer applying for relief must have been stunned by its dead hand.

Notes

[1] M.A.Crowther, *The Workhouse System 1834-1929* (London 1983), p. 41.
[2] 3rd Annual Report of the Poor Law Commissioners (1837), p. 73.
[3] K.D.M. Snell, *Annals of the Labouring Poor: Social Change and Agrarian England 1660-1900* (Cambridge, 1985), p. 116.
[4] *Morning Chronicle*, 10 Nov 1849.
[5] NRO: SO 17/1.
[6] *NC* 1 Aug 1846 & 17 Jul 1847.
[7] NRO: VIS 64/3.
[8] TNA: MH 32/48.

Conclusion - Mr Groom Pays a Visit

Not long after the riots Richard Groom came to Houghton. He was often there, and on 26 August 1835 John Drage sent in his bill for 'Goods for the Use of Mr. Groom when at Houghton'. He appears to have had a sweet tooth, as 3lb of loaf-sugar and 3lb of moist sugar had been supplied. There were also 1lb of currants and then mustard and a bottle of Reading Sauce.[1]

He did not come with the sole aim of discussing the riots. The repairs to the Bircham properties were well under way and the law had already taken much of its course as far as the rioters were concerned. His visit had to do, mainly, with improvements in Houghton village, and here he was influenced by the thoughts of Lord Henry Cholmondeley, the brother of the then Marquess. (He was later to become the third Marquess, when he became known as William.) Still kept at Houghton Hall are notes on the visit, which were written up in September.[2] The Marquess, his brother, Groom and even Stephen Reeve were remarkably silent on the riots. Nevertheless, in Groom's notes we have an inkling of a more enlightened attitude, a refreshing antidote to the vituperative rantings of some of the pamphleteers such as Trimmer and Godfrey, or the comments of Parry, Davy and Kitton.

He mentions various changes to the layout of Houghton Village Street, and concludes:

... the step will be a judicious one I think, by way of sounding the disposition of the Villagers, and giving them food for talk, from which it is not unlikely the best course of managing such a population may be discovered.

I am indisposed to take any abrupt measures towards the Villagers, particularly at this time, when the poor fancy the rich are conspiring to increase the privations of their condition by the New Poor Law System.

It is couched in very circumspect language, and is virtually devoid of emotion. There might also have been a touch of cowardice: those managing large estates could buy peace by treating their poorer tenants generously. It was not true democracy as we understand it. Can we, nevertheless, not hear the faint voice of reason here, in that willingness to talk to the Houghton villagers and to sound out their views? Shafts of light, however diffused, are certainly contained within the notes, and there is a distant prospect of the eradication of 'ignorance'. Writing of the new girls' school in the Square, Groom adds: 'I adhere to the Opinion I have expressed of the importance of elevating the minds of the Parishioners by a good rudimental education in reading, writing and arithmetic.' We can surely hang onto the idea of 'elevating minds'. It would take many years, but eventually educational standards would rise, labourers would be given the vote, and never again would a newspaper have cause to dismiss so contemptuously the population of a village as 'ignorant and uncultivated'.

The essential economic nexus, however, remained. On 17 February 1836, Stephen Reeve wrote to Richard Groom concerning a proposed reduction of ten per cent in farm rents. This section sums up exactly the farmers' situation:

The great reason is that the different expences of the Farmer have been by no means reduced to a level with the low price of grain. I cannot think there ought to be any further reduction in the wages of the Agricultural Labourers, but such is the effect the price of grain, wheat in particular, has upon agriculture that every Farmer feels the necessity for reducing his outlay, but is prevented doing so by a surplus poor, w^h he must either maintain or supply. A great deal of wheat has been consumed in this county in feeding cattle owing to the price being so low.[3]

Not all farmers saw it quite like this, and it would be a long time before labourers had anything like fair treatment from their employers; but it cannot be denied that farmers too were at the mercy of the rise and fall in prices, and of the vicissitudes of the weather.

Nonetheless, there was a huge gulf between the income of farmers and that of their labourers. There would be further struggles and further manifestations of the impotence of the poor (notably the burning of ricks) throughout the remainder of the nineteenth century and into the twentieth. Larry Banville, Lord Buxton's gamekeeper, was not the only contemporary of the Bircham Rioters to point out the hypocrisy of the attitudes of many of the great Norfolk families, such as those of his employer, with his Gurney and Fry connections. They had, with some justification, felt proud of their successful campaign against slavery, and yet were blind to the depressed and hopeless state of many poor families closer to home. Never again, however, would the farm labourers of Great Bircham assemble in large numbers and attempt to burn down farmhouses.

This book began with a visitor sitting outside the King's Head in the summer sunshine, unaware of what happened on that very spot at the end of June 1835. Let us finish by following the visitor down the road towards Docking. The route takes us past Church Farm and the site of Drage's shop. Shortly afterwards a right turn is reached by the bowling green, and it is a short walk, along Church Lane past the former post office and a number of houses which still bear the signs of having stood there in 1835, to reach the churchyard. Several of the players in our drama, all now equal in death, lie buried here.

The first gravestone presents us with a proud aspect; it is well preserved and is of Thomas Marsham, who died in 1884 aged sixty-eight, and of his wife Mary, who lived on until 1915, dying at the age of ninety. They were both related to rioters: Thomas Marsham's father slunk away from the village shortly after playing a minor part in the riots, and lived out the rest of his life in Lincolnshire. Mary was the niece of the rioter, John Pilgrim. Elsewhere there is also a gravestone for Rebecca Marsham, wife of the rioter, who died so soon after the riots, and her two daughters, Hannah and Maria.

A very short distance beyond the grave of Thomas and Mary, we come across two more. Their markers are placed with a symbolism, the poignancy of which cannot fail to strike anyone who has studied the Bircham Riots. John Shilling senior (the father of rioter John and his brother Horatio) and his wife Hannah face John and Rebecca Kitton. Shilling had spent some time in the workhouse before he died, a widower of some thirteen years, in 1849.

The Kittons' grave, behind rusting railings, looks a rather sorry sight. (There are much grander Kitton and Blyth slabs over tombs inside the church.) The stone's inscription is simple but fading. Next to it is the grave of their blind and unmarried daughter, Ellen; she died in 1885 and was seventeen at the time of the riots. Do they all feel confident facing John Shilling and were their consciences clear before they passed from this earth? We shall never know; but just a few yards away from their remains, in seemingly eternal defiance, lies the father of the young man who very possibly tried to burn their farmhouse down, and probably would have cared little if they had still been in it.

In the churchyard there is also a memorial stone to Luke Duffield, who lived on until the age of eighty-four, and his wife Mary. Duffield, a prominent Bircham Ranter, had been involved in the riots, yet had been discharged from the court when he was brought to trial. He worked as a groom for the Kittons for many years after the events of June 1835.

The Kittons are along the western wall of the churchyard. To the south of the church lie two more graves tellingly juxtaposed. Thomas and Susanna Hebgin lie in the ground under a coffin-shaped box, their headstone still clearly legible. Close behind them is the gravestone of the rioter John Pilgrim and his second wife, Elizabeth. It was Hebgin's identification of Pilgrim on 29 June 1835, when he was attempting, with Thomas Golding, to prevent John Hunter breaking the strike, that sent him off to Walsingham Bridewell for a month's hard labour. Pilgrim and his first wife, also called Elizabeth, were both Primitive Methodists.

It is not too far to walk from the church to Pond Farm. A visitor can sit by the pond, or look on the beautifully proportioned farmhouse. In the grounds of the ruined church of Bircham Tofts, visible from the pond, James Warnes Howlett and his wife, who both died in 1872, could be found, but it would take much effort to uncover their graves. It is best to let them sleep amongst the brambles, and walk back over the lanes to the King's Head. On the way there are many pictures to fill our minds: the seething mob ('monsters in the shape of men'[4] Godfrey called them) rushing down this very lane late on the evening of 29 June 1835, intent on destroying Howlett's farmhouse before the arrival of the civil force; the Howlett family cowering in the fields; the fleeing Kittons – with a blind daughter - and Hebgins, the latter with a very young child; a distraught Rebecca Marsham, close to death and with a baby not long born; and police constable Tilney lying helpless in Church Farm, believing his end had come. All were the result of acts, criminal then as now, performed by desperate men without a voice loud enough to be heard above the reforming clamour of the cohorts of the New Poor Law army.

There is one image which might linger longer in our brains, and that is the verse (from Psalm 37) on Pilgrim's gravestone:

Mark the perfect man and behold the upright
For the end of that man is peace.

The verse could have reminded those who read it of the shameless carnality of Thomas Hebgin, lying in the adjacent grave; but there was no perfect man in this drama. Most, if not all, would have struggled to be upright; but some, even among those desperate men (those drinking, cursing, wife- and child-beating men), must surely have found a measure of peace. It was a very ugly riot, and arguments may long continue as to its causes and as to its effects. As we make our way back to the King's Head, we can, if we pause a while, hear ever stronger the echoes of George Bennett's despair at the expectation that a labourer should live on 'half a stone and fifteen pence'; and we may wonder if the farmers who set that rate of pay ever found true peace.

Probably everybody in the three Bircham parishes and beyond, for many years after 1835, was compelled to reflect on the severe damage and injury that resulted from the riots. The rioters could hardly have achieved much more.

Notes

1 HH: M17
2 HH: M8; another copy is in the Cellar Documents (807k)
3 HH:M7c
4 Godfrey J. *The Poor Man's Friend or a Few Plain Words from a Plain Man* (Dereham), p.20

Appendix A

The complete list of rioters who appeared in court

There were eighteen men who appeared at the various trials following the riot of June 1835. It has been impossible to identify the person with certainty in all cases. The spelling of surnames had an inevitable fluidity at this time. Often a name was written as it was spoken; or an outsider attempted to write a 'correct' version. Where possible, alternative spellings have been noted.

The list gives some biographical details of the rioters, and where possible indicates where they were at the time of the 1851 census. Unless otherwise stated, it is assumed that baptism, marriage and burial took place in Great Bircham; and that the1851 census enumeration was in the same place. All cottages were of brick and flint and most had a pantile roof and a staircase. Thomas Marsham's cottage – a single dwelling 18ft x 14 ft 6 in. – had a straw roof. It was also described in the 1832 survey as 'in bad repair', and Carrington's cottage was in the same condition. Often the rioters and their families lived in properties divided into double or triple tenements. The amount of space available in them all was broadly similar to what Marsham had. Sometimes, however, there were lean-tos as well. Rooms in the principal dwelling were typically one or two downstairs with a pantry, and chambers above. Only the blacksmith, John Shilling, lived in a house, and its dimensions were larger than those of the humble labourers' cottages. It was 36 ft x 19 ft, with kitchen, parlour, stairs etc. on the ground floor, and had 3 chambers above. There were naturally other buildings including a detached shoeing shop, 45 ft x 17 ft; but this was an exception.

Unless otherwise stated the rioters were all agricultural labourers.

1. Thomas and William Bell; William Bullock

Thomas Bell was baptized on 6 January 1802, and his death was registered in 1872 in the Wisbech Registration District. He married Ann Bullock on 24 March 1823; both made their mark. By the summer of 1835 they had five children. At the time of the 1851 census, he was a widower, and was living in Tilney St Lawrence.

William Bell was Thomas's brother, and was born on 5 August 1805. He married Jane Matthews in 1829 in East Rudham, both signing with a cross. They had three children in 1835. They were still living in the village in 1851 and had six children. William was buried on 16 May 1881.

William Bullock was born on 12 April 1809 in Docking. He married Sarah Grange on 6 August 1840 in Docking, and they were both also unable to sign their names. They too were living in Tilney St Lawrence in 1851.

It is quite possible that William Bullock never moved from Docking. In May 1837 he appeared in the Docking Union Guardians' Minutes looking for work, for which he was granted a loan of 10s. It is impossible to say where he was in 1835, but he cannot be counted as a stranger from outside, given that he was the Bells' brother-in-law.

The mother of Thomas and William Bell – Elizabeth Webb – had been baptized in Great Bircham in 1772, but their father, also called Thomas, came from outside the parish.

In 1832 there were five families living in tenements within the Old Farm House. Thomas junior and Thomas senior had separate tenements, but not William. He probably lived with his parents. The 1836 rental shows the two brothers paid 16s. annually for a part of a cottage and an allotment, but their father (a widower since November 1832) paid just 10s. for his share of a cottage. They were all in arrears, and they still were in 1837: Thomas by as much as £1 2s. but he had been in prison for two years.

Hill's survey of 1800 mentions 'Bell's House'. It is tempting to think that the substantial property drawn by Hill, and situated in Church Lane, was the same one divided into five tenements by 1832.

Thomas Bell's imprisonment for his involvement in the riots was not his first visit to Swaffham Bridewell; nor was it his last (see below). In 1826 he served two months for stealing wheat from John Kitton.[1]

William made several appearances in the Guardians' Minutes: in 1845 and 1846, he was awarded relief in connection with his wife's illness. His father, too, was relieved in his infirmity. Thomas, however, appeared before the guardians more frequently than his brother and father. In November 1837, soon after his release from Walsingham Bridewell, he was given 3s. and one stone of flour for one week; but two weeks later he was out of work and had an order for the workhouse. In October 1838, he was again out of work, although his children earned 6s. a week, and received another order for the house. Later, in the early 1840s, there was relief for his wife, who died in February 1844; but the orders for the house began again at the end of that year. By early 1846, life in the Bell household must have fallen apart. His youngest son, George (3), was living with his grandmother, but she was very infirm. On 18 February, the child was given an order for the house; and his father was in Swaffham Bridewell. A month later, at the Quarter Sessions, he confessed to larceny and was sentenced to three months.[2] In May, another son, Samuel (14) was ill and had 2s. 6d. and half a stone of flour per week.

Thomas Bell senior, his wife and William appear in the 1839 Primitive Methodist class-lists.

2. George Bennett

George Bennett was born about 1778, probably in Brancaster. He married Margaret Park (who had been born in Lancashire) on 25 March 1805 in Thursford. By the time of the riots they were living with their married daughter, her husband and three grandchildren. In 1851 Bennett was no longer an agricultural labourer, but was enumerated as a baker; he was also a pauper. His daughter and her large family lived next door. He was buried on 20 April 1856.

The cottage where the Bennetts lived was let into three tenements. Another tenement was occupied by John Golding, probably Thomas Golding's brother. The rent for that year was £1 6s., and Bennett was 16s. in arrears at Michaelmas 1835, which was hardly surprising since he was in prison. By Michaelmas 1836, he was 6s. in arrears, and 12s. the following year.

George Bennett makes several appearances in the Houghton Farm Accounts kept by Stephen Reeve; but he was employed only at busy times of the year. He earned £1 4s. 3d. hoeing turnips and threshing oats in September 1833; and in August 1834 he and Golding earned £1 8s. for twelve days 'after turnips'. This must have been John Golding junior, the person who occupied another tenement in his cottage. The 1834 weekly wage worked out at 14s., considerably more than he normally earned. Nevertheless, despite being a pauper in 1851, he and his wife survived into old age.

His very many appearances before the Docking Guardians have been mentioned in Chapter 6. Of all those appearing in the courts after the riots he was the one who received the most relief, although given the age of his wife this was to be expected. No doubt the little relief they received – typically 2s. and a stone of flour per week – helped a little to lessen the poverty.

He does not appear in the Primitive Methodist class-lists, but his wife, daughter and son-in-law do.

3. Edward Carrington

He came from East Rudham where he was baptized on 21 December 1801. His parents, Thomas Carrington and Martha (Bussey), married in East Rudham in 1799, and probably moved to Great Bircham some time after Edward's birth. He married Martha Miles on 25 December 1824, both signing with x. There were four children in 1835. His working life is somewhat varied: in common with most men who appear in the Great

312

Bircham parish registers, he is given as a labourer; but that probably does not paint the complete picture. In 1851 he appears as a roadman. He was buried on 24 January 1865.

The 1832 survey does not show a separate dwelling house for Edward Carrington; but there is one for Thomas Carrington, who died in August 1836; after that his widow presumably went to live with her married daughter in Tower Hamlets, London, where two of her sons were also living. It was then, as we saw in Chapter 1, that the cottage was rebuilt. His mother must have settled in London and died there in 1846. The 1836 rental shows rent arrears of £2 owed on the property in 1835, but they were lost on the death of Thomas Carrington. In 1836 there were £3 14s. arrears, which can be partly explained by Edward's three months in Walsingham Bridewell.

In Chapter 1 we saw how Carrington worked in conjunction with his brother-in-law Robert Miles, shoemaker. In 1835 he was probably in the same cottage occupied by his parents. However, in the 1836 rental he and Robert Miles are jointly paying £2 6s. for a cottage and allotment (with arrears of £3 6s. at Michaelmas 1835). The rent was the same in 1837, but the arrears had become £6 6s.

Carrington was no stranger at the Docking Workhouse. His name first appeared in July 1842, when he was ill. He had three children under thirteen, and one earned 2s. 6d. He also received 8s. per week from his benefit club. He was awarded 2 stones of flour for one week. By November 1843, he was being offered the workhouse, although a week later he was awarded 2s. and 1½ stones of flour. Relief continued in December, when he was described as a cripple. In 1845, he was given relief on account of a bad foot; and around this time he left his wife and children in order to look for work. The rest of the family received an order for the workhouse. In January 1846, he was in the workhouse, but had left the boys outside to continue earning their 2s. per week. The last we hear of him is in the minutes for November 1846, when one daughter had gone into service and was allowed 10s. for clothing.

Carrington's son, Robert (born 1837), continued his father's radicalism later in the century. He was the local branch treasurer of the National Agricultural Labourers' Union; and he was also a trustee of the Bircham Primitive Methodist Church.[3] In 1871 he was living on Lynn Road, very close to his widowed mother, who was then living in one of the three almshouses created in the village by Lord Cholmondeley. She lived to a great age, having inherited the longevity of the Miles family, but she died (in 1893) in the workhouse.

4. Luke Duffield

It would appear there were three Duffield brothers – Luke, Walter and Robert – who were born in Flitcham and who came to Bircham early in the nineteenth century. There was also a John Duffield, probably a fourth brother, who married in Great Bircham in 1817. A probable sister was Elizabeth: she married James Morley in Great Bircham in 1823. Luke – born about 1788 in Flitcham - could well have been the first Duffield to come to Great Bircham, and he and his wife Mary were certainly there by the time of the 1811 census. Mary's maiden name was Saphy or Sapey, and she came from Holme next the Sea. They married in August 1808 in Bircham Newton and neither was able to do more than sign with a cross. The connection with Great Bircham, however, might be earlier than the beginning of the nine-teenth century: a John Duffield married Esther Royce in 1769; both were of the parish, and neither signed with a cross.

It is not easy to identify where he was living in 1835. He does not appear in the 1836 rental, but he is there in 1837 living with James Duffield, his married son. James is mentioned in 1836, and so we must assume that Luke was probably living with him in 1835 too. He had been widowed in 1834. There were no arrears of rent shown in either 1836 or 1837. In the censuses of 1851, 1861 and 1871 he appears as a groom at Church Farm.

We saw in Chapter 1 how Duffield had registered a dwelling house for worship in 1833. Whether this was the cottage where he lived is not clear. What is obvious is that the Duffields were prominent dissenters. The 1839 and 1841 Primitive Methodist lists, both of which have many names, do not show that Luke Duffield was a member of either of the two classes, but daughters Elizabeth Morley and Jemima Bowman are there in one class; and Robert and Ann Duffield are in the other one, along with other Duffields. It is evident that the Duffields had a considerable influence on Primitive Methodism in the Bircham parishes. Elizabeth Morley was a schoolmistress in 1851, and it should be recalled what was said at the time of the 1838 Visitation about the influence of the Ranters over the Bircham schools. (See Chapter 1.) A class was held at the Morleys' cottage, which (in 1851) was on the Lynn Road, next to the field barn occupied by Matthew and Jemima Bowman and their large family. Perhaps that was the dwelling registered by Luke Duffield in 1833. The 1851 Religious Census gave the details of the Great Bircham Primitive Methodist meeting house: a cottage 16ft x 14 ft. The dwelling where he lived in 1832, divided into three tenements, was 48ft x 18ft.

The other Bircham class was in Bircham Newton, and Robert Duffield was both leader and local preacher. Robert is of some interest in that he was described as a carrier in the 1851 census and a farmer of thirteen acres. The

314

Great Bircham farmers do not appear to have had any objections to the Duffields; although we cannot say how the servants viewed their masters. Luke Duffield was working as a groom with the Kittons in 1851 and 1861; and a Charlotte Duffield was a servant with the Hebgins in 1841. Relationships between the inhabitants of the three Bircham parishes were not simply determined by constant hostility between the labourers and their employers. There was a multitude of nuances, and the records can do no more than open a window onto some of them.

5. John and Thomas Golding

John or Jonathan Golding married Mary Wright in Great Bircham in 1801, both making their mark. John died in March 1844 and he had been a widower since 1826. The name was also written as Golden (occasionally Goldon) and Golding (or sometimes Goulding). In the 1851 census, Thomas is Golding and his brother is John Golden. For simplicity's sake Golding has been chosen as the preferred version, but it is impossible to give a 'correct' version.

No obvious birthplace has been found for the elder John Golding, nor for his wife. We must assume he came to Great Bircham around 1800, possibly earlier.

Golding senior paid £1 3s. for his cottage and half an allotment. It is very likely the other tenement in the cottage was occupied by Robert Ransome, shoemaker. Ransome also had half an allotment, and they must have shared the whole plot.

Thomas Golding, John and Mary's second son, was born on 25 October 1804. He married Mary Rippingale on 13 October 1823; neither of them could sign their name. He was buried on 17 September 1882. He paid a rent of £2 6s. but was in arrears by £3 5s. at Michaelmas 1835. A note gave the reason: 'In prison for Riot[g]'. The arrears had grown to £4 19s. by Michaelmas 1836. They were £7 5s. in 1837, although in February 1836 his brother did pay 6s. towards the rent bill, along with 5s. of his own rent, which came to £1 6s.

Shortly before he died, John Golding senior received relief from the Docking Guardians. Thomas appeared in the minutes in 1837 and 1838. There were funeral expenses for two of his sons, and then in April 1838 he was allowed 20s. as assistance with the funeral expenses of his wife. During his wife's final illness he had had the assistance of a medical officer, and also 21 bushels of coal. Thomas Golding was also relieved, in illness, in the autumn of 1846. Those appear to be the only occasions when the Goldings of Bircham were mentioned in the Guardians' Minutes.

Thomas Golding had one sister, Mary Ann, who married Robert Marsham in 1832; he must have been related to the rioter, Thomas

315

Marsham. She was one of the few women mentioned in the account of the trials and, called as a defence witness, she declared she had been with the mob for three or four hours on 29 June.

There is a Golding briefly mentioned in the Houghton labour accounts, but it is impossible to say which one he was. It might have been Thomas, but could also have been his brother, John. On 21 September 1833 Chapman, Golding, Rippingale, Bennett and Waddelow were paid 1s. 7d. each for one day threshing oats, and 2s. 3d. a day (over eleven days) for hoeing turnips.

Neither John Golding senior nor Thomas and Mary Anne appear on any Primitive Methodist class-lists, but John junior certainly does. Moreover, his wife (formerly Susan Curson) was a Local Preacher.

6. Richard Greeves

The name was possibly more correctly Greaves; sometimes it appears as Grieves.

Richard Greeves, the second of that name, was born in Great Bircham on 4 October 1805, but his parents – Thomas and Sarah (formerly Davey) – were married in Bircham Tofts in 1798. Thomas had been born in Docking in 1774, the son of Richard and Mary Grieves.

By the time of the riots, he was living - probably in one of the five tenements in the Old Farm House with the two Thomas Bells as neighbours – with his wife Frances and one child. He had married Frances Mitchell on 13 October 1830, both making their mark. In 1851 he was still living in Great Bircham with Frances and five children.

Greeves featured just once in the Guardians' Minutes: in December 1846 he was ill and a bill of 14s. was allowed for extra medical relief. His brother, however, was an inmate of the workhouse around this time. In November of that year James Greeves of Great Bircham was sent to the refractory ward for behaving badly.

There is no evidence of Richard Greeves being a Primitive Methodist, but his brother Thomas was.

7. George Harrison

The only positive thing we can say about George Harrison's family is that his sister was called Bathsheba Ewen. She was mentioned at his trial. (See Chapter 4.) We know that Bathsheba Harrison (daughter of William and Elizabeth Harrison) was born on 29 October 1802, and baptized in Sedgeford a month later. She married John Ewen in 1826. Baptisms of some of Bathsheba's other siblings are in the Sedgeford Parish Register, but not that of George. They seem to have been a literate family: William signed the register when he married and so did Bathsheba at her own marriage.

The burial of a George Harrison, aged 22, recorded in the Sedgeford Burial Register on 3 September 1836, must be that of the Bircham rioter; and in that case he died before the completion of his two-year prison sentence imposed in July 1835.

Here was a man whose young life was brought to an untimely end. Of course, men in their early twenties died of natural causes; their working conditions were hard and their diet often inadequate, but they were out in the fresh air. Suddenly George Harrison was confined to a small cell, and allowed no more than one hour per day for exercise. As for diet, the men had to be adequately fed because they were constantly at work on the tread-wheel. Displayed inside the old Bridewell is an extract from a report made by the Walsingham surgeon in 1842. He was proud of the health of the prisoners, and asserted that it could be attributed to the changes in diet he introduced after a man had been in prison for two months. His further statement is revealing: 'The ordinary diet is too low; you cannot keep a man here three months without injuring him, and rendering him incapable of that labour which is required of him to produce the means of self-support.' We can only wonder whether the prisoners of 1835 and 1836 had a diet unlikely to prevent physical harm, or whether a sympathetic surgeon supplemented it in some way. The 1842 report also indicated that it was after two months 'that the influence of the depressing passions are first observed'. Harrison's psychological state may have played a part in bringing him to an early grave.

Prisons, like workhouses, had punishment cells. Walsingham had its dark cell, which after the closing of the shutter allowed no light whatsoever. Punishment also involved cutting down on food. Sometimes prisoners were sentenced to be whipped. Five years before Harrison was sent to the Bridewell, Lord Townshend had been charged by fellow magistrates with introducing a whip of a very cruel nature. Such a whip, he declared, he had found there but 'he had substituted the naval cat, which could not injure any one'.[4]

Harrison may not have been the man who wielded the hammer and inflicted a deep wound on the side of Tilney's head, but he certainly had a bludgeon and very probably used it. His violence at Heath Farm is evident from the newspaper reports. Tilney was from Walsingham; is it too fanciful to suggest that some kind of revenge was taken?

8. William Hill

Of all the eighteen rioters he is the most difficult to identify. It is probable that his grandfather was Robert Hill, who married Elizabeth Marsters in Sedgeford in 1782. Elizabeth died in 1832, in Great Bircham, and Robert was probably living in one half of a cottage in the same year. Robert and Elizabeth had five

317

sons who lived into adulthood. Any one of these could have been the parent of William Hill; or he might even have been the illegitimate son of one of Robert and Elizabeth's daughters. No baptism has been found; but he was possibly born in Great or Little Massingham in about 1813.

The 1861 census for Great Bircham might have recorded him. There is a William Hill, married (his wife Ellen was from Ireland) and with three children. The age (47) certainly fits. If this is our man then his life after being released from prison is rather interesting. His eldest child, John (13), was described as a British subject and had been born in Kingston, North America. Perhaps this man went to Canada soon after leaving the Bridewell. There is no William Hill of an age to be the man who was active in the riots living in Bircham in 1841. Possibly this William took advantage of the Docking Union emigration policy. That probably was not from Great Bircham, however, as the parish does not appear to have supported any emigrants.

The family did not return to North America, but went to Beckenham, Kent; and he very probably died here in 1872. Here William must have worked for a water company, as he was enumerated as an assistant turncock in 1871. A guess has been made that this was the rioter. Although his birthplace in 1861 is given as Great Bircham, it appears as Massingham in 1871. Even that does not allow us to make a positive identification, as two of the sons of Robert and Elizabeth married in one or other of the two Massinghams; and the son of one was born there.

9. Thomas Marsham

Much has been written about Thomas Marsham and his children in Chapter 9. In a family which battled with poverty, and apparently came out well in the fight, he was no hero.

It would seem that his father was William Marsham, but the latter did not appear in Great Bircham until around 1780. It is not known from where he came. William fathered an illegitimate child (George) by Mary Webb (widow) in 1784; but he had married Mary by the time Thomas was born in 1787 (in Great Bircham). William was not in Great Bircham in 1811, but a John Marsham was there with his wife Frances and their four children. Given that Thomas married in Oulton – Rebecca Burton on 16 December 1813 – and that this John was born in Oxnead, it seems likely that the Marshams originated from that part of Norfolk. John, who was born in 1778, might have been a younger brother of William; or at least the two were related in some way. It was John's son, Robert, who married Mary Anne Golding.

Thomas Marsham's rent, in the 1836 rental, was £1 16s. He was in arrears by 6s. at Michaelmas 1835, and that had grown to £1 2s. a year later and £2 18s. in 1837. As was stated in the Guardians' Minutes, it was not long after this that he deserted his family, leaving them at the mercy of the New Poor Law.

It was left to his wife and daughters to support the Bircham Ranters.

10. William Miles

Even though Miles was an agricultural labourer, we now move to a family occupying a slightly higher social position than that of most other rioters. His brother was Robert Miles, shoemaker. (See Chapter 1.) They certainly were an old Bircham family, and several of them served as parish clerks. Given their long association with Great Bircham and this minor parochial role, they must have felt themselves in some degree to be a match for farmers like Kitton and Hebgin.

William Miles was born on 14 February 1789, and he married Mary Todd on 5 November 1829. They both signed x. In 1835 there were four children in the household, including his wife's illegitimate son. He and Mary, and five children, were still in the village in 1851.

William's sister, Martha, was married to Edward Carrington. Thus, with a brother who was a shoemaker (one of those traditional village radicals) and another rioter (with shoemaking connections) as a brother-in-law, he was well primed to join the Bircham Riots in some capacity. He cannot have played more than a supporting role, however.

Unlike some other rioters he did not fall into large rent arrears. His rent was £2 6s., and at Michaelmas 1835, and again in 1836, the arrears were 4s. They had become 10s. by 1837, but his brother and Carrington stood £2 18s. in arrears.

There were two mentions of his name in the Guardians' Minutes, and both in connection with illness. In August 1842, he was awarded 2s. 6d. and three stones of flour per week during his illness. Two of his children were earning 7s. a week during the harvest, and at other times of the year this was usually 3s. 6d. Next, in October 1847, one of his children was ill and the relieving officer ordered a surgeon. His brother had made a will and left everything to his second wife, Catherine (formerly Spooner). Robert and Catherine had produced a son, another Robert. The money was really for Robert junior, but he died an infant. Catherine followed him six years later, and thus any money in the savings account in the King's Lynn bank came to William, and to his sister Martha and brother-in-law Edward Carrington.

The fact that the office of parish clerk had been occupied by several generations of the Miles family clearly meant they were not going to be found singing from the Ranter hymn-book on Sundays.

319

11. John Pilgrim

By contrast, John Pilgrim was a very prominent member of the Primitive Methodist congregation. He appears in the class-lists of 1839, 1841 and 1843, along with his first wife. She died in 1849, and Pilgrim married his second wife, Elizabeth Bunning, in 1852 in Great Bircham. He was born on 24 July 1796 in Great Massingham, and his first wife was Elizabeth Dix; they married in Docking on 23 January 1829. He was able to sign his name. There were no children in 1835.

At the time of his first marriage his parish was given as Heacham; when he and Elizabeth moved to Bircham is not clear. In the parish of Bircham Tofts a son William was baptized, in May 1831; he died later in the same year. A death of an Anne Pilgrim, aged five, is recorded in the burial register in 1834. The child had been born in Docking in 1829, and in the register Pilgrim's occupation is intriguingly given as husbandman, not the usual labourer. There is no Pilgrim in the 1832 survey for any of the Bircham parishes, but John Pilgrim was paying 6s. rent on an allotment in Bircham Tofts in 1836. He was in arrears by the same amount in 1835. By 1837 he was paying £1 10s. (and had no arrears) for the late Thomas Carrington's cottage and allotment in Great Bircham. It is probable, therefore, that he was living in Bircham Tofts in 1835. In 1851 he was in Great Bircham, where he died in August 1876. Living with him in 1851 was his niece, Mary Ewer, who later married Thomas Marsham, a relative of the rioter.

He was in regular employment at Houghton at various times between 1833 and 1835, as is evident from Stephen Reeve's ledger. (See Chapter 1.)

His name has not been seen in the Docking Guardians' Minutes.

12. John Shilling

Something of the background of the Shillings, blacksmiths, was given in Chapter 1. Of all the rioters who appeared in court, he was the one who was clearly of a higher status than most men in the village. The rent on the house, garden and smith's shop was £10 per annum; and at Michaelmas 1835 John Shilling senior was in arrears by the same amount. John Shilling junior also belonged to that young and mostly literate group.

He was baptized on 14 April 1816 and he married Charlotte Scott – who could not write her name – in October 1836, in Bircham Tofts. He was still a blacksmith in 1851, and lived there with his wife and three children.

In July 1839, the Norfolk magistrates, especially those from the Docking area, must have been delighted when John Shilling junior and his brother, Horatio, appeared at the Walsingham Quarter Sessions. Four men in total stood charged with assaulting John Wilkinson and Richard Barnham, police officers at Docking. The men had been at the Rudham Fair and had been drinking over hours in a public house. The officers were in the act of closing the house when they were assaulted. Wilkinson came off worse than his colleague: he was thrown down, jumped upon and kicked. He was so badly kicked that he lost the sight of one eye. Three of the men were found guilty, and received sentences of imprisonment: Horatio to twelve months in Swaffham Bridewell and John to eighteen months in Norwich. The younger Shilling had tried to prove an alibi, but failed. His occupation was given not as blacksmith but as a carrier between Bircham and Norwich.[5]

1839 was not a good year for the Shilling brothers. In January the Police Report, read out at the weekly meeting of the Docking Guardians, stated that Horatio Shilling and Thomas Mindham of Bircham had been taken to Walsingham on suspicion of having stolen two deer traps. Edward Mindham had also been found in possession of ten rabbit traps. Most of the traps had names or initials on them. One wonders if the Shillings had had a hand in making them. It was clear that Bircham poachers had not only rabbits to catch, but Lord Cholmondeley's deer were also a tempting target. Venison would have made a welcome addition to the pot or have been sold on to third parties.

It is just possible that John Shilling was imprisoned in Swaffham Bridewell in June 1841 after being found guilty of felony and embezzlement. The sentence was three months and the last week was to be in solitary confinement.[6] No newspaper account of the Swaffham Sessions of 13 June has been found, and it is therefore not possible to be certain. The age (28) more or less fits, and even though the 1841 census was taken on the night of 6 June (when John Shilling junior was enumerated with his wife and two children in Great Bircham) he could still have been taken to Swaffham after the census night. There were, however, other Shilling families in Norfolk at this time.

It is interesting that John Shilling was able to escape imprisonment at his trial at the Assizes after the riots. Horatio had been equally fortunate in April 1827, when he too appeared at the Assizes; he was 'capitally charged with having on the 4th of Aug. last, maliciously cut and maimed a mare of Mr. Howlett, of Bircham Magna'. He was acquitted, no doubt much to Howlett's dismay, 'the evidence being very slight against the prisoner'.[7] (See Chapter 5,V.)

John Shilling junior does not seem to have made an appearance in the Guardians' Minutes; but his brother did. In January 1848, he was out of work, but nothing more than 'no entry' is written in the minute book.

After the 1851 census, John Shilling disappears completely; in the censuses of 1861 and 1871 Horatio was apparently carrying on the blacksmith's business from the same premises in Gaywood. Perhaps John fared better than his elder brother: Horatio was buried in South Lynn in September 1883, having died in the workhouse.

No Shillings were recorded in the Primitive Methodist class-lists, but Horatio married the daughter of the class leader and local preacher, Robert Duffield.

13. William Wanfer

Wanfer would have been the way everybody said the name, but it was also written Wanford (sometimes Wangford, Wanfor or even Walford). The same thing happened with Sanfer; but it is hardly possible to assert with any conviction what the 'correct' version was.

It is not possible to be certain of the identity of William Wanfer, but the most likely parents were Robert and Mary Wanfer (formerly Wakeman). They married in Bircham Tofts in 1792 and unusually this was by licence; they both made their mark. Eleven baptisms of children born to this couple have been found, mainly in Bircham Tofts, between 1793 and 1821; there might be two more appearing in the 1841 census. However, William appears on no census nor has any baptism been found for him. The only mention of a William Wanfer in any register is the burial in 1836 (Bircham Tofts) of William Wanford (26). Thus he must have been born around 1810, probably in Bircham Tofts. The age does not match that given in the records of the Quarter Sessions, however. (See Chapter 4.) Even so, the assumption has been made that the rioter William Wanfer was the son of Robert and Mary Wanfer; there does not appear to be any other family of that name in any of the Bircham parishes. As his death was in March and he had been sentenced in July 1835 to six months in the Bridewell, he must have died shortly after his release. Perhaps he was another victim of the prison conditions of the 1830s.

The tenement where Robert Wangford lived in 1832 in Bircham Tofts was in the same building occupied by William Hill, who was probably either the father or uncle of the rioter of the same name. The rent was £2 6s., and there were arrears of 6s. at Michaelmas 1835, a situation that was unchanged the following year.

14. Samuel Whitby

Yet again, the identity of this rioter is not certain, and all that can be done is to make a guess based on the available evidence. There is no Whitby in the 1832 survey in any of the three Bircham parishes and there is nobody of that name in the 1836 and 1837 rentals. It is still just possible that there was a Whitby living in Bircham Tofts in 1835, however. On 5 July 1837 the case of John Whitby, shepherd of Bircham Tofts, came before the Docking

322

Guardians. He was ill and his wages were 10s. per week. Since he had had £5 12s. 6d. for selling his lambs, the case was dismissed. Three weeks later he was still infirm and he was awarded 1s. and half a stone of flour per week. He was described as a widower. Next we come across the marriage of Jane Whitby to Isaac Bambridge in Bircham Tofts in 1840. The bride's father is John Whitby, labourer. In 1841 John Whitby was living with Isaac and Jane Bambridge in Bircham Tofts, and he was a shepherd.

It would appear that John Whitby had married Elizabeth Hunt in Harpley in 1805. Some children from this marriage have been found: Mary (1807) and John (1809) baptized in Bircham Tofts; Catherine (1813) and William (1818) baptized in Sedgeford; and it is also possible that there was a Sarah baptized in 1805 in North Creake. Unfortunately no baptism for Jane or Samuel has been found.

However, John Whitby was living with his son-in-law Isaac Bambridge in Bircham Tofts in 1851. Jane was in the same household, and her birthplace was given as Sedgeford. Now, it is possible that the Samuel Whitby, shepherd, aged thirty-six and born 'Setchford' enumerated with his wife, Martha, and their children in Worthing in 1851 was the son of John Whitby and the sister of Jane. There are certainly two neat gaps in the baptismal record for them to fit into. To give weight to this theory we might add that Samuel's eldest son was called John, and he had a daughter called Catherine. If this is the rioter, then he was probably the same Samuel Whitby who married Martha Whitrick in 1843 in the Mitford and Launditch Registration District.

Just like John Shilling and his family, the Whitbys seem to disappear after 1851. Little more can be said. John Whitby was described as a pauper in 1851, and two years later he was buried in Bircham Tofts having died in the workhouse. The apparent Sedgeford connection between the two young men (Samuel Whitby and George Harrison) taking part in the riots is intriguing.

15. James Williamson

The name is a common one and it cannot be said with complete confidence that the correct one has been identified; yet using baptismal and census records one man has been selected who fits the age given in the court records, and was not far from Great Bircham.

The James Williamson who was baptized in Great Bircham in 1813, the son of James Williamson and Mary his wife (formerly Everett), was possibly not living in the parish in 1835. According to the 1851 census, but not later ones, he was born in Bircham Tofts.

The James Williamson who married Ann Playford (Docking, 13 October 1837) was certainly the one enumerated in Docking with his family in 1851,

1861 and 1871. The Marriage Register is of some help. His father's first name, James, fits; but the surname has become Everet, his mother's name. His signing the register with a cross is consistent with the fact that the rioter of the same name was given as unable to write in the court records. He also made some appearances in the Guardians' Minutes. Though living in Docking, his parish was given as Great Bircham. Under the settlement law that was correct. In November 1841, aged twenty-eight, with a wife and two children, he was out of work and was offered the house. The same thing happened in October 1842. Then, in September1846, one of his children died and funeral expenses were allowed.

There were many Williamsons around at the time of the riots, and some were in Bircham. All that can be said is that James Williamson, baptized in Great Bircham in 1813, might have been one of that group of young and active rioters.

Appendix B: Relief in the Docking Union

An examination of the Docking Union Guardians' Minutes and Bacon's *Report on Norfolk Agriculture* (1844) makes it difficult to escape the conclusion that the three Birchams were pauperized parishes.

Since so few people were relieved inside the workhouse, compared to those who were relieved outside it, the figures for outdoor relief are the most illuminating. First it is useful to remember that there were far more women and children than men who received outdoor relief. The table below is taken from Bacon, and it is for the whole of the Docking Union during the early years of its existence.

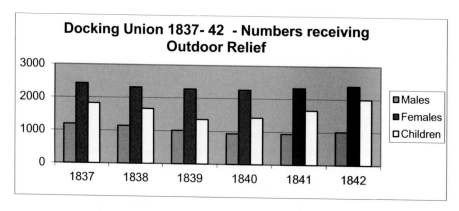

The numbers of men and women do not vary a great deal; but there is quite a rise in the children in 1842. From these few years it is not possible to point with any certainty to the trend towards giving men outdoor relief rather than offering them the house. As we saw in Chapter 6, there were some instances of this; but a much closer examination of the figures would be needed to show exactly what was happening in the Docking Union.

The next table, also from Bacon, shows the annual totals of indoor paupers for the years 1837-1842. There is a large increase in children in 1838, and again in 1842 and there are always more children than men or women. As well as infirm women and those incapable of looking after themselves, there were the deserted women and those with illegitimate children. No wonder that it became imperative to educate the children in the late 1830s. These years also covered the notorious period of the dress of shame, covered in Chapter 9.

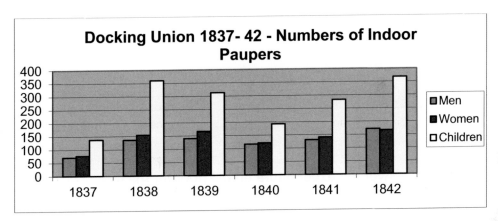

There were, naturally, seasonal variations, especially for able-bodied men, who were not in the workhouse in such great numbers in the summer months. It was the unemployment of the winter that brought them and their families into the house. The same pattern was repeated with outdoor relief. Every parish will have its own special characteristics; and given the numbers are small and relatively few years have been studied, there can well be odd results. By the mid-1840s, there are more paupers in the three Birchams than in other parishes with populations of similar size. Great Bircham may be compared, in size of population, with Hunstanton, Stanhoe and West Rudham. Similar groups have been created for the other two Bircham parishes. In 1838, not long after the start of the Docking Union, the amount spent on outdoor relief was broadly similar in the four parishes. However, ten years later Great Bircham had pulled away from the others. In the case of Hunstanton there was a huge difference: by 1847 just over £350 was being spent annually on outdoor relief in Great Bircham, but barely £100 in

Hunstanton. It might have been that the Great Bircham guardians were more generous – or less zealous in their task - than those in other parishes; but there seemed to be a compelling need in the Birchams, one which could not be ignored.

If the whole expenditure on the poor for the years 1842-45, including indoor relief and doles of flour, is considered, it becomes very apparent that the three Bircham parishes were distinctly pauperized compared with other comparable parishes

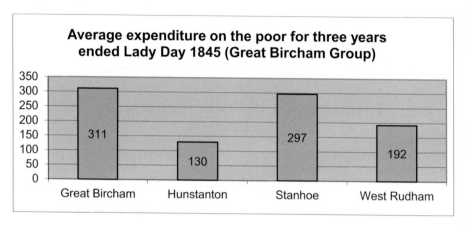

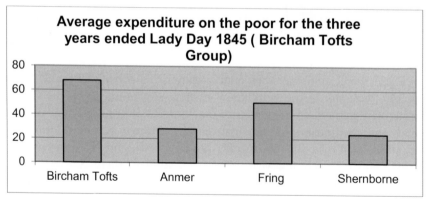

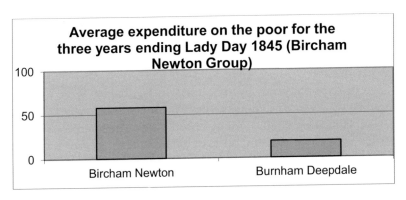

Average expenditure on the poor for the three years ending Lady Day 1845 (Bircham Newton Group)

An examination of the numbers of outdoor paupers, rather than the money expended on them, reveals that the Bircham parishes did not necessarily have the greatest number of people in receipt of relief outside the workhouse in all years. In 1838 Great Bircham had, in fact, the fewest outdoor paupers in its group; and over the next few years Stanhoe and West Rudham still had more. Not until 1843 did it have more outdoor paupers than the other three parishes. The same trend can be observed with Bircham Tofts and Bircham Newton. Unfortunately the figures are not available for all the quarters after 1843, but what survives in the Guardians' Minutes is still useful. There might be freak results in some quarters, caused by a sudden surge in relief payments, but a general pattern emerges. A closer examination of the minute books would reveal how many were being temporarily relieved, due possibly to a brief illness, or how many were receiving regular relief. In the latter category would be those too old or infirm to work, or widows.

To pay for relief a rate had to be levied. If Bircham rate-payers thought their bills would go down after the passing of the Poor Law Amendment Act they would have been disappointed. By 1847, the total annual rate bill for Great Bircham was nearly £600; whereas it was below £200 for Hunstanton.

Appendix C: Thomas Hebgin and Mary Anne Spanton

In 1835 Thomas Hebgin was the farmer of Town Farm, Great Bircham, where he had lived since at least 1800. He was born in 1789 (in Shouldham Thorpe), and he married Susanna Wright in 1832 in Saham Toney.

Susanna Spanton was the eldest child of Thomas and Susanna Spanton, and was born on 10 January 1810 in Great Bircham. Her parents had married, also in Great Bircham, on 30 October 1809. Coincidentally her mother's maiden name had also been Wright.

The illegitimate daughter of Thomas Hebgin and the younger Susanna Spanton, Mary Anne Spanton, was baptized in Great Bircham on 11 February 1827. Susanna had probably just turned seventeen when she gave birth to her daughter. Mary Anne Spanton married Stephen Doughty on 1 April 1849 in West Rudham. In the Marriage Register for West Rudham her father's name is given as 'Thomas Hibgin, Farmer'. Stephen Doughty was from a New Houghton family, and had been born there in 1822. Stephen and Mary Anne appear to have had at least three children before they married: William (1844), Hannah (1848) and Charles (1848).

Mary Anne's mother, Susanna Spanton, married Henry Johnson on 31 October 1831 in Great Bircham. She died in Houghton in 1845. Henry and Susanna had several children: Henry (1834), Charles Spanton (1836), Thomas Spanton (1836), Spanton (1839) and Maria (1844).

Thomas Hebgin evidently provided for his illegitimate daughter. In 1841, when the census was taken, she was living with her mother, stepfather and her half-brothers in New Houghton. In the occupation column she appears as 'Ind', which meant she was of independent means. As for her grandmother, Susan Spanton, she too appeared as 'Ind.' in the 1841 Great Bircham census; she had, however, been given an order for the workhouse in December 1840, which she refused. By then she was a widow, her husband having died in 1830. Later, in April 1841, she was granted 1s. and half a stone of flour per week in relief. It was established by the Docking Guardians that her son was able to assist her, and that could have been the reason for the 'Ind.' Her daughter, Sarah, was a dressmaker. By 1851, Susan Spanton was enumerated as a pauper.

According to the 1851 census, Susan Spanton was living quite close to Town Farm. It is very possible, therefore, that her daughter had worked as a servant for the Hebgins, although she was not given as such in the Great Bircham Register of Baptisms. It was common for the register to indicate if the mother of the illegitimate child was a servant. There was one woman, Elizabeth Abell, who had two such children (in 1816 and 1818); in both cases she was not simply given as a servant, but the name of her employer also appeared. This was Barker, another Bircham farmer; in 1818 his forename, Samuel, was also given. It is, of course, quite impossible to prove, but one wonders if the minister was going as close as he could to giving the child's father. In no other case of a servant girl giving birth to an illegitimate child was the employer's name given.

For Mary Anne Doughty things turned out well. In 1849 she, her husband and two children (William and Hannah) were among a group of eleven people – three married couples in their twenties and their children - who emigrated to Canada. All their expenses, including tickets and conveyance to Southampton, board and lodging in London, and boxes for their luggage were paid by Lord Cholmondeley. The Doughtys settled in Madoc, Ontario, and Stephen later became a farmer.[8]

1826 was not a year of good fortune for Thomas Hebgin. As has already been established (see Chapter 1), the decision not to continue with the farm had been taken by the autumn of that year. It would appear that this period of financial decline was accompanied by a moral one.

Appendix D: The dietary used in Docking Workhouse

On 18 November 1836 Francis Oakes, Clerk to the Docking Union, sent a letter to the Poor Law Commissioners in London enclosing a copy of the dietary which the Docking Board of Guardians proposed to introduce.[9] It had been adapted from the dietary of the Bosmere and Claydon Union; but in reality it was not greatly different from one of the Commissioners' standard dietaries.

Two notes accompanied the dietaries shown on the opposite page:

Old People of 60 years of age and upwards may be allowed 1 oz. of Tea, 5 oz. of Butter and 7 oz. of sugar per week, in lieu of Gruel for Breakfast, if desired Expedient to make this change.

The sick to be dieted as directed by the Medical Officer.

A note was added to the letter in London:

The Dietary appears in every respect unobjectionable.

On 15 August 1843, Oakes was writing to Somerset House again, and sending an amended dietary, 'which from repeated complaints of the able-bodied Paupers that they had not sufficient Bread, and more Cheese than was required, the Visiting Committee recommended the Board to take the subject into consideration'. The master, John Wilson, put the new dietary on trial for a fortnight, and reported to the board 'that the alteration was very much liked by the paupers, and no doubt would give general satisfaction'.

329

Dietary for able-bodied men and women

		Breakfast		Dinner					Supper	
		Bread	Gruel	Meat	Bread	Potatoes	Soup	Cheese	Bread	Cheese
		oz.	pints	oz.	oz.	lbs.	pints	oz.	oz.	oz.
Sunday	Men	6	1½	5					6	1
	Women	5	1½	5					5	1
Monday	Men	6	1½		6		1½		6	1
	Women	5	1½		6		1½		5	1
Tuesday	Men	6	1½		7			1	6	1
	Women	5	1½		6			1	5	1
Wednesday	Men	6	1½		6		1½		6	1
	Women	5	1½		6		1½		5	1
Thursday	Men	6	1½	5					6	1
	Women	5	1½	5					5	1
Friday	Men	6	1½		7			1	6	1
	Women	5	1½		6			1	5	1
Saturday	Men	6	1½		7			1	6	1
	Women	5	1½		6			1	5	1

Dietary for children under sixteen.

	Breakfast		Dinner					Supper	
	Bread	Gruel	Meat	Bread	Potatoes	Soup	Cheese	Bread	Cheese
	oz.	pints	oz.	oz.	lbs.	pints	oz.	oz.	oz.
Sunday	4½	1	3	4	½			4½	1
Monday	4½	1		4½		1		4½	1
Tuesday	4½	1		4½			1	4½	1
Wednesday	4½	1		4		1		4½	1
Thursday	4½	1	3	4½	½			4½	1
Friday	4½	1		4½			1	4½	1
Saturday	4½	1		4½			1	4½	1

Appendix E: The sale of Hebgin's stock, utensils and furniture

The following is an advertisement which appeared in *The Norfolk Chronicle* of 23 September 1826.

Flock of Prime Southdown Ewes, Cart and Nag Horses, Dairy of Polled Cows, and Agricultural Implements.

GREAT BIRCHAM.
By W. STURLEY
On Wednesday, Thursday, and Friday, the 4th, 5th and 6th of October, 1826, ALL the Live and Dead FARMING STOCK, Dairy and Brewing Utensils, and Household Furniture, of the late Mr. THOMAS HEBGIN, Great Bircham, Norfolk.
   Comprising 13 score of superior Southdown stock ewes, selected from some of the first flocks in the county, three score crones, five Leicester tups, two Southdown ditto, 57 Southdown ewe lambs, 12 valuable working horses and mares, brown five-year-old mare with foal at foot, bay ditto with ditto, four-year-old grey nag ditto by Fireaway, with ditto, six-year-old black gig mare, very fast and gentle, fine dark brown horse rising six, with fine action, either for road or field, bay mare five-year-old by Shales, roan nag horse five-year-old, a fast trotter by Golden Ball, brown four-year-old (off) nag mare by Trumpator, bay four-year-old nag colt, brown three-year-old cart filly, black yearling ditto, roan nag ditto, six handsome polled cows in profit, three two-year-old heifers in calf, two yearling ditto, one ditto steer, 44 strong store pigs, a brace of excellent greyhounds, two good road wagons, three harvest ditto; four large muck tumbrels, square luggage cart, water ditto, cup drill sowing machine, horse rake, drill roll, two-horse shaft roll, barley ditto, scarifier, four two-horse wheel ploughs, five one-horse ditto, large flag harrow, two pair of five-balked ditto, two pair of six-balked ditto, turnip ditto, 14 sheep troughs, turnip and straw bins, stacking stage, long and short ladders, about 20 dozen hurdles, cart and plough harness, saddle, two lady's ditto, gathering forks, pitching ditto, short ditto, long and short headed rakes, chaff cutting machine, pig troughs, wagon ropes, &c &c. also a neat gig and harness, with cushions, lamps, &c. complete.
   Dairy and Brewing Utensils, Household Furniture, &c. – Include treble milk lead, milk trays, churn, butter and milk keelers[10], pans, large brewing copper and furnace, mash tub, wort[11] ditto, two half barrels, 27 ten and twelve-gallon casks, ale stools, a very excellent patent mangle, folding iron board, large and small copper boilers, ditto saucepans, four post and other bedsteads and hangings, featherbeds and bedding, dressing and other chests of drawers, mahogany hair seated and other chairs, two Kidderminster carpets, large mahogany swing dressing ditto, eight-day clock in wainscot case, many volumes of books, an assortment of glass, china and earthenware, with every other household requisite, also 14 geese, 12 ducks, 12 turkeys, 12 guinea fowls, & about 50 hens & cocks.
   Catalogues to be had at the principal Inns in the Neighbourhood, Place of Sale, and of the Auctioneer, Dersingham.

Order of Sale. – Implements, Sheep and Working Horses, the First Day. Implements, Nag and Young Horses, Neat Stock, Pigs, and Fowls, the Second. Dairy and Brewing Utensils, Household Furniture, &c. the Third.

The whole will be Sold without the least Reserve, as the Family have declined carrying on the Farm any longer.

Each day's Sale will begin at Eleven o'clock precisely.

Appendix F: Details of Bircham farms

Susanna Wade Martins tells us that, in 1850, the majority of Norfolk farms were under 100 acres. In the light-soil area of North-west Norfolk, where some of the great estates were to be found, large farms of over 300 acres were common.[12] Clearly in 1835 there were larger farms in Norfolk than those in the three Birchams, but whatever scale is used there is no denying that the farms of Denny, Hebgin, Howlett and Kitton were huge. The buildings, including any barn conversions (as at Town Farm or Church Farm), are still impressive. Even a casual glance today points more graphically than any number of words to the wealth and power of the Bircham farmers in the nineteenth century.

The acreages are from the 1838 Tithe Apportionments:

> Church Farm – 825 acres.
> Town Farm – 608 acres.
> Heath House Farm – 940 acres.
> Pond Farm – 430 acres.

Annual rents were also high. The figures are from 1834:

> Church Farm – £400.
> Town Farm – £260.
> Heath House Farm – £450.
> Pond Farm – £280.

The 1832 Survey gives good descriptions of the farms. The farmhouses are what any progressive farmer who has invested much of his capital into the farm would expect. Pond Farm had a particularly impressive farmhouse: 72ft x 21 ft. There were an entrance, staircase, kitchen, keeping room, parlour on the ground floor; and five chambers and attics above. The others were very similar. All had lean-tos and other subsidiary buildings.

Naturally, in an area dominated by the cultivation of barley and wheat, the barns were substantial. Church Farm had three barns – one of them 84 ft x 27 ft – and Heath House Farm had an enormous barn measuring 144 ft x 20 ft.

All the farms had many horses, and the stables were impressive. Heath House Farm had farm horse stables (102 ft x 17 ft) and ride stables (46 ft x 16 ft 6 in.). Church Farm had three stables: farm, loose and ride.

Other out-buildings were on all the farms. There were, for instance, brew houses, bullock lodges, cow houses, waggon lodges, granaries and hog cotes. Sometimes there was also accommodation for farm servants: Heath House Farm had a double tenement with two rooms and a pantry on the ground floor, and two chambers above.

Heath House Farm, tenant Daniel Denny *(Photo 2011)*

Notes

The information on the eighteen rioters has been taken mostly from the Bircham parish registers, the 1851 and other censuses for the three parishes, Habbakuk Englestown's 1832 survey (HH: M24r), and the rentals for 1836 and 1837, kept at Houghton Hall. Details from other parish registers have been found online at FreeReg and FamilySearch; and censuses from other places and the General Registry Office. The 1811 census, the original of which is in the NRO (PD 34/43), has been consulted online on the GENUKI website. Indexes have also been consulted at findmypast.co.uk. The Primitive Methodist class-lists are at NRO (FC 54/461). The Docking Union Guardians' Minutes have been consulted online at FamilySearch. The originals are in the NRO.

Stephen Reeve's ledger is at Houghton Hall (M60).

Robert Miles's will is at the NRO (1843 - ME/20 284/2).

The detailed descriptions of the four farms are taken from Habbakuk Englestown's survey, 1832. The 1834 rents are taken from the 1834 rental, kept at Houghton Hall. The details from 1800 are from Joseph Hill's Survey of the Houghton Hall Estate, 1800 (Norfolk Record Society, Vol. L, 1984; edited David Yaxley); and those for 1838 from the Tithe Apportionments for Great Bircham and Bircham Tofts (NRO: DN/TA 155 & DN/TA 164).

[1] *NC*, 26 Jan 1826.

[2] NRO: C/S 1/24 (Quarter Sessions, Sessions Book 1830-35).

[3] N. Scotland, *Methodism and the Revolt 0f the Field:A Study of the Methodist Contribution to Agricultural Trade Unionism in East Anglia*, 1872-1896 (Gloucester 1981), Index of Agricultural Union Leaders in Lincolnshire, Norfolk and Suffolk 1872-92.

[4] *BNP*, 27 Oct 1830.

[5] NRO: C/S 1/25; NC, 20 Jul 1839.

[6] NRO: C/S 1/26.

[7] *NC*, 7 Apr 1827.

[8] I am grateful to Judy Mitchell of Thunder Bay, Ontario, and a descendant of one of the emigrants, for sending me information about the Doughtys in Canada. There is a bundle of papers at Houghton Hall which gives details of the emigration (HH: M17).

[9] TNA: MH 12/8249.

[10] keeler – a vessel for cooling liquids (OED).

[11] wort – unfermented beer (OED

[12] S.Wade Martins, *Norfolk: A Changing Countryside 1780-1914* (Phillimore 1988), pp 26-28

Bibliography

I. MANUSCRIPT SOURCES

Cheshire Record Office
DCH/X/11: Cholmondeley Papers; private correspondence, c. 1830.

Houghton Hall
Expenditure 1836.
Receipts 1836.
Rental 1834.
Rental 1836.
Rental 1837.

M6o: Farm accounts 1833-35.
M7c: Estate Letters 1835.
M8: Rentals c. 1800-35; also contains correspondence 1835-36.
M17: Estate and general vouchers and bills 1833-53.
M24r: Description of buildings on the Houghton Estate 1832.
M29: Houghton Parish Constables' and Overseers' Accounts 1738-1835.

Norfolk Record Office
C/GP/4/2-11: Minute Books of the Docking Poor Law Union October 1836 –
June 1854.
C/GP 4/39: Docking Poor Law Union, Ledger April 1839 – June 1840.
C/GP 4/96-97: Docking Poor Law Union, Parochial Ledgers, October 1835 –
December 1844.
C/GP 6/1: Minute Book of the Erpingham Poor Law Union, 1836-38.
C/S 1/24: Norfolk Quarter Sessions, Sessions Book 1830-35.
C/S 1/25: Norfolk Quarter Sessions, Sessions Book 1836-39.
C/S 1/26: Norfolk Quarter Sessions, Sessions Book 1840-45.
C/S 4/6: Norfolk Quarter Sessions, Minute Book 1833-37.
C/Saa 3/16-17: Petitions to Quarter Sessions against closing Walsingham
Bridewell, 1828.
C/Saa 5/1-4: Bundle of Reports and Petitions, 1839-42.
C/Scd 2/27: Smithdon and Brothercross Division, Land Tax Assessments
1777-1832.
DN/TA 40: Bircham Newton Tithe Map (1838) and Apportionment (1838).
DN/TA 155: Great Bircham Tithe Map (1838) and Apportionment (1839).
DN/TA 164: Bircham Tofts Tithe Map (1838) and Apportionment (1839).
DN/DIS 4/1: Register of Meeting Houses 1810-24.
DN/DIS 4/2: Register of Meeting Houses 1824-52.
DN/VIS 46/6: Visitation Questions (Heacham) 1813.
DN/VIS 53/1: Visitation Questions (Heacham) 1820.
DN/VIS 64/3: Visitation Questions (Heacham) 1838.
FC 54/461: Lynn Primitive Methodist Circuit, membership lists 1838-44.

SO 17/1: Records of the Docking Union Association 1840-50.

The National Archives
ADM 175/77, 78: Records of the Coastguard; Registers of Nomination for Appointment, 1827-41.
ADM 175/97: Records of the Coastguard; Indexes to Registers, 1819-41.
ASSI 33/12: Records of Justices of Assize, Norfolk and South-Eastern Circuits 1831-36.
HO 27/50: Criminal Registers 1835.
HO 41/12: Disturbance Books, Vol. 12, 1834-37.
HO 43/47: Domestic Entry Books, June – Dec 1835.
HO 52/26: Counties Correspondence (Bedford - Oxford) 1835.
HO 52/30: Counties Correspondence (Lincoln – Surrey) 1836.
HO 64/ 2-5: Criminal (Rewards and Pardons) Correspondence, 1831-35.
HO 73/3: Royal Commission Appointed as to the Best Means of Establishing an Efficient Constabulary Force; letters and papers 1836-38.
HO 73/7: Returns from Local Guardians to the Constabulary Commission, 1836-38.
MH 1/1, 2, 3: Poor Law Commission Minute Books, Aug. 1834 – Nov. 1835.
MH 12/8249 - 8254: Docking Poor Law Union Correspondence, 1834-53.
MH 12/8375: Freebridge Lynn Poor Law Union Correspondence, 1834-38.
MH 15/1: Subject Index of Correspondence, 1836.
MH 32/48: Correspondence of Assistant Poor Law Commissioners; correspondence with James Phillips Kay, 1835-36.
MH 32/60: Correspondence of Assistant Poor Law Commissioners; correspondence with Sir Edward Parry, 1834-36.
MH 33/4, 5: Poor Law Commission: Register of Correspondence, 1834-46 (J P Kay and W E Parry).

II. BRITISH PARLIAMENTARY PAPERS

1834, XXX-XXXIV, *Answers to Rural Queries*, pts. 1-5.
1835, *Reports of the Select Committee of the House of Lords on Gaols and Houses of Correction in England and Wales.*
1835–45, *Annual Reports of the Poor Law Commissioners.*
1843, XII, *Reports of Assistant Commissioners on the Employment of Women and Children in Agriculture.*

III. PERIODICALS

Bury and Norwich Post
Chester Chronicle, 1870
East Anglian, 1831
Morning Chronicle
Norfolk Chronicle
Norfolk Mercury

IV. CONTEMPORARY PRINTED WORKS (pre-1900)

Bacon, Richard Noverre, *The History of the Agriculture of Norfolk* (London, 1849).

Brereton, Rev. Charles D., *Observations on the Administration of the Poor Laws in Agricultural Districts* (Norwich, 1823).

Caird, James, *English Agriculture in 1850-51* (London, 1852).

Cobbett, William, *Rural Rides* (London, 1830), ed. George Woodcock (Penguin 1967).

Fellowes, John, *Short and Plain Address from a Clergyman to his Parishioners on some of the Chief Provisions of the Poor Law Amendment Act,* (Norwich, 1836).

Fulcher, George W., *Village Paupers* (1840-44), ed. E. A. Goodwyn (Beccles, 1981).

Godfrey, John, *The Poor Man's Friend or a Few Plain Words from a Plain Man* (Dereham 1835).

Hobson, Samuel, *The Nature and Design of the New Poor Law Explained* (London 1839).

Jessop, Augustus, *Arcady for Better for Worse* (London, 1887).

Kay, James P, 'Earnings of Agricultural Labourers in Norfolk and Suffolk', *Journal of the Statistical Society,* 1 (1839), pp 179-83.

Kent, Nathaniel, *General View of the Agriculture of the County of Norfolk* (London, 1796).

Loftus, Charles, *My Life: from 1815-1849* (London, 1877)

Marshall, William, *The Rural Economy of Norfolk* (two volumes) (London, 1787).

Nicholls, George, *A History of the English Poor Law* (London, 1898).

Parry, Rev. Edward, *Memoirs of Rear-Admiral Sir W. Edward Parry* (London, 1858).

Petty, John, *The History of the Primitive Methodist Connexion* (London, 1860).

Trimmer, Kirby, *The Folly, Sinfulness and Consequences of Stackburning* (Lynn, 1833).

Weyland, John, *Thoughts submitted to the Employers of Labour in the County of Norfolk with a few Words to the Employed* (Norwich, 1830).

— *Charge delivered to the Grand Jury of the County of Norfolk at the Easter Quarter Sessions 1834* (Norwich 1834).

Wood, John, *Letter to the Rev. George M. Musgrave containing strictures on a protest and a pamphlet by the Rev. Kirby Trimmer* (1838).

Young, Arthur, *The Farmer's Tour through the East of England* (Vol. II) (London 1771).

— *General View of the Agriculture of the County of Norfolk* (London 1804).

V. SECONDARY SOURCES

Ambler, Rod W., *Ranters, Revivalists and Reformers: Primitive Methodism and Rural Society South Lincolnshire 1817-1875* (Hull, 1989).

Archer, John E., *By a Flash and a Scare* (Breviary Stuff Publications, London, 2010).

— *Social Unrest and Popular Protest in England, 1780-1840* (Cambridge University Press, 2000).

Armstrong, Alan, *Farmworkers: A Social and Economic History 1770-1980* (London, 1988)

— *The Population of Victorian and Edwardian Norfolk* (Norwich, 2000).

Ashwin, Trevor and Davison, Alan, eds, *An Historical Atlas of Norfolk* (Phillimore, 2005).

Brundage, Anthony, *The Making of the New Poor Law (London, 1978)*.

— *The English Poor Laws 1700-1930*, (Basingstoke, 2002).

Burchardt, Jeremy and Cooper, Jacqueline, eds, *Breaking New Ground* (Milton Keynes, 2010).

Charlesworth, Andrew, ed., *An Atlas of Rural Protest in Britain 1548-1900* (London, 1983).

Checkland, S. G. and E. O. A., eds, *The Poor Law Report of 1834* (London, 1974).

Crowley, Jerry and Reid, Andy, eds, *The Poor Law in Norfolk 1700-1850* (Ely, 1983).

Crowther, M. A., *The Workhouse System 1834-1929* (London, 1983).

Digby, Anne, *Pauper Palaces* (London, 1978).

— 'The Rural Poor Law', in D. Fraser, ed., *The New Poor Law in the Nineteenth Century* (London, 1976).

— 'The Rural Poor', in G. E. Mingay, ed., *The Victorian Countryside*, Vol. 2 (London, 1981).

Ede, Janet and Virgoe, Norma, *Religious Workship in Norfolk: The 1851 Census of Accommodation and Attendance at Worship*; Norfolk Record Society Vol. LXII (1998).

Edsall, Nicholas C., *The Anti-Poor Law Movement 1834-44* (Manchester, 1971).

Edwards, George, *From Crow-Scaring to Westminster* (The Larks Press, 2008).

Englander, David, *Poverty and Poor Law Reform in 19th Century Britain, 1834-1914* (London, 1998).

Hamond, Mrs Philip, *Catherine Edwards Parry: A Record of her Life* (Norwich, 1900).

Harvey, John R., *Records of the Norfolk Yeomanry Cavalry* (Norwich, 1908).

Higginbotham, Peter, *The Workhouse Cookbook* (Stroud, 2008).

— *The Workhouse Encyclopedia* (Stroud, 2012).

Hobsbawm, Eric J., *Primitive Rebels* (Manchester, 1959).

— and Rudé, George, *Captain Swing* (Harmondsworth, 1973).

Holland, Michael, ed., *Swing Unmasked* (Milton Keynes, 2005).

Howells, Gary, 'Emigration and the New Poor Law: The Norfolk Emigration Fever of 1836', *Rural History*, 11, 2 (2000), 145-164.

Howkins, Alun, 'In the Sweat of thy Face: The Labourer and Work', in G. E. Mingay, ed., *The Victorian Countryside*, Vol. 2 (London, 1981).

Kendall, Rev. H. B., *The Origin and History of the Primitive Methodist Church*, two vols. (London, 1906).

King, Steven, *Poverty and Welfare in England, 1700-1850* (Manchester, 2000).

Knott, John, *Popular Opposition to the 1834 Poor Law* (London, 1986).

Lee, Robert, *Unquiet Country: Voices of the Rural Poor, 1820-1880* (Bollington, 2005).

Longmate, Norman, *The Workhouse* (London, 2003).

Mackie, Charles, *Norfolk Annals*, Vol. 1 (Norwich, 1901).

Obelkevich, James, *Religion and Rural Society: South Lindsey 1825-1875* (London, 1976).

Parry, Ann, *Parry of the Arctic* (London, 1963).

Peacock, A. J., 'Village Radicalism in East Anglia 1800-50', in Dunbabin, J. P. D., *Rural Discontent in Nineteenth Century Britain* (New York, 1974).

Pope, Stephen, *Gressenhall Farm and Workhouse* (Cromer, 2006).

Priestley, Philip, *Victorian Prison Lives* (London, 1985).

Reay, Barry, *The Last Rising of the Agricultural Labourers* (Breviary Stuff Publications, London, 2010).

— *Microhistories: Demography, Society and Culture in Rural England, 1800-1930* (Cambridge, 1996).

— *Rural Englands* (Basingstoke, 2004).

Rose, Michael E., *The English Poor Law 1780-1930* (Newton Abbott, 1971).

— *The Relief of Poverty 1834-1914* (Macmillan, 1972).

Scotland, Nigel, *Methodism and the Revolt of the Field: A Study of the Methodist Contribution to Agricultural Trade Unionism in East Anglia, 1872-1896* (Gloucester, 1981).

Snell, Keith D. M., *Annals of the Labouring Poor: Social Change and Agrarian England 1660-1900* (Cambridge, 1985).

Springall, L. Marion, *Labouring Life in Norfolk Villages, 1834-1914* (London, 1936).

Wade Martins, Susanna, *Norfolk: A Changing Countryside 1780-1914* (Phillimore, 1988).

Virgoe, Norma and Yaxley, Susan, eds, *The Banville Diaries, Journals of a Norfolk Gamekeeper 1822-44* (London, 1986).

Wheldon, F. W., *A Norvic Century* (Norwich, 1946).

Wrigley, E. A. and Schofield, R. S., *The Population History of England 1541-1871* (Cambridge, 1989).

Yaxley, David, ed., *Survey of the Houghton Hall Estate by Joseph Hill, 1800;* Norfolk Record Society, Vol. L (1984).

DISSERTATIONS

Allen, Barbara, 'Perspectives on Poverty: The Divergent Approaches to the Poor Law Amendment Act 1834 with Particular Reference to its Impact in the Docking Union', Third Year Dissertation (Cambridge University Board of Extra-mural Studies, 1990).

Archer, John E., 'Rural Protest in Norfolk and Suffolk 1830-70,' PhD thesis (University of East Anglia, 1982).

WEBSITES

The History of Parliament: http://www.historyofparliamentonline.org.
[Published as: *The History of Parliament: the House of Commons The History of Parliament 1790-1820*, ed. R. Thorne; and: *The House of Commons 1820-1832*, ed. D. R. Fisher, 2009 (Cambridge University Press)]
Norfolk Sources: http://www.norfolksources.norfolk.gov.uk
The Workhouse: http://www.workhouses.org.uk/

INDEX OF NAMES AND PLACES

Albemarle, Earl of, 188
Allen, George, 249
Ampthill (Bedfordshire), 163
Andrews, William, 228
Anmer, 106, 124
Appleton, 218
Archer, John, 70, 71, 185, 186, 189, 199, 206
Armstrong, Alan, 14
Astley, Sir Jacob, 111,113, 115, 117, 166
Ayres, Richard, 290
Ayton, Thomas, 242, 247
Bacon, Richard Noverre, 29, 49, 62, 65-66
Bagthorpe, 35, 40, 266
Bales, Daniel, 59, 60
Banville, Larry, 244, 306
Barker, John, 15; William, 232
Barmer, 241
Barwick, 103, 134
Bate, George, 48, 79, 85, 210, 300
Bathurst, Archdeacon Henry, 124
Beck Anthony, 14, 22, 97; Edward, 22; Fanny, 22; Frederick, 22; John, 158, 169, 175-176, 177; Kitty, 22; Margaret, 22; Mary, 22; William, 29
Bell, Jane, 56; Thomas, 50, 67, 104, 109, 136, 138-139, 141, 143, 151; William, 56, 137, 139
    See also Appendix A
Bennett, George, 59, 60, 105, 125, 134, 135, 136, 137, 139, 151, 159, 163, 212-213, 309; Margaret, 213; Mr & Mrs, 276
    See also Appendix A
Berry, Revd, 189
Bidewell, William, 115
Bilby, James, 277, 279, 280-281
Bircham, Great, 12-15, 20, 26, 27, 28, 31-50, 54, 55, 56, 58, 59, 60, 61, 63, 64, 67, 68, 69, 77, 80, 84, 86, 95, 97, 98, 100, 102, 103, 107-131, 133, 152, 165-166, 183-184, 189, 208, 215, 218, 226, 227, 229, 242, 257, 270, 273, 295, 300, 301, 302, 308, et passim
Bircham Newton, 13-15, 26, 41, 42, 45, 60, 67, 77, 84, 92, 93, 190, 242, 288, 301,
Bircham Tofts, 13-14, 15, 17, 22, 23, 24, 26, 27, 41, 45, 46, 60, 61, 77, 80, 84, 86, 95, 97, 10, 102, 107-131, 133, 172, 179, 183-184, 186-187, 189, 229, 259-260, 261, 272, 295, 300, 301, 309
Blyth, Anthony, 188-189; E.G., 282; Henry Etheridge, 17, 92, 188, 205-206, 208, 209, 211, 214, 217, 219, 222-223, 228, 231, 232, 236, 253, 256, 257, 267, 268, 269, 275, 278, 280, 285, 298, 300, 303; Samuel, 17; William, 15; family, 28
Blythe, H. E., 101
Booth, Thomas, 288-289
Boulton, Robert, 247
Bowman, Thomas, 300
Brancaster, 37, 82, 284-285
Brereton, Captain William, John, 11
Brett, Timothy, 178
Briston, 231
Brown, John, 94
Brundage, Anthony, 78
Bullock, James (aka Keeley), 303-304; John, 251-252; William, 137, 139, 140
    See also Appendix A
Burnham, Norton, 208; Overy, 56, 58, 129, 259; Thorpe, 218, 229, 290; Westgate, 17, 22, 53, 101, 104, 105
Burnham Westgate, 17, 22, 53, 101, 104, 105

341

Butcher, 58; Stephen, 106
Buxton, Lord, 244, 306
Caird, James, 13, 49
Caldwell, Henry, Berney, 117, 169, 170-171
Callaby, Christmas, 246
Carbrooke, 157
Carrington, Edward, 34, 105-106; Thomas, 60, 107, 134, 135, 137, 139, 151, See also Appendix A
Catley, Stephen Reed, 266
Chadwick, Edwin, 88, 89, 90, 157, 196, 198, 211, 217
Chapman, Dewing, 34, 46-7; John, 46-7; Sarah, 261
Cholmondeley, Lady, 71, 302; Lord George Horatio, Second Marquess, 11, 13, 30, 42, 43, 58, 60, 61, 62, 71-72, 79, 92, 93, 126, 128, 171, 180, 188, 190, 195-196, 210, 245, 300; Lord Henry, 305
Church, Mr, 284, 285, 290
Clarke, Mr, 105; Samuel, 21
Claxton, Ann, 42; Charles, 242; James, 42
Cobbett, William, 21, 87, 88, 90, 96, 164, 177, 198
Coke, Thomas, 232
Collinson (Collison), 103
Cooper, Ann, 137; John, 123
Covell, John, 243-244
Creake, North, 124, 206, 236, 242; South, 82, 214, 221, 229, 239, 242, 243, 248, 285
Crittenden, John, 283
Curry, Captain, 129; James, 210; William, 210
Curtis, John, 171, 185; Money, 106, 108, 136, 141, 149, 151,
Cutter family, 19, 27
Davies, Mr, 291
Davy, Captain John, 118, 173, 175, 179, 217, 246, 300, 303, 305
Daw, Phebe, 210

Denny, Bridget, Eleanor (née Clarke) 21; **Daniel, 14, 20-21, 28, 97, 102-3,105-106, 107, 115, 134, 135, 151, 178, See also Appendix F;** Samuel, 21
Dereham, 116-118
Dersingham, 82, 115, 208, 232, 240
Digby, Anne, 33, 40, 48, 56, 57, 81, 86, 158, 159, 177-178, 212, 228, 284
Docking, 14, 81, 82, 91, 92, 93, 108, 110, 116, 117, 118, 124, 129, 177, 189, 190-191, 205, 208, 21, 215, 218, 219, 224, 228, 234-235, 239, 241, 242, 246, 248, 258, 264, 265-271, 277, 280, 282, 283, 284 285, 290, 293, 294, 297, 299, 300, 303-304
Docking Union parishes, 92
Dodman, John, 225
Doughty, James, 243
Downham Market, 189
Drage, John, 32, 33, 56, 69, 127, 146, 300, 305, 306; John jun. 69
Duffield, Luke, 41, 107, 136, 137, 139, 308; Mary, 308, See also Appendix A
Dunger, 127
Dutton, Wingfield, 284-285
East Bradenham, 22
East Rudham, 26, 32, 53, 82, 128
Easton, 26, 16
Ede, Janet, 189, 190
Edsall, Nicholas, 162, 191-192
Edwards, George, 51, 71; Thomas, 71, 191, 117, 158
Eke, James, 248
England, Elizabeth, 40; Frances, 40, 109, 136, 195; George, 40, 53, 174; Martha, 40; Nicholas, 40
Englander, David, 86, 212, 284
Englestown, Habbakkuk, 16, 35, 59, 77
Evans, Mr, 138
Everard, Edward, 12

Everitt, Isaac 239
Ewen, Bathsheba, 137
Ewer, Mary, 257
Fakenham, 53, 114, 120, 124, 190
Fellowes, Revd John, 254
Ffolkes, Sir William, 156
Fisher, Mr, 283
Flitcham, 16, 82
Francis, James, 242
Frederick, Charles, 110
Freeman, Mr, 287
Garlett, Nelson, 35, 36
Gay, Margaret, 261
Gaywood, 37
George, James, 235
Gillingham, 21
Gimingham, 160, 244
Girling, Captain, 160
Godfrey, Ann (née Howlett), 24; John, 24, 174, 190-191, 201, 305, 309
Golding (Goldon), John, 35, 56, 59, 60, 63, 105, 137, 139, 308; 'Mrs' 50; Susanna, 42, 56; Thomas, 103, 104, 134, 135, 139, 152, 159, 173, 195, See also Appendix A
Goode, Revd Ambrose, 197-198, 220, 284
Great Massingham, 22, 53, 68, 169, 170
Greaves (Greeves, Greves),James, 227; Jane, 56; Richard, 60, 102-3, 134, 140; Thomas, 56 See also Appendix A
Gressenhall, 82, 238, 278
Grimston, 155, 158, 169-170
Groom, John, 32, 37-38, 126; Mary (née Spooner) 37-38; Richard, 11, 58, 60-61, 92, 93, 96, 126, 188, 305-307
Hamond, Ann, 256; Anthony, 196; Edward, 218; Sarah, 256
Harding, Mr, 226

Hare, Frederick, 124, 185, 278; Revd Humphrey John, 110, 131
Harpley, 22, 41, 81, 114, 218
Harrison, George, 105, 108, 136-137, 140, 141; Rebecca, 50, See also Appendix A
Harvey, Colonel John, 154
Heacham, 206
Hebert, 223-224, 227
Hebgin, Elizabeth, 30; John, 26; Robert, 26; Sarah, 31; Susanna (née Wright) 26, 27, 31; **Thomas, 14, 15, 16, 26-27, 28, 40, 69, 7, 78, 89, 91, 97, 103-104, 105, 108, 109, 115, 129, 134, 139, 140, 141, 178, 200, 219, 230, 258, 269, 270-271, 300, 301, 302, 308, 309, See also Appendix A, C, E, and F;** Thomas senior, 16, 30-31; William, 16, 26
Heckingham, 159, 160
Hempton, 117
Higginbotham, Peter, 246
Hill, Joseph, 17, 20, 22, 34, 35, 77; William, 105, 134, 135, 140, See also Appendix A
Hillborough, 117
Hillington, 155, 158
Hobsbawm, Eric, 42, 183
Hobson, Samuel, 255
Holkham, 232
Holland, Edmund, 29
Holloway, Revd Henry, 284-285, 287
Holt, 21, 111, 113, 117, 118, 133
Horsford, 17
Horsham, 17
Hoste, Captain Derick, 124, 125, 180
Houghton and Houghton Hall, 11, 16, 27, 30, 32, 34, 37, 39, 43, 46, 47, 48, 50, 52, 58, 59, 60, 79, 84, 85, 89, 114, 115,

116, 118, 126, 128, 145, 171, 209, 210, 214, 230, 231, 232, 245, 283, 301, 305
Howard, John, 146
Howell, Elizabeth, 56
Howells, Gary, 232
Howlett, Ann Warnes, 24; Elizabeth, Lucy (née Kitton) 17, 18, 19, 22; Fanny, 24; **James Warnes, 14, 22-24, 28, 97, 108, 115, 126, 129, 169 172, 171, 178, 179, 181-182, 186-187, 192, 219, 300, 308, See also Appendix F;** James sen., 23, 24-25; John Godfrey, 25; Sarah, 23; Sarah jun. 23, 24; other children, 24
Humphrey, Bloom 28, 32, 33
Hungerford, 191
Hunt, John, 50, 102-3, 134, 165
Hunter, John, 103, 108, 134, 308; William, 107, 108, 138, 140, 141
Ingoldisthorpe, 118, 179, 243
Ireson, Anne, 280, 285, 286; James, 285; Jane, 285, 286
James, Thomas, 239
Jarrett, Philip, 14, 26, 67, 69, 97
Jarvis, Lewis 11, 12, 77, 9, 126, 178, 179, 180
Jessop, Revd Augustus, 51
Kay, James, 49, 54, 60, 161, 176, 195, 203, 206, 215, 220, 222, 254, 255, 257, 273, 274, 275, 276, 277, 278, 279, 280, 283, 284, 297, 303
Kenninghall, 159, 160
Kent, Nathaniel, 200
King's Lynn, 22, 23, 24, 27, 54, 82, 118, 126, 133, 175, 190, 195, 198, 226, 277, 279, 291
Kitton, Charles, 20, 23, 24, 302; Edward, Wright, 19, 20, 27: Elizabeth, 17, 18, 19; Ellen, 17, 18, 19, 114, 307; Ellen,

Jane, (née Cutter) 19; Everard, 125; Henry, 18, 19, 20, 27: **John, 14, 16, 17, 18 19, 20, 24, 27, 28, 67, 72, 78, 89, 91, 94, 97, 98, 101, 104, 105, 10, 109, 111, 112-114, 126, 127, 128, 129, 135, 141, 143, 144, 145, 151, 158, 162, 166, 171, 178, 180, 181-182, 192, 200, 219, 230, 258-259, 274, 277, 300, 301, 305, 307, See also Appendix F;** John senior, 17; John (Revd, later Ketton), 18, 19, 20, 27-28; Lucy (née Blyth) 17, 23, 24; Margaret, Tillyard, 19; Rebecca, 17, 18, 19, 23; Rebecca Maria (née Blyth) 17, 92, 18 19, 20, 213, 302, 307; Mary, 17: Samuel Blyth, 17
Knatchbull, Revd H. E., 156
Lack, James, 32, 40, 127; William, 32, 242
Langley, 249
Leak, Ben, 111, 112, 113, 115-116, 119, 166
Lewis, Thomas, Frankland, 90, 101, 121, 122, 129, 130, 131, 167, 175
Little, Richard, 282
Livock, John, 302
Loftus, Lieutenant Charles, 116, 117-119; Frederick, 117
London, Bp of, 277, 279
Love, George, 126
Lown, Mary, 301
Manby, Frederick, 287, 294
Marshall, William, 200
Marsham, 37;Catherine, 258; Hannah, 50, 257-258, 307; Maria, 258, 307; Mary, 106, 136, 258-259, 283, 307; Rebecca, 152, 257, 258, 307, 308; Robert, 301: Thomas, 59,

60, 104, 138, 140, 152, 257, 307, 307, See also Appendix A; Thomas jun. 257, 307
Marsters, Thomas, 34, 59, 60
Massingham, Little, 158
Melbourne, Lord, 121
Melton Constable, 111, 116, 117
Mendham, James, 239, 288; Susanna, 288; Thomas, 239, , 288
Miles, Jane Maria (née Fox), 35; Robert, 32, 34, 35, 173, 176; William, 34, 35, 137, 140, See also Appendix A
Milles, Captain George, John, (later Lord Sondes) 116, 117, 118, 119, 129
Milton (Kent), 162
Mitchell, Michael, 238
Morston, 110, 115
Mott, Charles, 246
Murrell, Timothy, 160
Nicholls, George, 90, 243
North Creake, 124
Norwich, 24, 25, 37, 82, 116, 119, 125, 143, 146, 165, 190; Bp of, 282
Nurse, Ann (née Hebgin) 31; John, 14, 15, 16, 26, 69, 97, 115, 178, 300; John jun., 22, 26
Obelkevich, James, 39, 174
Osborne, William, 301
Oxley, 126
Palmer, Mr, 138
Parry, Sir Edward, 98-101, 104, 105, 109, 114, 117, 120, 121, 127, 129-131, 145, 152, 158, 160, 162, 165-6, 167, 170, 173, 175, 177, 196, 197, 198, 203, 207-208, 245-246, 305
Paul, Mr, 290-291, 292
Payne, 126
Phillipps, S.M., 144
Pickerell, 222

Pidsley, Revd Edward, 28
Pile, Martha, 256, 290; Susan, 256
Pilgrim, Elizabeth, 308; John, 46-7, 103, 105, 107, 134, 140, 159, 173, 174, 257, 307, 308, See also Appendix A
Playford, John, 280
Pratt, Revd William, 41, 172-173, 302
Priest, Edward, 41, 173
Pulham St Mary, 162
Quincey, Elizabeth, 24
Rainham, 116, 117
Ramm, Thomas, 210, 218
Ransome, Dinah (née Miles), 35; Robert, 32, 35; Thomas, 35
Raveningham, 2Reay, Barry, 271
Reeve, Stephen, 12, 26, 46, 47, 49, 50, 56, 58, 60, 92, 9, 127, 145, 188, 230, 305, 306
Rennie, Nathaniel, 241
Ricardo, David, 88
Ringstead, Great, 23, 61, 125, 261
Rhodes, Thomas, 236, 242
Rice, Edmund, see Royce
Rippingale, 47
Rix, Richard, 287-288
Robinson family, 35
Rodwell, George, 154; Mrs, 29
Rolfe, C.F.N., 293
Rollesby, 161, 192, 235
Rose, Robert, 242, 294
Ross, 277, 278, 279-280
Royce, Edmund, 32, 33; boys 46-7, 49
Rudé, George, 183
Rudham, East, 26, 32, 53, 82, 128, 215, 218, 235, 241, 242, 256, 287, 294, 303; West, 185, 206, 242, 256, 294
Rumbles, Hannah, 67
Rumbold, Robert, 34
Rush, Samuel, 247

Russell, Lord John, 96, 121, 122, 123-124, 125, 128, 136, 143, 144, 169
Saham Toney, 16
Salmon, John, 276
Sampher, Downing, 63
Sandford (Sanfer), 46, 58; William, 226-227
Sandringham, 12
Scholfield, R.S., 63
Sedgeford, 17, 23, 82, 124, 228, 247, 249
Senior, Nassau, 88
Senkler, Revd Edmund, 241, 266, 277, 278, 280, 285
Sewell, Sarah, 16
Seymour, Lady Charlotte, 71-72
Sharp, John, 37
Shaul, Mr, 285
Shaw-Lefevre, John, 90
Sheldram, John, 242
Sheringham, 160, 244
Shilling, Hannah, 37, 307; John jun., 32, 36, 79, 127, 137, 140, 141, 143, 145, 146, 152, 170, 176, 307, See also Appendix A; John sen. 145 176; children 37
Shipdham, 37, 157
Shotesham, 254
Shouldham Thorpe, 16
Simmonds (Simmons), John, 103
Smith, 228; John, 41, 190, 248
Snell, Keith, 49, 50, 86, 299
Snettisham, 12, 82, 190, 250
Spalding (Lincolnshire), 257
Spanton, Mary Anne, 270; Susanna, 270, See also Appendix A
Speenhamland, 83, 201, 220
Spooner, Catherine (née Brinn or Bunn) 38; Martha, 32, 56; Martha jun. 38; Robert sen., 32, 53, 79, 174; Robert jun. 38; William, 38

Spurgeon, Christopher, 42; Revd John, 270, 271
Sprowston, 16, 17
Stanford, 21, 41
Stanhoe, 37, 38, 107, 124, 185, 215, 221, 226, 227, 285
Stedman, ,r, 287
Stockton, 21
Stradbrooke, (Suffolk), 163
Swaffham, 67, 101, 133, 135, 139, 146, 149, 167
Syderstone, 103, 208, 242, 294
Taylor, Francis, 218; Mary (née Toll) 41; William, 41
Terrington St Clement, 197
Thornham, 208
Tillyard, Juliana, (née Kitton) 18, 19; Robert, 24
Tilney, William, 106, 108, 112-114, 115, 128, 134, 135, 137, 139, 140, 141, 144, 161, 175, 308
Tipple, James, 53
Toll, Dennis, 300
Tovell, John, 36, 56, 61; Martha, 36; Susan (née Curson), 32, 35-36, 56, 63, 126
Townsend, Edward, 242
Townshend, Lord Charles George, 116; Lord James, 133, 134, 138, 147 66, 67, 106, 110, 115, 124, 133-138, 146-53
Trimmer, Revd Kirby, 181-182, 278-279, 305
Twiss, Robert, 240
Twistleton, Edward, 211, 266-270
Upjohn, Mr, 289
Virgoe, Norma, 190
Wacey, Robert, 242; Thomas, 239
Wagg, Catherine, 242; John, 242
Walpole, 124
Walsham, Sir John, 213-214, 303
Walsingham, 64, 66, 67, 106, 107, 110, 115, 124, 133-138, 142,

146-152, 156, 167, 176, 224, 230, 235, 237, 251, 260, 308, 311

Wanford (or Wanfer), William, 46-7, 48, 105, 107, 134, 135, 137, 140, See also Appendix A

Wells, 110

Wells, Mr & Mrs, 285, 286, 287, 288

Weyland, John, 67, 96, 97, 121, 201-203

Whartons, 261, 263

White, George, 25

Whitely (Whitby), Samuel, 137, 140, 141, 145, 152, See also Appendix A

Whiting, J.B., 291, 292

Williams, Karel, 212

Williamson, Ann, 230; James, 46-7, 56, 105-106, 134, 135, 137, 140, 218, See also Appendix A;

Robert, 218, 219, 229-230, 231-232, 236; Thomas, 218; William, 230

Willoughby, three girls, 261, 262, 263, 278

Wilson, John, 220, 235, 248, 249, 251, 258, 261, 262, 26, 280, 286, 287

Wodehouse, Lord, 116, 121, 125, 169

Wood, John, 278-279

Wray, William, 123

Wright, Charles, 249, 250, 251-252, 259; Charlotte, 259-260, 261; Elizabeth, 250; Jane, 250; Joseph, 285, 286; Margaret, 250; Susanna, 16

Wrigley, E.A., 63

Wymondham, 146

347